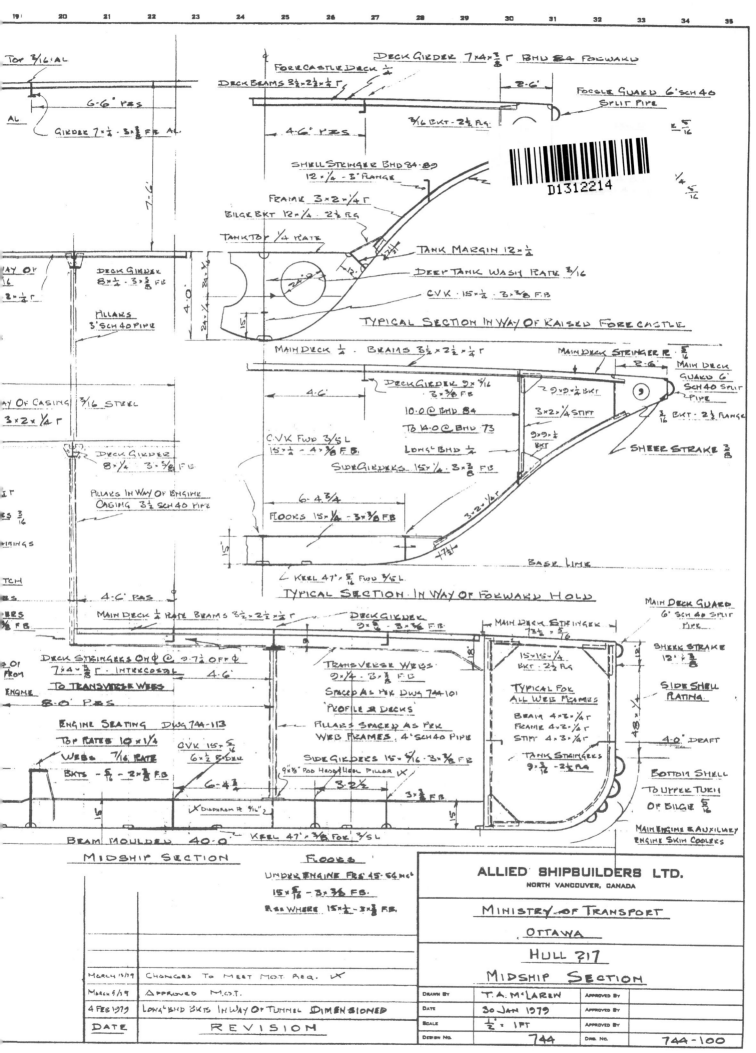

SHIPS OF STEEL

Arctic Nutsukpok in the Arctic Ocean, August 1982. Malcolm McLaren photo

Ships *of* Steel

A British Columbia Shipbuilder's Story

T. A. MᶜLAREN and VICKIE JENSEN

Harbour Publishing

Canadian Cataloguing in Publication Data

McLaren, T. A. (Thomas Arthur), 1919-1999.

Ships of steel

ISBN 1-55017-242-5

   1. McLaren, T. A. (Thomas Arthur), 1919-1999. 2. Allied Shipbuilders Ltd.—History. 3. Shipbuilding—British Columbia--Biography. 4. Shipbuilding—Building—British Columbia—History. I. Jensen, Vickie, 1946- II. Title.

VM301.A48M34 2000   338.7′62382′09711   C00-910767-3

Published by

Harbour Publishing Co. Ltd.

P.O. Box 219, Madeira Park, BC Canada V0N 2H0

Cover design and maps by Martin Nichols, Lionheart Graphics

Cover photographs: (front) launching of the *Lady Alexandra* (Hull #184), 1973; (back, clockwise from top) launching of the *Kootenay Park* (Hull #104), 1944; welder at work on the seiner–dragger *Tenacious*, 1980; main deck unit being set on the ferry *Spirit of British Columbia* (Hull #254), early 1990s (Avcom photo).

Page design and composition by Vancouver Desktop Publishing

Image processing, charts and graphs by Ron O'Connell

Printed and bound in Canada

Every attempt has been made to identify and credit sources for photographs. The publisher would appreciate receiving any additional information.

Harbour Publishing acknowledges the financial support of the Government of Canada through the Book Publishing Industry Development Program (BPIDP) and the Canada Council for the Arts, and the Province of British Columbia through the British Columbia Arts Council, for its publishing activities.

The Canada Council
Conseil des Arts du Canada

This book is dedicated to all the employees of Allied Shipbuilders Ltd., who by their skill and determined labour have created a fleet of good, safe, reliable ships that both builder and owner can be proud of.

Contents

Preface

Inspiration to produce this book came from a few different directions. Foremost was the shipbuilding career of my father, Arthur McLaren, and his writings about his childhood and early years in the shipbuilding industry. In the late 1990s, as we got ready to celebrate the 50th anniversary of Allied Shipbuilders, we decided the time was right to gather Arthur's papers into a simple chronological story, perhaps adding some photographs. To compile the story we approached Vickie Jensen, long known to our family through her work as editor of *Westcoast Mariner* magazine. Bright and eager, Vickie agreed to undertake the vaguely defined task of setting Arthur's writings into a "story" about Allied Shipbuilders.

As the project grew, it seemed important to go back even further in time. Our family had been in the shipbuilding industry for nearly a hundred years—almost as long as the industry has existed in BC—starting with my grandfather, W. D. McLaren. He got into shipbuilding by default: at the turn of the century he had intended to enter the brand new automobile industry.

Research began in earnest. I commenced sifting through both the company's and my grandfather's files, rooms of documents, and I interviewed and recorded my father at length about his history. He was seventy-eight years old, yet he had total recall of the most minute details from fifty years before. His recollections brought even more credibility and depth to the project.

Next came breadth. We had conceived the project as the story of Allied Shipbuilders, but ours is only one of many medium-sized British Columbia shipyards. Rollie Webb, a shipbuilder and historian who has spent much of his life in pursuit of Canadian shipbuilding facts, generously offered us his database of BC's metal ships and shipbuilders. These industry statistics provide context and background and they tell quite a story on their own.

Ever dauntless, Vickie worked with all of this material and did a wonderful job of weaving facts, stories and pictures into a cohesive story, combining a shipbuilder's technical outlook with the human touch.

Ron O'Connell helped in organizing and scanning Allied's many boxes of historic photographs and shipbuilding records, manipulating all of the data I brought forward from those records, and never complaining as he condensed and digitized a truckload of information into the photographs and appendixes that appear in the finished book.

Finally Mary Schendlinger, our wonderful editor, kindly advised us that it was time to stop writing and to begin publishing.

The firm of Allied Shipbuilders has prospered due to the efforts of a dedicated group of shipbuilding employees, each with significant stories, only a few of whom are mentioned in the book. I thank all of them. Many people have freely given of their time, memories and pictures. They include past Allied employees Bill Brown, David Cowie and Gunter Christophersen; fishermen John Lenic and Don Macmillan; aluminum builder Al Renke; naval architects Phil Spaulding and Rob Allan; Marc McAllister, Rob Lewis and Claire Johnston of the tugboat industry; the Vancouver Ship Registry; marine writer Alan Haig-Brown; my wife, Roberta McLaren; and my mother, Dorothy McLaren.

The photographs in the book are from Allied's files and friends. We have included credits wherever information was available.

Malcolm McLaren
July 2000

Like a lot of people, I first knew Arthur McLaren by his reputation. As the rookie editor of *Westcoast Mariner* magazine when it began in 1987, I was told that Arthur McLaren, president of Allied Shipbuilders, read each new issue of our magazine and our competitor's very carefully, circling any errors he found. Later I found out this was an exaggeration, but that first introduction to Arthur McLaren certainly had a positive impact on my own attention to detail.

When I took over the "Around the Yards" column, I met Arthur's three sons, James, Doug and Malcolm, and came to respect Allied in a new way. When I spent time in the yard talking or taking pictures, I'd see them in the thick of one project or another, but even when he was busy, Malcolm always answered my questions, adding his wry commentary on the latest news or political antics going on in the marine world. Like their father, all three sons have a biting wit that lightens the load of the serious work that goes on in a shipyard.

Over the years as I've stayed in touch with Allied, working on one marine story or another, I've come to rely on their knowledge of marine history, their contacts and suggestions, their take on the impact of political and economic trends. When Malcolm proposed compiling his father's writings into a book, I was immediately interested.

Producing a book, like building a ship, is always a saga of peaks and valleys. There were times when the task seemed daunting—Arthur McLaren was an extremely prolific writer as well as a stickler for facts. But throughout the process it was a delight to become better acquainted with Arthur and Dorothy McLaren and their sons. The McLarens have never been a family to toot their own horn, but readers can be grateful they made the commitment to this book. It is a rare insider's look at the work and history of an important BC industry.

I join Malcolm in thanking the many employees, family and friends of Allied Shipbuilders for generously sharing their memories, their knowledge and their photographs. They have enriched the story of BC shipbuilding in ways that would have made Arthur McLaren proud.

Vickie Jensen
July 2000

Steel Shipbuilding in British Columbia

Early in 1984, the naval architect Dick Walkingshaw asked Arthur McLaren for some information on the history of shipbuilding in British Columbia. Arthur fired back this succinct four-sentence reply:

The History of Shipbuilding in BC

- Wooden shipbuilding was carried out in British Columbia from the earliest days of European settlement.
- Steel shipbuilding was commenced some seventy-five years ago on a small scale but was greatly expanded during the period 1917–21 when some 30 cargo ships of 5,000–8,000 tons deadweight were built for the British and Canadian governments.
- The greatest shipbuilding activity in this province occurred during the 1939–45 war when about 250 cargo ships of 10,000 tons dwt and some 50 naval escort vessels were delivered.
- A viable steel shipbuilding industry continues producing annually about 30% of the total Canadian output.

Five years later, Arthur McLaren fleshed out a decade-by-decade description of "100 Years of Shipbuilding in British Columbia" for presentation at a meeting of the Society of Naval Architects. This longer history of provincial shipbuilding, along with the legacy of other papers he wrote over a period of twenty years, have served as the basis and guiding spirit of this book.

The Early Ships

The area now known as British Columbia was one of the last regions of North America to be settled by Europeans. British and Spanish navigators visited the area late in the eighteenth century, but it wasn't until 1843 that the Hudson's Bay Company set up trading forts and established what is now the city of Victoria. Even then, the outpost was still considered one of the most remote. It was a British possession, thousands of sea miles from London, a continent away from British colonies in eastern Canada, with no means of transcontinental communication.

If the fur trade opened the northwest coast to trading, it was the California gold rush that later triggered development of BC. After gold was discovered on the Fraser River in 1857, hordes of miners and settlers who had moved to California flocked northward to what is now British Columbia. Steamship links between San Francisco and Victoria were established, and when the American Transcontinental Railroad was opened in 1869, there was easier access to western North America via San Francisco. The demand for transportation up the Fraser River to the goldfields was enough to spark the establishment of shipyards in Victoria,

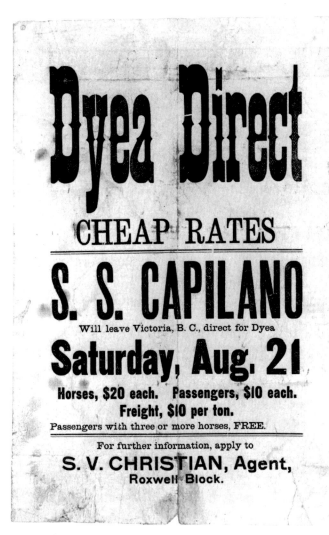

The Union Steamship Company vessel *Capilano* towing the steamer *Lightning*, St. Michael's Harbor, Alaska, 1898. VMM

Esquimalt naval base, commercial drydocking and repairs were undertaken by outside contractors.

In the 1890s a number of wooden vessels were built for coastal service, but most were constructed in the Puget Sound or San Francisco Bay areas. New sternwheel steamers began operating on four large lakes in BC's interior, linking railway branch lines with developing mines and farms.

Reports of a fabulous gold strike in the Klondike in 1897 brought a second influx of miners, all determined to secure passage on any craft heading north to the goldfields. The Union steamships, beginning with the *Capilano*, seized on the opportunity and entered into Alaskan service. Of the thousands of miners, speculators, merchants, entertainers and others who poured into BC from all directions to find gold, many stayed and settled in the province.

In 1914 Sir Alfred Yarrow, naval shipbuilder of the Clyde, bought the Victoria shipyard known as BC Marine Railway Company and renamed it Yarrows Ltd., thus establishing a branch of his family business in Esquimalt. The opening of the Panama Canal in 1915 brought more ships to western North America.

The Beginnings of an Industry

The fledgling economy of BC was strongly tied to the forest and fishing industries, both of which

where a few shallow-draft sternwheel steamers were built. Meanwhile rich seams of coal had been found on Vancouver Island, which along with timber gave rise to a brisk export business. By the 1870s, ships were being chartered to carry coal to San Francisco, and before long, machine shops began to appear on Vancouver Island.

Development of BC began in earnest with the completion of the transcontinental Canadian Pacific Railway in 1885. The history of BC's shipbuilding industry begins at about the same time, when the rail line joining the two Canadian coasts made for easier transport of steel and machinery to west coast shipyards. In 1865 the Royal Navy established a base at Esquimalt, adjacent to Victoria, and the Canadian government built a graving dock there during the 1880s. This was the first local facility capable of drydocking medium-sized ships. Although the dock was part of the

This is to Certify that we the Undersigned have examined the Schooner Alice of Victoria Vancouver Island and find her to answer the description given in the Builders Certificate and that she has One deck, Two Masts, Standing Bowsprit Shield Head & Iron Built

Victoria Jan 7. 8th 1852

Charles Dodd Ship Master
William Mitchell

Surveyor's certificate for the *Alice*, the first steel ship built in BC. It was assembled from sections brought out from England in 1851. The text reads: "This is to Certify that we the undersigned have examined the Schooner Alice of Victoria Vancouver Island and find her to answer the description given in the Builders Certificate and that she has One deck, Two Masts, Standing Bowsprit, Shield Head & Iron Built." VMM

required marine transportation. The early working vessels were made of wood and evolved to fit the needs of these resource industries. From the 1880s most logging was done along coastal inlets so that logs could easily be rafted into flat booms and towed to various sawmills. A distinctive type of tugboat developed to do this work: a wooden vessel, generally 60 to 80 feet in length, fitted with a single coal-fired Scotch boiler and a compound or triple expansion engine of 150 to 350 ihp. Although the first of these vessels dates back to 1889, in the early 1900s scores of utility steam tugs were launched. The developing fishing industry had its own requirements, just as specific. By 1910 some eighty canneries were operating up and down the coast. Fishing companies owned thousands of open wooden boats 25 to 30 feet in length, each outfitted with oars and a lug sail. A fisherman was allotted a boat and fished on a share basis. With the introduction of the gasoline engine, many fishermen saved up and acquired their own "gas boats."

Whether for forestry or fishing, all vessels tended to be small and built of wood. Timber was plentiful. The total construction time for some was often only one month—from tree to completed boat. Using green wood shortened the lifespan of these vessels, whereas tugs built of well-seasoned timber could be expected to last fifty years. For larger, ocean-going service, steel ships were the obvious choice.

The first new steel ships used on the BC coast were built in the United Kingdom, although some were sent to BC for re-erection. In 1891 the first steel steamers for the Union Steamship Company of British Columbia were built at Paisley, Scotland, and knocked down for shipment to Vancouver. They were then re-erected, launched and put into service as the sister ships *Comox*, *Capilano* and *Coquitlam*. These three small steel steamers are often cited as the first metal ships built in BC. However, marine historian and shipbuilder Rollie Webb says this honour should go to the *Alice*, which was brought out in sections from England in 1851. He quotes a letter he received from the late marine writer Norman Hacking, a

Employees of J. Coughlan & Sons shipyard, in front of the company's buildings at 1st & Columbia at the southeast corner of False Cre

few days after lecturing at the Vancouver Maritime Museum:

Apropos of your talk on Saturday, the little iron schooner Alice *was brought out from England in sections in the ship* Tory *and arrived at Victoria in 1851, and was the first vessel on the Victoria registry. Her certificate states that she was of 45 tons burthen and had "one deck, two masts, standing bowsprit, shield head and iron built."*

The Alice *was brought out from England by Capt. James Cooper who had been master of several Hudson's Bay Company vessels from 1844 to 1850, when he returned to England in command of the barque* Columbia. *He attempted unsuccessfully to organize the Vancouver's Island Steam Sawing Mill and Agriculture Company, and when this scheme was abandoned came out to Vancouver Island as an independent settler.*

I have seen no record of how he managed to put

the Alice *together, but she was not successful financially, as he ran up against the Hudson's Bay Co. trade monopoly. She made at least one voyage to San Francisco with lumber and one or two to the Hawaiian Islands where presumably Cooper sold her, for she disappeared from the records.*

1900–1910: The Industry Takes Root

In 1901, the first of the Canadian Pacific high-class steamers arrived from Newcastle for tri-city service between Vancouver–Victoria–Seattle. The *Princess Victoria* was the forerunner of the famous Princess fleet, which served the BC coast for three-quarters of a century. Establishment of the Grand Trunk Pacific Railway fleet provided a link between Vancouver and the Grand Trunk Rail terminal at Prince Rupert. The fleet of the Union Steamship Company, founded in 1889, carried

...ouver, May 9, 1918. The shipyard burned down in a spectacular fire on August 30, 1923.

freight and passengers to remote logging camps, fish canneries and small settlements all along the Inside Passage. At its peak, the company served more than 200 ports of call.

Although these new foreign-built ships did not directly assist the BC shipbuilding industry, the delivery of these vessels brought out scores of marine engineers, who then sent for their families and settled in Vancouver and Victoria. Many local families trace their origins in BC to the *Empress of Asia*, *Princess Charlotte*, *Prince George*, *Lady Cynthia* and other ships delivered to this coast nearly a century ago.

1910–1920: The First Shipbuilding Boom

Prior to World War I there were no yards on Canada's west coast capable of building ocean-

going steel tonnage. That would change quickly between 1914 and 1918 as World War I shipping demands encouraged shipbuilding in BC.

Early on, Victoria Machinery Depot Company was established in Victoria, J.H. Coughlan & Sons set up a yard on False Creek in Vancouver, and Wallace Shipbuilding Company of North Vancouver added new berths. These and other early BC yards began their wartime production with a series of four- and five-masted wooden auxiliary schooners. These vessels proved quite unsatisfactory for service in war zones because they could not maintain a convoy speed. Although they did transport timber from BC to Australia, the west coast of South America and other areas outside the war zone, they could not replace tonnage lost by enemy action.

The next wartime program was a series of wooden cargo vessels built to a standard 240-foot design, fitted with Scotch boilers and modest triple expansion engines of approximately 600 ihp. The existing yards and some six newly established ventures filled orders from both the British and French governments. Unfortunately, the order of the day was "in the forest one month; built into ships the next." Constructed with unseasoned lumber, these ships had an extremely short life, and coupled with their low carrying capacity, they turned out to be useless. After the armistice no ship owner would buy them, as a surplus of good, American-built steel ships was available by then.

Fortunately some provincial yards became involved in the much more practical program of steel shipbuilding that followed. The first orders came from Japan and Norway. Then the Imperial Munitions Board placed orders with Wallace Shipyards for 5,000-ton cargo ships and with Coughlan for 8,000-ton ships. These vessels were all named with the prefix War, a standard procedure for British government-built merchant ships. The benefits of the wartime shipbuilding boom were not limited to shipyards. Local boiler shops, machine shops and other manufacturing and subcontracting firms shared in the short-lived prosperity.

1920–1930: After the Boom

The end of the wartime program closed down all the large wooden shipbuilders. The steel shipbuilders carried on for a short time, when the Canadian government ordered some sixty steel ships. Vessels of several sizes were completed, from 2,500 dwt, built on the Great Lakes, to 8,500 dwt, built in eastern Canada and in BC at North Vancouver, Victoria and Prince Rupert. The Canadian Government Merchant Marine owned these vessels and operated them on many ocean trading routes, but with very little commercial success.

Steel shipbuilding in the 1920s was limited to coastal passenger and cargo vessels and a handful of small craft. Coughlan's False Creek yard ended operations after a spectacular fire in 1923. Yards in Victoria and Prince Rupert reverted to ship repairing only. Small-scale wooden shipbuilding activity was more brisk, with several small passenger ferries launched and a reasonable output of

Burrard Dry Dock, North Vancouver, as seen from the air, 1926. Note the Cates tug fleet and the passenger ferry dock at the foot of Lonsdale. The floating drydock is separated into two sections.

tugs and fishing vessels. Although the wartime and post-war shipbuilding boom was only a memory, the industry was well equipped to handle repairs to even the largest ships trading in the area. There was the new 1,100-foot Canadian government graving dock at Esquimalt (one of the world's largest), Wallace's new 12,000-ton drydock built in North Vancouver and the existing 15,000-ton floating drydock in Prince Rupert, along with two 2,000-ton marine railways in Vancouver and two 2,500-ton marine railways in Victoria.

1930–1939: Survival

The Depression years were very difficult. Some steel yards survived, only on repair work. Before the advent of radar, yards regularly got work fixing grounding damage to hulls of coastal steamers. A fraternity of itinerant steel shipbuilders supported themselves by moving from yard to yard as work was available. Builders of wooden ships competed fiercely for the very limited amount of new construction, and tight pricing put a number of these firms out of business.

Toward the end of the 1930s, the Royal Canadian Navy introduced a very modest steel building program of four 160-foot coal-burning steam minesweepers. Two such vessels were ordered in western Canada, one from Burrard Dry Dock and one from Yarrows.

Prince Rupert, March 6, 1934. The snag puller *Essington* is in front and the first *Prince George* is coming off the drydock at right.

The *Dunsyre*, built in 1891, undergoing conversion into a hulk to carry wood chips to and from the pulp mill at Ocean Falls. This photograph was taken December 4, 1935, at Victoria's Inner Harbour.

1939–1946: The Second Wartime Shipbuilding Boom

In 1939 Canada was a producer of raw materials rather than an industrialized society. Most engineering and manufacturing concerns were located

The Canadian navy minesweeper HMCS *Nootka* "going down the launchways" at Yarrows shipyard, Esquimalt, September 26, 1938. Courtesy R. Webb

The gantry at Yarrows, February 10, 1945. The sign reads: "Vessels under construction in this yard are urgently needed to replace losses by enemy action and to carry the war success fully to distant fronts. Every workman owes it to his country and his family whose safety is at stake to work full shifts from whistle to whistle every working day. These ships must be completed in the shortest possible time."

West Coast Shipbuilders Ltd., False Creek, Vancouver, 1944, as seen from the Cambie Street Bridge, looking east. Seven ships are under construction, three afloat and four on the building berths.

in eastern Canada, with only a few heavy industrial plants on the west coast. But the start of World War II precipitated a great shipbuilding boom of naval and merchant ships in BC and across Canada. Orders for naval vessels were placed in 1940, with the first deliveries following a year later. Ship construction was only part of the wartime story. Boilers, steering gear, winches, windlasses, masts, shafting, etc. were manufactured in BC. Eastern Canada supplied steel and engines, with pumps produced by the machine shops of the gold mines in northern Ontario.

World War II created a shipbuilding industry infrastructure in the province. BC shipyards produced over 250 10,000-ton freighters, 15 frigates, 3 landing ships, 10 corvettes and 22 Bangor Class minesweepers. Smaller craft included Fairmile patrol launches, wooden minesweepers and dozens of service craft for both the army and the air force. During the peak of wartime construc-

tion, 25,000 men and women were employed in provincial shipyards while an additional 5,000 manufactured components.

1946–1949: Period of Adjustment

There was no devastating economic slump in BC shipbuilding after World War II, but there was definitely a period of adjustment. BC yards took further shipbuilding orders, although certainly not enough to maintain the level of employment of the war years. Some yards folded their operations.

Burrard Dry Dock received an order to build a 7,500-dwt, 16-knot passenger and cargo motor ship, one of three ordered by the Canadian government on behalf of Canadian National Steamships. These vessels were built to replace CN's Halifax–West Indies fleet, of which four out of a total of five had been destroyed in the war. The same yard also contracted with French inter-

SS *Weston Park*, a Victory type ship, inbound Vancouver Harbour at the First Narrows.

ests to build a series of 4,500-dwt and 7,500-dwt coal ships. The French government ordered lighthouse tenders from Yarrows. West Coast Shipbuilders built the 180-foot ferry *Anscomb* for the BC Department of Highways and re-erected the vessel at Kootenay Lake. A contract to construct a fleet of two tugs and fifteen barges for service on the Mackenzie and Athabasca Rivers was shared by West Coast Shipbuilders and Yarrows.

The coastal passenger fleet certainly needed replacements. The CPR had lost the *Princess Marguerite* on war service in the Mediterranean, while the CNR's *Prince George* had been gutted by fire at Ketchikan. As well, the whole fleet was aging. By the end of World War II the newest CPR ships were fifteen years old; the latest of the Union Steamship fleet were twenty years old; and the remaining CNR vessel was thirty-five years old.

CPR ordered four new vessels from Clyde yards. CNR contracted with Yarrows to build a new *Prince George* for the BC Coast–Alaska trade. The Union Steamship Company purchased three war surplus Castle Class corvettes and converted them locally into passenger and cargo steamers. These three ships were among a large number of wooden and steel tugs, minesweepers, patrol vessels, landing craft and other vessels that were put up for sale by the Canadian War Assets Corporation and the US Navy and Army. Since little new construction had taken place in the towing and fishing industries during the 1930s and '40s, there was a rush to buy these diesel-powered war surplus craft. Their entry spelled the demise of the steam tug. Local wooden shipyards were fully employed converting minesweepers and patrol vessels into yachts and commercial craft, some of which are still in service.

SS *Prince George*, delivered by Yarrows in 1948, underway. The original specification and design plans were prepared by McLaren & Sons. George N.Y. Simpson photo

HMCS *Skeena* (2nd), a 2,000-ton St. Laurent Class destroyer-escort vessel, outbound from the Esquimalt navy base. *Skeena* was built at Burrard Dry Dock in 1957.

1950–1959: Slow But Steady

At the end of hostilities, the Canadian navy disposed of practically all its wartime-built ships, retaining only a few frigates and one or two Algerine minesweepers. Then, during the 1950s, the Canadian navy concentrated on building a modern fleet. This significant shipbuilding effort involved most BC yards and kept some occupied for more than a decade. The "new" navy operated destroyer escorts, non-magnetic minesweepers and trawler-type gate vessels, as well as several types of auxiliary vessels.

The post-war period saw a rapid expansion in the number of pulp and paper mills on the BC coast and the spread of new technology into sawmills. Logs were debarked before being cut, so the bark ("hog fuel") could be barged to mills for fuel. Sawmill waste, now free of bark, was diced into wood chips and barged to pulp mills. A variety of watercraft, including hundreds of chip barges, were now required. The side-tipping log barge was introduced in the late 1950s. This decade also saw the first small welded steel craft, used in the logging industry and later in the fishing industry. John Manly and Arthur McLaren were at the forefront of this change, with other yards soon following suit. By the end of the 1950s, steel had also replaced wood for most new small vessel construction.

1960–1969: Boom Times

In 1961 the Canadian government introduced a shipbuilding subsidy program for the construction of larger commercial vessels. The subsidy, which covered a percentage of construction costs, was intended to ensure that eastern Canadian shipbuilders produced the tonnage needed to ply the newly opened St. Lawrence Seaway, but it revitalized BC shipyards as well. A number of vessels were built for overseas customers, but most were for domestic owners.

Local tugboat owners took full advantage of

The *Great West No. 2*, a loaded log barge, 1960s. Commercial Illustrators photo

the subsidy during the 1960s and '70s, with new steel tugs and barges replacing most of the remaining wooden equipment on the coast. This work, coupled with the establishment of the provincially owned ferry fleet, kept some BC yards busy building ships for the next fifteen years.

1970–1979: Business As Usual

The principal new build orders in the 1970s were for offshore supply vessels, coastal forestry craft and fishing boats. Aluminum seiners were now commonplace, and fibreglass hulls were becoming more popular. This was a buoyant

A row of six seiners, all designed by Cleaver & Walkingshaw and built by Allied Shipbuilders, c. 1978.

Launching of the *Queen of Saanich* at Victoria Machinery Depot in Victoria's outer harbour, November 28, 1962. The keel was laid on April 2, 1962. The ship cost approximately $3.5 million and had its inaugural run on February 9, 1963. Jim Ryan photo

Offshore supply vessel *Lady Alexandra* on sea trials, prior to departure for the North Sea, 1974. Murray McLennan photo

decade with steady employment in BC shipyards.

Tug and barge construction for the forest industry continued, including the production of the first self-propelled log barge. New build activity for both the federal and provincial governments provided a substantial foundation of work.

In 1973 the price of crude oil leapt to record levels, which prompted oil exploration in the Canadian Arctic. BC shipyards produced the world's first fleet of private sector icebreakers, and the innovative, cost-effective designs developed during this period were later adapted by other countries.

1980–1989: Decade of Change

For BC shipbuilders, the 1980s began with full order books and the suggestion of a rosy future. New fishing vessels were in big demand, thanks to bountiful revenues from the salmon and herring fisheries. The price of crude oil was still high, sustaining the demand for Arctic Ocean exploration equipment. Caught up in the frenzy, the federal government built several new icebreakers. Although orders for commercial oil vessels were certainly more plentiful, the government vessels were always much more complex and expensive pieces of equipment than the private sector efforts.

Midway through the decade, the price of oil plummeted. Within a few years, oil exploration in the Canadian Arctic ended, and with it the dreams of BC shipyards. Plans for a Polar Class 8 icebreaker to exert Canadian sovereignty in the high Arctic went on until 1989, but the project was cancelled.

During 1986 and 1987, the order books of the principal BC shipbuilders were empty. The last two years of the decade saw a brief echo of the earlier boom, with the building of a good number of fishing vessels and some other private sector industrial orders. As well, there were a few government orders, including two 150-foot

A drydocking in the Arctic ice. Arctic Transportation tugs *Arctic Hooper* and *Arctic Nutsukpok* handle the ATL floating drydock containing Beaudrill's icebreaking supply vessel *Ikaluk*, c. 1984.

search and rescue cutters, two hydrographic and oceanographic vessels and four torpedo ranging and recovery vessels for the navy. As there was no shortage of competent builders or repairers in BC, the industry slowdown at the end of the decade resulted in too many shipyards chasing too few jobs.

POLAR CLASS 8 ICEBREAKER

Profile of the proposed Canadian Coast Guard Polar Class 8 icebreaker.

1990–1999: Ships Few and Far Between

The reality of the previous half-decade's lack of contracts and even bleaker prospects for the 1990s dictated the closure of many shipbuilding yards. Yarrows and Vito Steel Boat & Barge ceased operations after the second Spirit Class ferry was completed. Bel-Aire Shipyards Ltd. had already shut down its North Vancouver yard, as had the aluminum specialist Matsumoto Shipyards Ltd. West Coast Manly Shipyard Ltd., along with the 100-year-old BC Marine Shipbuilders, ceased operations partly in response to a federal initiative to close yards. Burrard Dry Dock in North Vancouver, which had become Versatile Pacific, was run down in the '90s until finally it was closed. Smaller yards such as Progressive Marine Ltd. in New Westminster folded after only a few years of operation. Over the decades, the veteran McKenzie Barge and Marine Ways Ltd. produced a goodly number of new barges, but in the early 1990s McKenzie

One of the two Spirit Class ferries, the largest ships ever built in BC at 18,000 gross tons each. The ships were built by consortium in the early 1990s. Avcom photo

began concentrating on barge repair, with no new construction.

In this decade, significant orders were few and far between, and there was no large construction work except for BC Ferry contracts. Two 550-foot, 470-car Spirit Class ferries were ordered early in the decade, with three different yards building various sections. Two 285-foot ferries and a number of barges were built by Vancouver Shipyards Company Ltd. In 1994 BC Ferries began its high-speed aluminum ferry construction program, eventually working with a consortium of companies to produce three high-speed catamarans. When built, the "fast cat ferries" were the second-largest of their kind in the world.

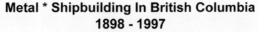

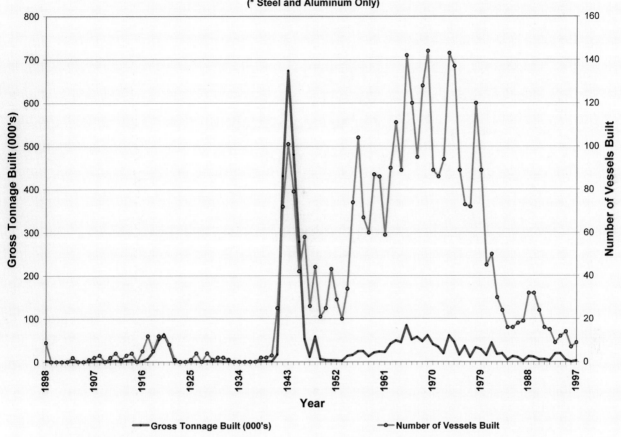

Metal * Shipbuilding In British Columbia
1898 - 1997
(* Steel and Aluminum Only)

Gross Tonnage Built (000's)   Number of Vessels Built

In fishing, the decline of the salmon resource coupled with the collapse of prices at the end of the decade precluded new vessel construction and reduced repair work significantly.

At the end of the 1990s, a worldwide commodity price slump and a decline in BC forestry and fishing economies combined to deliver a serious blow to provincial shipbuilding. There had been significant yard closures, and the scale of employment for survivors changed dramatically. For example, in earlier years Allied Shipbuilders routinely had a payroll of up to 300; at the close of this decade the yard employed only 100 tradesmen on a regular basis. In 1999 British Columbia no longer had any large yard employing 500 to 1,000 people; in fact, the province had only two medium-sized shipbuilding yards, Vancouver Shipyards Company Ltd. and the smaller Allied Shipbuilders Ltd.

Ironically, this decade saw a return to the ship-building situation of 100 years ago, when foreign ships were brought in to work BC waters. During 1998–99, twelve Chinese-built barges were imported for carrying wood chips, along with one for transporting pulp and one for moving fuel oil to Vancouver Island. Live-fish transporters were imported from Norwegian yards. Fishing vessels and a variety of used tugs and barges from the US were brought in under the duty-free free trade provisions of the North American Free Trade Agreement, while protective US government legislation known as the Jones Act prohibited any reverse flow of Canadian-built commercial vessels to the USA.

While the challenges of the new millennium are as tough as any the industry has ever faced, the legacy of BC shipbuilders is a strong one, and certainly British Columbia shipyard owners and workers can take a great deal of pride in the ships and boats they have produced in just over a century of work.

Those Shipbuilding McLarens

"By the time the boys each went off to work in the shipyard,
I was well steeped in Scottish tradition. You started early
and just kept on, generation after generation. It was hard
work and long hours, but we had good times."

—*Dorothy McLaren*

The McLarens are typical of many immigrant families who laid the foundation of shipbuilding in Canada. Such men often received excellent training, both academic and practical, in their mother country. Many came from shipbuilding families. The lure of far-off opportunities, coupled with a lack of economic opportunity at home, encouraged them to pack up little other than their skills, ambitions or dreams, and strike out for new opportunities.

Once settled, they quickly began building all manner of boats and ships. Many of their yards prospered, with sons, sons-in-law and eventually grandsons trying their hand and staying on in the business.

While the accomplishments of shipyards are

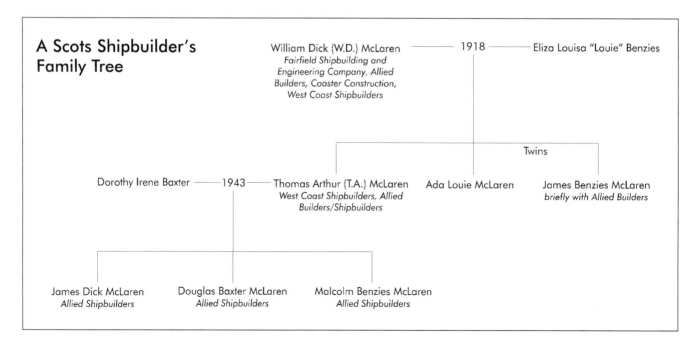

A Scots Shipbuilder's Family Tree

William Dick (W.D.) McLaren ——— 1918 ——— Eliza Louisa "Louie" Benzies
Fairfield Shipbuilding and Engineering Company, Allied Builders, Coaster Construction, West Coast Shipbuilders

Twins

Dorothy Irene Baxter ——— 1943 ——— Thomas Arthur (T.A.) McLaren   Ada Louie McLaren   James Benzies McLaren
West Coast Shipbuilders, Allied Builders/Shipbuilders   *briefly with Allied Builders*

James Dick McLaren   Douglas Baxter McLaren   Malcolm Benzies McLaren
Allied Shipbuilders   *Allied Shipbuilders*   *Allied Shipbuilders*

William Dick McLaren

Arthur McLaren as an infant, with his parents W.D. and Eliza Louisa McLaren, Montrose, Scotland, October 27, 1919.

measured in tonnage and hull numbers, the driving force of any successful yard is the experience, determination and sweat of those who work there. Strong family stock like the McLarens know well the marine tradition of long hours, financial gambles and perseverance, and the support and understanding of wives and families at home was crucial. Such maritime dynasties are at the heart of the shipbuilding legacy in this province and throughout North America.

W.D. McLaren
Patriarch of a Shipbuilding Family

William Dick McLaren was one of those young men who definitely showed promise. He graduated with honours from Glasgow & West of Scotland Technical College (now Strathclyde University), receiving degrees in mechanical and electrical engineering. He also became the King's Prizeman after taking first place in Britain in applied mechanics. He served a five-year apprenticeship with the engineering firm Mirrlees & Watson Ltd., where he worked on the first diesel engine built in Britain. Although he aspired to work in the embryonic automobile industry, he

was invited to join the staff of the prestigious Fairfield Shipbuilding and Engineering Company in Glasgow and took that position. At twenty-five years of age he was put in charge of Fairfield's Engine Design Office. He headed up night classes at the Engineering Department of Paisley Technical College for many years, providing technical instruction to working lads and men. In 1917 he accepted an invitation to take charge of the Engineering Section of the Chief Inspector of Shipbuilding in Scotland, established to accelerate production for the war effort.

In 1918 W.D. McLaren married Eliza Benzies and their family grew, first with son Thomas Arthur and then with twins Ada Louie and James Benzies. A vanishing breed of stern Scot raised in the Presbyterian Church, W.D. was known as "Mr. McLaren" to all but his family and closest friends.

During World War I, W.D. McLaren and his partner Welsh submitted designs to the Scottish Admiralty for building sea-going vessels 100' to 280' long. Malcolm McLaren found the vintage documents among the family papers. He comments that excerpts from the proposal reflect the business language of the day, as well as W.D. McLaren's advocacy of cost-saving straight frame construction and an oil-driven engine of their own manufacture. The prospectus also mentioned that negotiations were in hand for procuring a shipbuilding site at Montrose, Scotland.

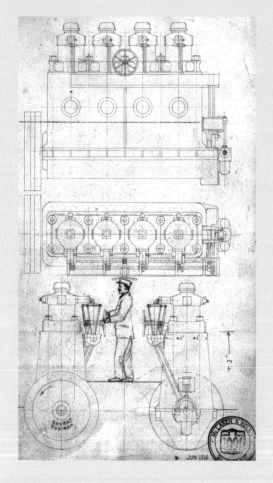

The prospectus has been compiled with the object of putting forward a scheme for the construction of small cargo vessels of a simple type. Since the government has standardized cargo vessels of 3,000 tons and upwards, the new designs proposed relate only to vessels of smaller size.

The present practice in the construction of these vessels does not differ from that employed for the larger sized. The hulls are usually formed of transverse frames, which are bent by furnacing. The shell plating is worked to bed against the frames by rolling and furnacing where necessary. The propelling machinery ordinarily consists of a compound or triple expansion steam engine driving a single screw, and supplied with steam from one or two cylindrical boilers, placed at about midship or at the stern of the vessel.

With regard to the cost of the vessel, one economy that may be effected is to so construct the hull that all the frames and floors are straight, and so that the shell and bottom plates may be readily attached to the transverse members without previous working to the requisite surface. The promoters of this scheme for building small cargo vessels of simplified construction have given this matter special attention and have produced a design which secures the above features . . .

The proposal to start a new yard would not be submitted if the only object to be secured were merely to have control of what promises to be a profitable line of business for some years to come. While all available energy and capital should be directed to replacing the commerce of this country on a sound foundation with the least possible delay, there must be some assurance that the energy and capital will continue to be employed usefully when conditions become more normal, and competition assumes complexity by becoming national as well as international. Consequently, any steps taken at the present time should be justified by making suitable provision for the keener competition which will come later.

When such a condition of the market has to be faced, the business which will weather it best is that which is able to produce most economically that class of vessel which combines low running costs with low initial cost. The latter is secured in the type of construction proposed.

This early proposal notes that "the attainment of low running costs . . . involves the adoption of an economical class of propelling machinery" and goes on to suggest the feasibility for developing an experimental high-compression oil engine. In comparison with the diesel engine, the proposed high-compression engine would be of simplified construction with consequent reduction in first cost, have lower compression pressure and simplified valve gear.

W.D. and Eliza with Arthur and the twins, c. 1923.

Coaster Construction

In 1919 W.D. McLaren and an associate, J.G. Johnstone, started a shipyard in Montrose, on the east coast of Scotland. They anticipated a great boom in shipbuilding after World War I as owners rushed in to rebuild coastal and short sea trade fleets that had been lost in the war. At the time there was a glut of sea- and ocean-going shipping vessels, but there appeared to be a market for smaller steel ships under 250 feet in length. The partners' intention was to build for this market, utilizing hard chine bilges and straight frames rather than the usual formed hull, in an attempt to lower steelwork costs.

The new shipyard was established on Rossie Island and named Coaster Construction Company Ltd. The fledgling yard started out with a bread-and-butter contract for small hopper barges destined for northern Chile. These craft were built, then dismantled and shipped abroad. Next Coaster Construction built a 200-ton steamer, on speculation, to get experience with straight-frame construction. This vessel was followed by two 800-ton coasters for Newcastle owners and two 750-ton island traders for Curacao, Netherlands West Indies.

The first few vessels that were built reflected Coaster's new straight-frame construction method. But all too soon there was a depression in the shipbuilding industry and owners spurned the hard chine bilges and straight frames for

Eliza and W.D. in Vancouver, 1929.

Coaster Construction Company ad for a self-dumping rock-carrying hopper barge, c. 1924.

One of five surplus Royal Navy Town Class minesweepers, March 27, 1924. Two of these were converted to the Union Steamship Company vessels *Lady Cecilia* and *Lady Cynthia*.

The *Lady Cecilia* and *Lady Cynthia* underway. VMM

"real" ships. So the partners abandoned the idea of simplified construction, and thereafter the yard built conventional hulls.

In 1920 Coaster bought five Town Class minesweepers from the Royal Navy surplus. In the post-war years it was possible to get such ships for next to nothing. These 220-foot ships were in new condition, having been built at the end of the war and laid up after completion of sea trials.

The first minesweeper, HMS *Wexford*, was converted to an excursion vessel and sent to Australia. Then, in 1923, Coaster secured a contract with the Union Steamship Company of Vancouver for a twin-funnelled, twin-screw excursion steamer. The result was the *Lady Alexandra*. The hull was newly built but the machinery for this vessel came from the second Royal Navy minesweeper, HMS *Cheam*. The *Lady Alexandra*

The launch of the 225-foot, 1,400-passenger excursion vessel *Lady Alexandra* at the Coaster Construction Company, Rossie Island, Montrose, Scotland, 1924.

The *Lady Alexandra*, outbound off Point Atkinson lighthouse, West Vancouver.

sailed through the Panama Canal and reached Vancouver in 1924. Shortly after, W.D. McLaren came to BC to meet the owners of the Union Steamship Company and see about the possibility of more work. He spent a short time travelling the coast to observe the company's operations and was favourably impressed with Vancouver, its environment and its people—who seemed to include a large number of transplanted Scots.

At that time Union Steamship was looking for new ships to service Howe Sound and the Sunshine Coast. W.D. was successful in getting orders for three additional ships, so the Coaster Construction yard converted the hulls of the third and fourth minesweepers, HMS *Swindon* and HMS *Barnstable*, to the two-funnelled *Lady Cecilia* and

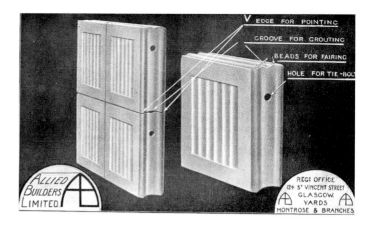

Lady Cynthia. An extra deck was added to each ship to increase capacity to 800 passengers. To provide buoyancy and stability for the additional height and weight of the superstructure, the hulls were widened by fitting sponsons on each side up to the main deck level.

The fourth Union ship was the steamer *Catala* of some 1,400 gross tons. The *Catala* was an entirely new ship, designed and built for weekly service between Vancouver, Prince Rupert and Stewart, Alaska. The vessel incorporated the boilers and some auxiliary machinery from the fifth minesweeper, HMS *Fisgard*. The minesweeper's engines were not used as they were considered "not heavy enough" for northern service. So two engines originally built for a pair of concrete tugs but never installed were purchased for the *Catala*. Normally a single-screw ship is given a right-hand turning propeller, while a twin-screw ship such as the *Catala* would get a right- and left-turning prop. However, in order to get the desired left- and right-hand rotation from the tugs' two right-hand turning engines, the starboard one was mounted forward and the port engine was installed backwards. This "making do" was typical of the ingenuity of the time.

After completion of the Union Steamship quartet, Coaster Construction built one final vessel, the single-screw motor ship *Kybra* for the government of western Australia. That vessel and the four Union steamships were all equipped with whistles taken from the five minesweepers, which explains why all the Union ships on the BC coast that came out of Coaster Construction sounded the same.

After that Coaster Construction ceased shipbuilding. Arthur McLaren was far too young at the time to know all the details of that decision, but later said, "I guess you could say Coaster just couldn't sell ships for more than it cost to build them. Father didn't appear defeated. Maybe he felt kicked, but not kicked down."

Allied Builders (Scotland)

In an attempt to keep men employed and maintain facilities, the two partners then set up a construc-

The "Montrose Bungalow," designed by Allied Builders, July 1925. The house could be built in six days from pre-made concrete blocks.

tion company under the name of Allied Builders Ltd. Their plan was to build prefabricated housing using large standardized concrete blocks. These houses were erected by mounting the square blocks atop and alongside each other and using steel tie rods to secure the blocks together. To make a publicity splash, the company's first four-room bungalow was built in six days. The conservative Scots of the east coast were not impressed. To them, a house should be built of stone. The prefabrication idea was an excellent one, but ahead of its time. It wasn't accepted with open arms until after World War II, some twenty years later.

The two entrepreneurs ceased all shipyard and concrete block manufacturing in 1927. In the years that followed, Johnstone stayed in Scotland and kept an office in Glasgow. He and W.D. shared some contracts and carried on that way. The name Allied Builders Ltd. was to surface again in Vancouver some twenty-three years later, as was the concept of modular construction.

On to Vancouver

Seeing no prospects in Britain, W.D. followed his ships to Vancouver in 1927. Over the course of the next fourteen years he practised as a consulting engineer, often with his partner W.N. "Bill" Kelly. W.D. focussed on designing and promoting steel vessels during the mid-1930s. Soon after the outbreak of war in 1939, he was approached by a group of Vancouver businessmen representing Vancouver Iron Works, Vancouver Machinery Depot and West Coast Salvage to establish a new

The *Lady Sylvia*, designed by W.D. McLaren and built in 1937 in Glasgow, Scotland, for Union Steamship service in Howe Sound. The vessel, renamed the *Lady Rose*, was still in service on the west coast of Vancouver Island in 2000.

four-berth wartime shipyard, in conjunction with Hamilton Bridge (later renamed Western Bridge), at a site on the southeast shore of False Creek in Vancouver. The enterprise, known as West Coast Shipbuilders Ltd., received orders to build 10,000-dwt cargo ships in early 1941. W.D.'s son Arthur, just graduating from the University of British Columbia in mechanical engineering, joined him in setting up this new shipyard.

Before the end of the war, West Coast Shipbuilders was sold to Frank Ross and Victor Spencer. In 1946 W.D. came to a parting of the ways with Ross and resigned his position as general manager. He continued consulting as a naval architect, however, preparing the original specifications and contract plans for the Canadian National Railway's 350-foot steamship *Prince George*, built at Yarrows and launched in 1947. Until his death in 1953, W.D. McLaren collaborated on ship design and regularly discussed shipyard matters with his oldest son Arthur.

The Ugly Rudder Syndrome

As a young man working at Fairfield in Glasgow, W.D. McLaren learned a great deal about the psychology involved in shipbuilding and in later years related these lessons to his son Arthur.

At that time, it was the practice of owners to circulate a list of the basic requirements for new

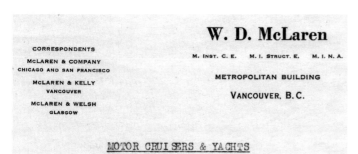

W. D. McLaren

CORRESPONDENTS

McLAREN & COMPANY
CHICAGO AND SAN FRANCISCO

McLAREN & KELLY
VANCOUVER

McLAREN & WELSH
GLASGOW

M. INST. C. E.   M. I. STRUCT. E.   M. I. N. A.

METROPOLITAN BUILDING

VANCOUVER, B.C.

MOTOR CRUISERS & YACHTS

Such great advances have been made in welding within recent years that it is now possible to secure in small steel ships the superiority over wood construction which was long ago recognized in comparing large ships. No longer is it necessary to worry over the early deterioration, leakiness, and fire risks associated with wood. Not only is a steel vessel free from these disabilities, but it can be constructed with proper watertight compartments, can provide greater accommodation within the same dimensions as a wooden one, and, in the larger sizes, can be built at less cost.

W.D.'s summary of the advantages of steel over wood for building yachts, 1930s.

tonnage amongst shipbuilders whom they considered to be reputable firms or whose directors were financially or socially integrated. The shipbuilder passed these outline specifications over to the hull and engine design offices. They in turn produced a proposed design, not only to prepare a construction estimate, but to suggest to the owners a design that would be the basis of a building contract.

There came, of course, the day of reckoning when a joint meeting of owners and builders was held to pass judgment on the new ship design. The general arrangement drawings were laid out on the board room table. Naturally the shipbuilder had designed a vessel that met the owner's wish list. But he had also incorporated features in the hull and machinery that worked best with his yard practices, equipment and outfit, and with which he had cost experience—thus allowing him to offer his most attractive proposal to the ship owner.

Far too often the senior owner's officials criticized the preliminary design mercilessly, suggesting more decks be added, accommodations and cargo handling gear be modified and important details, such as the rake of the funnels, be altered. To incorporate such suggestions required modifying or redrawing the design and re-estimating construction and outfitting. This meant spending time and money that was not likely to be recovered.

W.D. described a typical shipbuilder's ruse to avoid such a situation—to draw a most atrocious looking rudder on the ship's profile. Inevitably, at a very early review stage, the discussion would take the following course:

Managing director: *My goodness, what an ugly rudder. It should be shaped such.* (Penciling in his ideal form of rudder.)
Marine superintendent: *I remember the rudder we had on the Ben Nevis. She steered well. It was this shape.* (Redrawing sketch of the rudder.)
Superintendent engineer: *I do think we should install a balanced rudder, which would reduce torque and perhaps allow a lighter steering gear.*

Thus the whole afternoon was spent discussing rudders—past, present and future—until in the end they agreed on one rudder shape. Of course, it was the same rudder the shipbuilder had in mind in the first place.

At this point, the shipbuilder would interject: "Well, now that we are in agreement about the rudder, are there other points in our design which should be reconsidered?"

The owner's managing director would say: "Time is getting on. I think the rest of the design is very good. I have nothing more to offer, but I am certainly glad we corrected that ugly rudder. What do the rest of you think?"

All agreed the design was excellent save for that ugly rudder. The shipbuilder was well pleased his proposals were accepted and, as for the ugly rudder, an erasure and ten minutes of redrawing would put everything right.

Such is the case of the "Ugly Rudder Syndrome." Of course, the same psychology under different guises is practised many times a day by all sorts of people in different trades and callings!

The CNR coastal cruise ship *Prince George* in the graving dock, Esquimalt, BC, 1948. The vessel was built by Yarrows, using steel and machinery available after the end of wartime shipbuilding. George N.Y. Simpson photo

T.A. McLaren
"I Want to Build Ships!"

My love of ships and shipbuilding was probably the result of my upbringing. Father operated a shipyard in Montrose on the east coast of Scotland at the time of my birth, so it may truly be said that I have been in shipbuilding all my life. As a young boy I would head down to the harbour when I got out of school. Montrose was a seaport primarily concerned with exporting produce from the area. There were always a few fishing vessels tied up, too. I loved to walk the docks and look at the ships. Almost every Sunday I'd go to Coaster Construction with my father. I'd wander around the yard while my father worked. Some of my earliest memories are of people assembling ships out of steel, bolting up the structure and then putting rivets in the bolt holes.

Each summer of my Scottish childhood, I would spend two weeks on the west coast with my Grandpa McLaren, who lived in Helensburgh,

A Scotsman's Porridge

We lived in Montrose, Scotland. My Grandpa and Granny Benzies lived in Glasgow. So did my mother's brothers and one sister. On occasions, my mother would visit her family, taking me in tow. I hated Glasgow. My grandparents' house was habituated by adults. I was the only child and I did not fit into any of the activities. Except for Grandpa Benzies, he had been a builder and had benefited from the boom in tenement construction in Glasgow at the turn of the century and, though the business was now run by three of my uncles, he still liked to visit construction sites and I would accompany him. On one occasion, I was picking up nails. Grandpa wanted to see the length of the stray nails. When I showed him he said, "That's all right." Apparently he had instructed his crews that any nail $1\frac{1}{2}$ inches and longer should be picked up, any nails smaller were to be left. It did not pay to take time to pick them up. Grandpa came from Aberdeenshire where folks were known for their thrift.

One morning Grandpa and I were alone at the table having the usual porridge for breakfast. Now both my grandfathers and my father never poured milk onto their porridge, but rather had a small separate bowl of milk alongside and a spoonful of porridge was dunked into the milk before ingesting. On this particular occasion, as Grandpa and I sat at the table with our porridge plates in front of us, I took my spoon and reached for the sugar bowl.

"Arthur, what are you doing?"

"I'm going to put sugar on my porridge."

"No Scotchman ever puts sugar on his porridge."

I dropped the sugar in my spoon back into the sugar bowl and have never, never put sugar on my porridge from that day on. On occasions when I was away from home, the porridge has been so bland that I have sprinkled salt, but never sugar.

next to the great shipyards on the Clyde. In the 1920s the Firth of Clyde supported some thirty paddle steamers, and six of these vessels were operated by the North British Railway, which had a terminus close to Grandpa's house. From Helensburgh I could look south to Greenock, where deep-sea ships docked or where they stopped to pick up a pilot and escort tugs before proceeding the 20 miles up the dredged channel of the River Clyde to reach the Glasgow docks. Scott's Shipbuilding & Engineering Co. Ltd. was in

Arthur (rowing), James and Ada in a rowboat, 1928.

Thomas Arthur McLaren

- Born September 2, 1919, Montrose, Scotland
- Emigrated to Canada with mother, brother and sister, 1928
- During summer, employed as apprentice boilermaker with Vancouver Iron Works Ltd., 1937–41
- Graduated from UBC with degree in mechanical engineering, 1941
- Went to work for West Coast Shipbuilders, doing technical layout of yard and ship design with W.D., 1941
- Married Dorothy Irene Baxter, 1943
- Replaced W.D. as general manager of West Coast, 1946
- Incorporated Allied Builders (later renamed Allied Shipbuilders) in False Creek, 1948
- Relocated shipyard to North Shore of Vancouver Harbour, 1967
- Celebrated 50 years of shipbuilding, 1991
- Celebrated 50 years of Allied Shipbuilders, 1998
- Died Vancouver, February 19, 1999
- During his shipbuilding career, served in elected and appointed positions:
  - President, Association of Professional Engineers of BC
  - Fellow and Pacific Northwest branch chairman, Society of Naval Architects & Marine Engineers
  - Fellow, Royal Institution of Naval Architects
  - Fellow, Institute of Marine Engineers

W.D. on a swing with his children, c. 1929.

Immigrants with kilts, 1928. Left to right: Arthur, James, mother Eliza, Ada.

Arthur on board the *Cardena*, March 6, 1934.

Greenock, and in those days they always had at least one ship for the Blue Funnel Line under construction. These scenes and my father's work were my first introduction to ships and shipbuilding. I was well and truly hooked.

My father emigrated to Canada in 1927. He had visited Vancouver in 1924 and made the acquaintance of Henry Darling, a former superintendent for the Union Steamships Ltd. Henry's father was John Darling, who had come to Vancouver from the Union Steamship Company of New Zealand and assisted in establishing the company in British Columbia. The senior Mr. Darling brought the Union name and the familiar red funnel with black top from New Zealand to BC.

In 1928, a year after his arrival in Canada, Father sent for my mother and the three children. Amid a shower of tears and goodbyes from all the Scottish relatives, we boarded the Canadian Pacific liner Montclare *and sailed for Canada. I was not yet nine. In 1930 John Darling's widow visited my mother for tea. When I was introduced, Mrs. Darling asked me what I wanted to do when I grew up? I replied, "I want to build ships."*

A week or so later, three cardboard cartons arrived from Mrs. Darling, addressed to me. They contained the bound volumes of Transactions of the Institution of Naval Architects *for the years 1879 to 1896. Fortunately for me, these volumes tended to be descriptive rather than technical, so I could understand the text.*

When I was twelve, I went to the Vancouver Library, which was in the Carnegie building at Hastings and Main Streets. On a shelf at the

Arthur McLaren in his Sea Scout uniform, January 1935.

Arthur McLaren in 1941, as a University of BC graduate.

extreme southeast corner of the main floor was a copy of *Atwood's* Theoretical Naval Architecture, *published in 1899. The book covered the simpler calculations applicable to the practice of naval architecture. It was used by student draftsmen in Britain, guiding many a young man through an elementary course in naval architecture. I must have had that book checked out for three years.*

So it was by the age of fifteen I had gained an elementary knowledge of the principles of naval architecture. Poking around Vancouver's Coal Harbour, I became acquainted with the process of riveting, oxyacetylene burning and plating, thereby getting a general sense of shipbuilding procedures. As a young boy, I learned about ship recognition while visiting my Grandpa McLaren in Helensburgh. So when we emigrated to Vancouver, I could soon identify the local steamers, distinguish

between sister ships and tell a ship from the tone of its whistle on a foggy day. This boyhood interest in ship identification is one of my trivial pursuits that I have enjoyed all my life. I got my driver's licence at age fifteen and drove my father around the industrial area of the Vancouver waterfront. In fact, that's how I got to know most of the shops, waiting for Father to conduct his business. He was always hustling work and contracts.

When I completed high school in Vancouver, I mentioned to my father my desire to study naval architecture at Glasgow University, but there was no money for that. He had graduated from Glasgow Technical University with diplomas in mechanical and electrical engineering. It was decided that a degree in mechanical engineering from the University of British Columbia would provide me with a good basic engineering education. So it was that I entered UBC in 1936 to undertake five years of academic study.

During those student years, I spent the four summer months of each year as an apprentice boilermaker at Vancouver Iron Works Ltd., working for 18³/₄ cents an hour. While I did not absorb the skills of boilermaking, I did learn the technique of steel plate construction, and the use of tools and generally became familiar with boiler shop practice. More importantly, I worked amongst men. Prior to this I had only associated with people my own age whose thoughts and actions were like my own. Now in my later teens, I was working with men up to my father's age, working men whose outlook on life was not familiar to me. Being a university student isolated me from the others. I quickly learned to suppress my opinions and to accept with humour the tricks that were played on me. I also learned how working tradesmen thought. This practical education has been of great assistance to me over the years.

I enjoyed attending the University of British Columbia. In my final two years of mechanical engineering, there were only eighteen of us in the class and some four on the staff, so a real camaraderie grew between us. I was fortunate to take a primary course in physics from Dr. Gordon Shrum. He taught me to think, not just parrot back the expected answers. I remember one Christmas exam vividly—it had seven questions and each student was to attempt any five of the seven. I answered the first four questions with relative ease and confidence. But when I turned to the fifth question, I was stumped. The sixth question also seemed utterly hopeless, so I turned the page to question #7. It asked, "How many grains of sand are on the beaches of the world?"

This was an impossible question, so I went back to question #5 and then #6, but couldn't produce an answer for either. So I tackled #7 by making assumptions about the number of miles of sand beaches on each continent, the width of those beaches, how deep the sand was on those beaches. If all the foregoing were expressed in cubic yards and you could calculate the number of grains of sand in a cubic yard, I figured that the product of these calculations should give some guidance as to the answer.

Arthur sailing his Snipe sailboat, 1939.

On our return to classes in the new year, Dr. Shrum asked how we found his Christmas exam. One student boldly retorted, "How could anybody answer that stupid seventh question?" Dr. Shrum stated that he did not put stupid questions on exams. He went on to explain that indeed nobody could supply a fitting answer to that question, but at least two students had attempted something. And while their conclusions were not necessarily sound, nonetheless he had given full marks for the reasoning each had used to calculate an answer.

He went on to say that someday we would graduate from UBC's ivory tower and end up in the real world. While it was extremely unlikely that any of questions #1 through #6 would be asked, it was quite likely that we would encounter the equivalent of question #7.

Dr. Shrum was so right. In fifty-five years of shipbuilding, engineering and estimating, I have met question #7 daily.

A Shipbuilder's Wife and Life

Dorothy McLaren

Arthur and I met at a young people's church camp on Labour Day weekend in 1940. He was very shy, with only a bit of a Scottish accent—not like his father's. Arthur had a sailboat so we would go sailing on some of our dates. I remember once getting seasick off Point Atkinson! The motor on the boat wouldn't run and the wind wasn't up, but as soon as Arthur got the motor going to move the boat, I was fine.

I worked at a bank until we were married in 1943, some three years later. Then I resigned because in those days, wives didn't work. I was twenty. Arthur was already working long, long hours, so I sort of knew what to expect. When he graduated from UBC and the war started, he was hired by West Coast Shipbuilders. That was an around-the-clock job.

In those early years, Arthur's mother knew a great deal more about what it was like being a shipbuilding family than I did. At first I tried to plan meals for when Arthur came home, but it was impossible. On one of his trips to the Interior, I

ARTHUR McLAREN WEDS

Our Assistant Yard Manager, T. Arthur McLaren, puts in most of his time in charge of the Drawing Office, getting out plans for our Tankers, etc., and placing the new work into the hands of our associates—Hamilton Bridge.

Arthur served his apprenticeship as a boilermaker with our other associates, Vancouver Iron Works, and graduated Bachelor of Applied Science in Mechanical Engineering at U.B.C.

In spite of the fact that he has worked late most nights, Saturdays and Sundays also, since our work started, he has astonished his friends and associates by finding enough time for courtship and marriage.

The wedding took place at Knox United Church, Kerrisdale, on September 2nd, the bride being Miss Dorothy Baxter of this city.

The occasion was not allowed to pass without recognition by the Superintendents, Foremen and Staff, with whom Arthur has close working ties, and the couple were made the recipients of a silver tea service by the Day Shift, a handsome mantel clock by the Night Shift, floor lamp by the Drawing Office, linen by the General Office, and magazine table by the Guards. The young couple, after a few days' absence, have taken up residence in West Vancouver.

Arthur and Dorothy's wedding, as covered in West Coast Shipbuilders' bulletin *Down Our Ways*. Earl Mills and Arthur's sister Ada are attending.

phoned the office to inquire when my husband was expected to arrive home. Well, he didn't come and didn't come. I imagined him in every ditch along the way. When he finally arrived, of course he hadn't been in an accident—just building ferries and not thinking to phone home. He chided me, "You know about that in the construction business. Things come up." And from that day on, Arthur never would say when he might be home. There were always too many unexpected things happening. He just came home when he was finished, and that was that.

I was particularly fond of Arthur's parents,

especially his mother. His father was a real gentleman, but very stern. Anytime we went over to Arthur's parents' place to have dinner, there were always "discussions" at the table. I wasn't used to that. Sometimes it was hard to get a word in edgewise until Arthur and his father had finished talking. It wasn't always technical matters; sometimes it was politics or whatever came along. They used to talk frequently on the phone, too, about one shipping matter or another. When his father died in 1953, Arthur missed him tremendously.

Our first son James was born a few years after Arthur and I married. There's a Scottish heritage of handing down the family name through sons, so having a boy was quite important. With three sons, I did very well! For over twenty years I was domesticated and looked after the boys when they were little. I pretty much raised the family, although Arthur definitely had a part. Let's say he made most of the major decisions and I did the fiddly things, but that wasn't uncommon.

My independence began at a monthly meeting of the Cub Mothers' Auxiliary. I dutifully attended but when there was an urgent plea for a replacement for the leader, I realized how completely inadequate I felt for such a task. I just sat quietly and didn't say a word. Shortly after, I read in the newspaper about a new Toastmistress group being formed where one could learn about conducting meetings, public speaking and so on. At the first meeting when I had to stand up and say three things about myself, I said I was married, had three sons, and then stopped short, completely flustered and unable to say another word. Nevertheless I became a charter member of the club. That was the beginning of a life full of volunteer work with preschool, Cub mothers, Sunday school, cancer campaigns and Meals on Wheels. Helping out as a volunteer became my life theme.

At the time, Malcolm was only three years old, so in order for me to go out to a dinner meeting, Arthur had to come home and babysit. The boys know that Arthur's strong suit is building ships, not cooking, so it became the family joke that when Mother went out they always had "Toastmistress

1941

Dec. 24 Wed. Work proceeding on the vessels. Some of the men laid off midday through starting celebrations rather early. Blew whistle 4 P.M.

Visit from H.R. MacMillan and Van Dusen. Took them into yard and Hamilton Bridge. MacMillan appeared to be satisfied, but urged that we should improve upon the performance of four months for building.

Dec. 25 Thurs. Christmas Day. General Holiday. No men at work. Arthur and I in yard from 10 to 4 P.M. checking up drawings for cranes and other matters. Guards reported "all well". Weather: Frosty.

Dec. 26 Fri. Boxing Day. About 50 men at work advancing erection of 101 and 102, including two squads of riveters. Weather: Frost conditions.

Dec. 27 Sat. Resumed in full force this morning.

didn't show up, Arthur brought home a bell off a ship. He hung it from a hook at the back door. When I rang the bell, the neighbours knew that the kids were due home, and home they came. It saved screaming your lungs out, which I could do. The bell was more polite.

James and Douglas used to scrap like mad. I remember one time when they were teenagers, arguing in the living room. I was in the kitchen when I heard this whomp! I ran in quickly and could see that James must have annoyed Douglas, aged sixteen, one too many times. Even though Douglas was three and a half years younger, he'd just picked James up and literally thrown him across the living room. After that, peace reigned.

soup." That was their name for the split pea soup I'd make up ahead of time.

All three of the boys are different. James is extremely outgoing. Even as a toddler, if we were in a room of people, he'd be going around to everybody. Douglas wasn't like that. He was very shy, but felt he was invincible. He started to learn otherwise when he was three or four. He was hammering and hit himself in the head with the claw hammer; Arthur had to take him to emergency at Lions Gate. Malcolm is some of each.

In the wonderful long days of summer, the boys would just roam. They had a sort of time frame and a general geographic boundary, but they were allowed quite a bit of freedom. But with the long days, sometimes it was hard for them to know when to come home for meals. So, one time after we had to mount quite a search for James when he

TO MR. AND MRS. ARTHUR McLAREN

Since our last publication our Managing-Director has become a Grandfather, there having been born to son Arthur, our Assistant Manager and Naval Architect, and to Mrs. Arthur McLaren, a son, James Dick. However, in spite of the added family responsibility there is no evidence yet of Arthur getting home at usual quitting time. It was thought that with the end of the intensive shipbuilding programme the incessant grind of day and night work throughout the week, and with no let-up Saturdays or Sundays, would be eased. The opposite is the case. Arthur explains that his department turned out more than 500 plans and working sketches for the conversion of the "Menestheus," and now right on the top of that he is still day and night on the job of designs for new construction and conversions. He says that the problem of discussing with son James whether he wishes to become a shipbuilder, or would prefer to exert himself and lose his money in some other calling, can be deferred for a little while.

Mr. McLaren is a strong advocate of the old-time apprenticeship system, and saw to it that Arthur got that type of training by serving his apprenticeship as a boilermaker with Vancouver Iron Works, and graduating B.A.Sc. in Engineering at the University of B. C.

From *Down Our Ways*.

Arthur, Dorothy and son James (age two and a half).

Arthur's sons, June 1964. Left to right: Douglas, Malcolm, James.

Arthur McLaren, 1969.

By the time the boys each went off to work in the shipyard, I was well steeped in Scottish tradition. You started early and just kept on, generation after generation. It was hard work and long hours, but we had good times.

We used to call a business like ours a key-man industry, but I don't know if anybody uses that term any more. It meant that one person was the key man. When Allied started, Arthur was the owner, the designer, the purchaser—he was it, the key man. That went on for many years. And I guess that's how he got to be a workaholic. Arthur left for work at the crack of dawn, often stayed on through dinner and then went back on the weekends, although frequently not until noon. He kept that up until the mid-1980s when they were all working full out building Arctic icebreakers. After those jobs, he cut out weekends. That was a big change. Then came the bypass surgery in 1990 and he cut back a bit more. It was gradual.

Arthur McLaren and his sons James, Malcolm and Douglas in front of a Canmar supply vessel, June 6, 1981. Ian Lindsay photo, *Vancouver Sun*

cardiologist said or what, but he stopped cold turkey. I think everybody was glad when he quit.

Arthur didn't take holidays, except for every sixteen years. We just didn't go on holidays. But we did go to annual meetings like the Society of Naval Architects. They'd be held over a long weekend at Harrison Hot Springs or down at Gearhart on the Oregon coast. Other families like the Spauldings would bring their children and we'd all get together. For a long time, those were our only holidays.

Marine business is a lot like construction. If you don't have an order on your books, then not much happens. There were some really lean times when you had to be very careful with pennies. I'm not known for being careful. You give me $10 and I'll spend $9.98 or $10.02! But when you just didn't know which way the wind was blowing, you were very careful. One time Arthur sent somebody over who was selling deep freezes on the installment plan, but I knew we couldn't afford even the few dollars it would take for the monthly payments. It just wasn't there. It goes in cycles. There were a lot of years where you would just watch.

I remember one particularly quiet year in the yard when Arthur was president of the Professional Engineers, a job that involved visiting all the different branches in the province as well as

It was the same with smoking. He started out smoking cigarettes, but when he "quit smoking" that just meant he changed to cigars. He smoked ten cigars a day when he got going. Everybody hated the smell but the office had to put up with it. I used to buy them for him when I went shopping for groceries. I didn't get the very expensive ones, more the middle-of-the-road ones. They were tolerable. If Arthur bought cigars, they were the really cheap ones that would just stink. But even with the more expensive ones, he'd smoke them for too long and they'd become vile. When he got angina, he cut back from ten to two cigars a day. Then he had an angiogram. I don't know if it was something the

Arthur looks on as Dorothy breaks the bottle over the 120-foot floating drydock *Allied 208*, 1980.

Allied 208 being launched with the fishing vessel *Resolution* inside of it, 1980.

Arthur and Dorothy McLaren, Christmas 1998.

attending meetings and functions. I told him it was lucky that his turn in office coincided with a quiet year because other busier years he wouldn't have been able to do it.

Ship launches were always big occasions where you got to meet all the suppliers, owners and people from the other yards. You'd invite everybody, even your friendly rivals. I'd never christened any of the Allied ships until they built the floating drydock. They didn't give it a fancy name, just the hull number—Allied 208. The boys kidded me a lot about my speech, but when it came time to break the bottle of champagne, I just said, "I name this vessel Allied 208 and God bless all who work on her." Inside the drydock, they'd already built a fish boat—

a typical McLaren way to save space. So as soon as they were ready to sink the drydock, the fisherman's wife christened the fish boat. There aren't so many launchings now, and most of those people from the early days have retired or are gone.

During his last few years, Arthur's health demands meant we were together more than ever. He still went to the shipyard, but needed me to drive him to and from work. He used to say we married for better, for worse, but not for lunch. But by then I was making lunch for him every day. We were together for over fifty years and the shipyard was that old, too. Each decade was full of challenges, but I'd say the last decade was just as good as the first one!

CHAPTER 2

The Challenge of Wartime Shipbuilding

"We are going to have to work hard night and day to win."
—W.D. McLaren

The most powerful impact on the steel ship-building industry in this province was World War II. The initial orders were for naval vessels, including 190-foot single-screw patrol vessels (later designated corvettes), 180-foot steam twin-screw minesweepers (Bangors) and 118-foot wooden motor launches (Fairmiles). Federal government orders for the steel vessels were initially shared by the five steel yards operating in the province: Burrard Dry Dock, Yarrows, Victoria Machinery Depot, Prince Rupert Drydock and North Vancouver Ship Repairs (which rebuilt its maintenance yard to handle the new steel construction). Orders for the naval vessels were placed in early 1940 and deliveries began in early 1941.

World War II was largely a battle to control ocean transport, which was vital in all theatres of war, so there was a great need for merchant cargo ships. Supplies and war material had to be sent across the Atlantic in order to arm Britain and build up for the European invasion. To support the British 8th Army fighting in North Africa, ships were sent around the Cape of Good Hope and north to Egypt. Later on, ships went into the Mediterranean to supply the Italian campaign, to the Barents Sea to supply Russia, and across the Pacific to assist US forces in the re-conquest of Japanese-held islands. These ships were easy pickings for enemy forces. History had shown that the only way to protect merchant shipping against attack was to sail in convoy. However, at the outbreak of World War II, Allied merchant shipping was operating throughout the world, and it was not possible to bring all ships into convoys.

In the early years of the war, enemy submarines and aircraft took a toll of forty to eighty merchant ships every month. Despite new construction by British yards, the transfer of ships and crews from Norwegian, Danish, Dutch and Greek merchant fleets, and the release of World War I tonnage from the American reserves, it was quite obvious that replacement of considerable merchant tonnage was critical to Britain's survival. Some argued for the construction of wooden ships, but wiser minds prevailed. If the war was to be won, a sharp increase in the construction of steel merchant ships had to become top priority.

The North Sands Ship

Britain paid for the first warships in sterling. In 1940, when British funds were depleted, the US government introduced the Lend Lease Act to finance further building. The British Ministry of War Transport sent a team of shipbuilders and engine builders to the US and Canada. Their job was to determine the best way new merchant ships could be built in North America to head off the crisis. The team came armed with drawings for a 9,300-ton coal-burning cargo steamer made of steel. The drawings were prepared by Joseph L. Thompson & Sons Ltd., North Sands Shipyard, Sunderland, England; hence this wartime cargo vessel came to be known as the North Sands ship. The design was similar to that of hundreds of British tramp steamers and presented a simple, efficient, resilient cargo ship capable of carrying bulk cargo, baled cargo and deck cargo.

Propulsion was by a triple-expansion steam engine with three cylinders: 24$\frac{1}{2}$″, 37″ and 70″ diameter x 48″ stroke capable of developing 2500 ihp at 76 rpm. Steam was provided at 220 psi from three fire tube Scotch marine boilers, each with three corrugated furnaces and a heating surface of 2,380 sq. ft. Loaded, the ship could maintain a speed of 10 knots under favourable weather conditions, making it acceptable for fast convoys, which required at least 9 knots.

These plans became the basis of all US-built Liberty and Ocean ships (constructed for the US and Britain, respectively) and of the Canadian-built Park and Fort ships (constructed for Canada and Britain, respectively). The design was a rivetted shelter deck vessel with machinery amidships. The lines incorporated "V" rather than "U" sections

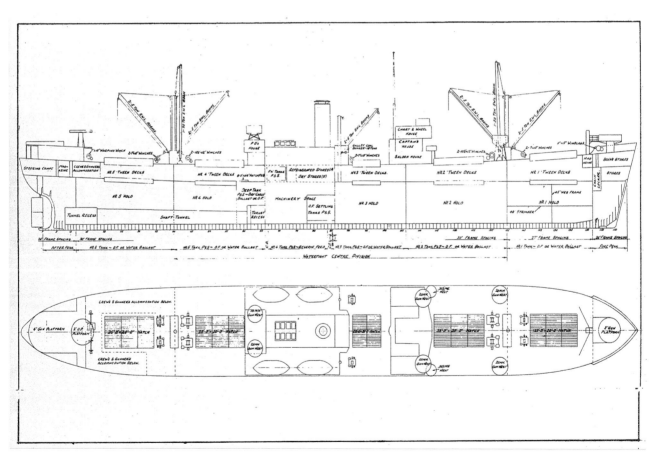

Inboard profile drawing of a North Sands cargo ship, 1940s.

forward and a "canoe" stern. The hull was an easy form to build, requiring no furnaced plates. The ships were designed to be built with a minimum of equipment. No extra large shipyard cranes were needed and the parts were supposedly interchangeable. The Americans kept the hull form, but adopted all-welded construction and eliminated the tumblehome on the hull. Canadian practice was to rivet the longitudinal seams and weld the transverse butts.

In the US, the naval architectural firm Gibbs and Cox redrew the British drawings suitable for welded construction and designed steelwork in prefabricated assemblies so that the hull could be built in panels or units of up to 30 tons. These units, built on slabs, could be turned over so that welding could generally be undertaken in downhand position and a great deal of the assembly labour could be done at ground level rather than on staging many feet in the air.

Further modifications resulted in the E-C2, the US Liberty ship, which Franklin D. Roosevelt dubbed the "ugly duckling." It had a hull and main engine similar to the North Sands ship, but incorporated two Combustion Engineering Company Inc. water tube oil-fired boilers in lieu of the three coal-fired Scotch boilers. Instead of the separate deckhouse structures, a single deckhouse of three levels was built over the machinery space. With the US prefabrication systems, this complete deckhouse could be built, outfitted and dropped onto the upper deck using a multi-crane lift. All told, some 2,700 US Liberty ships, 60 Ocean ships and 320 Canadian Fort and Park ships were built.

Building the Cargo Fleet

By late 1940 the British government had ordered a total of eighty-six North Sands ships, sixty to be built in the US and twenty-six in Canada. The US orders were split: thirty to the east coast and thirty to the west coast. The Canadian order saw eighteen assigned to the St. Lawrence yards (six to Canadian Vickers and

HULL PARTICULARS

LENGTH B.P.	416'-0"
BREADTH, M'LD	56'-10¼"
DEPTH, M'LD	37-4"
DRAFT SUMMER	26'-11⅞"
DEADWEIGHT AT SUMMER DRAFT	10310 ~ TONS
UNDER DECK TONNAGE	~ TONS
GROSS TONNAGE	~ TONS
NETT TONNAGE	~ TONS
WINCHES	6-7"x10" FOR 5 TON BOOMS, 1-7"x10" WARPING WINCH & 4-10½"x12" FOR 30&50 TON BOOMS.
WINDLASS	11"x13" STEAM WINDLASS.
AUX. CONDENSER	STRUTHERS-WELLS - 700 ∅ COOLING SURFACE
AUX. AIR & CIRC. PUMP	WORTHINGTON-10"x12"x12"x12" HORIZ. SIMPLEX.
DISTILLER	DAVIS ENGINEERING CO ~60∅ SURFACE.
WIRELESS	1-300 WATT TRANSMITTER (FEDERAL RADIO)
ACCOMMODATION	IN SALOON & MIDSHIP HOUSES & AFTER 'TWEEN DECK FOR 11-OFFICERS, 32 OF CREW & 16 NAVAL RATINGS.

MACHINERY PARTICULARS

MAIN ENGINES	SINGLE SCREW 24½"x37"x 70"x48" STROKE. TRIPLE EXPANSION. 2500 I.H.P. AT 76 R.P.M.
BOILERS	2-CROSS SECTIONAL SINUOUS HEADER STRAIGHT TUBE TYPE ~4852∅ HEATING SURFACE, FITTED WITH SUPERHEATERS ~2645∅ HEATING SURFACE.
FUEL	4-TODD BURNERS PER BOILER BURNING BUNKER 'C' FUEL OIL.
FORCED DRAFT FAN	CANADIAN SIROCCO ~ 10,000 C.F.M. AT 3" S.P.
CONDENSER	FOSTER WHEELER ~ 2700 ∅ COOLING SURFACE.
PROPELLER	BRONZE VARIABLE PITCH. 18-6" DIA. x 16'-0" MEAN PITCH, 117 ∅ SURFACE AREA.
AIR PUMP	24"x 26" SINGLE ACTING ~ON MAIN ENGINES.
BILGE PUMPS	2-4½"x26" ON MAIN ENGINES.
FEED PUMPS	2-WORTHINGTON 12"x 8"x 24" VERTICAL SIMPLEX.
CIRCULATING PUMP	MORRIS MACHINE WORKS ~ 14" ~3860 U.S.G.P.M.
BALLAST & G.S. PUMP	WORTHINGTON ~ 10"x11"x12" VERTICAL DUPLEX.
FIRE & BILGE PUMP	WORTHINGTON ~ 10"x11"x12" VERTICAL DUPLEX.
F.O. TRANSFER PUMP	WORTHINGTON ~ 10"x11"x12" VERTICAL DUPLEX.
F.O. SERVICE PUMPS	2-WORTHINGTON ~ 7½"x4"x10" VERTICAL SIMPLEX.
S.W. SERVICE PUMP	WORTHINGTON ~ 5"x8"x8" VERTICAL SIMPLEX.
EVAPORATOR	DAVIS ENGINEERING CO. ~ 25 TONS PER 24 HRS.
FEED HEATER	DAVIS ENGINEERING CO. ~ 48,000 # PER HR.
GENERATORS	3- 15 K.W. SETS ~8"x 4" HIGH SPEED ENGINE.

The *Fort Boise* (Hull #127), outbound at the First Narrows, Vancouver, September 18, 1943.

twelve to Davie Shipbuilding) and eight to Burrard Dry Dock in North Vancouver. All of the Canadian vessels were paid for by the British government and transferred to their Ministry of War Transport. The ministry assigned each ship to a British shipping company, which would operate it.

Within a short time, the US government placed orders for an additional 100 North Sands ships. These would be owned by the US Maritime Commission, but be built in Canada and delivered to the British Ministry of War Transport under the terms of the US Lend Lease Act. Later, ships were built for the Canadian government account. Some were loaned to the British Ministry of War Transport, while others were delivered to the Park Steamship Company, a Canadian Crown corporation.

Construction of the new West Coast Shipbuilders yard on the former site of the Coughlan & Sons shipyard, False Creek, July 1941.

Orders for standard vessels of smaller tonnage—7,500- and 4,700-ton cargo ships, 3,600-ton tankers, and 350- and 1,250-ton coasters—were placed with smaller Canadian shipyards. The overwhelming majority, however, were the 10,000-ton capacity ships.

To build a fleet of cargo transports and replace merchant ships lost through enemy action, more than 300 North Sands type cargo vessels were constructed in Canada between 1942 and 1945. The majority of these ships—some 255—were built in British Columbia. A total of seven shipyards in the province (five existing yards and two new ones) concentrated on wartime steel ship construction, and the summer of 1941 saw some twenty-two shipbuilding berths prepared. Six of these yards built 10,000-dwt cargo ships commissioned as Fort and Park vessels. Yarrows built two

freighters and then was reassigned to the frigate program.

The BC yards building 10,000-dwt ships were:

Burrard Dry Dock (North Vancouver)

This was the leading yard on the West Coast, with experience building cargo ships during World War I. Burrard produced the greatest number of cargo ships in Canada during World War II. Two sets of ways had been set up early in 1940 for building corvettes and Bangor Class minesweepers. Two berths from the World War I period were rebuilt and supplied with cranes and two new berths were built in North Vancouver to meet the cargo ship program.

Burrard South Yard (Vancouver Harbour, South Shore)

Burrard Dry Dock obtained a "greenfield" (vacant) site on the south shore of Vancouver Harbour, where it built four new berths along with the cranage, plate and fabricating shops necessary to build hulls. Installation of boilers, engines and general outfitting was done at Burrard's North Vancouver yard.

North Vancouver Ship Repairs Ltd. (North Vancouver)

This subsidiary of Pacific Salvage Company Ltd. was originally a small repair firm located just west of Lonsdale Avenue. Early in 1940 it had built three small construction berths and outfitting wharves for building Bangor Class minesweepers. On receiving orders for cargo ships, the company set up four building berths and enlarged the outfitting wharves.

West Coast Shipbuilders Ltd. (Vancouver's False Creek)

The promise of wartime cargo ship orders provided the impetus for a group of prominent Vancouver businessmen to set up a new shipyard just east of the Connaught Bridge (later renamed the Cambie Street Bridge). This property was the former site of J. Coughlan & Sons shipyard and was next to the bridge-building plant of Hamilton Bridge (later Western Bridge), which had a steel fabricating capacity greater than any of the existing Vancouver area shipyards. The Walkem family, who already owned Vancouver Iron Works, joined several others to establish West Coast Shipbuilders, a four-berth shipyard at First Avenue and Columbia Street on False Creek.

Victoria Machinery Depot Company (Victoria's Outer Harbour)

VMD had a complete engineering works, foundry, machine shop, boiler shop, marine railway and two building berths used in the early days of the war for building corvettes. On being awarded contracts for building cargo ships, the company erected a new two-berth yard in Victoria's outer harbour. That area is now occupied by the Canadian Coast Guard.

Yarrows Ltd. (Esquimalt)

This complete shipyard had a marine railway and two berths that were used for corvette construction in 1940. The company prepared a new two-berth yard on an open field site, north of the Esquimalt Public Works graving dock. This new yard was relatively close to the existing yard as the crow flies, but over a mile by road from the centre of activity. Complete steelworking equipment was set up in the new yard, and the wharves of the existing yard provided the facilities required for outfitting. Both VMD and Yarrows used the 50-ton crane at the Esquimalt Dock to handle engines and boilers. Yarrows built only two North Sands cargo ships and then was reassigned to build frigates as part of the naval shipbuilding program.

Prince Rupert Drydock & Shipbuilding (Prince Rupert)

Prince Rupert was chosen as the Pacific Terminus of the Grand Trunk Pacific Railway, with the first train arriving in 1914. City fathers envisioned Prince Rupert as a port and metropolis that would be the gateway to the Orient. Prior to World War I the railway company had a floating drydock of 15,000-ton lifting capacity built and installed as part of the city's shipyard facilities. From 1940 to 1942, Prince Rupert Drydock built four Bangor Class minesweepers. This yard was the only shipbuilder in BC readily equipped to build the North Sands type ship.

Shipyard production was only part of the wartime story. All boilers, steering gear, winches, windlasses, masts, shafting, etc. were manufactured in BC. Engineering plants in Vancouver were essential to the shipbuilding program. Vancouver Iron Works had a well-equipped boiler shop on the south shore just east of Alder Street; there employees built boilers for cargo ships, frigates and minesweepers at a rate of four per week. Vancouver Engineering Works on 6th Avenue immediately west of Cambie Street was a fully equipped engineering shop with steel foundry and heavy machine shop that turned out cast-steel stern frames, shafting and stern tubes. Progressive Engineering on 1st Avenue, just east of the Cambie Bridge, built cargo windlasses. Tyee Machinery on Granville Island turned out anchor windlasses. In fact, practically every component to fit out a cargo ship—except for main engines and pumps—was built in Vancouver, with the lion's share being delivered by False Creek shops.

As for materials from the rest of Canada, steel came from three mills in eastern Canada, engines were built by three eastern Canadian firms and pumps were produced by the machine shops of the gold mines in northern Ontario. Before the start of the war, Canada had been a producer of raw materials rather than an industrialized society. World War II changed all that.

Building a New Shipyard

WEST COAST SHIPBUILDERS LTD.

205 WEST FIRST AVE.
VANCOUVER, B.C.

W.D. McLaren and his son Arthur McLaren shared a common work history at West Coast Shipbuilders. On the south shore of False Creek in Vancouver was the former Coughlan yard site,

Hull #101, the double-bottom structure, on the launchways at West Coast Shipbuilders.

and adjacent to that was Hamilton Bridge, a structural steel building plant. When World War II broke out, it became apparent that peacetime pursuits such as bridge building would be put on hold. It seemed logical to exploit the greater fabricating capacity of the bridge-building plant. So a group of Vancouver businessmen, including the Walkem family, decided to set up a modern shipyard on the Coughlan site next door. They established a four-berth shipyard at 1st Avenue and Columbia Street, calling it West Coast Shipbuilders Ltd. In 1941 they asked W.D. McLaren to become the new shipyard's general manager, taking on the responsibility to lay out the new yard, recruit workers and begin producing ships. He accepted the challenge.

When the principals of the new yard went to negotiate with Wartime Merchant Shipping for a share of the North Sands ships, they were told to stand by while the "established" yards received orders. Some of the existing builders opined that there was not enough labour for another yard. West Coast's directors countered that the Hamilton Bridge company next door was much better equipped to fabricate steel than any of the existing shipyards. They pointed out that with commercial bridge building at a wartime halt, the plant was operating at less than 10 percent capacity. Their logic won out.

Beginning on May 12, 1941, W.D. McLaren kept a daily account of the activities of West

Hull #104, February 20, 1942. This view from the bow shows the margin plate at the side of the double-bottom tank top.

SHIPS OF STEEL

Coast Shipbuilders. His journals began with the setup of the new shipyard on its False Creek site in Vancouver. Unlike the existing BC yards building 10,000-ton ships, the new yard had to agree to maintain an "open shop." The unions did not accept that proviso easily.

1941

May 18 Sun.
Office-general. Meeting at Hamilton Bridge Plant. H.R. MacMillan, Austin Taylor, Capt. Vickery, USN, Mr. Smeltzer (Schmeltzer) USA Merchant Shipping, Mr. Thompson, Mr. Hunter, O'Hallern, Reps. for Hamilton: Spencer, Belyea, Lawson, Louden, Davis. Reps. for West Coast: Walkem, Cribb and self. All seemed satisfied.

Mr. H.R. MacMillan brought up matter of "closed shop" and concern of C.D. Howe on Union action. Had affidavits from men unable to get jobs in Wallace yard. H.R. MacMillan said he would tell Wallace and Burdick of arrangements with us.

May 19 Mon.
Office-general. H.R. MacMillan phoned to ask if we had placed orders for steel. I said no and expected help from his department. He asked that night letter be sent to Cowie. This I prepared and dispatched. H.R. MacMillan said he had told Wallace and Burdick that we were given contracts and I asked if we could now go out in open. Yes, could now keep head up but "mouth shut."

May 20 Tues.
At office and learned from Knox Walkem that Hamilton Bridge agreed on contract and road "all clear." Phoned Mr. Wallace that would meet him in afternoon to discuss arrangements.

At Burrard 1 PM and advised Mr. Wallace we are all set to build ships, and that we wanted to work on participation in templates, etc.

May 22 Thurs.
At Hamilton Bridge 8 AM. Again discussed progress with Cokely. Knox Walkem and Burbidge

called at 8:30 and I showed them around the place, and in particular outlined what I thought would be a good office arrangement, taking in the whole of the top floor and subdividing it by glass partitions. This could be done without disturbing Hamilton Bridge in the occupancy of the lower offices. Louden was asked to have the patterns removed from the top floor.

Arranged with the Telephone Co. to give us a phone immediately and to reserve us six lines and provision for a switchboard for 24 connections.

Cribb still engaged considering different ways and means of effecting the fill and getting the services of contractors. Louden arranging to clear away the steel, but it is possible the work may proceed rather slowly. Emphasized my desire that there should be two shifts daily, and that work should be continued over the weekend.

Phone call from Samson, Progressive Engineering, asking our launching dates. Told him that we would make the first launch in December, and would launch every five weeks thereafter as our requirement is to build and deliver ten ships before the end of 1942.

Arthur made sketch of the offices, and in the evening laid them out on 1/8" scale.

May 27 Tues.
. . . Evening: Back at office and then at yard where Bentall's men making very satisfactory progress on the top office. Worked all evening on the layout of ships and yard for the purpose of establishing rail tracks.

May 28 Wed.
8 AM at yard, Discussed matters with Cribb and Cokely and started Arthur on the layout of the ships and rail tracks.

May 31 Sat.
At yard 8 AM. Carpenters did not turn up as they wanted time and a half after 40 hours, and Cribb told them he had no authority to pay overtime till a 44 hour working week was completed. The

arrangement worked in very well. Weather was wet and the opportunity is thus provided for a clear understanding on the labour situation. Recommended that the men be paid 90 cents plus 4 cent bonus instead of 83 cents in the shipyards as all the shipyards had agreed to bring the carpenter's rate up to the same as other workers. We can start away with the 90 cents on the basis that this is the rate paid to the construction trades, and the men are really on construction work at present.

June 2 Mon.
. . . Had a call from J. McKinlay and Jack Evans of the Canadian Federation of Labour who say they are in the best position to provide shipwrights, joiners, boatbuilders, caulkers, electricians and helpers, also general labourers. They claim that the general membership of their Union, so far as woodworkers is concerned, is very much better than the A.F.L. Note that the other Unions in Vancouver are the Canadian Congress of Labour which is related to the C.I.O., and the American Federation of Labour, which is Bengough's union. McKinlay claims that Bengough could only provide a few carpenters.

I insisted that we must be an "open shop." We would consider workers only on their merit as workers. If one Union would work harmoniously with another that would suit us, but we can't pick from one Union to the exclusion of the other.

Agreed that the wages would be 90 cents plus 4 cents for cost of living bonus as intended after meeting Chase. Insisted that the working week must be 44 hours. We have no alternative.

June 9, Mon.
Telephones connected. Work proceeding satisfactorily, but still short of pile driving crews.

Visit from Miller of Canadian Federation of Labour who indicated his willingness to co-operate fully with us. Impressed him with the fact that we could not entertain the idea of a closed shop, and that we would wish to work impartially with any Union or none.

June 21, Sat.
Delegation from Brotherhood of Carpenters led by Stevenson. They object to carpenters working on Saturday without being paid overtime as they have a five day working week. Explained to them that we are shipbuilders and obliged to observe the 44 hour working week, and not general contractors, so agreements with general contractors are not applicable to us. Pointed out the impossibility of having to observe difference between building and ship work when our men would be carrying on both daily. Men left work about 10 AM merely because they were obliged to do so, not because they wanted. Feel that the interview was satisfactorily completed by understanding of the foregoing, and especially as the other Union—Federation of Labour—had tacitly agreed to recognize our position.

Aug. 1 Fri.
Call from Stevenson and Page of United Brotherhood of Carpenters and Joiners, who wished us to sign an agreement with their Union similar to Yarrows. Mentioned to them that Evans of the Amalgamated Builders, also, had a Yarrows agreement, and our reply would be the same as to him—that we would not sign with any Union.

As Arthur summed it up later:

Although it was never written down, the federal government at that time was concerned about labour stability. The steel shipyards were heavily unionized, with the Communist Party firmly entrenched in the union executive. Burrard Dry Dock had twenty-two separate agreements with steelworkers, shipwrights, machinists, pipefitters, coppersmiths, crane operators, etc., with new employees being recruited daily. So the federal government, through Wartime Merchant Shipping, offered West Coast Shipbuilders orders for North Sands ships, provided they kept an open shop. This challenge was accepted. Of course, we paid the wages and honoured the same terms as the other yards, but ours was the open shop. This matter of the union vs. non-union shop was seen as a holy war by some. As a result, my father was portrayed as a rabid anti-unionist. He was not. He was merely carrying out orders.

Arthur remembered his father listening to the radio on the day war was declared. "W.D.'s comment after the announcement was, 'This is going to be a long war. It will be won in factories and shipyards. We are going to have to work hard night and day to win.' There was nothing about whether the war was good, bad or indifferent, or whether we had suitable military personnel. Just that we were going to have to work very hard. That's the way he saw so many things."

The main deck of Hull #102, looking aft.

Joining West Coast by Default

Arthur went to work for West Coast Shipbuilders in 1941, within a week after completing his engineering studies at UBC. The new yard was just starting up. He recalled the frenzy to enlist and be a part of the action.

During the war all the young guys eighteen to thirty years old either enlisted or were conscripted into the services. I got drafted myself and spent a whole day down in Little Mountain army barracks, but they kicked me out and sent me home because I can only see with one eye.

I also tried to get into the navy. They were looking for engineering graduates so I went down to the navy base Discovery at Deadman's Island. Somewhere during the interview it came up that I couldn't see out of one eye. The officer said, "Well, that's it. You're not coming into this here navy." I reminded him that Nelson had only one functioning eye, but he said Nelson started out with two good eyes. So that was it for volunteering with the navy. In 1941 I went to work for West Coast.

Because West Coast was organized specifically to build the 10,000-ton steel wartime freighters, the new yard was set up so that four hulls could be laid at the same time. As part of his engineering duties, Arthur McLaren helped lay out the new yard. He recalled that E.F. "Jack" Cribb got the

project underway. Cribb was manager of West Coast Salvage Company Ltd., a wood-building shipyard owned by the Walkem family, and an expert in handling a project and dealing with men. One of the first men on the job was Leon Cokely, land surveyor. He not only surveyed the yard site, but laid out launching ways, recorded various measurements on ships during construction and measured shaft and engine alignments. Working with surveyor's instruments, Cokely did what was done in other yards by shipwrights using plumb bobs, declivity boards and battens—the age-old tools of shipbuilders.

Arthur McLaren with Earl Mills at West Coast, November 1943.

Launching of the *Kootenay Park* (Hull #104), West Coast Shipbuilders, June 11, 1944.

W.D. McLaren waves his hat at the launching of the *Mount Douglas Park* (Hull #122), April 26, 1943.

Unlike established yards, West Coast Ship-builders Ltd. hired carpenters and construction workers first. These men built the gantries, drove pilings for the wharves and set up the staging towers on the building berths. Most of them stayed with the yard after wood construction was completed and became part of the steel shipbuilding crew.

Arthur remembered that in the early days of World War II, when so many men were leaving to go to war, skilled tradesmen were pursued with offers of employment. But every morning there were also some two dozen men standing at the gates, waiting to be employed. Most of these men were not tradesmen, but workers who came from farms, logging camps and mines. Many had not found employment during the Depression. Others had left low-paying unskilled jobs, hoping for advancement. They were the raw material the

After launching, the 10,000-ton war ships were moved alongside the outfitting dock. After West Coast Shipbuilders closed, Allied Builders was originally located on the site of this outfitting dock.

shipyard had to work with in order to produce specialists—those men who learned one specific building task that was done over and over. The challenge was not so much to find workers, as to train them into a productive team who could work in harmony.

Whether dealing with labourers, tradesmen, foremen or engineers, the key was to ensure that everyone understood the language and requirements of the job at hand. Arthur described one brief communication snafu that his father encountered.

We had in our employment at West Coast the Smith brothers—Dick Smith was our maintenance engineer and Frank Smith was the maintenance foreman. My father was constantly coming up with ways to improve productivity and kept both Dick and Frank busy with his ideas. Dick developed hydraulic tools to aid in rallying up launching ways and later developed caulking machines for sealing the plate seams. Frank built sheds and other structures, as well as installing platforms so that special access could be provided in specific locations, all of which increased the efficiency of the shipbuilding process.

In building the first vessels, it was obvious

Lowering a 50-ton boiler into a Victory ship at the outfitting dock.

that access to the engine room should be available near ground level so that workers would not have to climb up 50 feet to the upper deck and 40 feet back down in order to work inside the engine room. Thus it was decided to leave off a bilge plate in the way of the engine room, closing the opening just before launching. Frank then constructed ramps reaching from the ground onto the engine room tank top.

My father approved Frank's arrangements but asked him to provide a hen run.

Frank scratched his head in puzzlement. "I'm sorry, Mr. McLaren, but I don't follow you."

"Make a hen run, Frank. Nail cross-cleats on the planks so the men can get a good toehold."

"Oh, I see, Mr. McLaren," Frank beamed. "You want a duck walk!"

Crews felt a tangible pride in helping with the war effort, a factor that instilled a certain dedication to the job. W.D. McLaren was particularly proud of being able to build ships with such a motley assortment of workers. He regularly invited visiting dignitaries from the UK to stroll

This photo was published in West Coast Shipbuilders' bulletin *Down Our Ways*, with the caption: "Here is 2496, Jacob Boles, one of our 150 men in the Burning Gang under Mr. Boutilier."

around the yard and see the wonder for themselves. But for Arthur McLaren, the main driving force was his wish to measure up to the expectations of his father (and boss). At 3:00 one Sunday morning, when he was in the yard checking out some work, the mechanic in charge asked him, "What the hell are you doing down here?" Arthur explained that he was just making sure they were getting ahead all right. "God, your father must be a son of a bitch," the mechanic commented. When Arthur asked why, the fellow said, "Fancy having his son down here at 3 o'clock on a Sunday morning." Arthur said later, "I didn't tell him, but I would have been disappointed if my father didn't expect that of me."

The Overnight Wonder
Hull #101

The first hull built at West Coast Shipbuilders was the *Fort Chilcotin* (Hull #101). Her keel was laid in August 1941; the ship was launched on March 7, 1942, with delivery in May. Most of the nine-month building period was taken up by the six months it took to build and equip the yard, a shortage of steel, holdups in the supply of templates, and the learning time necessary for all employees and supervisors.

By February 1942 the yard was under heavy stress to get the first hull launched. Hulls #102, #103 and #104 were all under construction and rapidly catching up. Hamilton Bridge had already fabricated half the steel for Hull #105, which was to follow #101 on the berth. A launching at the very earliest date was imperative, but there were still no deckhouses erected on the first hull except the boundary bulkheads of the engine casing. Since it was apparent that the deckhouse would have to be built after the hull was afloat, all the plating stiffeners and beams for this construction were dropped helter-skelter on the upper deck.

The drawing of the deckhouse, issued by the builders of the original North Sands ship, had been done on a scale of $1/4$ inch to the foot. This was rather small to reveal clearly all the steel-work detail and to include the markings for plates, frames, beams, etc. Furthermore, this particular drawing was difficult to decipher since it had been blueprinted from a sepia print of the original tracing.

"After launching, attention was given to shipping the three boilers and main engine," Arthur explained. "The piles of deckhouse steel were picked over, but the whole problem remained a Chinese puzzle. A week went by with no action on the deckhouses. The erection crew stood around as though waiting for guidance from some mystic spirit."

In those days the yard ran continuously on a three-shift basis. The day shift was fully manned by senior and older men. Younger men with less experience but more get-up-and-go ran the afternoon shift. The graveyard shift was normally for catching up.

One particular afternoon, we assembled gangs of younger men to blitz the deckhouses on Hull #101. The plan of attack was to retrieve the coaming bars for the deckhouses from the tangled piles of steel dumped on the deck. These would be bolted to the upper deck, flange up, thus establishing a datum for further erection. Next we'd tackle the look-out plates that formed the deckhouse sides. These were relatively small plates about 8 x 8 feet with seams on every third stiffener. A lot of the house sides, subdivision bulkheads, etc. could be manhandled into place. A crane was used for handling deck beams and deck plating. Using a gang of some forty fitters and ten welders, we started at 4:00 p.m. and worked through to 4:00 a.m. During that time we managed to erect 60 percent of the six deckhouses—indeed an overnight wonder.

In the course of erecting the steelwork, the pile of plates and angles diminished and the task of locating a given plate or steel section became much less arduous. The day-shift erectors who had been baffled were now in a position to continue and complete the deckhouse structures. Within two

The *Fort Chilcotin* (Hull #101), the first vessel built by West Coast Shipbuilders, on trials in English Bay, June 1942. She was launched March 7, 1942, and became a war loss when she was sunk off Brazil on July 24, 1943.

more days, deckhouse steelwork was completely erected, ready for welding and rivetting.

This exercise was a challenge to teams of younger men working on their first ship. They tackled the job with extreme enthusiasm, knowing it was vital that deckhouses be complete for joiner and electrical work to proceed. Nonetheless, this overnight wonder caused bad feelings amongst the senior men on the day shift, to whom the work had originally been entrusted. They felt humiliated that a crew of young men had done on one twelve-hour shift what they had failed to get started in one week.

Should we have consulted with the seniors first, I doubt such parley would have made any difference. We were a bunch of smart alecks who had gone out of our way to embarrass older, experienced men. We didn't apologize. There was a war on, and ships were being sunk at twice the rate of replacement. We had cleared a building stoppage on Hull #101.

Each subsequent West Coast ship, starting with Hull #105, was turned out from keel to launching in eight weeks. From keel to delivery took only twelve and a half weeks. With the second series of hulls, West Coast crews delivered a new ship through the False Creek bridges every second Sunday until the program eased off. The other three Vancouver yards met the same schedule: from mid-1942 to late 1943 two new ships per week were dispatched from Vancouver. During World War II, British Columbia shipbuilders constructed an amazing total of 255 10,000-ton ships.

In about 1943, when West Coast Shipbuilders was sold to Frank Ross, W.D. McLaren was asked to continue as general manager for West Coast Shipbuilders and to handle Western Bridge (formerly Hamilton Bridge) as well.

Workers and Wages

At the outbreak of war in 1939, there was a fraternity of itinerant steel shipbuilders in BC who supported themselves by moving from yard to yard as work was available. Most of this work was repair and maintenance. That changed with the advent of the naval shipbuilding program in 1940, which employed about 1,800 men. During this two-year period, a nucleus of skilled workers knowledgeable in special steel shipbuilding skills served as foremen while constructing patrol vessels, minesweepers and wooden motor launches with less experienced and less skilled crews.

Prior to 1939, employees in shipyards, shops and foundries all worked a forty-four-hour week: five weekdays and Saturday morning. Carpenters only worked a five-day, forty-hour week. When shipbuilding expanded during the war and carpenters were taken into the yards in large numbers, first for yard construction and later into the steel trades, they reasoned that they should get overtime pay, at $1^1/2$ times hourly wages, for the extra hours they had to work on Saturdays. "They never got any special consideration," Arthur remembered, "although there was a lot of fuss about it and threats of strikes."

Tradesmen (machinists, boilermakers, moulders) working in heavy industry in the Vancouver–Victoria area and employed fairly steadily under shop conditions earned 75 cents per hour prior to World War II. Helpers received 50 cents. Those journeymen carpenters, rivetters and shipwrights employed in outside work, subjected to inclement weather and layoff, earned 90 cents per hour. At the beginning of the naval shipbuilding program in 1940, wages of 90 cents per hour were established for all tradesmen, with a rate of $67^1/2$ cents for non-skilled workers. In 1942, the rising cost of living was recognized by the government, and a bonus of 10 cents per hour was added to all wages.

After the Japanese attack on the US navy base at Pearl Harbor in December 1941, Canadian shipyards were instructed by Ottawa to carry out continuous production, twenty-four hours a day, seven days a week. Each employee was to work eight hours per day, six days per week, with one day off per week (not necessarily Sunday). Maintaining the seven-day work week was extremely difficult at a time when the Lord's Day Act was enforced and no shopping or commercial activities were permitted on Sundays. For many employees, Sundays were for church and family. For others, Sunday was a day of rest following a bacchanal Saturday night.

"At that time union agreements were based on a forty-four-hour week," Arthur said later. "Men were then told to work forty-eight hours; the additional four hours were paid at time and a half. Thus the weekly wage was based on fifty hours' pay. This gave a tradesman $50 per week. For most, this was a bonanza compared to pre-war wages."

In order to train welders, several entrepreneurs set up shops to teach welding techniques. Students paid for their tuition and went on to work in shipyards as improvers. As such, they earned 67 cents per hour until they gained experience and a recognized status as qualified welders.

Rivetting was hard, dirty manual work. The best recruits were younger men with stamina and the experience of working with pneumatic tools in mines. To train rivet gangs—rivetters, buckers up (holders) and heaters—a series of plates, angles, etc. were set up. This gave new workers the opportunity to practise rivetting downhand, on the vertical, and overhead. Subsequently burners got practice by burning out those rivets. Older men were trained as caulkers, where the work and tools were lighter.

Reading from left to right, front row: J. De Francisco, T. Holt, Alex. Greer (Rivet Foreman), F. Barter, G. Karens and R. Nesbit. Back row: J. Goranko, E. Elhert, W. Bogle, J. Potinjak and A. Cross.

Two years ago West Coast Shipbuilders came into being. We were the baby of the shipbuilding fraternity on the Pacific Coast, and, like all babies, we have had to take what our big brothers did not want. The riveting department of this yard was no exception, and from the farms, general labor, and ex-office workers, we had to draw our material to form our rivet gangs. Rome was not built in a day, nor were the West Coast riveting gangs formed in a day, but after months of hard labor and patience, we have at last developed riveting gangs second to none throughout the shipbuilding industry of Canada.

Today we are justly proud of the men comprising these gangs and the records they have brought home to West Coast, and we take this opportunity of showing our appreciation for their efforts by publishing the above picture of our ten high riveters for the month of July.

L. MacDonald was our first Riveter to drive a record for any one shift, then Bill Robbins took the top spot by driving 2154 bottom shell rivets in a $7^1/_2$-hour shift. Since that time we have not gone out for individual shift records but have concentrated on raising the average for the yard as a whole. The past eight months have shown a steady increase in these averages, and July put us over the top

with an average never attained by any other yard in Canada. Our average was 401 rivets per shift per gang; a long cry from the 200-rivet average of a year ago. To Mr. Frank Barter, who drove an average for an all-time high of 700 rivets. per shift for July, and the other nine men and their gangs who gave him a close run for top honors, we say, "Well done, and may you all go on to bigger and better records, if such, are possible, in the future."

We should like also to pay special tribute to our buckers, heaters and passers for their splendid co-operation, without which the above records would not have been possible.

From the West Coast Shipbuilders yard bulletin *Down Our Ways*, September 15, 1943.

For each trade there was a small core group of experienced tradesmen working as lead hands. New recruits were taught to master one phase of the work and do it repeatedly. This method of training specialized crews was also carried out for pipefitters, steamfitters and plumbers.

Paper Ships

Training workers to build ships was one job; ordering and paying for ships was another. To that end, several separate agencies were involved in establishing the Canadian Merchant Shipbuilding Program. The British Shipbuilding Mission assigned the ships to be built. Early on, the USS Maritime Commission undertook financing through the Lend Lease program.

Aerial view of the West Coast Shipbuilders yard in the southeast corner of False Creek, Vancouver, looking south.

Burrard Dry Dock crewman using a pneumatic bolt tightener. The ship's plating was bolted together, then rivetted. VMM

Other parties dealt with commercial and legal aspects. Shipyard staff had to struggle with all the various government departments involved, as well as the endless instructions and regulations and an abundance and variety of inspectors. As more yards became involved in output, C.D. Howe, federal Minister of Munitions and Supply, assumed responsibility for streamlining the shipbuilding program, which was eventually incorporated under the Department of War Production.

As director, Howe set up Wartime Merchant Shipping, a Crown corporation to run the merchant shipbuilding program. He chose H.R. MacMillan, a former chief forester of BC and probably the foremost leader in the BC forest industry, as president. The program had its primary office in Montreal and a branch office in Vancouver. Austin C. Taylor, a well-known BC industrialist, headed up the Vancouver office. William S. Dey, newly appointed general manager,

This photo of George Simpson appeared in *Down Our Ways*. The caption said he was "doing a day's work six days a week and which he picked up very quickly—sorting rivets. George, who was blinded in the First World War, came to us three weeks ago. He says he is happy to work and glad to be able to do something to help the Allies along."

had managerial experience and had sailed as chief engineer with the Canadian Merchant Marine on vessels with machinery installations similar to the North Sands ships to be constructed. Not only were his qualifications excellent, but he glowed with humour and disarmed people with his friendliness. In the days before political correctness, Bill Dey asserted that the three most common things in this world were Swedish matches, French prostitutes and Scotch engineers.

The Montreal office of Wartime Merchant Shipping administered program policy and handled legal and accounting activities. The main functions of the Vancouver office included purchasing, scheduling, taking care of local matters and expediting the delivery of hundreds of components, a job the office performed in an excellent manner.

OUR FIFTY 10,000 TONNERS

FREIGHTERS

NORTH SANDS TYPE

No.	Name	Date of Launch	Year
101	S.S. FORT CHILCOTIN	March 7,	1942
102	S.S. FORT CONFIDENCE	May 16,	1942
103	S.S. FORT CHIPEWYAN	April 30,	1942
104	S.S. KOOTENAY PARK	June 11,	1942
105	S.S. FORT MAUREPAS	July 1,	1942
106	S.S. FORT NORMAN	July 25,	1942
107	S.S. FORT SLAVE	August 15,	1942
108	S.S. FORT SOURIS	September 8,	1942
109	S.S. FORT BRULE	September 25,	1942
110	S.S. FORT FRANKLIN	October 16,	1942
111	S.S. FORT LA TRAITE	October 30,	1942
112	S.S. FORT FINLAY	November 17,	1942
113	S.S. FORT RAMPART	December 5,	1942
114	S.S. FORT STAGER	December 23,	1942
115	S.S. FORT FITZGERALD	January 9,	1943
116	S.S. FORT NAKASLEY	February 6,	1943
117	S.S. FORT ENTERPRISE	February 24,	1943
118	S.S. FORT GLENLYON	March 10,	1943
119	S.S. FORT GLENORA	March 24,	1943
120	S.S. FORT GLOUCESTER	April 5,	1943
121	S.S. FORT GRANT	April 19,	1943
122	S.S. MOUNT DOUGLAS PARK	April 26,	1943

VICTORY TYPE

123	S.S. FORT ASTORIA	May 21,	1943
124	S.S. FORT KULLYSPELL	June 5,	1943
125	S.S. FORT CREVECOEUR	June 21,	1943
126	S.S. FORT KASKASKIA	July 6,	1943
127	S.S. FORT BOISE	July 21,	1943
128	S.S. FORT LA BAYE	August 5,	1943
129	S.S. TECUMSEH PARK	August 25,	1943
130	S.S. WINDERMERE PARK	September 14,	1943

TANKERS

131	S.S. MOUNT BRUCE PARK	October 17,	1943
132	S.S. SILVER STAR PARK	November 3,	1943
133	S.S. WILDEWOOD PARK	November 22,	1943
134	S.S. MOOSE MOUNTAIN PARK	December 10,	1943
135	S.S. ARLINGTON BEACH PARK	December 31,	1943
136	S.S. WILLOWDALE PARK	January 20,	1944
137	S.S. QUETICO PARK	February 12,	1944

VICTORY TYPE

138	S.S. SUNNYSIDE PARK	March 1,	1944
139	S.S. PARKDALE PARK	March 23,	1944
140	S.S. QUEENS PARK	April 11,	1944
141	S.S. ATWATER PARK	May 9,	1944
142	S.S. TUXEDO PARK	May 23,	1944
143	S.S. DOMINION PARK	June 19,	1944
144	S.S. MOUNT ROBSON PARK	July 6,	1944
145	S.S. WESTON PARK	August 4,	1944
146	S.S. CORNISH PARK	August 31,	1944
147	S.S. QUEENSBOROUGH PARK	September 28,	1944

CANADIAN TYPE

148	S.S. WINONA PARK	October 21,	1944
149	S.S. MONTEBELLO PARK	November 21,	1944
150	S.S. WAVERLEY PARK	December 19,	1944

TANKERS

Listing of the first fifty 10,000-ton standard ships built at West Coast Shipbuilders during World War II. The astonishing pace of production can be seen by the launch dates.

"... and that's our department for filling out government reports." —Courtesy of Colliers.

Cost-Minus Contracting

The first North Sands ships ordered at Burrard Dry Dock, to British account, had a contract price of $1,860,000 each, which covered the purchase of machinery and an allowance to offset the extraordinary costs of yard construction. With very minor changes, this amount became the initial contract price on all BC-built ships.

After the program was underway, it soon became apparent that the fixed price was quite generous. A revised pricing policy was put in place, which stipulated a price of $1,350,000, exclusive of boilers, engines, generators, etc. If the final cost of the ship came to that amount or less, the shipbuilder would be awarded a 2.5-percent management fee of $35,000. If the cost of the ship went over $1,350,000, then the management fee was reduced according to a formula until it was eventually nil. Thus, contracting was done on a cost-minus system.

Under Fire!

Arthur remembered one alarming incident that took place on one of West Coast's new cargo ships during its passage out of False Creek.

Under wartime regulations, no name or any other form of identification could be exhibited on a ship. However, atop the wheelhouse on each side of the rails was a heavy board bearing the ship's name. This board was hinged so that when folded, the top half covered the lower portion and the name was obliterated.

We always made the run from the east end of False Creek to open sea at English Bay on Sundays, so as to cause the least inconvenience to traffic held up by opening the various swing span bridges. On this particular Sunday, we had cleared False Creek with a new ship and were sailing toward First Narrows. The Army had installed a coastal defence gun at Ferguson Point in Stanley Park, midway between False Creek and the First Narrows.

As we proceeded, a signalling lamp at the gun emplacement rattled out a speedy Morse code message. Those of us on the ship's bridge asked, "What's up?" There was another unintelligible dash of code, then another. Finally, there was a puff of smoke, a scream through the air, and a splash in the water about a quarter of a mile ahead of us—all quickly followed by the sound of a gun firing!

We had an Aldis Lamp on board, so somebody who at least understood Morse code tapped out, very slowly, "What's the matter?" The reply came back flashing at a mile a minute. So our Aldis man tapped back a request for the sender to signal slowly. That did the job. Back came the question, painfully slow: "What ship is that?"

We showed our name board and that was that. End of story.

One of Burrard Dry Dock's ships was not so lucky. Returning from sea trials, the vessel was similarly challenged from the gun emplacement at the north side of First Narrows, under the Lions Gate Bridge. The warning shot ricocheted

10,000-ton Cargo Ship Output from BC Shipyards During World War II

Burrard Dry Dock, North Vancouver & Vancouver yards	111
West Coast Shipbuilders, False Creek, Vancouver	55
North Van Ship Repairs, North Vancouver	54
Victoria Machinery Depot, Victoria	20
Prince Rupert Drydock, Prince Rupert	13
Yarrows Ltd., Esquimalt	2
Total	255

off the surface of the water and actually punctured the hull of the brand-new cargo ship. The vessel was beached on the sand bank on the north side of First Narrows. Fortunately it was subsequently refloated with only minor damage.

"So," Arthur concluded, "if you ask if I've ever been under fire, I'd have to say yes, but presumably only from friendly forces!"

Changing Needs

By 1944 it was apparent that the war at sea had finally seen the defeat of the U-boat, so the requirements for merchant shipping replacements were much less urgent. Each Vancouver yard was instructed to close one of its berths. In 1945 a second berth was closed with the idea of rationalizing production. That year West Coast secured one of its last wartime contracts: to build five maintenance ships for the Royal Navy. The yard also completed conversion of one of the British Fleet Train's existing Blue Funnel ships, the *Menestheus*, from mine layer to amenities ship. Yarrows, Burrard South Yard and West Coast Shipbuilders were contracted to build transport ferries (LST Mark III); however, only two were launched, in Esquimalt, as the four under construction in Vancouver were later cancelled.

The final wartime program was the construction of 15 Type "B" China coasters, six of which were assigned to Burrard Dry Dock in North Vancouver and to North Vancouver Ship Repairs, and three went to Victoria Machinery Depot. These were small, 214-foot 'tween-deck steamers, with machinery aft. None was complete at war's end, so all were taken over by private owners and finished to the purchaser's specifications.

W.D. McLaren's journals describe the effect of the end of the war on the day-to-day life and work at West Coast Shipbuilders:

1945
Aug. 10 Fri.   Weather: good
Broadcast carried the news that Japan will probably agree to the Potsdam Ultimatum and surrender early in the forenoon. Reports came through that they are already celebrating in London. Instructed Mr. Brown that the work in the Yard will continue but should be interrupted long enough for a brief service and observance . . .

Rumours current throughout the day of a Japanese surrender but official position seems to be that they have offered to surrender on a stipulate condition and the matter is now under consideration by the Allies.

Took note of progress while on the Menestheus *and Arthur has prepared listing of about 68 major items of jobs yet to be done.*

In the course of the evening nothing further could be learned regarding the reception of Japanese application for peace.

Sat. Aug. 11   Weather: good
News came through in the morning of the likelihood of the Allies agreeing to the Japanese request to recognize the Emperor provided that he will work under the control of the military establishment to be set up by the Allies in Japan. Got a phone call from Sutherland of CMS and as a result prepared a notice to make clear that we could not pay the men in the event that Mayor Cornett declares a public holiday. Sent copy of this to Western Bridge after notifying Hogg.

In evening attended launch of Mull of Oa *at North Van, the last of their Maintenance ships, also reception thereafter at Hotel Vancouver. Later stood by radio in expectation of something definite re Japan's surrender.*

Sun. Aug 12   Weather: fine
Was at radio 4:30 in the morning expecting surrender news would come through at any time.

Started work on a $^1/_{16}$*" scale plan of the Transport Ferries with the idea of making a proposal to use the hull in whole or part in the event of cancellation. On return home still waited for news regarding Japan's surrender. Got false report in the early evening which was contradicted later.*

Mon. Aug. 13   Weather: good
*Walkem looked in for a short time this morning
and we talked about the effect on our employment
resulting from Japan's surrender. At that time we
had no notice of cancellations.*

*About 9:30 got a phone call from Bell-Irving
that work had to be stopped on the floating dock
and later a telegram came here addressed to Knox
Walkem cancelling our Ferries 158, 159, 160,
161. Instructed Lancaster to circulate to all our
sub-contractors this cancellation.*

*At 2:30 PM attended board meeting with Col.
Spencer, Lawson, Walkem, Martin and with Bell-
Irving and Mrs. Maxwell present. The matter of
these cancellations was thoroughly discussed and
Bell-Irving wanted to lay off 300 men
immediately. I asked that this should not be done
precipitously; that he should try and fit them into
other jobs and if possible put them on work for
Hulls 156 and 157.*

*Walkem said he would try and contact Dewar as
to how we could observe no publicity of cancellations
and at the same time give notices of dismissals to
workers. Also spoke to Dey who felt there was no
alternative but to make dismissals whereas when I
returned to the yard, Tyrwhitt phones up to say that
we should not do this immediately.*

Tues. Aug. 14
*Overnight uncertainty continued regarding
Japanese situation and we had no further word
when work started.*

*Walkem present and had talk with him about
cancellations etc. and on the matter of receiving
goods after the cancellation notices have been
served. Sent a note to Western Bridge to stack up
all cancelled fabricated steel from the Ferries in
our yard 1st & Columbia.*

*Learned that Atlee would speak at 4 PM and
the message came clearly through from London
announcing Japan's surrender. After he finished,
Truman's speech was recorded and after "God
Save the King" made an announcement to the
men on the second shift to carry on with their
work and tomorrow would be holiday.*

Wed. Aug. 15   General holiday

Thurs, Aug. 16
*Had another telegram from Dewar cancelling
remaining Transport Ferries and gave instructions
all round to advise sub-contractors. Attended the
Foremen's meeting and after making presentation
to Davidson told them of the necessary layoff
procedure. Asked them to reconvene for supper at 5
and at 5:30 PM we would go into the subject again.*

*Went over to Western Bridge and had a talk with
Bell-Irving and Hogg on the matter of laying off the
additional men, which means that all men on ship
work at Western Bridge will not be laid off and
consequently we agreed to start work immediately on
the Kootenay Lake Ferry (Anscomb).*

Fri. Aug. 17
*Walkem arrived and we spent the time discussing
our arrangements for laying the men off, and
possible application of our cancelled Transport
Ferry hulls to BC coastal requirements. He
introduced the subject of the Gulf of Georgia and I
explained that I am a director of the Island Tug &
Barge Co. and had already discussed with
Elworthy a use for these Ferries, and also showed
him that I had in 1938 made a report to the
Powell River Co. on newsprint transportation and
would wish to revive with Powell River some of
the proposals then made.*

*Asked Elworthy round for lunch. Showed him
our work on the Transport Ferries and model
drawings. We came to the conclusion that the work
in our Yard on the Ferries is not sufficiently
advanced to make it practicable to get low cost in
completing as a freight car barge and formed the
opinion our best course would be to snub the after
end off and make a tanker barge.*

Sat. Aug. 18
*At 9:20 AM received a telegram from Dewar
cancelling Nos. 153 and 154 and to rush work on
#152 and 155. Passed this information round*

BULLETIN OF

WEST COAST SHIPBUILDERS LTD.
VANCOUVER, B. C.

A NOTE FROM OUR MANAGING DIRECTOR

With the completion of the "Cape Wrath" at the end of the month our Wartime programme of building 10,000 Ton Cargo Ships for the Government of Canada, and Maintenance Ships for the Royal Navy, comes to an end, and the Management takes this opportunity of expressing thanks to all Employees of West Coast Shipbuilders Ltd., Western Bridge and Steel Fabricators Limited, and of all Subcontractors, for the splendid job they have done in turning out all the Cargo Ships precisely according to timetable, and all ships in the best traditions of good workmanship.

With the near completion of this work the necessity for laying off the large majority of our Employees has been placed upon all department heads, and, while it is a job that none cared for, it speaks well for our Employer-Employee relationship that arrangements have proceeded without rancour. Many Employees have expressed their pleasure in having worked with this Company, and the Management hopes that they will secure other employment to their liking.

What the future holds for us in shipbuilding is hard to assess at the present time. It seems clear, however, that with excess of world tonnage in the type of cargo vessels we have been building, we needn't expect work along that line. The Company is laying its plans for something different in the hope that West Coast Shipbuilders may continue helping to its utmost in providing effective employment.

With a greatly reduced payroll, and corresponding reduction in circulation, it has been decided to discontinue the publication of our Bulletin, "Down Our Ways." To the Editor, Major Conway Brown, O.B.E., Personnel Manager, and to all others who have helped to maintain interest in our work, and knowledge of our employees, we tender thanks for a worthwhile job well done.

W. D. McLAREN,
Managing Director.

Words from W.D. McLaren to the employees at the end of the war.

immediately. Arranged that Lancaster should send out letters of cancellation.

Decided to launch #155 7 PM Friday 24th.

Squire estimates that we shall now have to cut down our strength to 700 men on each of the three ships: #152, Menestheus *and #155 for completion in that order.*

Spent the time with Squire discussing ways and means of dealing with the layoff and started a plan of proposals for converting the Transport Ferries for scow and car barge service.

Tues. Aug 21

A good deal of the forenoon was taken up with matters relating to the cancellation of contracts, payoff, etc. etc. and things now proceeding in orderly fashion with another batch of men getting their cheques at 2 o'clock. Hereafter the layoff will be only in small numbers as different jobs finish up.

The end of the war brought to a close the most remarkable shipbuilding era for BC yards. During World War II, 25,000 men and women were employed in the construction of some 255 10,000-ton cargo ships, 15 frigates, 2 LST Mark IIIs, 10 corvettes, 22 Bangor minesweepers as well as Fairmile patrol launches, wooden motor minesweepers and dozens of service craft for the military. There is no doubt that the massive wartime shipbuilding effort had a major impact on Canada's transition to an industrialized country. It is also unlikely that the shipbuilding industry in this country will ever see a recurrence of those days.

CHAPTER 3

Postwar Downsizing and Adjustment (1946–1948)

"The men who built ships during the war became proficient at their jobs, but the experience they had was doing the same ship fifty-five times, not building fifty-five different ships. It became obvious that our wartime crews were specialists, not shipbuilders."

—Arthur McLaren

At the end of World War II, shipyard activity was reduced dramatically. The Canadian government was faced with the problem of cutting back on shipbuilding and at the same time not dumping large numbers of wartime employees into the ranks of the unemployed. There was employment in BC shipyards, but for a vastly reduced workforce.

If there were plenty of surplus workers after the war, there were also surplus boats and ships. A large number of wooden and steel vessels—tugs, minesweepers, patrol vessels and landing craft—were put up for sale by the Canadian and American governments. These war surplus diesel-powered craft were quickly snapped up, spelling the final demise of the steam tug. Local wooden shipyards were fully employed converting minesweepers and patrol vessels into yachts and commercial craft, some of which are still in service.

To renew an aging coastal fleet, the Canadian Pacific Railway ordered four new vessels from yards on the River Clyde in Scotland. Union Steamships purchased three corvettes and engaged local yards to convert them into passenger and cargo steamers. Other vessels needed to be replaced: the CPR's *Princess Marguerite* had been lost in war service in the Mediterranean, and the Canadian National Railway's *Prince George* was gutted by fire in Ketchikan. The CNR contracted with Yarrows to build a new *Prince George* for the BC coast–Alaska trade, and the well-known W.D. McLaren landed the design contract.

Burrard Dry Dock received an order from French interests for one of three 7,500-dwt passenger and cargo motor ships to replace war losses, as well as a series of coal ships. Yarrows got orders for lighthouse tenders for the French government. Yarrows and West Coast Shipbuilders shared a contract to build two tugs and fifteen barges for work on the Mackenzie and Athabasca Rivers.

With most of the Canadian naval fleet disposed of immediately after the war, the federal government embarked on a plan during the 1950s to build a more modern fleet. This new defence program involved most BC yards and kept some occupied for a decade.

Canadian Naval Vessels Built on the West Coast 1950s to mid-1960s

Category	Builder	Output
Destroyer escorts	Burrard Dry Dock	2
	Yarrows	1
	Victoria Machinery Depot	1
Wooden minesweepers	Yarrows	2
	Victoria Machinery Depot	2
Gate type vessels	Burrard Dry Dock	1
	Victoria Machinery Depot	1
Ammunition lighters	Allied Builders Ltd.	2
	Yarrows	1
Water lighter	Victoria Machinery Depot	1
Steam crane barge (non-propelled)	Pacific Drydock (on site of North Van Ship Repairs)	2
Tank cleaning barge (non-propelled)	Allied Builders Ltd.	1
Deperming barge (non-propelled)	Star Shipyards (Mercer's) Ltd.	1
78-foot wooden personnel launches	Star Shipyards (Mercer's) Ltd.	3
	Withey Shipyard (Gabriola Island)	3
45-foot steel harbour launches	Allied Shipbuilders Ltd.	2

CITY COMPANY BUYS 4 SHIPS FOR $80,000

Union Steamship Gets 'Sweepers'

Four Bangor minesweepers —each 180 feet in length— have been bought by Union Steamships Ltd., and will be converted for peacetime B.C. Coast use in a project worth $800,000 in new work for Vancouver shipyards.

In announcing this new venture Carl Halterman, vice-president of Union Steamships, said the firm paid War Assets Corporation $20,000 for each of the four veterans of war service.

Postwar Work for West Coast Shipbuilders

January 1946 was a time of turmoil at West Coast Shipbuilders. The last three 10,000-ton ships were afloat: one was being completed as a coastal force maintenance ship for the Royal Navy; two had work suspended. Two transport ferries (LST Mark III) occupied berths, but work on them had been stopped since VJ Day.

Design drawings were in hand for the conversion of two corvettes into coastal passenger steamers for the Union Steamship Company. Negotiations were underway with Sir Walter Carpenter of Sydney, Australia, who had a large trade in the South Pacific Islands; he was interested in acquiring the two standard 10,000-ton ships (Hulls #153 and 154) and finishing them as specialized cargo steamers to suit his South Pacific trade. The Western Bridge Company

Ltd. (formerly Hamilton Bridge) had subcontracted West Coast to build the *Anscomb*, a 180-foot twin-screw ferry. Although these jobs and prospects represented a fair volume of work, it was only a fraction of the yard's wartime work load. Furthermore, these contracts were not the repetitive work of the wartime cargo ships. There were many lessons to be learned.

Learning the Hard Way

Anscomb

In the late summer of 1945 the provincial Department of Public Works called for tenders to build a forty-eight-car twin-screw passenger and vehicle ferry to cross Kootenay Lake, a link in the future southern Trans-Provincial Highway. The tender documents called for the completed vessel afloat on Kootenay Lake, with the government-supplied machinery package (engines, shafting, propellers, etc.) installed.

Western Bridge won the contract to build the *Anscomb*. At the time West Coast was still under the control of Wartime Shipbuilding, so was not allowed to pursue commercial contracts. Western Bridge was a steel fabricator but, because of union agreements, had to subcontract all of its field work. In this case the re-erection, rivetting and welding of the hull at Nelson, as well as the out-fitting, machinery installation, launching and tri-als, all conveniently went to their wartime shipbuilding associates, West Coast Shipbuilders.

The bridge company applied structural steel practices rather than shipbuilding techniques. This meant detailing all steelwork in the drawing office. The design drawings called for rivetted construction throughout, but the owner granted permission to use the more familiar wartime practice of rivetting seams and welding butts. Somewhere along the line it was decided to pre-erect the ferry hull on one of the vacant West Coast berths. The theory was that this would allow the steelworkers to check out errors in fabricating and permit the lifting of some dozen shell plates with compound curves, which the drawing office had declined to detail.

Arthur McLaren noted that it was a mistake to erect the vessel before shipping it, something West Coast realized only after the fact. The steelwork detail drawings were excellent with all rivet holes in alignment, and the few lifted shell plates could have been done in the field. Pre-erecting took some ten weeks. Consequently, after the hull was "proved," the structure was dismantled and shipped off to Nelson with great haste. Unfortunately the opportunity to fabricate and install piping or other outfitting was lost. That was the second mistake, as West Coast learned later when piping work had to be done under much less favourable conditions in the field.

The ship's two Vivian engines, producing 400 bhp at 600 rpm, weighed some 18 tons each and were well beyond the capacity of the crane. This had been anticipated, so instructions were given to leave an access hole in the ship's side and to provide a timber structure that would permit the engines to be skidded into the hull sideways. The operation was successful, but for some reason the shipwrights built a framework that could have supported a CPR Mountain Class locomotive. Expenses rose and more days slipped by, as crews took two and a half weeks to erect the hefty ways, skid the engines and then dismantle the entire structure.

There were more challenges to come. Once the superstructure and boat deck were erected, the crane boom could no longer reach across the

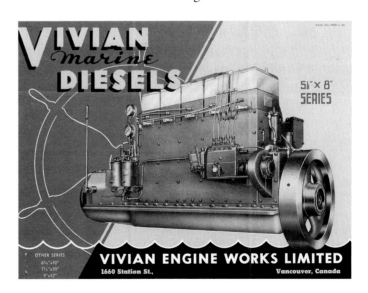

VIVIAN *marine* DIESELS

5½" x 8"
SERIES

OTHER SERIES
6½"x10"
7½"x10"
9"x12"

VIVIAN ENGINE WORKS LIMITED
1660 Station St.,   Vancouver, Canada

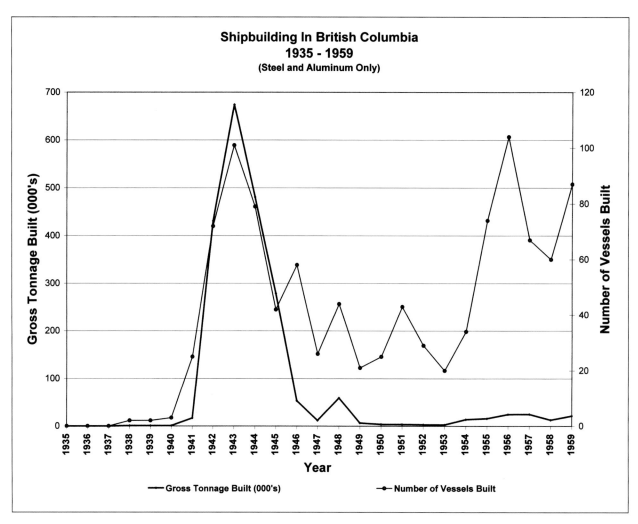

Shipbuilding In British Columbia
1935 - 1959
(Steel and Aluminum Only)

Gross Tonnage Built (000's) — Number of Vessels Built

centreline of the ship, so all lifeboats, davits, etc. had to be manhandled across the boat deck. The wooden wheelhouse, built as a complete unit in Vancouver, had to be landed on falsework, then skidded to its final location on the ship's centreline. Piping, which should have been fabricated and lined up while the hull was pre-erected in Vancouver, was now assembled piece by piece. Joiner work, machinery and electrical installations then followed in a labour-intensive, on-site fashion.

"The fault was ours," Arthur McLaren said later. "West Coast had trained its unskilled men to build one type of ship over and over in the yard. While they became proficient at their jobs, the experience they had was doing the same ship fifty-five times, not building fifty-five different ships. It became obvious that our wartime crews were specialists, not shipbuilders. What we needed now was men who could build a vessel in a remote area under conditions that taxed experience and ingenuity."

In ordinary shipbuilding, crews work eight hours a day, play eight hours a day and sleep eight hours a day, striking a good balance between working life and social life. But working on a field job is intensive and requires a more single-minded attitude. Indeed, the controlled discipline of a remote site is more akin to a military campaign than civilian life. Crews must be prepared to work ten to twelve hours a day, at least six days a week. They have to be able to put up with fellow workmen and, above all, maintain a sense of humour.

Most field jobs are done in remote locations, but the *Anscomb* was assembled at Nelson, the hub of the west Kootenay district, so the project took on the mood of a holiday rather than a race against time. The superintendents rented living quarters and brought their families in for the duration. West Coast leased space in auto camps to provide accommodation for a fifty-man crew. The caterer set up a kitchen and mess hall at the building site. The field supervisor corresponded regularly by letter with the yard in Vancouver, but it was hardly the type of communication that was useful. "What we expected was a weekly progress report," Arthur explained. "What we got was the weather, and that the superintendent had visited the mayor, the CPR manager, the Presbyterian minister, etc."

The assembly job in Nelson started at the beginning of May 1946, with completion expected by the beginning of September. But the ferry wasn't launched until late September and wasn't handed over until mid-November—two and a half months over estimate. As Arthur noted, "This is a story of tears. What should have been a straightforward job was mishandled through lack of experience. Financially the job was a disaster, but we certainly learned what building in remote areas was all about. If the re-erection of the ferry was painfully slow, it was exceedingly sound." The *Anscomb* sailed continuously on Kootenay Lake for over fifty years.

Even the most disappointing job has its humorous moments, and sea trials of the *Anscomb* certainly provided some. Prior to building this ferry, the provincial government operated the large sternwheel steamer *Nasookin* on the Kootenay Lake crossing. When the *Anscomb* was ready for her sea trials, the captain of the *Nasookin* came on board to take command. Captain McKinnon was quite an elderly man, who obviously came from the western isles of Scotland and had lost none of the beautiful soft accent of the West Highlander. Upon entering the wheelhouse, he announced to Arthur McLaren, "I was once on a screw steamer, the *Scot* of the Union line, trooping to South Africa during the Boer War."

After a look around the wheelhouse, he inquired, "Where's the gong and jingle?" He was referring to the bridge-engine room communication system common on sternwheelers and steam tugs of a bygone era. "We don't have a gong and jingle," Arthur replied. "We have an engine room telegraph." He then proceeded to explain to the elderly captain the operation of this basic signal system.

The *Anscomb* sailed forth on trials "Royal Navy style"—that is, with Captain McKinnon giving the orders and Arthur ringing the telegraph.

"*Nasookin* in the Kootenay River near Fraser Landing. This steel sternwheeler ferry was fabricated at Port Arthur Ontario and shipped by rail in sections to Nelson where she was launched in 1913. In 1933 the Ministry bought the ferry, modified it and ran it until 1947. *Nasookin*'s vehicle capacity was 30 cars and one bus. The picture was taken in 1946." From *Inland Coastal Ferries* by Frank A. Clapp, Victoria: Ministry of Transportation and Highways.

Side launching of the *Anscomb* from the CPR ways at Nelson, October 17, 1946, as shown in *Inland Coastal Ferries* by Frank A. Clapp, Victoria: Ministry of Transportation and Highways.

They proceeded 20 miles down the west arm of Kootenay Lake and then came back. The building site had no wharf, so the CPR had one of their laid-up wooden railcar barges moored against pilings and extending at right angles to the shoreline. Captain McKinnon approached this make-do wharf at full speed. Three times Arthur suggested that he slow down, but McKinnon was happy. Finally, when Arthur could stand the situation no longer, he said, "Captain, we must ring down for full astern." Hoping that there was nodded agreement, Arthur rang for full astern on both engines. It seemed an eternity before the engines stopped and the cams reversed, followed by the welcome sound of an air blast as the engines started astern. During this time the *Anscomb* was rapidly bearing down on the old wood barge. With the engines going full astern, there was some measure of deceleration, but not enough. The new ferry plowed right into the side of the old barge. Arthur remembered there was no crash or shattering of timbers, just a hollow thud like the squashing of a ripe watermelon. The barge crumbled and rotten wood flew in all directions. Fortunately there wasn't a scratch on the *Anscomb*.

Railway on the Lakes

Canadian Pacific Lakes and River Service operated basically on four Interior BC lakes (east to west): Kootenay Lake, Slocan Lake, Upper and Lower Arrow Lakes and Okanagan Lake. Service

on these waters dates back to the 1890s, when sternwheel steamers were put into service between railway terminals and intermediate points on the lakes. The steamers carried passengers and light carry-on freight. Subsequently, to handle bulk freight in carload lots, rail barges and low-powered steam tugs were built to service each lake. Service increased until the 1920s, when buses, trucks and automobiles started to replace the branch line railways. West Coast won the contract to build one of the first new steel river tugs for the CPR.

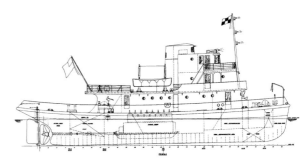

Inboard profile of the *Okanagan*, built in 1946.

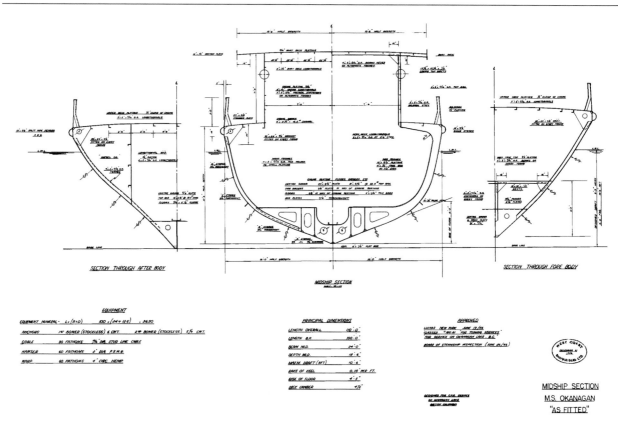

Midship section of the *Okanagan*.

Okanagan

The 110-foot tug *Okanagan* was designed and built by West Coast Shipbuilders in 1946 for handling CPR rail barges on Okanagan Lake. The tug was built as a complete hull in Vancouver and then split longitudinally into three sections for transport. The main engine, built in Seattle, developed 800 hp at 250 rpm and weighed 50 tons. The 18-crew tug was intended to move railcar barges while alongside, rather than from astern or forward. The high wheelhouse allowed the captain or pilot clear visibility over the tops of railway cars on the barge.

Early in the summer of 1946, Arthur McLaren made a visit to Okanagan Landing to size up the chosen site for re-erection. As he walked around the site taking photographs, he noticed an elderly gentleman hovering in the background who was obviously very curious about his presence. To be polite, Arthur introduced himself and explained that West Coast was starting construction of a new tug for the CPR and would be erecting the sections locally at Okanagan Landing. By way of response, the old gent gave his name as Del Burgoyne and said that he was a shipwright and caretaker of the CPR premises. (Arthur found out later that he made pike poles for the CPR services on all four Interior lakes.)

"Is this tug going to be steel?" he asked me.

"Yes."

"I like wood, myself; wood has got life in it."

"I am sorry, but CPR ordered a steel tug."

At a later date, when carloads of equipment and parts began arriving, Mr. Burgoyne observed one specific carload and proceeded with more questions.

"Is that the engine?"

"Yes."

"Where is the boiler?"

"There is no boiler; it is a diesel engine."

"I like steam. You can see what is happening with a steam engine."

Later still, he noticed the absence of rivets.

"Is this tug all welded?"

"Yes."

"I like rivets. You can feel them harden up as you drive them, and besides welded ships are not safe."

Well, old Del had a point. This was 1946 and a number of the US-built all-welded Liberty ships had fractured in cold weather conditions. However, the *Okanagan* proved to be a fine, trouble-free

The 800-hp CPR tug *Okanagan* on a trial run. The caption that originally accompanied this photo went on to say: "The vessel is 110 feet long, has a beam of 24 feet and a draft of 10 feet six inches. It has accommodation for a captain, four officers and a cook, all in single berth cabins, and 12 crew members in double berth cabins. Total cost is over $200,000. The *Okanagan* was so constructed that it could be broken down into large sections, weighing from 10 to 18 tons, for shipment to Okanagan Landing."

The *Okanagan* preassembled in Vancouver.

vessel servicing the CPR on Okanagan Lake for thirty years. She was laid up when the barge service was abandoned in the mid-1970s.

We ran sea trials for the Okanagan *on a freezing, windy day in February 1947 on a very choppy lake. The forward deck was covered in ice, such that we had to use an oxyacetylene torch to free up the windlass to undertake anchoring trials. In spite of this weather, the trials proved successful, with one very embarrassing exception. When we set out, the CPR trials skipper turned on the wrong course and was taken to task by numerous CPR officials, who had crowded into the wheelhouse to avoid the inclement weather. However, it became immediately obvious that the fault was ours. We had originally arranged that the helm was to be directly connected to a sprocket pulling the steering chains. During detail design, it was deemed desirable to gear the steering wheel shaft onto the chain sprocket to obtain a 2:1 reduction, but no account was taken of the fact that this would reverse the steering motion. There was no excuse for the oversight, but this is why shipbuilders perform trial trips.*

Northern Transportation Company Ltd.

After the war, Burrard Dry Dock, North Van Ship Repairs, Victoria Machinery Depot and Prince Rupert Drydock had, between them, orders for fifteen steam coasters of some 1,500 tons dwt originally intended for the Pacific war. These vessels suited commercial requirements and were completed in 1946. This meant that while West Coast and Yarrows had a few private contracts, they were the only large shipyards without government work.

Fortunately Northern Transportation Company Ltd. planned a sizable expansion of its fleet. NTCL was a subsidiary of Eldorado Mining and Refining Company, a company with a mine on Great Bear Lake. The Eldorado Mine originally produced radium, but during the war it proved to be a source of strategically important uranium

ore. The Canadian government made both the mine and transportation company Crown corporations, with an eye to considerable expansion of uranium production. New steel tugs and barges would be needed, with funding for the new vessels coming from Ottawa.

Frank Ross, president of West Coast Shipbuilders, approached NTCL about the possibility of getting those orders. One Saturday afternoon Captain Kelly Hall, marine superintendent, and Jack Houston, superintendent engineer, of Northern Transportation came to visit West Coast with a shopping list:

- 1 - 120'-0" 800 hp Tug 3'-0" draft for Mackenzie River
- 1 - 120'-0" 480 hp combined Tug/Cargo Vessel 4'-0" draft for Great Bear Lake
- 11 - Barges 120'-0" x 30'-0" x 7'-6" for River Services
- 3 - Barges 100'-0", 27'-0" x 5'-0" for Great Bear Lake
- 1 - Barge 75'-0" x 24'-0' x 5'-0" for Bear River

Hall and Houston had pencil sketches of what they were looking for. W.D. McLaren, general manager, took the visitors for a tour of the yard after first instructing his son to have something to look at when they returned. Arthur McLaren attacked his drafting table with earnest resolve. Some two hours later he had outlined scale drawings for both river and lake tugs. The sketches were clear enough to land West Coast Shipbuilders the entire order for two tugs and fifteen barges. With few changes, these drawings became the basis for the river tug *Radium Charles* and the lake vessel *Radium Gilbert* (1946).

However, some two weeks later the NTCL order was split with Yarrows Ltd., who were assigned the river tug and the four small barges. West Coast retained the lake tug and eleven 400-ton barges. This was a disappointing turn of events, but Yarrows had no new construction at the time and the government wanted to balance orders.

The entire fleet was to be shipped by rail to Waterways, Alberta, near Fort McMurray, where

Prefabricated sections of barges being loaded on rail cars at West Coast Shipbuilders' Vancouver yard, 1946.

all tugs and barges would be reassembled and launched into the Clearwater River, at the northeastern rail terminus of the Northern Alberta Railway. In rearranging the building program, the government awarded West Coast Shipbuilders the field reconstruction of all five Yarrows vessels, in addition to the twelve they themselves were building. This work for NTCL set a pattern of informal contracts between NTCL and West Coast Shipbuilders, and later Allied Shipbuilders, that lasted twenty-three years. Most jobs were secured on the basis of a phone call and built on the strength of the yard's track record of solid design and vessels delivered on time.

West Coast assigned the shop fabrication of its barge sections to Western Bridge, which turned them out at the rate of $1^1/_2$ per week. The barges were to be of lightweight construction, incorporating corrugated longitudinal and transverse bulkheads as well as corrugated side shells. All barges were built from detailed drawings prepared by Western Bridge.

The eleven 120 x 30 x $7^1/_2$-foot barges were set up for two longitudinal cuts and one transverse cut so that each one consisted of four outboard pontoons and four centreline panels. This breakdown allowed each 60-foot pontoon to be carried on a 52-foot flatcar, loaded so that the overhangs faced each other, and separated by 41-foot idler cars carrying miscellaneous piping and outfitting components. The lake vessel built by West Coast was designed to be cut longitudinally on the centreline,

Steel barge sections at Waterways, Alberta, near Fort McMurray, 1946.

West Coast Shipbuilders crew at Waterways, 1948. Part of a 400 Series barge is on the rail car.

with both port and starboard sides cut transversely at midships. Thus the 120 x 28 x 8-foot tug hull could be shipped in four blocks on edge, plus an additional three sections for the deckhouse and wheelhouse. This breakdown avoided disturbing the shaft lines, seatings, stern tubes, etc. of the twin-screw vessel. Yarrows used a similar method of pre-erecting and dismantling their vessels.

In the Field

This job, unlike the *Anscomb* construction, proceeded on time with no problems.

We put Dick Smith, our maintenance engineer, in charge of the project; he was a man with long experience in installing engines and systems. For an assistant, we had a young steel fitter who had shown an aptitude for doing this work and was good at handling the men. Bert Slade had a joke to cover every situation. If you ever wondered what happened to the humorous fillers in the Reader's Digest, *he remembered them all and could quote any one to suit any situation. The field crew were men in their early thirties who needed money to buy a house or a car and with wage rates of $1.25/hour with time and a half for overtime, many did. They tackled the job with a single-minded determination.*

Times were busy and I only had one opportunity to visit the job at Waterways. About nine o'clock one morning, I heard a whoosh! whoosh! whoosh! It was the exhaust of the Hudson's Bay Company sternwheel steamer Athabasca River, *travelling upstream to Waterways, which was some half mile away. I was lured into following the vessel and while watching from the riverbank, I was hailed by a happy, friendly man who introduced himself as Captain Alexander. We talked, and he told me about the river and the intermittent passages from one woodpile to the next. I told him details of the work we were undertaking. As I left, he invited me to dinner on board at six o'clock that evening.*

At lunchtime in the mess hall I told my table mate, Jack Houston, that I would be away on the Athabasca River *for dinner. Jack asked, "Did you wear your Sunday suit when you travelled up here?" I replied, "Yes." He said, "Then you better wear it to dinner tonight." Now this bothered me because Jack loved a practical joke; a whole day could be spent setting up a practical joke and that was time well spent in Jack's view. I was in a dilemma. To dress or not to dress, that was the*

Bert Slade at the West Coast field office, Waterways, Alberta, 1948.

The reassembly site at Waterways consisted of numbers of launchways leading down to the Clearwater River. Timbers extending into the water had been installed; crews used these for skidding flat-bottomed vessels into and out of the river. A railway spur ran across the head of the berths. West Coast Shipbuilders used one of Western Bridge's locomotive cranes with the capacity to lift barge sections from the deck of the flatcar onto the ways. A former US army camp with kitchen, mess hall and barracks for over 100 men was also available at the site, so Northern Transportation was able to arrange room and board for the field crews required to reassemble its order of barges and tugs.

The sternwheel steamer *Athabasca River* pushing a barge.

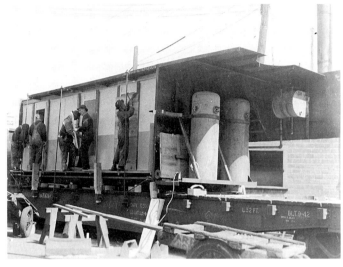

Crew protects a pre-built hull section for transportation on a rail car, June 1946.

Launch of the *Radium Gilbert*, Waterways, Alberta, summer 1946. It was launched into the river as a bare hull in order to minimize draft for its delivery trip up the shallow Bear River.

question. Is it better to dress when all around you are in working clothes, or to be in working clothes amongst the formally dressed? I decided to dress for dinner, and just as well, because the captain and engineer were in uniform, several members of the RCMP all in scarlet, Catholic priests and nuns in their best habits and a handful of northern entrepreneurs all in suits. The dinner table occupied a space on the centreline of the vessel on the upper deck and was laid with sterling silver cutlery and fine china crockery, all with the Hudson's Bay Company crest. Captain Alexander explained that they dressed for dinner because for most of the passengers heading north it would be the last formal occasion for at least one year.

Radium Gilbert

Arthur remembered the challenge of getting the *Radium Gilbert* up to its final destination.

The 120-foot tug was to operate on Great Bear Lake, about as far north as you can get. It meant proceeding down the Mackenzie River to Fort Norman, and then up the Bear River to Great Bear Lake. The hull of the Radium Gilbert *was completed in Vancouver, then cut into sections and sent by rail car to Fort McMurray. The sections were then welded together and the hull launched at Waterways, while the tug's engine, deckhouses, etc. were loaded onto one of the new barges. Next the equipment barge and hull were towed to Fort Fitzgerald, portaged and relaunched at Fort Smith. After travelling down the Mackenzie*

River, both the hull and equipment barge then navigated the Bear River's portage without difficulty. However, there is a stretch of river from the portage to Great Bear Lake that is extremely shallow, and there both hull and barge ended up hard aground.

We had been told the river was very, very shallow, but people had also reassured us we would have no trouble. They said there would be a couple of feet of water at least. Certainly there was 2 feet of water, but only in certain places. In other places there wasn't much except great big boulders. Well, fools rush in where angels fear to tread, and the Northern Transportation crew took bulldozers into the river and with a blade hard against the

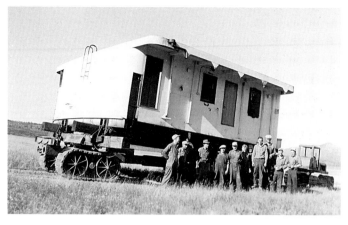

The deckhouse of the *Radium Gilbert*, on portage, summer 1946.

The *Radium Gilbert* underway, 1946.

to locate the babbit, metal alloy that gets melted and poured into the cast fittings to secure the wire rope, we realized it had been left 2,500 miles behind. Fortunately Jack Houston was looking after NTCL and he assured us he would come up with a solution. Soon after, the mine manager produced a few ingots of something that looked like babbit, saying, "that should work." It did. Afterwards I asked him was it was, and he said, "Oh, just some silver." There must be few ships using silver for securing wire rope sockets, but then necessity is the mother of invention, especially when working in the field.

Changes at West Coast Shipbuilders

In 1946 W.D. McLaren and Frank Ross came to a parting of the ways, which left only one McLaren on the payroll at West Coast Shipbuilders. As Arthur recalled:

A problem had developed with my father being an inflexible Scot and Frank being an equally inflexible Scot. They could not agree on anything. Consequently, things got sharper and sharper until in August of 1946 my father quit. Retired. Then I found out what a nice guy Frank Ross was!

Of course, all I had heard was my father's point of view. But when it was all over, Frank Ross sent a Mr. Brown over to see me, a friend of his from Ottawa. This Mr. Brown was the fellow who was involved with the White Pass and Yukon Railway. We talked about this, that and the other thing and he asked me a lot of questions. Then two days later, Frank called me into his office and said, "Mr. Brown suggests that I could do a lot worse in finding somebody to carry on this shipyard." So I was asked to take it over under the direction of a fellow called Sydney Hogg, a Frank Ross man. He was a heck of a nice guy, let me go in and do what I could do and never bothered me at all. So in August of 1946 I took over my father's job of shipyard manager for West Coast Shipbuilders. I think he was very proud that they had asked me. Mind you, he didn't say so, because he's a Scot and they don't say things like that.

transom of the vessel, pushed the unit up the river. By the time we got to our destination, the bottom of the Radium Gilbert was badly dented, but remarkably there was only one short fracture in the plating. We solved that problem by driving a wooden wedge into the split.

It was a relief when the Radium Gilbert hull together with a barge carrying the deckhouse and machinery were towed across Great Bear Lake to the Eldorado Mine site at Port Radium. There the tug was engined and outfitted, but not without another opportunity for creative problem solving. The Radium Gilbert had a steel foremast rigged with booms for handling cargo, and the shrouds for the mast had not been made up. We had sent up galvanized wire and sockets, but when it came time

Arthur McLaren and crew with the rail barge *Canadian National No. 112*, at the north end of Okanagan Lake, just before launching in August 1948.

Locomotives to the Rescue

In 1948 West Coast Shipbuilders received an order from Canadian Pacific Lakes & River Service for a 240 x 38-foot ten-car rail car barge for service on Slocan Lake, which runs north and south between the Arrow Lakes and Kootenay Lake. Access is from the south, at Slocan City. It was serviced by a branch line from Nelson and from the north at Rosebery by another CPR line between Nakusp on the Arrow Lakes and Kaslo on Kootenay Lake. This short line was originally built in the 1890s to service Slocan district mining, as well as the local forest industries.

As part of the building contract, the CPR agreed to provide building facilities at the site on Slocan Lake at Rosebery and to transport steel and contractor's equipment from Vancouver. The CPR had built a haulout slip for their existing wooden car barges at Rosebery, consisting of a series of transverse ways with cradles spanning alternate pairs of ways. These cradles were built up so that there was a flat, level grid on which the barge could be erected. There was very limited open space between the head of the ways and the single-line railway.

After surveying the building site, Arthur explained, the decision was made to build the barge in twenty-four pontoons (eight in the length of the vessel, three in the width). Each pontoon was a complete box consisting of bottom shell, deck, side shell and/or longitudinal bulkhead, and weighed about 18 tons, an ideal load for a 41'-6" flatcar.

There were no sidings, and the head of the ways abutted the main line running from Rosebery to Kaslo. At that time, mobile cranes capable of 20-ton lifts at 40-foot reach were not available so plans were made to skid each pontoon from the deck of the rail car to its appropriate position on the launching grid. The idea was to use railway track, supported by blocking and liberally greased, as skidways, with a small gasoline-powered two-drum winch yarding the sections.

Arthur explained:

When the first train arrived with three of our flatcars at the rear, the conductor uncoupled them as directed and proceeded with his train to Kaslo, announcing that it would be the next day before he returned. We set to work placing and greasing rails, etc., but by that evening we had only unloaded one car. Next morning we were struggling with car number 2 when the train returned. The conductor sized up our struggles and offered to help. He asked how many snatch blocks we had and how much wire rope, cable, clamps, etc. We were not sure what a freight train conductor knew about shipbuilding, but fortunately we took his advice.

He backed up his train and uncoupled the engine. A line was secured to the barge section sitting on the car and led through snatch blocks to the point on the ways where we wished to spot the section; then the line returned and was secured to the locomotive couplings. We soon discovered that a steam locomotive in the hands of an experienced engineer and under the guidance of a veteran conductor is the gentlest of machines. As the locomotive backed down the track, the barge section slid softly along the greased surfaces to the desired spot. It took them minutes to do what had taken us hours.

In fact, we assembled the whole barge in this manner. The train crew laid over at Rosebery two nights a week, where we hosted them for some three weeks with what I consider to be the cheapest beer I ever bought.

The End of an Era

Although there was continuous work for BC shipyards, the second half of the 1940s certainly did not have the tempo of the wartime boom. Some yards folded their operations. The first one to close was the yard in Prince Rupert. The next was North Van Ship Repairs, located on the site that became the Seabus ferry terminal in 1976. The company was sold to Burrard Dry Dock in the late 1940s.

The shipyards that persevered after the war had some hard lessons to learn, many of them financial. Securing new work orders was one thing; bidding wisely and carrying out the work on time and on budget was quite another. During the war, West Coast built fifty-five 10,000-ton cargo ships in assembly-line style and did it very well, but it became apparent that these competent wartime crews were not as adept at "one off" shipbuilding as were the old-time tradesmen. Similarly, West Coast's technical staff was not experienced in estimating, nor were supervisory personnel adept in controlling manpower in nonstandard production situations. All of these factors proved detrimental in the transition from wartime to peacetime shipbuilding.

In the summer of 1948, the directors of West Coast Shipbuilders decided to fold their operation, retaining only their interest in Western Bridge and Steel Fabricators. Western's shop was well suited to building barges, but the directors were not interested in constructing self-propelled ships. The closure of West Coast's yard effectively finished off one chapter of Arthur McLaren's working history, but it certainly provided the impetus to start another.

CHAPTER 4

No Assets, No Overhead: Starting a New Shipyard

"When people talk about being an expert in this and that, really they're saying they made a lot of mistakes but overcame them and learned from them. Well, that's what we did, too."

—*Arthur McLaren*

In 1948, when the decision was made to close West Coast Shipbuilders, Arthur McLaren was shipyard manager. The conversation he had with Frank Ross, owner of the yard, changed his life.

Ross came to me and said, "Look, McLaren, we're not going to carry on shipbuilding. That's a losing game. There's far too many shipbuilders in this world and far too many ships, so we're going to close it down. What do you want to do?"

I told him, "I want to build ships."

Ross studied me and asked again, "I know you want to, but what do you really want to do?"

And I told him, "I really want to build ships."

"Well," he said, "there's no future in it. I know you're a bright young fellow. Why don't you choose something else?"

To make a long story short, around September or so in 1948, I ended up asking Frank if I could make arrangements to lease a small corner of their False Creek yard to carry on building ships. He doubted the wisdom of this but in the end he came through and I started building steel vessels on my own.

My father, W.D., also warned me about the

folly of shipbuilding. "You should get out and do something else," he said. "Don't build ships. I'm not sure there's any market for it." But I protested. And finally he allowed that he didn't really think that other people were building ships all that well. And I decided right then and there that that's what I was going to do—build really good ships.

Fortunately he gave me some good advice about the business of shipbuilding, in typical Scots fashion. He said the first thing I had to do was find a lawyer. "Your mother and I have a very good friend called Judge Smith who is connected with Bull, Housser and Tupper. They will be your lawyers." He didn't ask me if that's what I wanted. He didn't ask Bull, Housser if they wanted me, either! "Then the second thing is you have to have an accountant, and I have a very good friend called Andrew Rathy." So Andrew Rathy through his son Bill Rathy became our accountant. Eventually they sold out to Coopers & Lybrand.

The third thing he told me to get was financial support. Of course I had none, so the business started off in a very, very, very meagre way. I

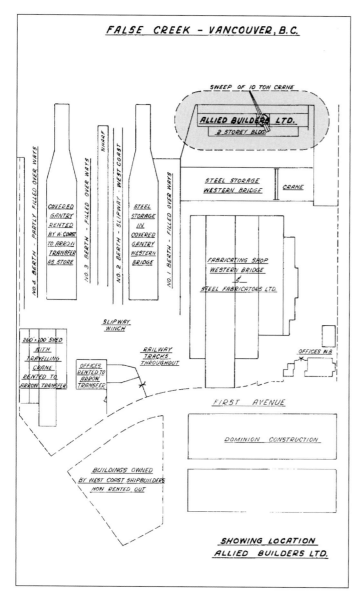

FALSE CREEK - VANCOUVER, B.C.

SWEEP OF 10 TON CRANE

ALLIED BUILDERS LTD.
2 STOREY BLDG.

NO. 4 BERTH - PARTLY FILLED OVER WAYS
NO. 3 BERTH - FILLED OVER WAYS
NO. 2 BERTH - SLIPWAY - WEST COAST
NO. 1 BERTH - FILLED OVER WAYS

WHARF

COVERED GANTRY RENTED BY W. COAST TO ARROW TRANSFER RR STORE

STEEL STORAGE IN COVERED GANTRY WESTERN BRIDGE

STEEL STORAGE WESTERN BRIDGE

CRANE

FABRICATING SHOP WESTERN BRIDGE & STEEL FABRICATORS LTD.

260 x 100 SHED WITH TRAVELLING CRANE RENTED TO ARROW TRANSFER

SLIPWAY WINCH

OFFICES RENTED TO ARROW TRANSFER

RAILWAY TRACKS THROUGHOUT

OFFICES W.B.

FIRST AVENUE

DOMINION CONSTRUCTION

BUILDINGS OWNED BY WEST COAST SHIPBUILDERS NOW RENTED OUT

SHOWING LOCATION ALLIED BUILDERS LTD.

Site plan showing the location of Arthur McLaren's new company, Allied Builders Ltd. Allied leased premises on the site of the former West Coast Shipbuilders yard at the foot of Columbia Street on the south side of False Creek.

dealt with the Toronto Dominion Bank and they were quite interested because of the connections our family had. My father worked with Island Tug & Barge over in Victoria and that enabled us to use them as a reference. At the time he was also a director of Crown Zellerbach, which owned the Ocean Falls Paper Company. Those kinds of connections meant we did get accommodation from the bank. It wasn't very much, but in those days you didn't need an awful lot.

A New Allied Builders

SHIP BUILDERS – SHIP REPAIRERS – ENGINEERS
"SPECIALIZING IN SMALLER STEEL VESSELS"

On St. Andrew's Day in November 1948, Arthur McLaren established his own shipyard. Initially he had proposed using the name McLaren for the new venture, but his father was strongly against the use of the family name for a risky business where it was extremely likely that the firm would go out of business in the next year or two. The senior McLaren knew of what he spoke, since in 1919 he had set up Coaster Construction, a yard for building ships up to 250 feet in length. Although the shipyard did build a number of new vessels to a modern design, W.D. McLaren was forced to withdraw from shipbuilding in 1926. Hence he argued for a name not so closely connected to the family and suggested the name Allied Builders—the same name he had used years earlier when setting up his own construction company in Scotland. That firm built prefabricated houses out of concrete blocks and had attracted favourable publicity by completing a four-room bungalow in just six days.

My father suggested we use the Allied name again. It had some historical meaning and I knew what it was all about. Also, in 1948, my brother had finished up with the Air Force and was now in his second to last year at university, studying civil engineering. He was a structural engineer and I thought he just might want to join forces and we could build houses and do construction. As it turned out, he wanted to be on his own, which was just fine. But that's how I went with the name Allied Builders in the beginning. It wasn't until around 1961 that we changed the name to Allied Shipbuilders.

The new company got barge erection work in northern Alberta right away from Northern

Transportation Company Ltd. NTCL had been a customer of West Coast Shipbuilders, so it was like the work was just given to us as a continuation of that. I thought it was a wonderful way to start out in business! It doesn't happen that way very often, but it did that time and again the next year.

We made good use of Frank Ross's offer to lease us part of the West Coast yard, along with tools and equipment such as the welding machines and the crane. When we'd first discussed the arrangement, he'd said, "McLaren, do you think you can afford to pay me $200 a month rent?" I said, "Certainly, Mr. Ross," although at the time I hadn't the foggiest notion of where that $200 was going to come from. We continued paying $200 for a fair-sized chunk of property for several years. We got the new yard up and running with just $5,000 in the bank. I put in $3,000, my brother Jim put in $1,000, and several founding employees like Bert Slade and Bill Arthur chipped in enough to come up with the last thousand. Allied started with less than ten people and gradually built up to twenty.

Unions

When Allied Builders had been in business for about a year or so, the Marine Workers and Boilermakers Union advised the company that they wanted to open negotiations for a collective agreement. West Coast Shipbuilders had been the only non-union yard in the province during World War II.

It had been the stipulation from Ottawa—West Coast Shipbuilders workers could not join the union. That caused all kinds of problems when I worked there. My father had a reputation as a union breaker because of his association with West Coast, but he told me, "If you want to live with the people who work with you, you're going to have your people in the union." I said something like "Who needs them?" And he told me, "It's not a question of need, it's just the way it is." That's how we signed up with the Marine Workers and Boilermakers Union.

We drew up a list of all the people that would be covered by the collective agreement and it was everyone in the yard except the pipefitters and electricians. Within a couple of weeks we had a request that they wanted to organize, too. One by one we settled with each union to a closed shop agreement.

Allied had the same union agreement as the steelworkers at the other shipyards, including Burrard Dry Dock. Then in the late 1950s the union wanted a wage increase of 5 cents an hour. At the time wages were about $2.00 an hour so a nickel increase amounted to about 2.5 percent. The management at Burrard refused to raise wages. But I thought that the increase was a reasonable request and I agreed to pay it.

Shortly after, the boss at Burrard, Mr. Claude Thicke, called me over to talk. We all sat down over coffee. At that time no one in a small yard like ours got coffee breaks so the coffee service really made an impression on me. Anyway, they explained all their problems. Burrard Dry Dock was doing the naval work on a cost-plus basis so it seemed to me it really didn't matter what they paid their tradesmen. But to Burrard it was a matter of principle, and the suggestion was made that the government of Canada wouldn't stand behind a nickel-an-hour increase. They also said I had to understand they couldn't have a little guy like me upsetting the whole apple cart.

Building Small Steel Vessels

In the late 1940s, Manly and Allied had begun building small steel vessels.

Initially Allied's rent was $200 a month and that included the welding machines, what was left of the burning equipment, and one of the small mobile cranes, as well as the launching ways. Then there were wages, but in the early '50s we operated with only ten to twenty people most of the year. It was a real no-assets, no-overhead operation.

John Manly was our earliest competitor. He started out a couple of years ahead of us, with a

Arthur McLaren (seated, second from left) aboard Allied's Hull #9, the 20-foot launch *Kildala*.

small shop in downtown New Westminster. Gradually he built up his equipment and managed to get a yard built at the foot of 20th Street in New West. There was enough work that we didn't really have to cross each other. John stayed in New Westminster and his first years of work were more or less building 30-foot tugs or smaller for working the Fraser River. We built for the saltwater fleet. In 1959 the Mercer brothers with Star Shipyards switched over from wood and built some steel tugs. Later McKenzie Barge switched from building wood scows to steel ones.

Allied's low costs allowed the company to compete against the larger established steel shipbuilders such as Victoria Machinery Depot, Yarrows and Burrard Dry Dock. McLaren's outfit was considered the new kid on the block.

We had the advantage of having production-oriented people who had built fifty-five ships in three years—and who were still young. When we were just building 20-foot boom boats, the big yards like Burrard didn't even know about us. But by 1954 when we started doing the 100-foot ammunition lighters, that was a different story. And when we began constructing log barges in the late '50s, it was a totally different story. They didn't like it at all. Back then Allied was the "new" spoiler; fifty years

later we were the established yard and the little guys were chasing us.

Building Upside Down

From early on, Allied built small, self-propelled vessels upside down because we thought it was easier to align everything and jig everything together that way. It certainly was easier to do most of the welding with the boat upside down. John Manly did the same, but Bensons never did. They built their steel vessels right side up, the same way they did wooden vessels.

Designing for Convenience

A lot of naval architects seem to draw a picture of a vessel first and then put the machinery inside it. But I had a different outlook on design. I thought it far simpler to put a vertical line and a horizontal line on a sheet of paper. The horizontal line represents the shaft line and includes the engines and the shafting. The vertical line represents the exhaust pipe. The right thing seemed to be to set the exhaust pipe over the engine exhaust flange so you didn't have to bend it very much. Of course there are times when it isn't convenient to put the exhaust pipe straight out of the engine, but I used that method quite a bit. Over the years our vessels have enjoyed a good reputation for being convenient to access when it comes time for repair or refit work. This design approach saves the owner time, money and frustration.

Lofting

I think I lofted the early vessels. We did most on a $1/12$ scale, although certain parts of the thing got done full size. Most of the early rudders, tail shafts and stern tubes were made at Howard Leeming's Western Machine Works. We'd buy a shaft from them and weld the rudder blade and stiffeners onto it. They were simple boats but they still had pipes in them, and I'd make a drawing of the pipes. It was just a schematic for the early ones. Later we got into making scale drawings, so what was drawn was representative of what was actually put in the ship.

New Ideas for Hull Shapes

Arthur described how he handled the hull shape in a different way from other local builders. He remembered getting the idea from "Developable Surfaces for Plywood Boats" by Chas. P. Burgess, published in *Rudder* magazine in February 1940:

In this issue Burgess talked about building boats of developable form. This included how to make hulls that had plating or plywood put on in geometric forms. I applied what I read to building small steel vessels. Basically it meant trying to develop the hull as a series of cones. There are certain lines along the bottom of a ship which you could say were conic developments, and when you build the thing that way, you get a development in the bottom of the boat which allowed a round bottom forward and a shape that flattened out aft. It meant you could build quite an acceptable form of hull without having to do any difficult, expensive double curvatures. This approach was similar to the one my father had tried with Coaster Construction back in Scotland—but back then the economy didn't favour the acceptance of such new ideas.

Our method of building was to draw the small ship out on a good-size scale and determine the details of the shape we wanted to make it. While we were doing that, we drew down the body plan in a manner such that the shape was formed out of a cone or cylinder to eliminate the need for compound curves in the plating.

The other architects and builders were doing it with compound curves, but that wasn't satisfactory at all. A wooden boat doesn't have that problem because it's made from narrow planks. You can steam bend a plank and do almost anything you want with it. A big steel ship with curves on it, like a 10,000-ton ship, doesn't have to have much bending done on each plate because the hull is very large. But a smaller steel boat is made from far fewer wide sheets, and you have to put a lot of form into every plate. The problem is that the actual plate won't follow a twisted line. However, I found that if the plate is put into a form such as a round cone or cylinder, it will bend easily. Of course this saved us both time and money. And that allowed us to gain the advantage over others who were doing it the harder way.

For a long time, it seemed that I had the only copy of Rudder *magazine. Even in the '60s people still didn't catch on to the geometric development of a hull. It took a while before the naval architects caught on to the fact that we weren't duplicating their drawings exactly. I remember a few being most upset that we weren't doing what they had asked to have done. With the introduction of computer lines fairing programs in the 1980s, many more naval architects began using "conically developed" ship's lines due to the fact that this was the way the computer worked.*

Building Boats that Sell

At first the company had minimal assets, so the principals raised operating capital by giving first security on accounts receivable.

Every year it became more and more important to raise money, so we built what we could sell—lots of little piddlepots. These weren't complex vessels. Of course, they all had to meet the steamship inspection requirements, but you wouldn't say the government regulations were complicated to the extent they are now.

Welding

Our steel vessels were welded. Bill Envik was in charge of welding for Allied; he served as foreman from the start of wartime shipbuilding in False Creek in 1941. We relied on his experience and just welded the same way as during the war. Some of the other builders who wanted to keep a nice smooth appearance held back on the welding. They'd just put in very small tacks so they didn't distort the plating. We always put in the welds to the sizes dictated by the American Bureau of Shipping Rules—that meant lots of weld.

Design/Build Boats

In the early days there weren't that many naval architects around to design vessels. It wasn't like today, when there are far more architects than builders. Many of our first eighty or so hulls were obtained on a design/build basis. That means we offered a complete package—the design and the construction—to our customers. If the design and price we quoted were acceptable, we'd get the job.

Allied had no master plan for finding customers. The contract to build the *Bering Straits*, for example, came in because West Coast Shipbuilders had done jobs for the client, Straits Towing, who knew they could expect good work. The same was true for all the tugs and barges that Allied built for Northern Transportation Company.

I don't ever remember having a formal contract with Northern Transportation. They'd phone up and tell us what they had in mind. We'd draw it up and give them an idea of the price. Two days later they'd phone back and say, "Go ahead. Get it done."

As Arthur put it, "In this business, your reputation is as important a factor as the price."

Allied's First Steel Tug

Bering Straits (Hull #1)

This steel tug was the first hull built by the fledgling shipyard. Arthur got a phone call from Fred McKeen, general manager for Straits Towing:

He phoned me up one day and wanted to know if we would be interested in building him a steel tug. I told him, "Yes!"

At the time, John Manly had built some small steel tugs, but the 55-foot Bering Straits was to be one of the larger steel tugs constructed locally. Prior to this, most tugs of that size had been imported or made of wood. We designed the tug and built it from scratch, but our wartime experience had been in building much bigger vessels.

The building went smoothly but when we went on sea trials it was a different story. We had a hell

Launching the *Bering Straits* (Allied Builders Ltd. Hull #1) into False Creek by crane, June 1949. Charles Wishart photo

of a hammering sound from the propeller, to the extent that the vessel was not usable. We tried to improve it but weren't getting anywhere. A lot of people gave us their ideas for solutions. Fortunately in the end we fixed the problem by pulling the shaft back a long distance out of the hull. As the vessel was built it had a fairly full structure around the stern so the water was simply not getting to the propeller fast enough. We never did that again. When people talk about being an expert in this and that, really they're saying they made a lot of mistakes but overcame them and learned from them. Well, that's what we did, too.

Small Tugs

Wee MacAdam (Hull #2), Wee MacAlpine (Hull #3)

Allied built many of these small 20-foot tugboats on speculation.

We didn't have anything to do for a couple of months and could build these small tugs for something on the order of $3,500, so we did. We turned around and sold them for only a couple of hundred dollars more. At that price, you were able to sell boats fairly easily.

The *Wee MacAdam* (Hull #2), a typical steel "boom boat" tug designed and built by Allied in the 1950s to meet the needs of logging camps and sawmills for an inexpensive boat, capable of towing booms up to eight sections and yarding logs. Charles Wishart photo

1ST AVE. & COLUMBIA
VANCOUVER 10, B. C.
CANADA

PHONE EMERALD 1718
CABLE "FORWARD" VANCOUVER

SHIP BUILDERS — SHIP REPAIRERS — ENGINEERS
"SPECIALIZING IN SMALLER STEEL VESSELS"

WORK ORDER

Job No. __1995__   Date __March 13, 1958__

To Order of: L & K Lumber (North Shore) Limited
P.O. Box 219
North Vancouver, B.C.

P.O. No. 6981   15'-0" STEEL BOOM BOAT

The following dimensions will be acceptable:

Length   15'-0"
Beam moulded   7'-6"
Depth moulded   3'-1½"
Draft   3'-0" approx.

This vessel will be registered!

SPECIFICATIONS

Hull: A steel hull for a 15'-0" x 7'-6" steel boom boat of 3/16" plate with 3" split pipe fenders at the deck level, water level, and in way of the heat exchangers with additional stiffening as required. The vessel to be complete with bow post, towing post, engine seat, cockpit, 50 gal. gasoline tank, and rudder all completely installed. All steelwork cleaned and primed with two coats red oxide primer.

Completely outfitted as follows:

Chrysler Crown 110 h.p. gasoline engine with 2.95 to 1 reduction gear, hydraulically operated.
Instruments and controls completely installed on the above engine.
12 volt electrical system complete with battery, generator, starter, voltage regulator, lights, etc.
Vessel to have 2" monel metal shaft, cast steel propeller of suitable size.
Stern tube with cutless rubber bearing.
Navy-type hand bilge pump.
Manual Steering gear.
Vessel complete in all respects, painted to owners' colours, etc., afloat after trials alongside our dock.

Price quoted $4,725.00

Delivery approximately 5 weeks.

In the 1950s, the work order for a 15-foot steel boom boat was only one page long.

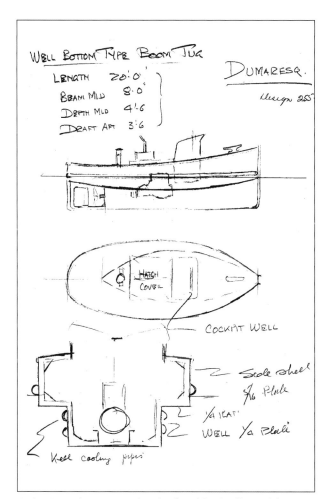

Arthur's early concept sketch of *Debby* (Hull #35) for Dumaresq Bros. of Squamish. This vessel was a "well-bottom type boom tug," known today as a pod boat.

Again, only Manly and Allied were building these small steel tugs or boom boats at that time. I designed these ones—they were very simple, with no sophistication at all. For power, they had whatever engine we could get from an engine supplier. The first three or four were mostly gasoline, not diesel. Two were Chrysler Crowns, one had a Packard engine. And then there was a Gray Marine engine. We'd go see various engine suppliers, tell them we were building this boat and ask if they'd like to supply the engine on spec. A lot of people were ready to do that. These small tugs and work skiffs were more or less our stock boat that we could build when things were quiet in the yard.

Rosalie (Hull #22)

The arrangement of this 22-foot steel tug was typical of many that Allied built in the early years of the yard. The *Rosalie* was delivered to Dumaresq Bros. of Squamish, BC.

A 15-foot boom boat, the *Sandy L II* (Hull #97), powered by a Chrysler Crown gasoline engine, 1959.

The 25-foot *Canim Clipper* (Hull #14) on the way to the Cariboo, blocked and stopped on a Pacific Great Eastern rail car. Charles Wishart photo

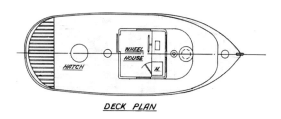

PROFILE

DECK PLAN

PRINCIPAL DIMENSIONS

LENGTH O.A.	22'-6"
BEAM MLD.	8'-0"
DEPTH MLD.	3'-4½"
DRAFT EXT.	2'-4½"
POWER · GASOLINE	100 BHP.
MAX'M PROPELLER DIA.	27"

MCLAREN & SONS CONSULTING ENGINEERS & NAVAL ARCHITECTS VANCOUVER, B.C. – CANADA		
22'-6" STEEL TUNNEL STERN WORK BOAT		
DRAWN	DATE	SK.NO.
T.A. McLAREN	DEC. 52	161-1

Profile and deck plan of a typical early shallow-draft tugboat built by Allied Builders. Arthur McLaren designed his vessels to suit the standard size of construction materials. The hull was developed to complement a simple arrangement of machinery, so as to minimize construction labour and longer-term maintenance.

We tried to develop a series of standard designs for various vessels, but people weren't really interested except in cases where the vessels were doing the same work. Basically they wanted what they wanted. Nobody thanked you for being able to standardize or duplicate things. But as a builder you want to do the same thing over and over. That's what brings economy into shipbuilding.

Steel Fish Boats

Spica's Spanker (Hull #5)

In the late 1940s and early '50s, most fishing vessels were constructed of wood. Arthur remembered a Scotsman, David Thom Scott, who had his own shipyard on Mitchell Island, at the end of Fraser Street in Vancouver. He single-handedly built steel fishing boats with rivetted hulls, the first of which was the *Pursuit*. Other than that, steel fishing vessels were still the exception.

Allied's first steel fishing boat was Hull #5, *Spica's Spanker*. "We built it for a fellow called McCormick of Vancouver," Arthur recalled.

He was interested and we talked him into it because we wanted to build a steel fishing boat. It was about 50 feet long with a Gardner engine in it that was about 60 or 70 hp. It didn't have any special innovations. The fishhold, for example, was

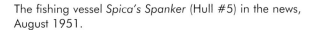

FIRST OF ITS TYPE LAUNCHED in Vancouver is this 55-foot steel fishing vessel built by Allied Builders Ltd. for David McCormack of Vancouver. The boat was christened Spica's Spanker by Mrs. McCormack in a novel crane launching at the firm's False Creek yards Saturday. It carries its own refrigeration plant to increase its sea range in tuna and general trolling operations, is completely outfitted with modern electronic navigation gear, and can be run from both the wheelhouse and a cockpit aft. It was designed by T. A. McLaren.

The fishing vessel *Spica's Spanker* (Hull #5) in the news, August 1951.

The fishing vessel *Pacific Ocean* (Hull #58) under construction, 1957. The aft hull section is being lowered into position on the mid-body after being built upside down in the shop. Allied built steel vessels in blocks, rather than frame by frame in place.

The 76-foot *Attu* on sea trials in English Bay, Vancouver. At the bow: George Arnet. On the bridge, left to right: Jim McLaren, Edgar Arnet, Arthur McLaren, unidentified.

just a compartment that was painted inside. It had no lining at all. But it was one of the first of the modern steel fishing boats built. Later Norman Ryall ran it for quite a while.

Attu (Hull #103)

Designed by Robert "Bob" Allan, this well-known fishing vessel was built for Edgar Arnet in 1959 and was later taken over by his son George. Its original purpose was to fish halibut in the Bering Sea. The *Attu* was equipped with a Dutch Stork-Werkspoor engine. The owner chose this particular engine because it came with a controllable pitch propeller, so the crew could feather the propeller and run slowly while picking up halibut gear.

The hull was steel and the superstructure was rivetted aluminum because, according to Arthur, "we didn't have the equipment to weld aluminum in those days." The *Attu* was a successful vessel, he said, "although thirty years after it was delivered, George came in one day and complained that the galvanized steel shrouds we put on the mast were starting to rust away. Thirty years later!"

Ammunition Lighters

Y.S.F. 217 (Hull #25), Y.S.F. 218 (Hull #26)

When the navy called for three 100-foot ammunition lighters to be built on the west coast, Allied pursued the job. "When the bidding was all over and done with," Arthur recalled, "the people in Ottawa said, 'You've got the lower price so we'll order two from you, but we want Yarrows to build the lead hull, so that they do all the experimenting.'" Arthur and Hubie Wallace had a talk about that arrangement.

Hubie's real name was Hubert; he was the number two son of Alfred Wallace who started Burrard Dry Dock. About two years after the war was over, Burrard bought out Yarrows. Alfred had two sons: Clarence stayed with Burrard and Hubert went over to run Yarrows. So it was Hubie I talked to about ammunition lighters.

Y.S.F. 218, an ammunition lighter built to service warships at the Esquimalt naval base, on sea trials, 1954. Commercial Illustrators photo

Hubie warned me, "Don't do anything these people ask until we tell you what we are going to do. That way you'll come out much better." He also said, "There will probably be hundreds of experts on this and we don't want to spoil their fun. So we'll tell you what price we think is realistic." He was right. I probably would have done the lighters too cheaply and there were many change orders, disrupting progress. I think the changes came to about a third of the original cost. We just followed Yarrows' lead, so when they quoted a price, we gave the same price for the changes. We worked on the theory that we had been told Yarrows was to be the lead yard. Well, we let them lead!

Hubie was also right about the experts. There were probably four people who constantly oversaw the job. That was four people overseeing the ten who were doing the building! When we came to sea trials on the Y.S.F. 217, we had some twenty-eight people on board. Each one had a different job to do. One had to check the navigation lights, another the fire hoses, etc. I thought one guy could have done it all, but apparently I didn't understand how the military worked.

Hubie had one other piece of advice for me when the conversation about pricing and government ships was all wrapped up. He said to me, "Arthur, you're a government contractor now, so you have to smoke cigars." So I did. That was in 1955 and I smoked cigars for the next thirty-five years.

Same Company, New Name

```
1ST AVE. & COLUMBIA
VANCOUVER 10, B.C.      ALLIED SHIPBUILDERS LTD.
CANADA
        SHIPBUILDERS  —  SHIP REPAIRERS  —  ENGINEERS
```

Around 1961, Arthur changed the name of the company from Allied Builders to Allied Ship-builders. He felt it was smart to identify the company a little closer to what it was actually doing. The name change was not earthshaking. "If you look at the mail sent to us, it's got every name under the sun," he said later. "Somehow it all gets delivered here."

Lessons in Finance

Money is always an issue in shipbuilding, and Arthur remembered one lesson in particular that the bank provided.

It must have been in the early '50s. The provincial government had a job to take a little ferry boat that had been on a lake in northern BC and move it down to Salmon Arm. It seemed pretty straightforward. It was just a matter of pulling the boat apart, loading it onto railway cars, unloading it and putting it back together. We needed to submit security with our bid, so I went in to the bank and explained about this excellent job and my need for $6,000 or something like that. The next day I got a call from a Mr. McCormick, superintendent of the Toronto Dominion Bank. "I've got all your statements and accounts here in front of me," he said, "and it looks like there's a lot of money owing to you." I had to agree with him. "And you're not collecting it," he commented. I had to agree again. "Well, the reason we loan you money," he explained, "is so we can do business and get the money back again. That's the way the world operates. If you're not collecting the money, we won't get ours back either."

I hadn't thought of it working quite that way, but he was right. He didn't give us the loan, but he did give good advice. "The only reason your customers haven't settled up is because you haven't pushed them," he said. In the end I didn't go after that job, but I did go after the customers who hadn't paid their bills.*

Later, when another job came along, I went back to him. I told him I'd collected the money that was owing and I asked if he could advance me money for a new project. After a time he called and said no again. "The bank has looked over this project and we don't think it's a good deal for you. It looks pretty risky to us." I told him, "Well, I'm the shipbuilder; I'm the guy who's got to do it." "Possibly, possibly," he answered, "but we're the bankers and we don't think you should do it." So we didn't. Afterwards I realized the job wouldn't have gone very well. That refusal was one of the best pieces of advice I got from anybody. Today you might be tempted to tell that banker to stuff it, but way back in the beginning, the third piece of advice my father had given me was to go with a good banker. He conducted his affairs with the same bank, so naturally I did, too. Sometimes it was a marriage made in heaven and sometimes one in hell, but it was not to be broken.

As each job progressed, Arthur worried about where the next ones would come from. He spent long days working in the yard—twelve- and fourteen-hour stretches were normal.

I knew that if we were going to make a success of this business, I would have to work hard. I felt that since I had the opportunity to do the most interesting job there was, I shouldn't stint on it. Eventually I found that worrying about the next job was a waste of time. The jobs would come. You might have to stretch yourself a little bit, but the work would be there.

My wife Dorothy would probably agree that I was a workaholic. Very few women would have put up with what she did. Very few. She kept the house going and looked after the boys and backed me a hundred percent. I don't think I ever discussed work matters with her to any great degree; it was just sort of how things were done. After the boys got a bit older, she got very involved being superintendent of the Sunday school and doing volunteer work. She didn't expect very much. Maybe she didn't get very much, I don't know. But she was always there for me.

A Hardworking Team

A popular quip goes: "Happiness is liking what you get; success is getting what you want." By this measure, Allied was successful. The company was building the right product at the right time, but more important, all of the founders and employees worked very long and hard. While some are included in Arthur McLaren's lively stories, it would be impossible to list all the people who made this yard successful, many of whom gave decades of dedicated service. In shipbuilding it is more appropriate to speak of the many skilled people working together to produce well-built vessels. These include:

- Metal workers who cut, form, fit and weld steel and aluminum
- Pipefitters who make and install all kinds of piping—copper tubing, screwed pipe and welded pipe—for all ship services: bilge, ballast, fire, vents, fuel, oil, cooling, water, compressed air and hydraulics
- Machinists who make propulsion shafts, stern glands, babbit bearings, rudders and stocks, as well as all sorts of machined equipment to "make" the machinery run
- Engine fitters who install and align the diesel engines, shafts, pulleys and belts, hydraulic machinery, winches and controls
- Woodworkers, including cabinetmakers, who produce and install furniture, linings, etc.
- Shipwrights who mill and fit wood keels and planks, caulk seams, etc.
- Electricians who install and connect cabling to diesel generators, switchboards, motor controllers, alarms, lighting, electronics, computers, etc.
- Painters who prepare and/or sandblast steel surfaces and apply paint

Bill Arthur, with the recently launched *Dumit* and *Miskanaw* behind.

- Crane and crane mobile operators who move equipment and all the pieces of the ship
- Drydock operators who ensure that ships are safely lifted and returned to the water
- Storesmen who receive and distribute all the different materials required to construct, refit or repair a ship
- Designers and draftsmen who create concepts and transform ideas into buildable reality
- Support staff who handle payroll, invoice preparation, purchasing, accounts payable, record keeping, overall financial management and all the routine yet essential tasks that must be done.

Arthur had these recollections about some of Allied's founders and/or long-term employees:

Bill Arthur came to West Coast Shipbuilders just a few days after Arthur got there. The crew were clearing stumps on the site and Bill had a dynamite blasting certificate.

He was employed as a powder man, blowing up stumps left, right and centre, and enjoying it thoroughly. Then when the yard got started, he trained as a rivetter and ended up as a rivet foreman during the war. At the end of the war Bill left to go gillnetting. He wasn't away too long before he came back. He said that fishing was not all it was cracked up to be and asked if he could come back to the shipyard. Bill was one of the founders of Allied Builders and was instrumental in the yard's success.

Ed Steffensen was a Norwegian immigrant who had been farming on the Prairies, then moved west.

He was looking down in False Creek one day and saw us building a ship. He came by and said that's what he wanted to do. He had served his apprenticeship in a shipyard in Bergen, Norway, back when the Germans were controlling things, so he had a good deal of experience. Ed worked at Allied from 1954 to 1994.

Guenter Christophersen is another forty-year veteran with Allied.

He came along to see me for a job back in 1957. He told me he was a draftsman. I said that I spent my time doing that, too, and did he expect to take over my job? He said, "Yes!" Guenter had a great roll of his drawings with him, and after I had a good look at them, I hired him. A few years later I told him about some articles from Germany I had been reading where people were using a 1 to 10 scale. Normal shipbuilding made a full-size template of everything, but I figured this would work so I gave Guenter the job of doing all this 1 to 10 stuff. From then on Guenter single-handedly produced all the lofted construction drawings that the workmen used for every vessel Allied built until he retired in 1998. He was so proficient that his manual production was faster than modern computerized methods.

Guenter added his own recollections of working at Allied:

Arthur McLaren was an excellent marine engineer and naval architect. He could be very tough at times, but he also had a good sense of humour. We worked together really well. I can't tell you how many times we leaned over the drawing table together, discussing things until we arrived at a solution.

Guenter Christophersen in Allied's loft.

Arthur was a real workaholic. I'd go home on Friday and when I came in on Monday morning, there would be four drawings on the table that he had done over the weekend. He didn't like to see people just standing around. And he didn't like to see people measuring everything or using the burning torch, cutting a little bit off here or there. Everything was supposed to be cut exactly to size so measuring wasn't necessary. It was supposed to fit the first time. When Arthur McLaren made daily rounds, he could spot a mistake a mile away. You couldn't hide it from him. He was really hands-on. In the forty years I worked for Allied I never had to collect unemployment insurance and never had a paycheque bounce. I think that's saying a lot."

Buying a Repair Yard

Burrard Shipyard & Marine Ways Ltd.

DRYDOCKING — MARINE REPAIRS

CAPACITY 1600 TONS

All Agreements are contingent upon strikes or delays beyond our control. Quotations subject to change without notice.

1729 GEORGIA STREET WEST,
VANCOUVER 5, B.C.

In 1961 Allied bought Burrard Shipyard and Engineering Works from Jack MacDonald. This yard was in Coal Harbour, across from the auto testing station on Georgia Street. "I bought it because Jack told me I should," Arthur noted.

Coal Harbour, Vancouver, once a prime site for BC shipbuilding and repair, shown here c. 1950. The area was home to many of Vancouver's marine industries. The 1700-block of West Georgia Street runs along the bottom of this photo, the engine builder Easthope Brothers is at left, Burrard Shipyard is at centre and A.C. Benson Shipyard is at right. Osborne Propellers, May Marine Electric, Pilkington Blacksmith and Vancouver Shipyard were located in Coal Harbour as well. Gordon Moodie photo

A steel deep-sea freighter on the marine railway at Burrard Shipyard, 1930s.

Burrard Shipyard & Marine Ways, looking south. The wood tug *Mary Mackin* is on the No. 1 cradle, at left. Burrard was one of many shipyards once located in Coal Harbour, Vancouver. The yard was torn down in 1979 to make way for an enlarged parking lot for the Bayshore Inn Hotel.

One day Jack asked me, "Say, Arthur, how many boys you got?" I told him I had three. "Well, I've got just the thing they want," he announced. "What's that?" I asked. "It's my shipyard," he said. "I'm getting ready to retire and I've got two girls. The shipyard is no earthly use to them. How would you like to buy it?" I thought it over and told him, "I'm very interested but what would I use for money?" He assured me that we could reach some sort of agreement. And sure enough, he came up with an arrangement I couldn't turn down, basically a relatively small down payment and annual payments for some time afterwards.

It was a very good little yard with a marine railways on it so we could drydock vessels. We couldn't do that at our False Creek yard. We mainly did repair work there. Jack had only done repair work before us. Mostly it was tugs and fishing vessels. It was a good bread-and-butter business. We renamed it Burrard Shipyard and Marine Ways Ltd. and stayed there until it was torn down in 1979.

The Third Generation

"Jack MacDonald was right," Arthur said later. The repair yard was a good place to get sons started in shipbuilding.

They all got their beginnings at the bottom. Jim came in on Christmas vacation, just before he turned sixteen. Jim had learned a lot when we went up north to Alberta and to Kelowna, where we took a ferry out of Okanagan Lake, brought it to the coast and reassembled it. Mostly he learned how to live with people who weren't his age. I think that's one of the most important lessons a young person can get. His mentor was Bill Arthur, one of our founders. He was the one who made Jim toe the line.

Then Doug came along. He worked in the Coal Harbour yard for a couple of summers until he got out of high school. Then he went to work with the electrical people and did his apprenticeship. That and studying electrical engineering at BCIT put him in line for what he is today, our electrical superintendent.

Then Malcolm came along. When he got out of school, I figured he wasn't quite ready to go to work because he had so much hair. I figured that working people cut their hair. He figured that was none of my goddamn business and went welding. None of my sons seemed to mind starting off on the tools.

Jim McLaren remembered his first taste of shipyard work. It came in 1958, when he was twelve years old.

Ad for Burrard Shipyard & Marine Ways Ltd. repair yard,
from *Harbour & Shipping* magazine, January 1962.

*My father took me with him up to field jobs near
Fort McMurray, Alberta, where the shipyard was
doing a lot of work assembling barges. I remember
it as a lot of travel, but it got interesting when we
were working on commissioning new boats or when
there were problems with a launching or at the
yard site.*

*Some years later, over Christmas holidays I
started at Burrard Shipyard & Marine Ways
doing labouring work. I also worked under the
joiners and finishers over at Allied in False Creek,
helping with finishing work such as wooden doors,
casings and things like that for whatever vessels
they were building.*

Doug McLaren started at Burrard Shipyard by
scraping barnacles off the bottom of boats, wiping

the oil out of tanks and similar tasks. Many years
later, his own son started out the same way, cleaning out old fuel tanks.

*I didn't get too much flak about being the boss's son
because they saw I was starting out at the bottom.
Of course, no matter where you start, as a
newcomer you do take a lot of ribbing from the
guys. But I was wise to a lot of it, like the first
time they sent me to go find the electric cable
stretcher. I said, "No. Nice try, guys." I knew that
one.*

*I remember working in the repair yard fixing
wooden scows. When it was raining, we used to
have to dry the hulls of the boats before we could
paint them. There was this big pot of kerosene that
they'd connect to a sort of paint sprayer with
compressed air supplied to it. That turned it into a
flame thrower! You could get a 15-foot flame
coming out of the end for drying off a boat. As a
kid, I thought that was interesting and fun.*

*I also remember when the guys would take their
coffee break. They'd be sitting outside, looking at
the spot where they'd just taken a broken timber
out of the side of a boat, and they'd bet on how
long the new piece of timber would have to be to
fill the hole. One guy would say, "Well, it's 15'-
$3^1/_4$." And another guy would say, "No, it's 15'-
$4^1/_2$"." These guys would be guessing down to the
half inch, and they'd be right!*

Malcolm McLaren didn't see much of his father,
except for the occasional weekend, until he started to work in the yard.

*In the summers I had already worked in shipyard
stores passing out materials. After high school I
spent a year at college taking science and math, but
after that I'd had enough of school for the time
being so I started working at the North Van yard
as a welder improver. It's not quite like being an
apprentice. You're welding but you're not a
versatile welder, so you're called an improver
because you have a lot of improving to do. My
brother Jim was the one who first taught me. He
said, "You're going to weld. Hold this rod. Put this*

helmet on. When the screen's dirty, spit on it and wipe it off so you can see again. Here's the stinger, now weld."

I started off doing what is called production welding or "duck welding"—head down, ass up. Then you worked into competence at all positions, including overhead welding. The foreman would give you guidance and show you what to do. I did that for a while at the new yard site and eventually got sent to the repair yard in Coal Harbour. That was enjoyable. It was much dirtier work, but it was a different dirty job every day.

When there wasn't anything for Malcolm to weld at the repair yard, he would help with planking or docking vessels or taking a propeller off. He did a variety of tasks, such as working with pipefitters and helping install engines. He notes, "It was quite interesting and a good introduction to ship repair and shipbuilding."

There was a lot of humour working at the repair yard. It might be gruff humour but there were always good laughs through the day, even when things weren't always going well. Nick Lovrich would always have the right joke. Or the time we caught Zeb draining one of the work floats—he was bailing it out at one end while not realizing the other end was under water. It was coming in as fast as he drained it out! Without humour, work can get pretty dismal.

CHAPTER 5

Building for Remote Areas:
The Northern Rivers

"The big yards had other work they were doing. They were established. We weren't. So we had to go up north and do the work that nobody else wanted. And eventually, we became known for that. That's how we got established."

—*Arthur McLaren*

Building steel vessels for remote areas is not a recent enterprise. British and European shipwrights were constructing light iron and steel rivetted steamers for service on Asian, Indian and African rivers and lakes some 135 years ago. The first steel vessels in British Columbia—the little 45-ton iron schooner *Alice* and the better-known *Comox*, *Capilano* and *Coquitlam*—were built in Britain, knocked down for shipment and then re-erected in Vancouver.

The introduction of welding greatly speeded up the work of erecting and dismantling a ship in one location and re-erecting it in another. Shipbuilders could construct a complete hull and then cut it into the sections most advantageous for shipment, regardless of construction seams and butts. Early Canadian examples of welded reconstruction were the *Radium King* and *Radium Queen*, built in 1937 at Sorel, Quebec, for Northern Transportation Company Ltd. After construction, the ships were sliced transversely, like a loaf of bread, for rail transport to Waterways, Alberta. The circumferential welded hull meant that the structure's strength depended 100 percent on welds, a fact that caused some misgivings among those familiar with rivetted construction. Their fears were unfounded.

Western Ships for Remote Locations

After the close of World War II, the Canadian government set up the Northern Transportation Company Ltd. as a Crown corporation, with funding for new construction coming from Ottawa. C.D. Howe, who had served as minister of munitions and supply during the war—with such extensive powers he was dubbed the "minister of everything"—concentrated on industrializing the

The *Comox*, near Bowen Island, c. 1892. VMM

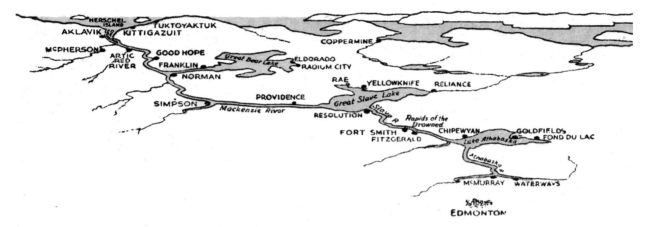

Canadian economy. As minister of trade and commerce in the 1950s, he carried on with this work, pushing to expand Canada's trade activity, to encourage a trans-Canada pipeline and to develop the north. There were no roads and few rail lines, so transportation of goods, services and people to the northern territory required a new fleet of ships and barges.

Between the late 1940s and mid-'70s, BC builders such as West Coast, Allied, Burrard Dry Dock, Yarrows, Western Bridge, Bel-Aire, Vito Steel Boat and others all built steel vessels designed to be re-erected at northern sites. Work was plentiful and jobs were bid at reasonable rates. Efficient yards did quite well and even the mediocre ones could survive.

Early smaller tugs and barges were built in support of the Eldorado Mine on Great Bear Lake, the Norman Wells oil refinery and the Distant Early Warning (DEW) line. Northern Transportation, associated with the Eldorado Mine, ordered many of the northern ships.

The Territory

The Athabasca River, the Mackenzie River and Great Slave Lake are parts of an extensive complex of waterways that stretches thousands of miles across northwestern Canada. From the 1940s to the mid-'60s, all freight movement started with a transfer from rail to water at Waterways. Supplies and equipment were then barged north along the Athabasca River to Fort Fitzgerald. All northbound freight was then portaged by road to

The "rapids of the drowned," on the Athabasca River between Fort Smith and Fort Fitzgerald.

A Northern Transportation Company Ltd. barge on the sixteen-mile portage between Fort Fitzgerald and Fort Smith on the Slave River.

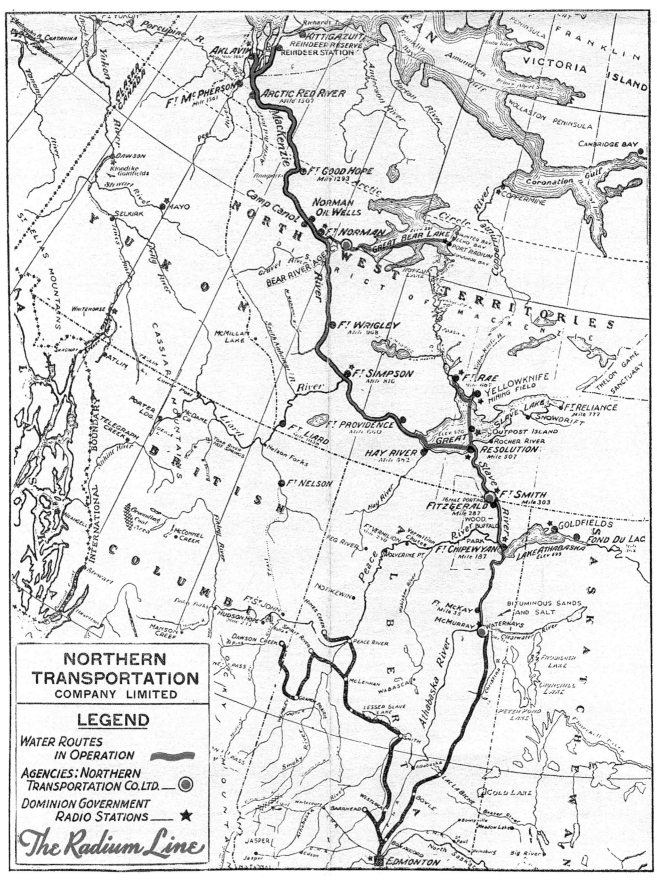

Map printed with the 1947 schedule of sailings for freight shipments from Waterways, Alberta, to northern Canada.

Bell Rock Camp, 9 miles north of Fort Smith, and relaunched upstream of the "rapids of the drowned." Finally the freight was barged down the Mackenzie to destinations such as Norman Wells. At the time, sailing completed vessels to the northern rivers site was not done due to the long distance and because insurance was not yet available for vessels transiting by water from the Pacific Ocean, around Point Barrow, Alaska, to the Arctic waters.

In 1942 the US Army Corps of Engineers undertook to lay a 4-inch pipeline from the Norman Wells oil field, developed by Imperial Oil in the 1920s, to a new refinery at Whitehorse in the western reaches of the Yukon Territory. This high-priority job required massive supplies and equipment, all of which had to travel by rail or river. For this pipeline project the American army brought in small tugs and barges from western US rivers, either as single units or broken down into parts for shipment. This equipment was reassembled and launched at Waterways. Downriver, the Fort Fitzgerald–Fort Smith portage road was improved and a 40-wheel trailer was installed so that tugs and barges could be portaged around the rapids as complete vessels.

Learning to Build Twice

Arthur McLaren first learned about transporting sections of vessels and re-erecting them at distant sites in the post-war period. All together, the building programs of West Coast Shipbuilders, Western Bridge, Allied and others with which he was involved, totalled some 150 vessels, so he knew first-hand that bidding, designing and building ships for remote sites can be either a costly learning experience or a satisfying challenge.

The design must be as simple as possible: transporting and rebuilding can add 25 to 35 percent to the cost of the vessel. Equally important is proper outfitting of the vessel prior to dispatch. In a typical case, half of the total hours spent building a ship are expended on the hull. The balance is spent on the outfitting trades, such as piping,

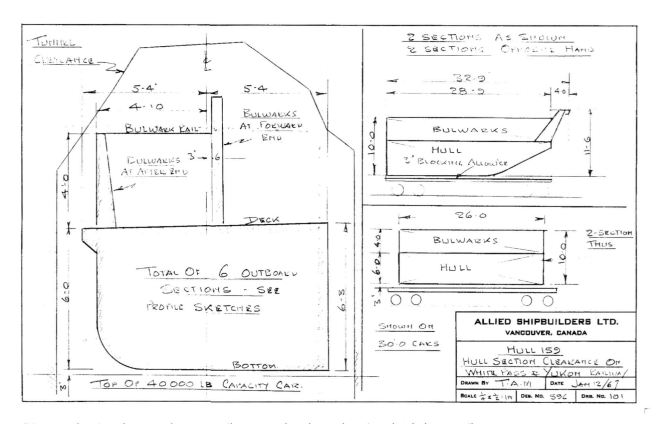

Diagram showing clearance between railway tunnel and vessel sections loaded on a railcar.

electrical and joiner work. Effective construction is achieved when the vessel is designed so that a large portion of outfitting can be completed before shipment.

Designers and builders must also be completely familiar with railway (and later road) bridge and tunnel clearances on the route, as well as weight restrictions. Arthur McLaren explained:

Often we modified the design drawings so that sections for shipment were as large as possible. We also discovered there were several standards of clearance involved when shipping sections of ships by rail. One standard allows any train to move through a tunnel without restriction of speed, with sufficient margin to allow for the car rocking on its springs. A second kind of clearance permits hauling on a local train during daylight hours with speed restrictions at various tunnels to avoid rocking. Finally there is a third, very limited clearance where the loaded rail car is under direct observation of the brakeman and speed is reduced to a creep while negotiating a tunnel. To get accurate clearance data we dealt with the yard foreman and track superintendent, because they knew every inch of the line intimately. District engineering staff were seldom up to date, and the customer relations types who solicited business were out to lunch on this critical issue.

Building ships twice poses the additional challenge of re-erection. The size and weight of modules must also reflect facilities at the rebuilding site, as well as the size and capacity of cranes available. As for the field site itself, it's necessary to consider logistical matters such as where and how the crew will be housed and fed. Then there is the matter of materials and tools, most of which must be shipped out with the vessel sections. Realistically, this means being able to calculate how many and what size of bolts are necessary, how many bottles of oxygen and gas, etc. are required.

Because procurement of equipment and materials is difficult at a remote site and therefore expensive, pre-planning and field experience are critical in keeping construction costs down. As Arthur explained: "When you're building at a remote site, basically everything you need has to be sent along. If you haven't brought it with you, you're not going to find it there. With the smaller jobs it wasn't too much of a problem, but with big jobs such as re-erecting three 165-foot tugs at Fort Smith, it was impossible to take all the parts and pieces you'd need."

If something was forgotten, or it was lost or broken or used up sooner than expected, it could take days to get a replacement. "This caused a lot of trouble," Arthur remarked. "Getting everyone to understand how the procurement system worked was always difficult."

But there was a humorous side to the challenging business of ordering supplies for field camp. As Doug McLaren recalled, "Up north somebody would say they needed another half box of a certain type of screw. So you'd give the order to the on-site foreman who'd say, 'We're not going to bring up a measly half box of screws. If the guys need 25, we'll order 100.' The order would get sent down to our yard in Vancouver, where somebody would say, 'Wow, they need 100 of these. We better send some extras.' When the supplies finally arrived up north, we'd scratch our heads and say, 'Who in heck are these 500 screws for?'"

On the other hand, with so many ships and barges being re-erected, there was usually a considerable amount of material left over. "So if you couldn't find what you needed," Doug said, "often you made do with what you had. You

A postcard showing the town of Waterways, Alberta.

know, 'Heck, we've got five hundred of these screws. Let's use them!'"

Arthur became extremely well versed in this kind of design and planning—knowledge he passed on. Allied foremen and superintendents also transmitted remote site knowledge and experience to workers. During the late 1950s and early '60s, contracts for ships and barges for the northern rivers made up nearly half of Allied Shipbuilders' business. "We had other work," Arthur noted, "but the NTCL contracts provided the big sales that bought equipment." From time to time, other shipyards in Vancouver did northern work and then left. "The big yards had other work they were doing," Arthur pointed out. "They were established. We weren't. So we had to go up north and do the work that nobody else wanted. And eventually, we really became known for that. That's how we got established."

Living in Field Camps

Aside from the complicated business of assembling ships in remote sites, there was the matter of housing and feeding the crew. Jim McLaren, the eldest of Arthur's three sons, got his first look at field camp life at age twelve, when he travelled north with his father and helped cook in the camp for several weeks. Later he made the trek north as a crew member on many of Allied's northern contracts. By 1970 he was project manager at Hay River, doing the final outfitting of an NTCL tug. For that job, the crew actually lived on board some laid-up boats; the cold, wet, sleeting weather didn't make the work any easier. The tug and barge re-erection site at Waterways was only a few miles away from Fort McMurray. As Jim recalled, "All the activity was in Waterways primarily because that's where the Legion was!"

Allied's field crews ranged in size from ten to sixty men. Arthur often travelled to field camps when jobs were getting started, and Bert Slade went up practically every time, starting in 1946. Early on, crews were sent north and housed in decrepit bunkhouses, equipped only with metal cots. As time went on, people expected better

accommodations and got them. "People knew it was hard work but they went up north for the money," Arthur explained. "Wages were about $1.20/hour in the beginning, but we often put in long days. So at the end of the year a worker could add an extra $500 to his total income. That was a lot of money in those times; it was enough to buy a car or use as a down payment for a house."

Occasionally, small issues at field camps grew to become official issues, and the result could be a "wobble," which Arthur described as a work stoppage protest: "We had a wobble with the field crew up in McMurray in 1955. Somebody made a fuss about the fact that there wasn't any butter on the mess table, and it degenerated into a 'down tool' situation. So we got butter in the mess room and the men went back to work. It was really an oversight, I think. Nobody thought of offering butter, and then there were technical reasons—a shortage of refrigeration meant we had trouble keeping it. It wasn't a survival issue, but in field conditions sometimes small issues could quickly blow up into big ones."

Fortunately there were always one or two crew members who offered some comic relief to the relentless grind of field camp. Jim McLaren recalled two brothers, Jerry and Woody Woods, from Newfoundland, who worked on his crew in 1970 during the completion of a Northern Transportation tug. The men were living on board some nearby laid-up boats in cold, wet, snowy weather. "All the guys were getting pretty tired. One day I was going down to the boat when Woody walked past me heading the other way, going for the highway. 'Where you going?' I asked. 'To get my coat,' he mumbled. 'Well, where's your coat?' I asked. 'Vancouver.' We brought him back."

Another time when Woody was welding underneath the engine room control booth, his clothes got soaked with oil and he set himself on fire. "I came into the engine room and could smell this burning cloth," Jim remembered, "so I started following what turned out to be a trail of burning clothes that went from the engine room, up the stairs, down the passage, through the galley and up the next deck. When I caught up to him, Woody was still pulling off burning layers as he headed down the hall for his room. His clothes ended up burnt right to his shorts!"

Even though the Woods brothers got into lots of trouble, Jim said, "they were the sort of people you really needed on a heavy job like that to keep the crew's morale up and keep them moving. They didn't take life so seriously."

Design and Planning

In the early years, Arthur designed almost everything he built. He would usually sit down with the customer, talk over their needs and then produce a concept drawing. If the customer thought it looked good, they usually bought it. Northern Transportation Company vessels were a good example of customer and builder working together. NTCL's marine engineering superintendent, Henry Christopherson, lived in Vancouver during the winters and met with Arthur regularly to talk over vessel plans.

As a twelve-year-old boy, Arthur's youngest son Malcolm spent many a Saturday kicking around his father's yard. He remembers his father sitting on one side of the drawing board, drawing a tug, with Henry sitting on the other side, making suggestions and telling jokes. "I can still hear him saying, 'Well, Arthur, why don't you put the vents over here? Well, Arthur, why don't you put the sea chests over there so air won't get in?' They'd talk back and forth and change the boat around. Henry knew 'hands-on' marine engineering and the work the tugs would be doing; Arthur knew structural and engineering reasons why things were built the way they were. The result was a wonderful vessel. NTCL got an excellent series of tugs that worked up and down the Mackenzie River handling a whole fleet of barges. Up north, breakdown wasn't an option, there wasn't room for failure."

This shared expertise was typical of Arthur's work with all his customers. It wasn't necessarily the same as drawing what the client thought he wanted, which could result in instability or other problems. Instead it meant listening to the customer and figuring out a way to incorporate his needs while getting the job done.

Allied's First Northern Vessels

Radium Franklin (Hull #7)

In 1951 Allied got an order from Northern Transportation Company Ltd. for a 70-foot vessel slated for service on Bear Lake, moving in barges loaded with supplies and taking out barges loaded with uranium.

Arthur noted that the dimensions of this vessel made breakdown for shipment a relatively simple matter: the bow section was cut about 12 feet from the stem and shipped "nose up" on a flatcar. The remainder of the hull was split down the centreline and the halves shipped on flatcars. The deckhouse, of rivetted aluminum construction built on a steel coaming, was a box with an aluminum deck. This unit, complete with linings and joiner bulkheads, was shipped on edge on a flatcar. The rivetted aluminum wheelhouse was also a complete unit. The *Radium Franklin* was a straightforward job that broke down into five well-outfitted units for shipment.

The *Radium Franklin* gave Allied crews their first experience in building a vessel that included aluminum construction. The hull was made out of steel, but the deckhouse and everything above the main deck was aluminum. "We rivetted it together because nobody could tell us how to weld it together," Arthur recalled. "The tug cost about $200,000, which was about twice what it should have because it was elaborate and a lot of people got involved. Things were done the hard way; it would have been a lot simpler not to put all the beautiful round curves in the plating. Still, it was a successful ship and stayed up working that area for nearly fifty years."

Barges for Western Bridge

In 1955, construction and maintenance of the North American Air Defense Distant Early Warning (DEW) Line generated more shipbuilding

The following letter from W.D. McLaren to his son Arthur is typical of the mix of shipbuilding business and day-to-day life that father and son regularly discussed. It is interesting to note that even though Allied had been in business since 1948, the address at Waterways was still West Coast Shipbuilders. In these days of instant communication by fax, e-mail and cellular telephone, it's hard for younger people to imagine the complexity of doing business in remote locations such as this. Not only was it hard to get equipment in, but even simple communication was difficult. As late as 1951 it simply was not possible to contact Waterways directly.

May 18, 1951
T.A. McLaren, Esq.
c/o West Coast Shipbuilders Ltd.
WATERWAYS, ALTA.

Dear Arthur:

I have been attending the yard and things seem to be going along satisfactorily. There are no men working on the Fishing Boat today. Apparently your requirements for doors and stairway monopolized first attention. I saw Ross Neilsen working on a stairway with stringers about $1^1/_2'' \times 8''$—enormous. What on earth are you doing with a thing that size where otherwise you are going in for light construction?

The Workmen's Compensation Board were about to put you onto a very high premium because you failed to attend to their request for three safety ladders at the dock. Fortunately, Miss Cokely got the man into an easier frame of mind and promised that the work would be done today. This has been done and the Board notified.

I have had talks with Walter regarding the equipment of the fishing boat. I have been told to call it a "fishing boat" as there is no such word as a "fishboat"! It certainly isn't so easy to say. With regard to the equipment, Walter feels that we would be far better to stay with

32 volts and I think he is right. I went over the requirements and we agreed to order a 2 k.w. generator from Magneto Sales & Service at a price which comes just a little under $300 with the 20% discount they allow us. Walter will put in a battery charger so that when the vessel is alongside a dock you can plug in at 110 volts, which current will go to charge the batteries and thus avoid any complication with the equipment in the vessel.

However, the main purpose in writing you this letter is to let you know that your brother Jim had a meeting with Granger last night and learned from him today that the Sun Life would be prepared to give you a mortgage on the house at up to $8500 at $4^1/_2$ to 5%. I think it works out to about $59 a month. Do you want us to tell Granger that will be satisfactory and let him go ahead with the preparation of the papers?

I learned that you were in Edmonton yesterday and would be back in Waterways today. Drop a line and let us know how things are going.

Miss Andrews has found that you failed to sign your name on the Declaration of Ownership regarding the "Wee MacAlpine" and "Wee MacAllister". The forms are enclosed herewith—please sign and return them.

Sincerely,
Dad

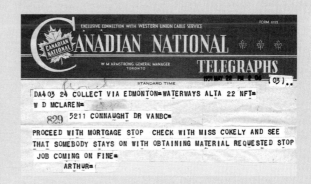

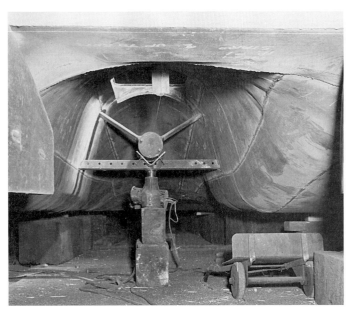

A propeller "tunnel" of the *Radium Franklin* while under construction.

work for BC yards, and Western Bridge contracted Allied to build ten barges, 600 Series, 150 x 35 x 7 feet. The barges were designed with two longitudinal bulkheads so that in section there were 10-foot wide pontoons port and starboard with 15-foot wide interconnecting deck and bottom panels. These were built in Vancouver, then transported by rail to Waterways. Each barge shipment consisted of six pontoons 50 x 10 x 7 feet, shipped on edge on flatcars, while the centre panels were stood on edge in gondolas. Upon arrival, Allied handled the complete erection for Western Bridge, along with supplying and installing the cargo oil piping, deck fittings, etc.

"Since we had contracted on a firm price basis to do this field work," Arthur explained, "we became concerned when man hours expended on the first barge were well in excess of our estimate. Fortunately, hours on the second barge were satisfactory. Those on subsequent barges were even lower than anticipated, perhaps responding to the learning curve. However, barges 5 to 9 each showed a slight increase. We wondered if the men were taking longer and longer because boredom was setting in. Fortunately the tenth barge was completed in 85 percent of the hours for barge 4—the best performance of the series. Probably at the end the crew simply wanted to go home!"

Radium Dew (Hull #34)

In 1955, in the same year Allied was carrying out their barge construction contract with Western Bridge, the company received an order from NTCL for a 150-foot twin-screw tug. The 1,500 hp *Radium Dew*, an improved version of the *Radium Charles* and *Radium Yellowknife*, was needed to push barges on the Mackenzie River system and from the delta of the Mackenzie River west to Herschel Island and east to Baillie Island.

This tug was designed by the owner's consulting naval architects and was not an ideal model for breakdown and shipment. Consequently Allied was not able to benefit from pre-outfitting to the extent they would have liked, and crews had to do more detailed outfitting in the field than Allied had estimated. Nevertheless, the *Radium Dew* was a satisfactory job.

In 1956 NTCL contracted with Western Bridge for an additional twenty-six 600 Series barges and one 100-foot barge. The fabrication of these barges was subcontracted to Dominion Bridge in Winnipeg. At the same time, NTCL contracted with Yarrows for three 95-foot shallow-draft tugs, the *Radium Miner*, *Radium Prospector* and *Radium Trader*. Once these vessels arrived on site, Allied undertook the re-erection, piping and outfit of Western Bridge's barges, as before. They also undertook the steelwork in reassembling Yarrows' tugs, with Yarrows completing the outfitting with their own crews.

As the 1956 season advanced, Gunnar Mines ordered the 90-foot tug *Johnnie B* from Russell Hipwell of Owen Sound and three 150-foot barges similar to the NTCL Series 600. By agreement, Allied completed these barges, reassembling the hulls, and finished outfitting the tug. Thus, 1956 was Allied's busiest year in the north, with its crews assembling four tug hulls and some thirty barges.

Naval architect's perspective drawing of the 150-foot *Radium Dew*, the largest self-propelled vessel that Allied had built to date. It was ordered to support building the DEW (Distant Early Warning) line stations. Arnott & Rogers

Trials and Tribulations

Dumit (Hull #65), Miskanaw (#66)

Arthur described vividly the lessons learned with these two vessels.

In late 1957, Allied Shipbuilders tendered on and won a contract to construct two small shallow-draft buoy vessels for what was then the federal Department of Transport. The Dumit and Miskanaw were to be delivered at Waterways, Alberta, after satisfactory trials. The design, prepared by a well-known firm of Montreal naval architects, called for vessels 60 feet in length, 18 feet in breadth and 5 feet 6 inches in depth, with a working draft of 2 feet.

One of the first requirements of such a contract is for the shipbuilder to check the design. Using his schedule of weights and the naval architect's lines plan, he confirms that the completed vessel will meet the specified draft restrictions. We pursued

this matter and discovered that, as designed, the vessel would exceed draft restrictions. So we concluded that a larger hull would be required to adequately float engines, equipment and outfit. In order to make a complete presentation, we drew a new design with the length increased to 67 feet 6 inches and the beam to 20 feet 4 inches, which increased the displacement of the hull by 25 percent, thus meeting the 2-foot draft requirement. We then forwarded the complete report to the shipbuilding branch of the Department of Transport, showing our schedule of weights, horizontal and vertical centres of gravity, draft and trim conditions resulting from various loading criteria, etc. The submission ended with a price for undertaking the revisions.

Several days later I received a phone call from Alex Watson, the doyen of the Department of Transport fleet, instructing me to be at his office at 10 a.m. on the following Thursday. In my naiveté, I muttered, "Is that in Ottawa?"

Bow section of the *Miskanaw* inside rail car, arriving at Waterways for assembly. The *Dumit* can be seen on the ways beside it, just to the right of the rail car.

"Of course it is," was the reply.

Now, I had never dealt with directors in Ottawa. The first thing that bothered me was the cost of the trip. A trip to Ottawa was what big yards did. We certainly did not budget for such expenses and at that time we were struggling to meet the payroll for some two dozen men. But of course I went to Ottawa and, at 9:50 a.m. on the appointed day, entered Alex Watson's domain. One of two secretaries directed me to be seated in the outer office, where I could watch the door leading to Mr. Watson's inner offices. For half an hour, nobody entered that inner sanctum and nobody left. Eventually I was shown into the office and the chief of the DOT fleet got down to business. He asked me, I had sent him a letter?

"Yes."

"The letter was in reply to the design check requirement?"

"Yes."

"In the letter I had quoted prices for modifications?"

"Yes."

Then he wanted to know, "Who asked for such prices?"

I paused and then said, "Well, I thought it would help to settle the matter if I gave prices."

There was another pause before he demanded, "Do you know what happens to letters that come into my office?"

Well, I had no idea whether they were copied in beautiful script or shredded, but Mr. Watson brought me back to reality.

"They go into the file. And do you know what happens to my files?"

No, I really did not.

Pointing in the general direction of the Parliament Buildings, he continued, "Any son of a bitch in that building has access to my files, so there is nothing going into the records without my full approval. So, Mr. McLaren, in future you will contact me by phone and we will discuss matters. Then you will write a letter covering the items I tell you to and in a manner I can accept."

It was excellent advice, and I followed it when dealing with Alex Watson and most other *government officials. The meeting ended in a friendly vein, and Mr. Watson remarked that I had a bit of an accent. He inquired as to my origins. When I told him about my Scottish boyhood, he said that I was amongst friends—the Canadian shipbuilding fraternity was known as the Scotch Mafia.*

As builder for all but one of the Coast Guard vessels on the northern rivers, Arthur was often frustrated when presented with government designs that he felt were inadequate. In 1979 Rollie Webb was working in Ottawa at the Department of Supply and Services. He remembers a long distance phone call after Allied landed the contract to build the second *Dumit*. Arthur's voice announced definitively, "This one won't float either."

The *Dumit* and *Miskanaw* were built simultaneously and shipped to Waterways. Upon completion, Alan Webster from Ottawa headquarters came out to Fort McMurray to observe sea trials. Arthur met him at the airport and drove him to the Northern Transportation camp where the Allied crew was staying. On the way he explained that space had been booked for Webster in the camp. As an alternative, a reservation had been made at the one and only hotel in Fort McMurray. Today Fort McMurray is a bustling city, but at that time both Waterways and Fort McMurray had a total population of under 1,000. There were no roads and no telephones. The entire community consisted of wood frame buildings and it had been many years since a paint salesman had plied

The *Dumit* landing at the edge of the river, 1958.

his trade there. Mr. Webster was not ready for this scenario, as Arthur recalled.

The next day was one of trials and tribulations. I organized the trials and Webster organized the tribulations. "Where is the measured mile?" he asked. I explained there wasn't one. "Well, how will we measure speed?" he wanted to know. I explained we would choose two points on the riverbank which we could measure from the District Survey Plan. "This will nae do at all," he said in disapproving Scots accent. We ran the trials but we could not satisfy Allan Webster.

Finally he said, "Fa're ye frae?"

I told him my birthplace was Montrose.

"Montrose, ye dinna say. I frae Aberdeen." At that moment the sun broke through and he smiled. I knew Allan Webster for the next thirty years until his death, and we were great friends. His severest admonition to me was, "Dinna gie me that. You're not in Montrose now."

Arthur noted that the first pair of buoy vessels had problems steering a straight course. "The little vessels lacked keels, or skegs; as a result they had little or no directional stability. In due course Allied modified the hydraulic steering by fitting a power pump and a jog lever for fast response. With power steering, the problem of yawing was overcome to some extent. Some two or three years later, Allied built an 80-foot barge for each of the two buoy vessels to push. Once the buoy vessels were connected to their new barges, their directional stability was excellent."

Eckaloo (Hull #115)

In 1961 Allied received a contract to build a third buoy vessel. The *Eckaloo*, which was to service aids to navigation on the Great Slave Lake as well as parts of the Mackenzie River, was 84 feet in length with a 20-foot beam and a loaded draft slightly under 4 feet. Several bothersome features evident in the previous buoy vessels were overcome. Sea trials were scheduled for Vancouver, after which the vessel would be cut apart and shipped north.

"We ran the trials in English Bay, over the measured mile at Spanish Banks," Arthur remembered. "To perform the shallow-water trials, we sounded the very shallow sand bar off Spanish Banks and marked a suitable depth of water. As the vessel sailed over the shallow water and speed was gradually increased, a squatting effect took place. The stern waves peaked up into short high crests. The bow dropped until presently the whole forward deck was awash and the hull was dragging the bottom. Once the ship lost speed, the bow rose again."

This squatting effect is well understood by river pilots, but it is not appreciated to the same extent by their sea-going brothers. Observers on the sea trials were alarmed to see the ship settle in the water until the forward deck was awash. The phenomenon is no doubt due to the Bernoulli principle: higher velocity between the hull and the river bottom reduces the pressure and causes a vessel to squat. It is more noticeable in flat-bottom vessels than in those having a pronounced dead rise of the bottom. The *Eckaloo* was in good company—squatting has been observed when large crude carriers navigate the Maas to Rotterdam, in loaded condition and with less than 6 feet of water under their keels. Similarly, in August 1992 the *Queen Elizabeth II* grounded with some 6 feet of water beneath her. Fortunately the Ottawa officials attending trials accepted Arthur's explanation that shallow-draft vessels squat.

The contract for *Eckaloo* called for delivery at Hay River in the Northwest Territories. The vessel was shipped in sections by rail to Waterways, where it was re-erected and launched. Then it was taken down the Athabasca River to Fort Fitzgerald and the portage to Fort Smith. The beaching and launching facilities at both ends of the portage were crude affairs, consisting merely of a series of 12 x 12-inch timbers, well greased with tallow, running into the river. Bulldozers hauled out and launched the vessels as required.

When it came time to relaunch *Eckaloo* at Fort Smith, Arthur McLaren told interested parties that they would set a record: the ship would be launched, generators and both main engines would be started with compressed air and the vessel would be underway in less than five minutes. Alas, it was not to be.

Our electrician Ced Hope, who at that time had been with us for twenty years, wanted to ride the vessel down the ways. I agreed. Ced took a commanding position in the wheelhouse as the cats started to push. He pulled the ship's whistle lanyard and blew it and blew it while the vessel travelled down the launchways.

Finally the whistle died off to a whisper. Ced had used up all the air.

We set no records that day. Eckaloo *lay at the bottom of the ways for a full twenty minutes while Ced was given the task of hand cranking the small diesel-driven start-up compressor to fill the air reservoir.*

The 84-foot *Eckaloo* (note misspelling on ship) on maiden sea trials in Vancouver Harbour.

Tembah (Hull #135)

In early 1963 Allied was contracted to build a fourth shallow-draft buoy vessel, a much more sophisticated design than the previous vessels, with an overall length of 130 feet and a beam of 26 feet. The *Tembah* was a twin-screw vessel, powered by Cummins 12-cylinder engines. Electrical requirements were met with two 38 kW 440/3/60 diesel alternators with static excitation.

One of *Tembah*'s two main engines being lowered into the vessel during initial construction in Vancouver, July 22, 1963.

The steering system was electrohydraulic with electric level control. The salient item of deck machinery was a 5-ton capacity HIAB hydraulic crane with folding boom, which could handle buoys and anchors either on board or overboard.

The contract called for performance trials in Vancouver, with particular emphasis on shallow water trials, before dismantling and shipping the vessel north. "There were a number of senior Department of Transport personnel attending the trials," Arthur recalled, "and we were anxious to demonstrate the virtues of our latest vessel construction. The Sperry electric steering controls had not been delivered in time for sea trials so these manoeuvres were carried out using manual hydraulic steering control. We put the vessel through steering and astern trials, a six-hour full-speed endurance run and speed runs on the measured mile, where we achieved a very credible 13.5 knots. As for the shallow water trials, we had to explain the predictable squatting effect yet again to nervous officials."

Finishing off the hull and outfitting in Vancouver proved to be a very efficient way to build this ship. In fact, a crew of six put the vessel back together and launched her at Waterways in just three weeks. In addition to Allied's regular crew, Tom Davies, a Sperry technician, travelled to Waterways to install and test the electric steering system. Arthur McLaren thought that the control

circuit Tom brought with him resembled a sheet of cardboard on which somebody had squeezed a glob of toothpaste in some offbeat design. "I asked him, 'Tommy, what is this?' He explained, 'This is what steers your ship, Arthur.' I disagreed, reminding him that a steering system is a big heavy assembly on which the smallest fitting is a 3/4-inch hex nut. But Tommy just connected the printed circuit panel, manoeuvred the steering lever, and everything functioned perfectly."

That was in September 1963. After launching at Waterways, the ship departed for Fort Fitzgerald one afternoon with Arthur and a trial team on board. The group included a shipbuilding supervisor from the Victoria office of the Department of Transport, one Captain E. Alfred Arneson, who had retired from the Royal Canadian Navy and was now with the DOT. Arthur's old friend and the company's electrical foreman, Ced Hope, was on board as well. During lunch the next day, Captain Arneson said, "Ced, there's one trial you have yet to perform. I want you to parallel the electrical generators." Arthur explained:

Now, these generators were statically excited, and Ced just wasn't too clear on the functioning of the exciter so he deferred. Arneson rose from the table, announcing, "We are going to do this test, now." Ced protested. Arneson headed down to the engine room. I told Ced he had to follow, but felt some unease so I stayed at the mess room table,

Tembah, afloat on a northern river.

During sea trials on calm shallow water, the bow of *Tembah* takes water due to squatting effect.

addressing my thoughts to a cup of coffee. A few minutes later the lights went out—the ship had undergone a complete blackout. I continued to make a thorough examination of my coffee cup. I certainly was not about to make my presence known in the engine room. When you have a foulup, it seems wise to involve as few people as possible. After my fifth cup of coffee, I went outside and joined Captain Arneson at the rail. Finally I asked if Ced was having a problem. "He has lost the residual magnetism on both generators," Arneson replied, and the subject was changed.

By this time it was obvious that the ship was without electrical power. We had main engines and radio, but no steering, no lighting, no gyro compass, no heating, no domestic or galley services. We could drive the vessel but not steer. Furthermore, we were well down the Athabasca

River, approaching the delta, a stretch of the river that winds like a corkscrew.

Our Coast Guard captain was attempting to steer using the engines, but with poor results. Now, I am not trained in ship handling, but I think I know how ships run and steer. So with some degree of placating of the captain's ego, I explained that we could not proceed the way he was handling the ship. I asked him to put both engines about one-third speed ahead and not touch the port engine; then by increasing or decreasing the speed of the starboard engine we would be able to maintain a course. The Tembah had a length-to-beam ratio of nearly 5 to 1, which ensured a good degree of directional stability and made this method of steering effective. We could never have accomplished this on the Dumit *or* Miskanaw *unless we were pushing a barge.*

SHIPS OF STEEL

Fortunately Tom Davies, the Sperry technician, understood modern electronic circuits. He opened up the generator enclosures, checked the circuitry with his electronic instruments, and found an error in one of the connections. He corrected it quickly, but still couldn't get current.

Tom then proceeded to check the three diodes in each of the generators and discovered that two diodes had failed on each unit. However, by fitting the three working diodes on one generator, we could reactivate one unit and run all ship services again. Thus we reached Fort Fitzgerald and the portage to Fort Smith. We sent a radio message to the Coast Guard in Hay River, asking them to send replacement diodes. They were on board a plane that evening.

When we relaunched at Fort Smith, nobody—but nobody—blew the whistle this time. On the trip from Fort Smith to Hay River we did synchronize the alternators. At Hay River Ced Hope spent a day with the appointed ship's engineer, familiarizing him with the new electrical system. Tembah was a good ship, and thirty years later there had been very few failures in hull machinery or equipment—and none in the steering system.

The 130-foot shallow-draft buoy vessel *Tembah* being trundled along the portage to Fort Smith, 1963, after reassembly at Waterways, Alberta.

The *Knut Lang* afloat at the Bell Rock ways, near Fort Smith, May 15, 1969. This 4,200-hp tug was one of three Allied built simultaneously for the Northern Transportation Company Ltd.

Big Power

Angus Sherwood (Hull #168), Kelly Hall (#169), Knut Lang (#170)

In January 1969 Allied Shipbuilders received orders for three tugs for Northern Transportation. These twin-screw vessels were not only intended to operate on the Mackenzie River, they were built to Home Trade Class II specifications, permitting operation in the Arctic from Tuktoyaktuk to Cambridge Bay. Each one was of 700 gross tons, two and a half times the size of the *Radium Dew*, and was equipped with General Motors EMD main engines of 2,250 hp a side. Their free-running speed was about 12 knots. They were the biggest and most powerful tugs on the river. Arthur McLaren designed and built them, based on a gentlemen's agreement with NTCL's managing operator, Henry Christopherson.

The third tug was 5 feet wider and longer than the others. "We built the first two vessels," Arthur recounted, "put them in the water and then NTCL starting loading stuff in them—all sorts of gear and some 60,000 gallons of fuel oil. The boats went down and down, down and down into the water. The owners became quite alarmed and wanted to know what we were going to do about it. I suggested they take some of the gear out of the boat, but they weren't interested in that, of course. To make a long story short, I suggested we widen the third tug and lengthen it. So we did."

Arthur McLaren in the wheelhouse of an NTCL tug, summer 1969.

Vic Ingraham (Hull #173)

Allied's Hull #173, the 1970-built *Vic Ingraham*, was the last NTCL vessel re-erected in the north. Other vessel orders for the northern rivers came in the early 1970s, in response to the oil discovery at Prudhoe Bay. This second lot of vessels could now get to their final northern destinations by sea, thanks to the removal of earlier insurance restrictions. After that, vessels were completely finished in BC and delivered via the Pacific and Arctic Oceans.

"The *Vic Ingraham* was a Robert Allan design," Arthur recalled. "He got the job because he told Mr. Monpetit at NTCL he could design a vessel that would have much better performance than the ones we had designed and built. With this tug he had 4,500 hp from four diesels and four propellers. The vessel also had an aluminum superstructure so was lighter, which meant less draft."

In terms of performance, the bollard pull of this tug was almost identical to that of the three tugs Allied had done the year before. "I suppose the propellers were smaller," Arthur noted, "so the power was just spread over four propellers instead of two. Regardless, it had plenty of power and any of those tugs could push up to a dozen NTCL barges, each of which was 200 by 50 feet."

The one peculiar thing about the job, he said, was that Allied shared the building contract with Bel-Aire Shipyards. "They did the deckhouse and

Allied did the hull, machinery and everything else. That arrangment happened because the tug didn't come out for bidding until March and NTCL wanted it by September."

Nahidik (Hull #186)

This shallow-draft buoy and supply vessel was built for the Department of Transport. The 175-foot ship had an aluminum superstructure and was equipped with EMD main engines that delivered 2,100 hp a side. Arthur explained, "The design came from the drawings we had done of the three 1969 NTCL tugs, so modifications weren't any problem."

The government put the vessel contract out to tender but Allied was the only yard that bid on the job:

That caused some problems for me, because I had thought George Fryatt, owner of Bel-Aire Shipyard, was going to bid against us. It wasn't until they opened the tenders that we discovered that George's letter said he wouldn't bother bidding on it just now because he was busy. If I had known that, we might have gone just a bit higher.

In the end it worked out. A fellow from Ottawa came out and told us he would have to review our bid since we were the sole bidder. He wanted to know the price for this and that and the other thing. Eventually we gave him a breakdown of our price and based on that, they gave us the contract. We had a bit of an argument on the overhead we were going to apply against the job, which I had put down at 60 percent. He challenged that, saying we didn't need anything like that. But I told him we did since we didn't have any other work to do at that time. Finally we settled on a figure that was somewhat less than the 60 percent. That review of our bid was done according to what they used to call the Sole Source Bid Regulations.

The *Nahidik* was built for buoy work in the Arctic, on both the rivers and the ocean. It was very similar to the *Knut Lang*, except there was a crane on the forward end for handling buoys. It was the first vessel Allied built that sailed around Point

The 175-foot shallow-draft navigation aid tender *Nahidik* at work in the Canadian Arctic. Canadian Coast Guard Fleet News No. 22

Barrow, rather than being shipped up and reassembled as previous insurance requirements had dictated. Arthur recalled, "In 1973 the Northern Transportation people said to hell with insurance and sailed a flotilla of tugs and barges around Point Barrow to the Arctic. You can do that when you're the government, you know? They didn't have any trouble, so that was the way it was done after that."

Dumit (Hull #217)

The 160-foot buoy vessel *Dumit*, built for the Canadian Coast Guard, was similar to the *Nahidik* in that James Kirk again provided a preliminary general arrangement and bids were based on that drawing. A design change made the replacement *Dumit* much wider and longer than specified. "We did that in order to meet the requirements the owners had laid down," Arthur explained. "Longer gave them speed; wider gave them more buoyancy in order to meet their load and draft restrictions."

A.M.E. Biname (Hull #251)

In 1988 Allied beat out the Rivtow Group to build the *A.M.E. Biname*. Peter Hatfield designed the 42-foot twin-screw pusher tug for Esso Resources Canada Ltd. It was a little shallow-draft tug with a very high wheelhouse, specifically designed to push service barges at the Norman Wells oil refinery. "That was really the last ship on which I

The 42-foot shallow-draft pusher tug *A.M.E. Biname* under construction—upside down on the jig. Arthur (at front) prepared the winning bid for the job. The *Biname* was the last vessel for which Arthur made the working drawings.

The *Biname* was completely assembled and painted in the yard, then underwent machinery trials on dry land. After all of this, the vessel was split in half lengthwise and taken by rail car to Hay River.

The *Biname* was reassembled and launched by crane at Hay River, NWT.

The *Biname* in service. This short, stubby pusher tug was designed to push barges carrying trucks and other equipment around the various islands at the Norman Wells oil field.

Flotilla of newly built Northern Transportation Company Ltd. tugs and barges on their way to northern Canada, July 10, 1973. The vessels, which left Vancouver and travelled all the way around Alaska to the Mackenzie River, were the first NTCL river vessels delivered by sea instead of being shipped in pieces and reassembled in the north. This photograph was taken from the Lions Gate Bridge (First Narrows), looking east. Murray McLennan photo

did working drawings," Arthur stated. "It was also the most recent vessel we did for the north that was completely assembled at our Vancouver yard and then cut into pieces for transport."

Barges for Northern Rivers

Building tugs, supply vessels and buoy tenders constituted only some of the shipbuilding work for northern rivers. The other work was building barges. After World War II, Northern Transportation Company Ltd. ordered a 100 Series, each with a 100-ton capacity. Fifty years later, some of these barges were still hard at work.

Over the years, the size and capacity of the barges increased. By 1955, NTCL was operating its 600 Series, with a 600-ton capacity. By the time the company launched its 1000 Series,

barges were carrying ten times the amount of the first ones that had been built. Finally, they commissioned a 1500 Series, each with a capacity of 1,500 tons. New, more powerful tugs were required to handle moving this increased mass of freight. All of this took place in the name of economy—fewer trips carrying more goods always meant a better return on the owner's investment.

At the end of fifty years of shipbuilding, Arthur McLaren regarded the vessels Allied built for the northern rivers as some of the best challenges for himself and for the shipyard. "The vessels we built for Northern Transportation in the latter part of the 1960s and early '70s tested our mettle," he said. "The challenge came from the fact that they were looking for more complicated ships. We rose to that challenge and did it."

CHAPTER 6

Landlocked Vessels
(1950s–1970s)

"There is little point in practising a procedure that must be done perfectly the first time."

—*Arthur McLaren, quoting a Canadian commanding officer*

Interior Ferries

Since the province was first settled by Europeans, an impressive array of ferries have crossed various bodies of water that cut through major trading routes. These craft were powered by an equally interesting variety of propulsion systems. Simple manual methods ranged from rowing to poling to pulling on overhead ropes. Mechanical means included paddlewheels, outboard motors, a tug and barge, conventional screw propulsion and guided cable operation. A novel river type was the reaction ferry, utilizing river current to propel the vessel from one side to the other.

In the 1940s and '50s, the BC Department of Public Works maintained some forty-eight miscellaneous ferry barges at various river crossings throughout the province. The largest craft were located at Nelson and Castlegar, but there were small ferries at crossings on the upper Fraser, Columbia, North Thompson and Skeena Rivers. Most of the first freshwater ferries were built out of wood, so ferry builders were supplied with ongoing work, as timber hulls deteriorated regularly and had to be replaced.

Beginning in the late 1940s and early '50s,

most of the cable ferries and reaction ferries were replaced with steel-hulled vessels. As Arthur lamented, steel hulls were practically indestructible in a freshwater environment; this quality combined with the determination of civil and structural engineers to replace economical ferries with expensive bridges has had a severe impact on the prospect of new ferry work. "Indeed, our success at building, shipping and re-erecting these vessels may have precluded such work in the future. We may have been the authors of our own misfortune!"

From the 1950s to the 1970s, Allied built a number of vessels for service on short routes on the province's interior waterways. Those contracts for the northern Canadian river vessels had been primarily for transporting goods over long distances, but landlocked vessels—Arthur called them "across-the-pond" types—were designed to travel short distances. Many were ferries built for the BC Department of Highways. Other contracts ranged from small excursion boats to an updated paddlewheeler destined for Calgary. These vessels all presented opportunities to contribute to the province's development.

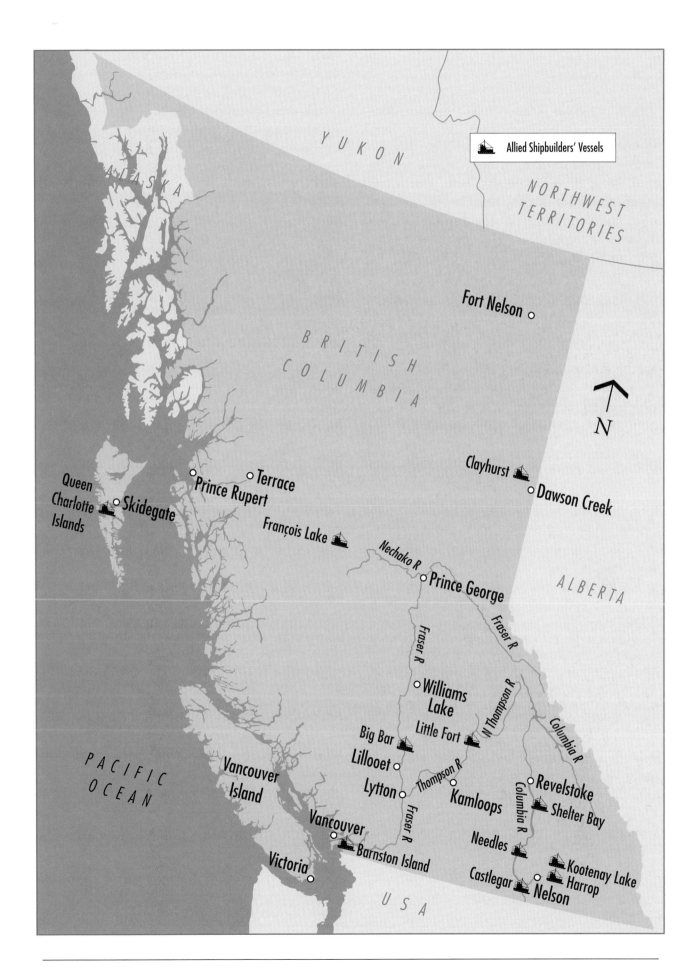

Cable Ferries

A crossing such as those at Nelson and Castlegar, with little or no river current to deal with, called for a cable ferry—a pontoon hull with a winch, reeling a cable stretched from riverbank to riverbank. In addition to this live cable, one or two guide cables were fitted to resist any lateral movement due to river current. The ministry operated many cable ferries over the years, but most have been replaced by bridges.

Reaction Ferries

Crossings with stronger river currents and light traffic were served by reaction ferries. In a typical installation, an overhead cable line spanned the river stream and was supported by a tower on each bank. This skyline had a bicycle, consisting of two large pulleys, travelling on it. A lead from each side of the bicycle ran down to each bow of the catamaran hull and then wrapped around a winch drum controlled by a large steering wheel. By turning the wheel, the ferryman could incline the pontoons to the river current, thus producing a component of force to drive the ferry across the

The Harrop ferry (Hull #123), a cable ferry built to run across the west arm of Kootenay Lake, unloads cars at the north landing, near Highway 3A.

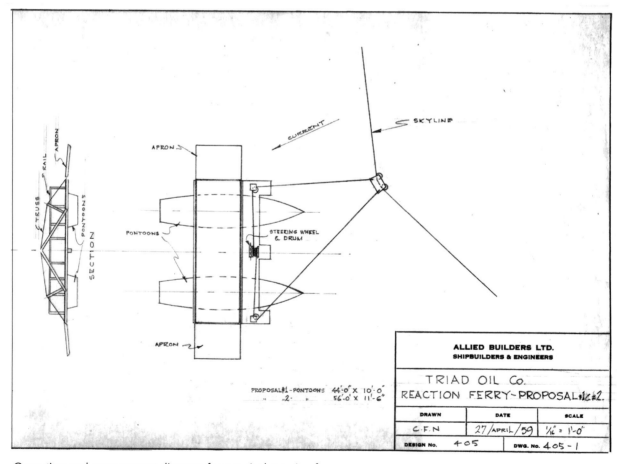

Operating and arrangement diagram for a typical reaction ferry.

The reaction ferry at Big Bar on the Fraser River, near Clinton, is located in a remote area.

The Big Bar reaction ferry approaching the landing. Note arrangement of cables from the bow up to the bicycle at upper left of photo.

The tourist excursion boat *Schwatka*, built in 1960, travels through Miles Canyon, Yukon. During the Klondike gold rush at the turn of the century, this was the way to Dawson City.

river. Speed control was obtained by varying the angle of incidence to the river current.

The reaction ferries themselves were catamarans consisting of two boat-shaped pontoons, each approximately 45 feet in length with an 8-foot beam, interconnected by a steel and timber vehicle deck.

A Good Little Excursion Boat

Schwatka (Hull #110)

Unlike most Allied projects for service in BC's Interior, Hull #110 was not a ferry. However, the 48-foot *Schwatka* was designed to carry passengers. The excursion boat was a retirement project for John D. Scott of Whitehorse. His dream was

to run tourists a few miles upriver, through the rapids to Miles Canyon, so they could see local pictographs and visit other areas of interest. Back in the days of the Klondike gold rush of 1898, people set off from what is now Lake Bennett to go to the goldfields near Dawson City on the Yukon River. The trip was a challenging one, and Miles Canyon was the first point they had trouble. A lot of people lost their lives there.

Arthur McLaren described the *Schwatka* as a "handsome little boat that did very well." In order to comply with regulations and run with one master and no mate, the vessel was limited to just forty passengers and crew. It was built at the Allied yard, then loaded onto the freight ship *Clifford J. Rogers*. At Skagway the boat was off-loaded onto a rail car and taken by rail all the way to Whitehorse. Finally it was transferred onto a truck for the final leg to the launch location. By 2000 the *Schwatka* was as reliable as ever, still transporting tourists on the same route every season.

A Ferry for Dawson City

George Black (Hull #159)

The *George Black* was a public bid, which Allied won in 1967. The all-steel ferry, a Robert Allan design, was to run across the Yukon River at Dawson City. To deliver the ferry to its landlocked destination, Allied crews cut the hull into six sections—three in the width and two in the length. These were shipped by Whitepass to Skagway, along with three sections of wheelhouse; there they were off-loaded onto rail cars and taken the rest of the way to Whitehorse.

Erection of the ferry at Whitehorse was straightforward, but Arthur described the trip downriver to Dawson City as a real headache. "The vessel didn't want to go in a straight line; it wanted to go in circles! The problem was that it was flat, like a saucer. There was nothing in the structure of the vessel to encourage it to go in a straight line. There was a propeller at each end and a separate engine driving each propeller, but unfortunately they were in a tunnel."

The solution was to alter the shape of the rudder, creating more drag at both ends of the vessel. The idea was that enough drag on the rudder would help the ferry to go in a straight line. Fortunately that took care of the problem.

A Hydraulic Paddlewheeler with Expensive Coffee Service

Moyie (Hull #150)

This paddlewheeler was built in 1965 for the Heritage Park Society in Calgary. Phil Spaulding designed the 80-foot sternwheeler and referred the job to Allied. It was built as part of the Heritage Museum in Calgary and slated to carry passengers on the Glen Bow Water Reservoir. The name *Moyie* was taken from a sternwheeler that had run on Kootenay Lake.

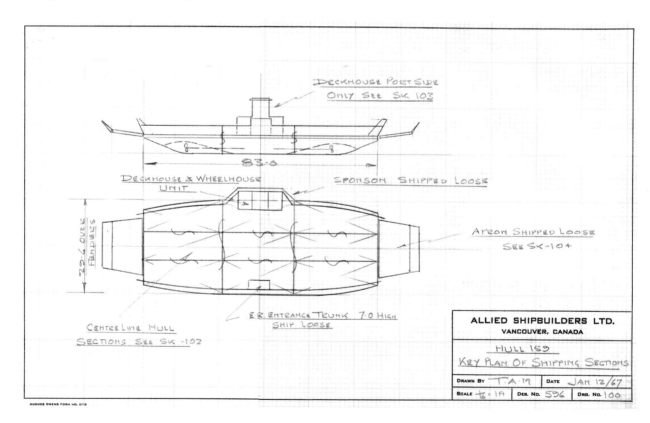

The lines on the Shipping Sections diagram show the position of the cuts on the *George Black*. The hull of the Yukon ferry was shipped north to Dawson City in nine sections.

The paddlewheeler *Moyie* at Heritage Park, Calgary.

The vessel was steel with a wooden super-structure and was half the length of the original *Moyie*. The steel hull was built upside down so that it could be plated easily. It was even launched upside down, then rolled over and towed to Allied's Coal Harbour yard where, as Arthur put it, "we let the fellows loose on the woodwork." The paddles were turned by a large radial-piston hydraulic motor, which in turn was driven by a diesel engine.

The vessel was built, broken down, transported and reassembled in Calgary without any difficulty. The trouble started when the vessel was ready for commissioning. Arthur told the story:

When the Moyie *was ready, some important people from Calgary came down for a trial run. The captain was a fellow named McPherson who had been on Kootenay Lake long before. The deckhand was a nice kid but I don't know if he'd ever been on a boat before. Well, the captain told the deckhand to go downstairs to the coffee bar and bring him a cup of coffee. When the kid came back, he said, "Here's your coffee. That will be 15 cents, Captain."*

"What the hell do you mean, 15 cents?" the captain roared.

"That's what the guy downstairs charges for a cup of coffee," the deckhand explained.

"Well, he doesn't charge me 15 cents for a cup of coffee!" was the final word.

With that, they tied up the boat and

McPherson went traipsing up to the office, making a noise about everything he saw. "I've just been told that the price of a cup of coffee on that boat is 15 cents!" he blustered. "That's fine, but it does not apply to me! That's the way I've run boats for years, and that's the way I will continue to run them." Once it was agreed that the captain could have his coffee for nothing, he calmed down and the boat ran just fine!

Harrowing Launch, Happy Ending

Galena (Hull #163)

In 1968 Allied Shipbuilders received an order for a fifty-car diesel electric ferry with Voith-Schneider propellers. The double-ended *Galena* was designed by John Case of Case Existological Laboratories Ltd. It was to make a 6-mile crossing from Shelter Bay to Galena Bay, south of Revelstoke.

This single-deck vessel measured 165 x 61 feet, with deckhouse casings port and starboard. Its high-level wheelhouse was located midships on the ship's centreline and supported by a bridge gantry. Although it was the first vessel on which Allied had used Voith-Schneider drives, there were no complications installing the two drives.

The ferry was designed with a system of longitudinal bulkheads and longitudinal girders, which favoured splitting the hull longitudinally for shipment. All steel was sent by road. The hull was completely pre-erected in Allied's North Vancouver yard and the piping completed there. However, due to the large number of field butts and seams, no electric cabling was installed. Deckhouses were built as units apart from the hull, and all insulation and lining, doors, portlights, etc. were completely installed prior to shipment.

By the date of this order, the Keenleyside Dam had been completed and the Arrow Lakes above Castlegar were flooded. A re-erection site on the foreshore of the east side of the lake was selected, a mile or so above the dam. The site had previously been a field, so it had fairly soft ground. There was still a construction camp at the dam site, so Allied arranged to house and feed their crew there. Construction and re-erection at the south end of Arrow Lake proceeded in a satisfactory manner, until it came time to launch the *Galena*.

Every shipbuilder knows that launching is one of the most critical procedures in ship construction. The technology involved may be simple, but the risks are great. Arthur was fond of quoting a Canadian commanding officer's response to a US query about parachute training in the 1940s: "There is little point in practising a procedure that must be done perfectly the first time."

So it is with launchings. You need to get them right the first time.

Details of successful launches are kept deep in the files of the shipbuilder's drawing office or, more often, in well-fingered black notebooks kept by the launching foreman. The launching options are to slide the new ship either lengthways or sideways from the building berth into the water. An end launch in a tidal situation permits working on the ways clear of the water or in relatively shallow water when the tide is low. A non-tidal site provides no such advantages. With a side launching, the ways are run in a right angle to the keel. The vessel must attain sufficient launch speed to clear rapidly and drop off the end of the ways and right herself.

It was decided that the *Galena* would be side launched. Alas, things did not go smoothly. As Arthur said later, "The constant fear accompanying all side launchings was realized. When we let go, one end slid faster than the other, so the vessel ended up off the ways with one end in the water, but not yet buoyant. The other end was still hard ashore with a tangle of collapsed timbers under the bottom." Luckily the 360-degree Voith-Schneider propulsion drives had not yet been installed, so they suffered no damage. However, that was scant consolation in the face of the immediate problem of a half-launched ferry stuck on the ways.

In order to start clearing the area, a small tug attending the launch hooked onto some projecting timbers. Someone observed that its propeller wash was quickly eroding the sand and gravel

The *Galena* on the run, at the north end of Upper Arrow Lake near Revelstoke.

bank. So the tug was put to work as a dredge, with its towline secured onto the immersed end of the ferry. After two days, the *Galena* finally floated free with no damage.

Now crews could proceed with all the cabling for the electric installation. However, there were more challenges to come. The reassembly area was hit with a record snowfall, which seriously interfered with production. This was followed by minus-20°C weather and more record snowfall, and the lake froze completely. Completion of the job was a slow and costly business. But despite that harrowing start, the *Galena* went on to prove most successful, providing continuous service at the north end of the Upper Arrow Lake.

The Largest Ferry Built Twice

Omineca Princess (Hull #193)

In 1976 Allied Shipbuilders undertook to build a 192-foot car ferry for service across François Lake in northern BC. The Talbot Jackson & Associates design was a twin-screw vessel with a single deck, two-tier superstructure and wheelhouse on the port side.

The transverse framing of the vessel suggested cutting the hull transversely into sections for easy transport. The two 565-hp engines were installed in canoe-like pods extending below the hull; this permitted each pod to be outfitted with engine, shaft and rudder installed, and shipped as a complete unit. The long, narrow deckhouses were shipped with two transverse cuts along the length. The upper houses and wheelhouse were sent as separate units.

Paying attention to previous experience and with an eye to minimizing field labour, Allied built and outfitted the $2.4-million vessel in North Vancouver prior to shipment. Before cutting, all electrical cables and lines were run through the ship's structure and then pulled back to a central point. Similar efficiency was achieved in the engine room. Since the cutlines were predetermined, all piping and auxiliary equipment was prearranged within specific sections so that only interconnecting spool pipes fitted in the way of those cutlines required removal and replacement. When the hull was completed, shipyard crews cut it transversely into 10-foot-long sections, prompting one reporter to compare it to slicing chunks off a mighty hunk of bologna.

Because the nearest rail access was still some 20 miles from the lake site, Allied chose to transport the huge 18-ton sections of the hull by road from North Vancouver to François Lake. The challenge was that the hull depth was so great that the sections could not be loaded onto flatbed trailers without exceeding highway height limits. Allied overcame this problem in a rather innovative manner: each section was made into its own trailer. Two sets of wheels were welded at the end of each section and a fifth wheel-bearing plate was fitted to the opposite end onto which the tractor could couple. Altogether, thirty-four loads were shipped by road; twenty-three sections had wheels attached.

The ferry *Omineca Princess*, under construction at Allied's North Vancouver yard.

The hull of the *Omineca Princess* was sliced transversely into pieces. Each piece had a fifth wheel welded on one side and a two-axle rubber-tired bogey welded on the other side. A tractor trailer then pulled each section, via road, right to the assembly launch location. Note wheels attached to hull sections at right of picture.

Smaller pieces of the *Omineca Princess* were loaded onto 40-foot flat decks for the trip north. Welding foreman Henry Smart is at right.

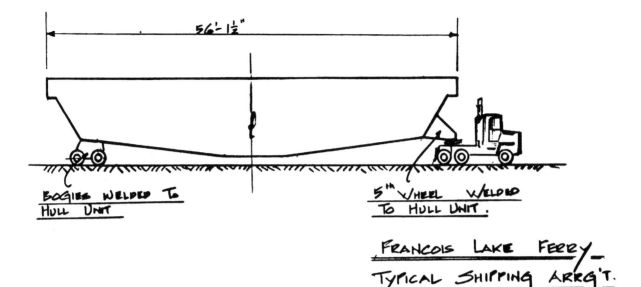

56'-1½"

BOGIES WELDED TO HULL UNIT

5ᵗʰ WHEEL WELDED TO HULL UNIT.

FRANCOIS LAKE FERRY - TYPICAL SHIPPING ARRG'T.

The decision to build the *Omineca Princess* in the North Vancouver yard proved to be a good one. Construction time was five months. A further two months was required for cutting the hull apart for shipment and subsequently refitting the sections and welding them back together.

The *Omineca Princess* was an excellent example of the type of construction Arthur McLaren had been aiming for since 1946, with most of the work being done in the yard where tools, stores and other facilities were most accessible. The goal was to minimize field work and, particularly, reduce the amount of outfitting work left to be completed at the remote site. Over several decades, Allied's extensive experience with pre-planning work for remote sites secured a strong reputation for the shipyard.

The *Omineca Princess*, reassembled and ready for launching on François Lake, 1976.

CHAPTER 7

Building a Saltwater Ferry Fleet

"Over the past fifty years we've found that ship construction means you're always resolving problems that come up. You're working with the tradesmen and the pressure is on to come up with on-site decisions so that the work can carry on unhindered."

—Arthur McLaren

The First Ferries

From earliest days, the inhabitants of British Columbia have moved goods and people across bodies of water. The boats that accomplished these tasks varied dramatically in size and configuration. Once European settlement began, vessels tended to be operated by individuals or small private companies who came up with creative solutions for hauling an assortment of passengers, freight, livestock and vehicles. One favourite was the 51-foot *Senator*, which offered luxurious crossing of Vancouver Harbour in 1881, charging 10 cents per passenger and 50 cents per head of cattle.

By the early 1900s, larger companies such as Canadian Pacific and Union Steamship Company had evolved, with fleets of ships providing regular service to coastal communities. Connections between the mainland and Vancouver Island became the domain of the CPR. The increasing popularity of the automobile was grudgingly accepted, with some CPR ships adapted to carry a small number. But loading and unloading arrangements on the CPR Princess vessels were cumbersome, and the 'tween deck heights on these ships precluded carrying trucks.

Private entrepreneurs played important roles.

Saltspring Island businessman Gavin Mouat operated a ferry service to the Gulf Islands. Oswald "Sparky" New moved from log towing operations to coastal freight services with his Gulf Island Navigation Co. In the 1950s other private companies entered the ferry business. The American Black Ball Line, headed by Captain Alex Peabody, built ferry terminals and began offering more efficient passenger and vehicle service between Nanaimo and Horseshoe Bay, as well as service to the Sunshine Coast and Jervis Inlet.

BC's transition from an assortment of private ferry companies to a single provincial fleet was sudden and unexpected. Premier W.A.C. Bennett was well aware that Vancouver Island was dependent on the vagaries of the CP steamers operating between Victoria and Vancouver and the more efficient Black Ball roll on/roll off service between Nanaimo and Horseshoe Bay. But the importance of that transportation link became front page news in May 1958, when contract negotiations with CP ferry crews failed and workers went on strike. Days later, Black Ball unions issued a strike warning to their company management. Premier Bennett met with the three unions involved and then invoked the Civil Defence Act,

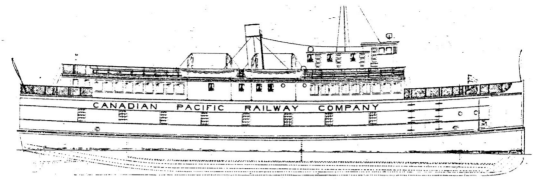

Motor-Car Ferry Steamship, British Columbia Coast Service, Canadian Pacific Railway.

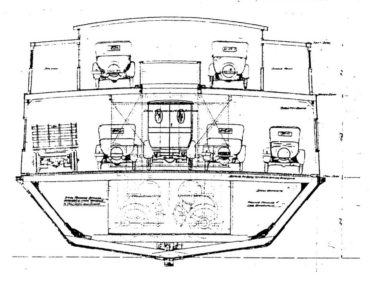

CPR car ferry *Motor Princess*, built of wood by Yarrows Ltd., 1923. The 170-foot, 35-car ferry initially ran between Sidney, on Vancouver Island, and Bellingham, Washington, USA.

which put Black Ball under trusteeship. But discussions with business leaders, including Black Ball and CP officials, offered little hope for any greatly improved, profitable services between the mainland and Victoria.

Captain Harry Terry, President of Northland Navigation Ltd., disagreed. He gave the premier a solid professional understanding of marine operations, providing optimism and suggesting an alternative. On July 18, labour negotiations floundered and Black Ball crews defiantly went out on strike, severing connections between Vancouver Island and the Mainland. Premier Bennett responded with an announcement that the government would take the unions to court for their defiance of the Civil Defence Act. Far more stunning, however, was his declaration that the provincial government was going to provide a proper ferry service. The news was greeted with disbelief, ridicule and political cartoons, but to little effect. The premier had made up his mind.

The Start of the Provincial Fleet

Implementation of W.A.C. Bennett's vision was turned over to his highways minister, Phil Gaglardi. "Flying Phil" had a reputation for achieving the impossible, and he would have to prove it again in order to design and construct both ships and terminals in just two years' time.

First priority on this project was ship design. There was little time to shop for a naval architect but there was a new US flag vessel, the *Coho*, plying the Strait of Juan de Fuca between Victoria and Port Angeles. This was proven operating experience that government decision-makers could assess. The *Coho* had been designed by Phillip Spaulding and Associates of Seattle. Soon Spaulding was engaged to draw up a similar vessel that could carry 100 automobiles and run at 18 knots, to provide two-hour service between the southern Lower Mainland and Vancouver Island. The government stipulated that Spaulding work with a BC partner to assist with modifications and follow the ships through to construction. Thus began the first of several collaborations with his friend and fellow designer, Arthur McLaren.

Once modifications to the design were completed, tenders were called. When the bids were opened, Fairfield's (of Glasgow) had bid the job at $3,800,000; Burrard Dry Dock was at $3,750,000 and Victoria Machinery Depot came in at rock bottom with $3,250,000 for a single vessel. Arthur remembers that VMD's Harold Husband looked at the bid spread and muttered, "Oh my God, lowest in the world!" Two vessels were ordered—one from VMD and the other from Burrard. In March 1960, less than two years after Bennett's decision, the *Sidney* and *Tsawwassen* were delivered, and they commenced operations when the shore terminals were completed early that summer. With two ships and 191 employees at the ready, the British Columbia Ferry Authority was officially open for business.

Designing the *Sidney* and *Tsawwassen*

Arthur traced his early association with government ferry work back to 1946, when he was working for West Coast Shipbuilders and the company was building a ferry for Kootenay Lake.

John Armstrong was the gentleman in charge of that ferry for the government. He would often come around and talk about other ideas he had and things he wanted done. I became quite friendly with John and made proposals for him on one thing and another. I guess you could say I was acting more or less as a designer for the Provincial Department of Public Works, as it was known in those days.

The new superintendent of ferries was a fellow called Ken Gann. His background was engineering rather than shipbuilding, so he used to call on me and I would make drawings for him of the ideas he had for ferries. One day he called me up and told me that Mr. Gaglardi, the minister of public works, wanted a proposal for two ferries that would run between White Rock on the mainland and the lower end of Vancouver Island near where the gravel pit had been.

Gaglardi had several requirements. One of the things he wanted was a vessel that would do at least 35 knots. "You can't do that," I told Ken. "Well," he said, "Gaglardi won't believe that."

A number of discussions ensued, and Arthur produced an outline sketch of a vessel he thought would suit them.

Then I realized that I was doing the wrong thing because Black Ball Transportation was building a ferry that would take care of everything that BC Ferries wanted. It only had to have the side loading changed. The design belonged to Phil Spaulding, so I told them the ethical thing to do was to approach Phil and deal with him. It was settled that they would go with Spaulding and I would make the changes. If you want to call that a joint effort, you can, but actually I didn't contribute very much. Phil had all the thinking done before we started.

I remember that when we actually got the contract signed with BC Ferries, Phil Spaulding said, "You know, this is going to be lots and lots of fun." Not many people say that when you start a big job, but Phil did. And he was right. He saw to it that it was lots of fun.

Phil Spaulding is a great naval architect. You can always tell one of his designs. Some people can tell a Picasso, but I can tell a Spaulding. He has a style about him that you can't copy. It was easy for us to get along. I guess we were cut from the same mould. When we had problems that took us all night, they took us all night. There was no argument about it. That's the way we got along. And that's the way we started off on what turned out to be the Sidney *and the* Tsawwassen.

Arthur McLaren, 1958, with the model of the 320-foot, 105-vehicle ferries *Sidney* and *Tsawwassen*. Bill Cunningham photo

Arthur's job was to look after construction of the vessels and make sure they were built the right way. It wasn't until the ferries were underway that discussions about building terminals began. The matter was controversial, particularly the proposal to build a terminal at Tsawwassen.

Finally the government handed the terminals over to civil engineers and appointed Captain Terry, president of Northland Navigation, and Alex Peabody, who had been in charge of the Black Ball ferries between Nanaimo and Horseshoe Bay, as advisors. When construction of both the ferries and the landings was completed, the vessels went into service in June of 1960.

Phil Spaulding described working with Arthur:

Arthur and I were both active in the Society of Naval Architects and Marine Engineers (SNAME). It was more than just a technical society in those early days, it was also a social opportunity. So our families got to know each other, as well. We'd have meetings at Harrison Hot Springs or down in Oregon and always bring the kids. Sometimes those SNAME conferences were the only family holiday

we got. Later it got very technical, very businesslike, with meetings run like a convention of engineers. But in those days there was a lot of social life and getting to know one another. It was great.

We worked hard back then, sometimes twenty-four hours a day. My wife Peggy can tell you about that. She'd bring up a bacon and egg sandwich to me at midnight. I don't think people are that driven today. But when you've got five kids, a mortgaged home, a payroll to meet and a very understanding wife, you break your tail. In the marine business, the work comes in blobs. A lot for a while, then a dry spell. So when there's work you go at it hard, and when there isn't, you work even harder.

Arthur and I had a lot in common. I admired him for his design work. I admired him for the shipyard.

The first major project the two men worked on together was the construction of the *Sidney* and *Tsawwassen*.

That really goes back to about 1957, I guess, when I met Bob Atchinson in Rotary. I was well aware of his business at Black Ball Transport in the freight service. Over lunch we began brainstorming a new ferry boat. He told me his thoughts and I started to sketch them up on a napkin. Eventually I completed the design of the Coho. That ferry was a long time gestating because Bob didn't have any money. The Black Ball Line had actually moved to Canada, and Bob had the residual run that was left in the U.S. It carried newsprint to Seattle, Port Townsend and Port Angeles and then one trip to Victoria and back. But Bob persisted and got the financing for the vessel. I had to take stock for my fee.

Anyway, the vessel got quite a bit of publicity because the ferry strike happened in BC at about that time. John Wallace, with Yarrows in Victoria, came down to Seattle. He had been talking with Phil Gaglardi about a ferry boat design, so he made arrangements for me to come up and meet Gaglardi. Naturally I rode the Coho to Victoria.

The *Sidney*, built by Victoria Machinery Depot. This vessel and the sister ship *Tsawwassen* were powered by two 3,000-hp Mirrlees V-16 diesel engines, giving a service speed of 18 knots. The keel of the *Sidney* was laid March 9, 1959, the launch took place October 6, 1959, the ferry was completed March 6, 1960, and service began in June 1960.

Gaglardi requested some modifications to the *Coho*, including changing the side port loading that was necessary for Victoria's inner harbour. But the basic design was approved.

> It was a handshake deal. When we got to serious negotiations, I knew there had to be Canadian content in this whole program. So naturally it was my good friend Art McLaren. And that's the way it's been in every project we encountered in BC. We did the working drawings for both the Sidney and the Tsawwassen. Having Arthur as our representative at the shipyard was the most wonderful arrangement.

"Phil had lots of other design work to do and I had a shipyard to run," Arthur said later, wondering whether he and Phil Spaulding should have put in all those sixteen- to eighteen-hour days. But they did.

Two changes to the ferry plans came about quite unexpectedly. One time I took a bunch of drawings home and my wife Dorothy looked at them. "What's this?" she asked. I told her, "That's the gents' washroom." "And that?" she persisted. "Well, that's the ladies' powder room," I explained. "Well, it's no good," she told me. "There's no ledge there to put your purse on." It had never occurred to me that there should be a ledge in a washroom, but thanks to Dorothy the ferries had an ample shelf right above the wash basin.

Another time I was walking around one of the ferries under construction with my youngest son Malcolm. We went into the gents' room where they had installed one urinal. Well, it would do all right for a giant, but I had a little guy who was only six years old. There was no earthly way he could use it. So I told them to drop it way down . . . lower, lower, lower. And the ferries have had one urinal accessible by little boys ever since. That was Malcolm's contribution.

Growth of the Fleet

In 1960 the BC government passed an order-in-council setting up an independent management structure for BC Ferry Authority with Monty Aldous as general manager. Despite a prediction that the new provincial ferry service would not divert more than 5 percent of Vancouver–Victoria airline traffic, by 1961 BC Ferries had captured 95 percent of the business. That same year the government purchased Gavin Mouat's Gulf Islands Ferries, adding four small vessels to the BC Ferries fleet. The company also purchased Peabody's Black Ball ferry operation for $6,690,000. The deal for the northern service included staff and vessels, but more important, the terminals at Nanaimo, Horseshoe Bay, Langdale and Jervis Inlet. The government was definitely in the ferry business.

Due to the influence of World War II, the people creating engineering solutions had a mindset of rapid delivery, hard work and KISS ("Keep It Simple, Stupid"—or, when dealing with higher ups, "Keep It Simple, Sir"). The people who built the ferries were the same. The early BC ferries reflected the values of efficiency, utility and pragmatic simplicity. These vessels were designed to get the job done. There was a sense that public money should be spent wisely, and the mandate was always to find more cost-effective ways to meet the requirements of a particular route. Arthur McLaren's saying, "The job of an engineer is to do for a nickel what any damn fool can do for a dollar," reflected that view.

These first BC ferries reflected the beauty of a simple design that was inexpensive to produce. BC ferries were among the most efficient traffic movers in the world. The rapid roll on/roll off design contrasted dramatically with the cumbersome side-loading arrangement of the earlier CPR vessels. They were easy to load and crews did so skillfully; the resultant 15 mph unloading speeds were hard to match and turnaround time was amazingly short.

The convenience of those first two provincial ferries and the dramatic increase in the quantity of goods transported by truck rather than barge quickly escalated the demand for service. Spaulding's original design served as the basis for seven more BC vessels. The *Queen of Victoria* and *Queen of Vancouver* were launched in 1962. They were followed a year later by the *Queen of Esquimalt* and *Queen of Saanich*. The last three of the original generation, the *Queen of Nanaimo, Queen of New Westminster* and *Queen of Burnaby*, first sailed in 1964 and 1965.

Yet demand for passenger and vehicle space on ferries continued to rise. The result was some enterprising engineering achievements that involved adapting existing ships. Platform decks installed inside the car decks during the mid-1960s increased car capacity from 106 to 150. Even more unusual at the time was the subsequent decision to "stretch" seven ships by adding 84-foot midships sections. By 1972 the seven ships had more than twice the car capacity, and their outlines bore little resemblance to the original Spaulding design.

"C" Class Vessels

By the 1970s, the BC Ferry Corporation was looking for even bigger vessels. They wanted workhorses that could handle the Nanaimo–Horseshoe Bay run. Impressed by the success of the new Spaulding-designed Washington state

Arthur McLaren and naval architect Phil Spaulding, 1996.

ferries' *Spokane* and *Walla Walla*, Arthur McLaren accompanied a BC Ferries rep to Seattle for a first-hand look at the new double-ender jumbos. Over a decade after the original contract, Spaulding was again hired to design the three Cowichan "C" Class vessels. Arthur served as owner's representative, overseeing construction and reviewing design/cost changes.

In the middle of the work, Phil Spaulding's office was destroyed in an arson fire. The target of the fire was the building's owner, but the arsonist was a real pro. Fire broke out at noon on all floors and water pressure in the regular fire mains was so low that they had to bring in the fireboat. Phil's son Bill quickly called his father in Tacoma, where he had gone on business. "When I came in to Seattle on I-5, the traffic was absolutely jammed and I could see flames coming out of my fifth floor window. I knew then that everything was gone," Phil recalled later with emotion. "I lost everything. The working drawings for the two ferries and for five tankers we were doing for Gunderson's in Portland. My library. My collection of museum quality model ships. Everything."

The fire happened on June 14, 1974, shortly after the new firm of Nickum & Spaulding had been formed. Somehow no insurance had been secured in the transition, so the loss was not covered. With shipyards and companies concerned about delays, Spaulding pulled his old office lighting fixtures and surplus equipment out of storage. The shipyards returned all of the last prints they'd been sent and within a week Spaulding was back in business. "The fire was disastrous, but Art McLaren was fighting for our side in Vancouver," he commented later. "He was the man on the scene and saved our bacon."

At the time, the 457-foot ferries were the largest double-ended ships in the world. Two of these jumbo vessels, the *Queen of Cowichan* and the *Queen of Coquitlam*, were capable of carrying some 360 automobiles. A third, the *Queen of Alberni*, was built to accommodate overheight vehicles. Each of these double-ended ferries had

The "C" Class ferry *Queen of Alberni* on the launchways at Vancouver Shipyards Company Ltd., December 29, 1975. Colin Bradbury photo

two engines producing a total of 11,000 bhp. Fitted with single controllable propellers, one each fore and aft, they were capable of 20 knots and maintained two-hour service on the Mainland–Vancouver Island crossing.

In 1981, two more "C" Class ferries, the *Queen of Oak Bay* and the *Queen of Surrey*, were delivered. Later the *Alberni* was converted to provide additional vehicle capacity, and the government ferry fleet boasted five such jumbo vessels.

Taking Over the Smaller Routes

Originally BC Ferries handled only the major routes in the province. Some eleven smaller ferries on shorter runs were operated by the Department of Highways. Then, in 1979, the Ferry Corporation Act was passed, establishing the British Columbia Ferry Corporation as a Crown corporation. By the mid-1980s the BC Ferry Corporation controlled all of the highway ferries operating in salt water (mostly smaller vessels).

Allied's Ferries

Island Princess (Hull #72)

Allied Shipbuilders' first saltwater ferry was the *Island Princess*, later renamed *North Island Princess*. This Robert Allan design was built for Sparky New's Gulf Island Navigation Company, prior to the establishment of BC Ferries. When the CPR boat was taken off the Gulf Islands run, Sparky was eager to expand his domain and used the *Lady Rose*. To handle vehicle traffic he ordered the ferry

Island Princess. Originally it ran from Steveston around several Gulf Islands and back again. The following day it alternated to the other Gulf Islands. The new vessel was all steel construction with two Rolls Royce diesels that delivered a service speed of about 10 knots. It boasted four double staterooms as well as a twenty-car capacity.

In July 1960, newspapers reported that a furious "row" had erupted over private sector vs. government-subsidized ferry service for people flocking to the "paradise" of the Gulf Islands. Chambers of Commerce from the various islands

The *Island Princess*, as built, sailing from Steveston at the mouth of the Fraser River on a routine trip to the southern Gulf Islands. Note the twin cargo booms, rigged Union Steamship style, for handling cargo when alongside a conventional wharf.

suggested the government take over services between Vancouver Island and the Gulf Islands, which were already getting government subsidies of $101,000 per year. Sparky New, who operated the two-year-old $300,000 ferry *Island Princess*, said government should let private enterprise rule the waves. His run had previously included Vancouver Island, but he cut it out after the government began subsidizing the competition. His opinion: "The government should get out of the ferry business. Otherwise, in due time, private enterprise will not be able to provide the necessary funds (taxes) to pay the deficits on government operations."

In 1971 Case Existological Laboratories came up with a design to widen the *Island Princess*. Burrard Dry Dock undertook this work. First the ferry was sliced in half both lengthwise and transversely. Then a new section of deck was inserted on centre in order to make a catamaran hull configuration. The result was a forty-nine-car catamaran ferry servicing the northern tip of Vancouver Island. She was renamed *North Island Princess*. When the Vancouver Island highway from Kelsey Bay to Port Hardy was completed in 1979, the ferry was no longer required. By the late 1990s it was running between Powell River and Texada Island.

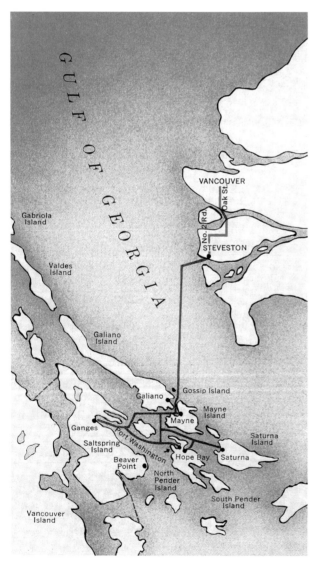

The routes of the *Island Princess*, sailing from Steveston to the Gulf Islands when operated by the Gulf Island Navigation Company.

CATAMARIZING * THE ISLAND PRINCESS

THE ABOVE ILLUSTRATION SHOWS THE
CATAMARAN "M.V. ISLAND PRINCESS"
RUNNING STERN TO STERN WITH HER
OLD MONO-HULLED SELF.

GENERAL PARTICULARS

BEFORE		AFTER
131'-3"	LENGTH O.A.	186'-6"
35'-0"	BEAM	57'-0"
11'-0"	DEPTH	13'-6"
422	△ LOADED FULL	731
700	B.H.P.	700
11.5	V(k)	10.5
20	CAR CAPACITY	49

* A WORD AND IDEA CONCEIVED AND PURSUED THRU DETAIL ENGINEERING BY C.E.L.L.

The *Island Princess* became the larger *North Island Princess* after an imaginative stretch designed by John Case of Case Existological Laboratories Ltd.

Quadra Queen (Hull #108) *and* Garibaldi (Hull #117)

The *Quadra Queen* was one of the Department of Highways' early small saltwater ferries. Arthur McLaren designed the 110-foot steel auto ferry in 1959 and prepared the specifications at the request of Ken Gann, superintendent of ferries. Subsequently Allied won the public bid for construction. The all-steel vessel was powered by two 200-hp Cummins diesels and twin screws, giving a service speed of 10 knots. It could accommodate fifteen cars and ninety-nine passengers.

This ship, later renamed the *Cortez Queen* and then the *Nicola*, was the first of several ferries built to the same general design. Arthur recalled one incident resulting in a change to future ferries of similar design: "I drove my big blue 1959 Pontiac up to Campbell River for the maiden voyage ceremonies. It was as wide as a car could be, and when I tried to go down the outer lane of the new ferry I found I couldn't get around the corner. So I quietly backed up and went down the centre lane instead. I didn't say anything to anybody, but the next three ferries built to that basic design had a 2-foot wider hull."

Besides the *Quadra Queen*, Allied also constructed the first *Garibaldi* (which later ran as the *Westwood* and then the *A.J. Savoie*) in 1960.

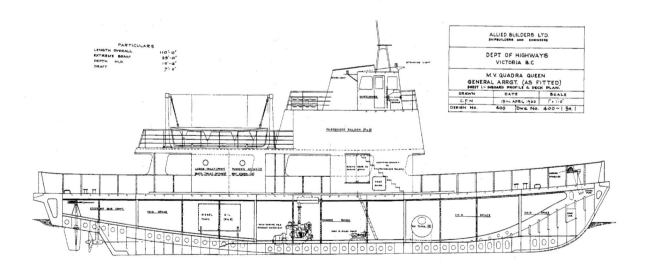

Inboard profile drawing of the *Quadra Queen*.

The newly built *Quadra Queen* on sea trials, 1959. Forty years later Scott Lang, a Prince Rupert marine engineer, wrote to the *Westcoast Mariner*: "The vessel is now registered as the MV *Nicola* and is known under its service name, the *Spirit of Lax Kw'Alaams*. The *Nicola* provides service between Prince Rupert and the village of Lax Kw'Alaams [Port Simpson] . . . It must be satisfying for Mr. McLaren and his workers to know that years after construction of Hull #108, it is still playing an active role in west coast transportation." Commercial Illustrators photo

McKenzie Barge built the *Garibaldi II*, still running at Woodfibre, and BC Marine Shipbuilders did the *Nimpkish*, for a total of four 110-foot ferries to the basic McLaren design. In 1964 Arthur designed the *Bowen Queen*, *Powell River Queen* and *Mayne Queen*. Victoria Machinery Depot was the low bidder and built all three vessels.

Texada Queen (Hull #164), Quadra Queen II (Hull #165)

1969 was a busy year for Allied Shipbuilders. In addition to building three big tugs for Northern Transportation Company Ltd., the yard also built the *Texada Queen* and *Quadra Queen II*. Arthur was hospitalized for weeks because of a car accident, but continued working from his hospital bed. The design of these 165-foot ferries was done by Greenwood McHaffie, following on Arthur's earlier design of the *Garibaldi* and *Quadra Queen*.

A twin order in 1969 produced the 165-foot ferries the *Quadra Queen II* and *Texada Queen* (later renamed *Tachek*).

Building Ferries by Consortium

Spirit of British Columbia (Hull #254), Spirit of Vancouver Island (Hull #255)

The Spirit Class ferries were part of a $440-million (Canadian) capital expansion program for the BC Ferry Corporation. $268 million of that budget was committed to construction of two new Spirit Class vessels, beginning in 1990. The outfit of these ferries was much more luxurious than the spartan approach of earlier vessels, and travellers responded enthusiastically. The basic design was developed by Knud E. Hansen in Denmark, with detailed drawing work by local naval architects.

As the number of large-capacity provincial yards had dwindled and the size of ferries grew, the innovative approach was to arrange the building of these large vessels by a consortium of shipyards. To this end, the first Spirit Class ferry was packaged into several blocks for bidding purposes. Versatile Pacific Shipyards of North Vancouver bid for overall management of the project, but their financial difficulties prevented them from obtaining bonding for the project. Instead the Crown formed a company, Integrated Ferry Constructors (IFC) to run it. The project engineering firm

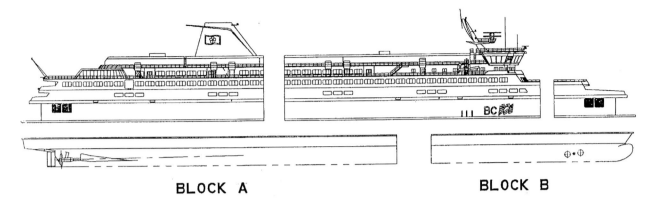

BLOCK A   BLOCK B

Diagram of an "S" Class BC ferry to be built by consortium. Separate sections were built by different yards. The forward hull was built by Allied, the aft hull and mid-body by Yarrows, and the superstructure by Pacific Rim Shipyards, Delta.

A main deck panel is lifted into position on the *Spirit of British Columbia*. Avcom photo

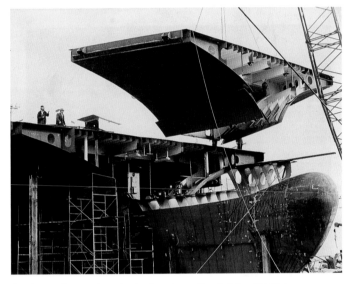

Setting a forward main deck unit on the *Spirit of British Columbia*. Note the unit is pre-outfitted and the interior painted. Avcom photo

Sandwell administered IFC at first, but later experienced shipbuilders took over. Rollie Webb was hired as general manager. He became known as "the guy who got the job done."

After the selection process for construction of the various component parts of the ferry, the seven initial packages were rationalized into three blocks: the bow section of the hull, the mid and aft section and the superstructure. This third package was later divided into three units for ease of installation on the ship. One of the most daunting aspects of construction was ensuring that the various individual parts would fit together. Indeed, the press dubbed the ship *Queen of Lego!*

Allied Shipbuilders put in a successful offer to build the $6-million 200-foot forward hull section of the new *Spirit of British Columbia*. Integrated Module Fabricators–Yarrows Ltd. built the 340-foot stern section of the hull. These two sections were joined in the Public Works graving dock at Esquimalt and then towed to Fraser Surrey Docks to receive the superstructure. Pacific Rim Shipyards Ltd. (a joint venture between Vito Steel Boat and Barge Construction and Purvis Navcon) built the superstructure in three parts. Once the superstructure was slid into position, welded in place, and related work on it completed, the assembled vessel was towed to Esquimalt

Chuck Ko, Allied Shipbuilders technical manager, and Ed Steffenson, steel superintendent, in front of the forward hull section of the *Spirit of British Columbia* (Hull #254), just before launch. Avcom photo

Launching the *Spirit of Vancouver Island*. Allied built the same forward hull section as on the sister ship, the *Spirit of British Columbia*. A crew of 100 worked on the 200-foot project. Upon completion, it was towed to Esquimalt, where it was joined with the stern section built by Integrated Module Fabricators–Yarrows Ltd. Murray McLennan photo

so that the two shafts could be fitted and aligned, the balance of the machinery added, and the final outfitting completed.

"The concept of building such a complex vessel by consortium took some getting used to," Malcolm McLaren said later. "We did our best, but sometimes we wondered about the other guy. In the end, the various sections of the ship went together like clockwork. It only took six days to fit and weld the massive forward and aft hull sections into one vessel. Everything fit beautifully." While the costs to construct, operate and maintain these Spirit Class vessels are higher than the simpler Spaulding-conceived 457-foot "C" Class ferries, the ships are well built and loved by the travelling public.

The second Spirit Class ferry was initially a build or not-build question. An editorial in the *Vancouver Sun* promoted building smaller, faster

Bow view of the *Spirit of Vancouver Island*. Avcom photo

ferries, and other media attention encouraged a public outcry against building another of the large vessels. But the newly elected New Democratic Party government went ahead with construction because they felt the vessels would work most effectively if paired on the run—as has proven to be the case.

The Competent Century Class Commuter Ferry

Skeena Queen (Hull #257)

The mandate for this 1997 commuter-run ferry was "cost-effective and spartan." McLaren & Sons, the design division of Allied, won the design contract for the 360-foot Century Class vessel. BC Ferries' criteria for the 100-car, 600-passenger commuter ferry included a 14.5-knot service speed at 4,500 hp. Thrust was to be provided by four 360-degree rotating right-angle drives, with the vessel able to hold direction and position in high-current areas.

Working with Joe Gruzling, a local hydrodynamic specialist, McLaren & Sons completed the design in five months. Input from crew members familiar with the high-current, high passenger-volume runs was also critical. The design work included a number of different design concepts, model testing the hull form and a complete re-do of BC Ferries' new construction specifications. To increase manoeuvrability, propulsion nozzles were fitted on the drives. The hull was then uniquely shaped to align the water flow directly to the propellers. This provided greater propulsive efficiency than was available from any of the fleet's other ferries fitted with right-angle drives.

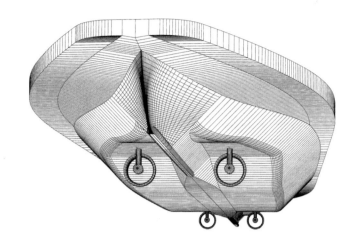

The innovative hull design of the *Skeena Queen*. The shape of the hull directs the water flow right to the propellers, giving the vessel good propulsive efficiency. This ferry barely throws a wake in service.

Allied Shipbuilders subsequently won the tender for construction. Their bid of $20.5 million was considerably lower than the construction costs of similar capacity vessels in the fleet. The utilitarian style of the *Skeena Queen*'s design and construction harkens back to the post-World War II get-the-job-done engineering ethic. This commuter ferry was built on time and to budget.

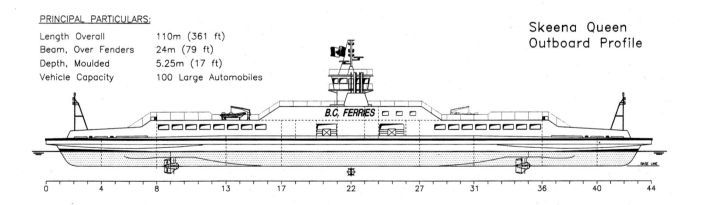

PRINCIPAL PARTICULARS:

Length Overall	110m (361 ft)
Beam, Over Fenders	24m (79 ft)
Depth, Moulded	5.25m (17 ft)
Vehicle Capacity	100 Large Automobiles

Skeena Queen
Outboard Profile

B.C. FERRIES

Outboard profile drawing of the *Skeena Queen*, the eighth ferry designed by McLaren & Sons and the sixth vessel built by Allied Shipbuilders for BC Ferries.

Assembling the *Skeena Queen* on the launchways, winter 1996. Avcom photo

Crane operator Paul Amaral.

Placing the first deckhouse section onboard the *Skeena Queen*. Avcom photo

Turning the right-angle-drive hull unit on the *Skeena Queen*. Steel superintendent Ron Campo is in foreground. Avcom photo

SHIPS OF STEEL

Ben Brizee, foreman engine fitter, inside the propeller nozzle of the *Skeena Queen*.

The *Skeena Queen* on the run, fully loaded.

High-Speed Aluminum Catamaran Ferries

PacifiCat Explorer (#1), PacifiCat Discovery (#2), PacifiCat Voyager (#3)

By the early 1990s there were growing complaints about the traffic snarls created by large ferries unloading high volumes of cars onto highways. About this time Australia had launched a revolutionary innovation—large, lightweight high-speed ferries. With many voices in the province pushing for such technology, and with government policy embracing the concept, BC Ferries

pursued the project. The Crown corporation assessed population growth, rising demand for service, prognosis of aging vessels and the evolving regulatory environment.

During 1993, Sam Bawlf, who was involved in provincial transportation planning, met with many industry people. One meeting was with Malcolm McLaren to discuss the possibility of building high-speed aluminum ferries. Bawlf championed the Australian fast catamarans as a model for the evolution of the BC Ferry Corporation. Malcolm's notes from this meeting record a discussion of construction methodology possibilities ranging from one yard with a large shed doing serial production to multiple small yards in joint venture scenarios. Bawlf was a strong proponent of the fast cats, predicting low initial cost, berth construction costs lower than those of large steel ferries, and cheaper overall operation. He backed up his opinion with extensive computer modelling and studies to show the advantages of the new vessels. Bawlf contended that the earlier BC ferries were overbuilt and expensive, due to the influence of Scottish shipbuilders with their very traditional approaches to designing and constructing ships. Ironically, "overbuilt and expensive" would later come to haunt the high-speed aluminum ferry project.

BC Ferries' decision to introduce fast ferries to the fleet was announced to the industry and to the general public in 1994. The need to utilize existing double-decked terminals dictated service-specific dimensions and layout for the new vessels, including a beam limit of 87 feet. Fast turnaround of passengers and vehicles also required a drive-through arrangement using bow and stern doors like those of the fleet's conventional ferries.

BC Ferries selected a catamaran proposal submitted by Incat Designs of Australia, in a joint venture arrangement with Robert Allan Ltd. Construction of the 398-foot high-speed aluminum ferries was arranged by establishing Catamaran Ferries International (CFI), a subsidiary of BC Ferry Corporation. Essentially a shipbuilding management company, CFI organized all work

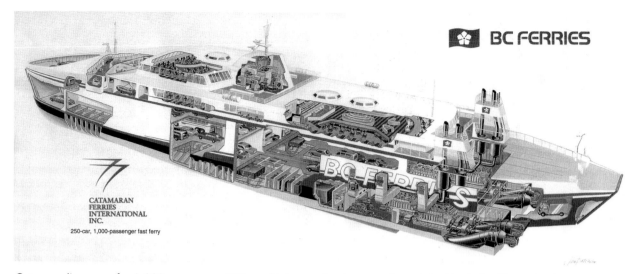

Cutaway diagram of a 1,000-passenger, 250-car high-speed catamaran ferry. John Batchelor illustration/courtesy BC Ferry Corporation

The PacifiCat *Explorer* underway. Courtesy BC Ferry Corporation

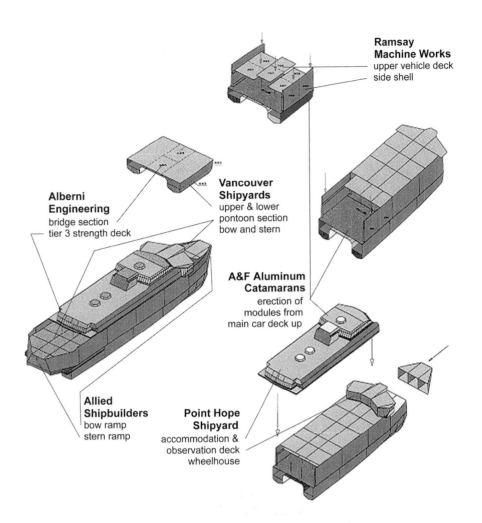

Ramsay
Machine Works
- upper vehicle deck
- side shell

Alberni
Engineering
bridge section
- tier 3 strength deck

Vancouver
Shipyards
upper & lower
pontoon section
bow and stern

A&F Aluminum
Catamarans
erection of
modules from
main car deck up

Allied
Shipbuilders
bow ramp
stern ramp

Point Hope
Shipyard
accommodation &
observation deck
wheelhouse

Block building diagram of a high-speed ferry.

and awarded contracts to private facilities. Significant players included Alberni Engineering, Allied Shipbuilders, A&F Aluminum Catamarans, Point Hope Shipyard, Ramsay Machine Works and Vancouver Shipyards. The various sections were then joined at a new assembly facility in North Vancouver. The first PacifiCat ferry began carrying passengers and vehicles in the summer of 1999.

Certainly the high-speed ferry program was interesting technologically, but it was a massive project that allowed BC shipbuilders very little preparation time. The Australians had begun by constructing high-speed aluminum catamarans 20 metres long, then moved on to 40- and 60-metre vessels, building their expertise gradually as they went. BC builders were familiar with aluminum construction, thanks to pioneers such as Sam Matsumoto and later Al Renke, but the leap to building high-speed catamarans—the second-largest in the world at the time—was a huge one for provincial yards.

After the PacifiCat ferries had been in service for about six months, the BC government advised the public that the high-speed ferries did not "fit the service requirement" and that all three would be sold on the world market. The announced target sale price was about $40 million per vessel, a considerably lower figure than their all-in project cost of about $150 million each.

Fleet at the Crossroads

At the start of the new millennium, BC Ferry Corporation remains one of the world's largest ferry operators, serving forty-six ports along more than 700 miles of coastal BC. During the 1999–2000 season, forty vessels carried 21.4 million passengers and nearly 7.9 million vehicles on twenty-six routes.

CHAPTER 8

Boom Times: Government Subsidies and a New Shipyard Site

"I don't know if the subsidy has increased orders for ships, but I do know that if you threaten to withdraw it, the orders come pouring in."

—*Arthur McLaren*

Almost every decade in shipbuilding has a story. The feature story of the 1940s was the massive shipbuilding effort for World War II. Concern over the possibility of another war led to the events of the '50s: the building of a new navy for Canada. As for the '60s, the story was one of turnaround—from bleak prospects to a shipbuilding boom—in part due to the federal shipbuilding subsidy.

By the end of the 1950s the shipbuilding industry had completed many of its naval contracts. The looming question was what would happen with the massive talent pool of experienced shipbuilders. With the opening of the St. Lawrence Seaway in 1959 came a need for new ships to service the projected increase in trade. For the most part the domestic shipping industry of the late 1950s and early '60s was still using the tonnage it had bought for next to nothing at the end of the war, and after twenty years of use, those ships were all aging. In 1961 the Canadian government stepped in to stimulate the marine economy with a federal shipbuilding subsidy program that matched the subsidies available to Canada's competitors. The strategy worked. The result was a boom in shipbuilding that lasted more than two decades, in the context of

a strong North American post-war economy. The domestic fleet was renewed and the industry achieved export sales as well.

The Basis of the Subsidy

Until the St. Lawrence Seaway was completed in 1959, only relatively small freighters could travel from the Atlantic Ocean to the Great Lakes. The result of this monumental engineering and construction feat was that cargo volume went from an annual average 11 million tons in the 1950s to 45.1 million tons in 1983. However, this success depended on replacing small, aging bulk carriers with a large new fleet of cargo ships that could transit the new seaway, loaded with grain, iron ore, coal, bulk cargo and finished goods.

Construction of the seaway had been set in action by the Liberals, but they were no longer in power when it was completed. Canadian shipping companies looked to Ottawa for help. The federal government's Shipbuilding Industry Assistance Program was introduced in 1961, but not without some political tinkering. Leon Balcer, the Conservative minister of transport, realized that Canadian inland merchant fleets could not

Canadian Federal Shipbuilding Subsidy

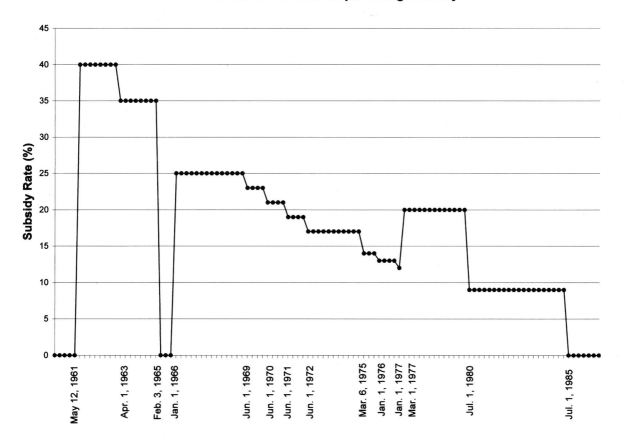

From 1961 to 1985, the federal government operated a subsidy program that paid Canadian shipbuilders a percentage of the audited construction cost for pre-approved shipbuilding projects. Compiled from Canadian Shipbuilding & Ship Repairing Association data.

remain competitive unless they were modernized. He also wanted the work to go to Canadian shipyards. So he introduced a generous 40-percent subsidy for Canadian-built ships. Originally the subsidy was slated to be in effect from May 1961 to March 1963, after which it would be reduced by 5 percent per year.

When the Conservatives were defeated in the general election of April 1963, the Liberals kept the program with some modifications. The subsidy continued at 35 percent until February 1965, at which time it was suspended for eleven months. Reintroduced in January 1966 at the rate of 25 percent, it was reduced periodically until it reached 12 percent in 1977. The rate was increased to 20 percent in March 1977 and reduced to 9 percent in July 1980. There it

remained until the Mulroney Conservatives abolished it entirely on June 30, 1985.

An impending subsidy reduction always resulted in a flurry of new build orders as the principals rushed to qualify for the existing rate rather than the lower one soon to follow. As Arthur recalled:

When the rate was slated to change on January 1, in December we'd be scrambling to send off subsidy applications. One New Year's Eve we didn't even have anything typed up yet for one order, so we phoned the people in Ottawa to ask how we could get it to them in time. It was long before faxes and things like that. Finally we got ahold of someone back east who said it would be OK so long as we got it turned in to their Vancouver office by 1:00 that afternoon. We talked them into 2:00, but no further. Then we flew at it, and about 1:45 we made a mad dash for downtown. Their people were all hanging around the office, wanting to go home, but we got it turned in. That was the way these things got done!

A Canadian-built ship was eligible for subsidy if, after completion, it met these minimum requirements:

- 100 gross tons if self-propelled
- 200 gross tons if not self-propelled
- 50 gross tons if a tug
- 75 feet in overall length if a fishing vessel not used by owner primarily for personal recreation

Effects of the Subsidy

The subsidy program was intended to bolster employment within the Canadian shipbuilding industry, but it also significantly encouraged the development of Canadian-made marine equip-ment. To this end, the subsidy was not paid on the cost of any material, components, equipment or services obtained outside Canada where, in the opinion of the minister, they could have been obtained at a competitive cost in Canada. This mandate was one of the significant benefits of the subsidy program. In a typical commercial ship, one half the value of the vessel is materials and equipment supplied by companies outside the shipyard. The program's made-in-Canada requirement helped create an industry that produced all types of marine equipment, such as winches, doors, windows, control systems, linings, electronics and steering gear, all of which significantly raised the level of economic activity across the country. Even after the demise of the subsidy there remains a healthy marine manufacturing industry that sells Canadian-made marine products worldwide.

The Canadian content requirement was no paper promise—government officials really did check to see whether or not there was a suitable

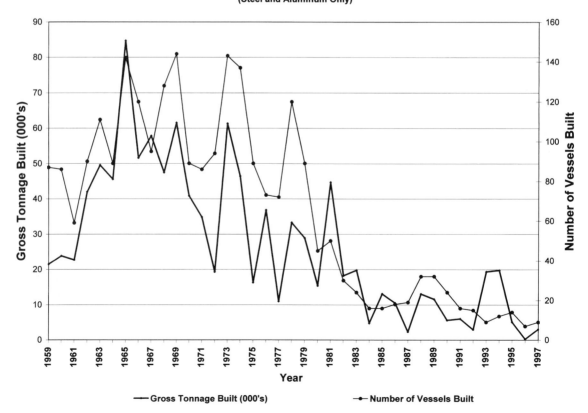

Shipbuilding In British Columbia
1959 - 1997
(Steel and Aluminum Only)

——— Gross Tonnage Built (000's)   —•— Number of Vessels Built

SHIPS OF STEEL

Allied Shipbuilders Ltd. completes steel tug, launches car barge

VANCOUVER — The scheduled cut in federal construction subsidies in March led to a flurry of work for estimators at smaller shipyards here at year's end.

The subsidies will be cut from 40 percent to 35 percent — and those planning vessels that would qualify want to get in under the wire.

"Pricing and tendering has been hectic," reported T. A. McLaren of Allied Builders Ltd. "There have been a great many enquiries. Result is that we've got some work lined up and more that we hope to acquire."

Allied Builders — which has done very well in small-tonnage construction for the past two years — has sufficient work on hand to carry the yards through the summer.

"Generally, this next year looks okay," said McLaren. "We expect to keep just as busy as we have been."

Allied in 1962 built the largest tug launched during the year in B.C. — a 93-foot job powered by a 900-hp Werkspoor-Stork with a controllable-pitch screw. Owners are Straits Towing Ltd.

On the ways at writing were a 2,000-ton self-loading barge for Evans, Coleman & Evans and a 65-foot tug for Gulf of Georgia Towing Co. Ltd.

Activity over the year called for a small increase in staff, though mostly it meant steady employment for regular workers.

It also brought Allied and others up against a labor problem:

"It's hard now to get experienced men," said McLaren. "A skilled man would have no trouble whatever finding work in coast yards right now. There's a distinct lack of them."

Smaller coast yards were up against it as well when the subsidies that stimulated their increased volume of work were not forthcoming in good time.

Subsidy payments were behind as much as six months and operators had to borrow from banks to pay their bills. Interest on loans, amounting to thousands of dollars in some cases, forced several small yards to curtail business until federal money arrived.

For instance, West Coast Salvage & Contracting, owed $50,000 in subsidy money for two vessels built in its yards, laid off men and borrowed $25,000 to meet bills. Owner F. J. Whitcroft said he spent $700 traveling twice to Ottawa for his money — and in vain.

The subsidy delays — blamed on government austerity — were being corrected at year's end and the situation was not so depressing as it had been.

Complaints against the delays were made to Transport Minister Leon Balcer in a wire from Arthur Mercer, of Star Shipyards (Mercer's) Ltd. and chairman of the boatbuilders' section of the Canadian Manufacturers' Association.

An article in the *Canadian Marine and Engineering News* about business at BC shipyards in 1962.

Canadian supplier for materials and equipment. However, Arthur recalled one amusing occasion when rule prevailed over logic. Allied had a large northern vessel under construction intended for work in the Arctic Ocean. The tug had to be equipped with a gyroscopic compass, since in the Arctic a magnetic compass is not a reliable instrument—the needle simply doesn't know which way to point. Arthur applied for a subsidy on a foreign-made gyro-compass, citing the fact that Canadian manufacturers only made magnetic compasses. The federal government administrator wouldn't hear of it. "Since there was a Canadian compass manufacturer, we were to buy a Canadian-made compass, and that was that." In the end, the tug got its foreign-made gyro-compass, without benefit of subsidy.

The subsidy program injected new life into shipbuilding in British Columbia. Some felt it was a drain on the public purse, but at a rate of 20 percent, the direct cost of the subsidy was equivalent to the taxes collected from the shipbuilder, without even counting the economic stimulus to the area and the development of various marine manufacturing companies. In total, 2,353 vessels were built under subsidy in Canada. A number of ships were built for overseas accounts, but most were for domestic owners. Arthur McLaren often said, "I don't know if the subsidy has increased orders for ships, but I do know that if you threaten to withdraw it, the orders come pouring in."

A New Site for Allied

Booming sales in the 1960s gave BC yards great optimism about future business. Some of them expanded or relocated, and Allied Shipbuilders was among them. Allied's False Creek yard had been set up for building wartime ships: the launchways were all set for standard hulls 440 feet long and 37 feet deep, with a 58-foot beam. But those facilities didn't suit the sort of ships Allied was building by the 1960s, which made it difficult to achieve any efficiency. More significant, the owner of the property wanted the shipyard out of the False Creek location. So in the mid-1960s, Arthur started looking for a place to re-establish the yard.

I got along quite well with a fellow called Jack Lawson. He was a business agent for the Marine Workers & Boilermakers Union. One day he asked, "Do you ever think of getting onto a better site?" I told him I'd been considering just that for two years. He told me that he was planning to leave union work and go into real estate. And his first project was going to be finding a place for us to situate a proper shipyard. So he did that, but the possibilities he came up with didn't seem to be what we wanted.

Finally, I told him I'd had my eye on some waterfront property on the far side of the Second Narrows bridge and described it to him in detail. "It's as flat as anything can be, there's nothing on it that would have to be torn down and there's a great big hole alongside where you could launch ships into the water. I think it would be the best place in the whole of British Columbia." Jack went away and came back four days later. He said, "You can have that property if you want. It's for sale." "I haven't seen it advertised," I replied. And he told me, "It hasn't been. It's only for sale through me."

At the time, the property was owned by a contractor by the name of Jameson. He'd dredged this great big hole in order to provide clean fill for the approaches to the Second Narrows bridge and highway. Anyway he was getting on in years so offered the property to us. I hadn't the foggiest notion of how I was going to come up with the money and told Jack so. "Nobody mentioned cash," he explained. We negotiated a down payment and a certain amount over the next few years. And that's just what we did. It kept us going hard, but we paid it off and the move was a good one.

Big shipyard slated for N. Vancouver

Plans have been prepared by Allied Shipbuilders Ltd. for construction of a modern shipbuilding and repair yard at North Vancouver, at the mouth of Seymour Creek, just east of the Second Narrows Bridge.

T. A. McLaren, president of Allied, says that his company has acquired 11 acres of waterfront property, and construction will start as soon as zoning authority is approved by the North Vancouver district council.

The land is presently zoned for industrial purposes, but application has been made for zoning under a new category of waterfront industrial.

The company at present operates two yards in Vancouver, a shipbuilding yard on False Creek, and Burrard Shipyards and Marine Ways Ltd. in Coal Harbor, which specializes in ship repair work.

The False Creek yard was built during the war and constructed a large number of Fort and Park ships for the Canadian government. The property is held on sub-lease from Western Bridge Co. The Coal Harbor property is held under lease until 1969.

McLaren said that his company plans to build a yard with the most modern equipment which will permit it to meet world competition, building ships up to 5,000 tons capacity.

The Allied yard in False Creek will be the first to move its operations to the North Shore, and it is expected that the Coal Harbor repair yard will move after its present lease expires.

From the *Province*, Thursday, October 27, 1966, written by Norm Hacking

Allied moved to the Seymour River site in North Vancouver in 1967. The site met the needs of a shipyard: it was on flat ground ("because you don't build ships on the side of hills"), and there was access to the right kind of water.

We needed water with some depth to it and some variation so we could start off on dry land at one end and end up in deep water at the other. The location of the new yard meant there was no hope of launching ships in the usual manner, which would be endways. So we decided to launch vessels sideways. This is not particularly common in the world, but it is in eastern Canada, on the Great Lakes.

The other thing we intended to do was to keep on building vessels that were then shipped to remote locations and re-erected. So we wanted a rail access; fortunately it was already close to hand. We also needed good road access to deliver materials. All in all, the Seymour River site looked to be workable and that's why Allied Shipbuilders ended up there.

The Move

The idea of moving the contents of a shipyard from False Creek to North Vancouver may seem daunting to most, but according to Jim McLaren it wasn't such a big production. "My uncle Jim McLaren looked after all of the civil engineering, and my other uncle Don Berry was in charge of constructing all the footings and erecting all the buildings on site. I was working up north in 1967, and when I came out in late summer I did some work in the new yard, preparing for the concrete and then building the slabs that the rolling sheds are on. We didn't have that much equipment to move. The biggest job was probably shifting the office building, and we hired someone to do that. It all happened smoothly over the space of a few weeks. There were many loads of equipment and supplies to bring over. The only exciting part was unloading the old crawler crane off a barge at the new shipyard."

By the time Allied moved onto the new site in

Moving the Allied office from False Creek to the North Vancouver site. The building was moved over the water by barge, then trucked to the new location.

1967, Jim had left university and decided to work full time in the shipyard.

One of my first jobs was setting up the initial stores—that's the supplies you keep in inventory for the day-to-day tasks of building or repairing vessels, as opposed to the specific equipment you buy for a particular project. My uncle Don and I put in all the shelving and bins first. Then we moved load after load of the supplies and stock that was spread throughout many different shops at the False Creek site. That meant hauling steel, pipe, pipe fittings, welding rods, ship's spikes, oakum, wood, electrical materials and cabling, right down to nuts and bolts and cotter pins. We consolidated all that stuff into one area in the new yard and set up the basic inventory systems. Even so, we still had a lot of material that was just piled under our big shelters.

The North Vancouver site was built as a new construction yard. "We still had a repair/refit yard in Coal Harbour," Jim explained. "It seemed best to keep new construction and repairs separate. If we had it to do all over again, the yard would probably look very different. At the time our interest was in building log barges and very large structures, which were built in panels and then

Aerial view of Allied's North Vancouver shipyard, looking west, summer 1969. Hulls #164 and #165 are on the ways; Vancouver harbour is in the background.

quickly transferred onto the launchways, where they were erected into modules."

When building large panels, Allied was able to move one 11- to 15-ton panel out of a work area every day. There were five basic work areas on the covered assembly slab, and the yard ran two shifts. Basic assembly of each panel happened on the day shift. The panel was welded at night and cleared out the next morning, and the cycle was repeated. "We were able to move a tremendous amount of steel with a very limited facility and just one crane," Jim said.

To build the ideal type of steel shop, we would have had to spend more money on that one shop than we did in preparation of the entire new yard. Our idea was "pay as you go" or "don't build any more than what you can pay for directly." The other factor is that development permits take time, and each time we wanted to expand or build, it was always just after we'd secured a contract and there wasn't any time for the permit process. We needed to get to work immediately. So over the years and jobs, we'd often build portable buildings or do our work under very simple sheds that could be funded by the job we were doing.

SHIPS OF STEEL

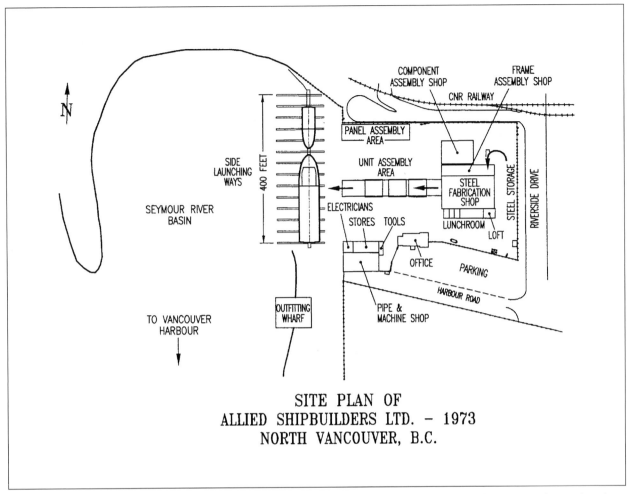

COMPONENT ASSEMBLY SHOP

FRAME ASSEMBLY SHOP

CNR RAILWAY

PANEL ASSEMBLY AREA

N

SIDE LAUNCHING WAYS

400 FEET

UNIT ASSEMBLY AREA

STEEL FABRICATION SHOP

STEEL STORAGE

RIVERSIDE DRIVE

SEYMOUR RIVER BASIN

ELECTRICIANS

STORES

TOOLS

LUNCHROOM

LOFT

OFFICE

PARKING

TO VANCOUVER HARBOUR

OUTFITTING WHARF

PIPE & MACHINE SHOP

HARBOUR ROAD

SITE PLAN OF
ALLIED SHIPBUILDERS LTD. – 1973
NORTH VANCOUVER, B.C.

Plan view drawing of Allied's North Vancouver yard, 1973. Arthur McLaren did a good job of laying out the yard and process flow of construction modules. Unlike many existing BC shipyards (and the old Allied site), which had been set up for piece-by-piece shipbuilding, Allied's new yard was laid out for unit construction. The company didn't have fixed overhead cranes for materials handling, but the flow was efficient. It facilitated assembly and easy handling of relatively large sub-assemblies; consequently Allied was able to be much more productive than by traditional methods.

Other Shipyard Expansions

Business was good in 1967. That year alone, three shipyards set up modern yards in North Vancouver. Allied moved to the mouth of Seymour River, Bel-Aire moved underneath the Second Narrows Bridge and Vancouver Tug & Barge set up Vancouver Shipyards at the foot of Pemberton. In the early 1970s, Vito Steel Boat and Barge opened up a new shop on the Fraser River and began building standard 40- and 60-foot tugs. For the previous twenty years no new significant shipyards had been built in BC The expansion took place because order books were full and looked to stay that way for a number of years.

The Work Must Go On

In 1969, two years after the North Vancouver shipyard site was set up, Arthur McLaren was involved in a head-on automobile collision that broke his knee and left him confined to a hospital bed. The yard was swamped with work. "We were building three tugs for up north and had won the bid for the *Quadra Queen II* and the *Texada Queen*," he recalled. "I was in that blessed hospital under traction for seven weeks. It came at a time when I didn't feel I could spend even seven minutes there." He confounded nursing staff by turning his hospital bed into a drafting table and turned out daily construction drawings, as well as sheaves of memos. The smell of his cigars reputedly stunk up the entire hospital floor. Arthur's son Jim became involved in all aspects of management and materials—from procurement and major purchases to dealing with suppliers and expediting.

Buying Two Companies

In 1971 Arthur bought a large portion of Howard Leeming's machine shop business, establishing Coast Engineering Works Ltd. Initially Howard retained control of the name Western Machine Works so he could continue selling his world-renowned patented towing pins. Two years later, when Howard retired, Arthur acquired this company as well. "First we bought Burrard Shipyard & Marine Ways and then we bought Western Machine Works," he said later. "They all complemented what we were doing."

Coast Engineering Works includes Allied's marine machinists, who specialize in tail shaft work. Western Machine Works continues its strong tradition of supplying tow pins for towing vessels of all sizes. The division manufactures hydraulic tow pins with cable hold-down and stern roller combined in one unit.

Moving Repair Work to North Vancouver

Repair work wasn't a priority for Allied's North Vancouver site before 1979: repairs were handled at the company's Coal Harbour yard, which Arthur had purchased in 1961 from Jack Mac-Donald. Coal Harbour was the marine area that stretched along four blocks east of Stanley Park and was filled with shipyards, chandleries and machinery facilities. "It was quite a sight, and most of them got along very well," Arthur remembered. "They'd even borrow tools from one another. We were in the middle of the 1700 block of West Georgia Street and our driveway came out right in the middle of the block. Western Machine Works was right next door. We used to pull shafts out of boats that were drydocked and take them to the machine shop. That meant loading them on a little cart and stopping the traffic on

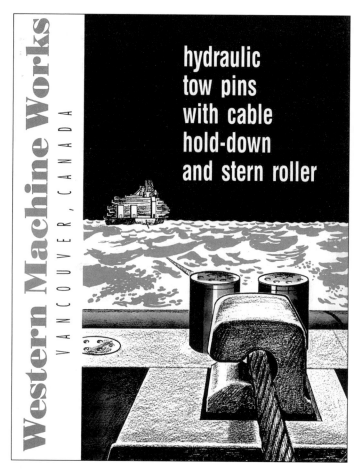

Western Machine Works
VANCOUVER, CANADA

hydraulic tow pins with cable hold-down and stern roller

A 10,000-ton dwt barge in tow by the icebreaking tug *Arctic Nanook*. The towline is led between the towing pins.

Georgia Street while we turned this great long thing to enter the shop. You wouldn't do that today!"

Urban development spelled the end of an era for that historic marine district. In 1979 eviction papers were served to the Coal Harbour businesses, giving thirty days' notice to firms that had been operating there for sixty years. Even though the notice period was later stretched to three months, the die was cast. More change was in store for Allied.

Drydocks

For many years Allied's Coal Harbour repair yard had relied on "the Boeing drydock," one that had quite a history. The Boeing plant, located right at the end of Georgia Street just before the entrance to Stanley Park, produced aircraft and yachts. The biggest yacht built was Mr. Boeing's last one, the *Taconite*, and a new drydock was specially constructed for it. But things didn't go according to plan, and the dock couldn't lift the boat high enough. "They pumped and pumped and pumped and pumped," Arthur said, "but the yacht still wasn't clear of the water, so the drydock was looked upon as one of the goofs." The Boeing Aircraft shipyard division used it for some years until Jack MacDonald bought it in 1942; Allied inherited it when they purchased the repair yard. After the Coal Harbour site was closed down, the aging drydock was towed over to the North Vancouver site.

Arthur immediately set about designing a new, larger floating drydock for the North Vancouver yard. The steel for it was purchased, but got used for other vessels before construction could start. Finally, in the fall of 1979, Allied completed the orders that were underway, and construction began on the new 120-foot drydock that could lift vessels of up to 750 long tons. That drydock is a registered vessel, officially named *Allied 208*.

At first, little repair work was done at the new North Vancouver site. Most of it consisted of vessels in for a dock, clean and paint or propeller work. The repair foreman, John Manahan, and his relocated crew from Coal Harbour attended to most of it. In the early 1980s Arthur tabulated the dimensions of the major vessels on the BC coast that would require repair work and then designed a second drydock (Hull #244) that could

The tug *Seaspan Chinook* in floating drydock (Allied Hull #244). Courtesy *North Shore News*

accommodate most of them. It was 160 feet long and could lift 1,800 long tons. This new drydock greatly expanded the yard's capacity for repair work. After the large drydock was completed, ship refit and maintenance became the mainstays for Allied Shipbuilders.

The Allied Design Team

Today many marine architects in this province are independents, operating separately from the yards that eventually construct the vessels they design. However, Arthur always preferred a hands-on approach, with the designer no more than steps away from the tradesmen that have to work with the design. That tradition remains strong, with the design team McLaren & Sons an integral part of Allied Shipbuilders.

McLaren & Sons spans three generations. W.D. McLaren's training as a mechanical and electrical engineer, combined with the practical experience he gained as an engine builder, ship designer and shipbuilder, was invaluable as a foundation for the next generations. W.D. first used the name McLaren & Sons when preparing original specs and contract plans for the CNR's *Prince George* and collaborating on ship design with his son Arthur. The name also included W.D.'s younger son Jim, who was trained as a civil engineer.

Designing ships was Arthur McLaren's side job, one that he often started after coming home from the shipyard. He built a drawing office in the basement and worked at night, free from the interruptions of phone calls or visits. Dorothy McLaren recalled, "He'd be working away on that huge drawing table and singing! Mostly it was whatever was popular, but sometimes Scottish songs. It was companionable just to hear him."

Chuck Ko, Allied's technical manager, took over from Arthur as the shipyard's in-house designer; he has often been referred to as "the young Arthur."

Chuck came to see me in 1980 when he was going to BCIT and wanted a job. I hesitated until he showed me his marks. He didn't have anything but A's all the way through. I said, "You don't expect me to say anything nasty about that, do you?" He didn't say a word. Well, Chuck was with me quite a long time before I knew whether he could speak or not. All he ever said was "OK." It turns out he was just shy, but he sure was a worker. He tackled every task we gave him and got most things exactly the way we wanted. At the end of the year when it was time to go back to school, I asked him if he'd like to work for us again next summer. He allowed that he would, and he went back to BCIT and

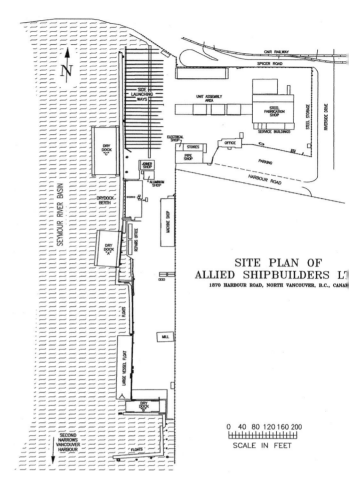

Site plan for the Allied yard in North Vancouver, 1993, when repairs had become a higher proportion of the company's business.

Engine fitters who worked to repair Voith-Schneider drives fitted in a navy berthing tug. Left to right: Frank Christophersen, Bob Adams, Voith-Schneider technician, Airie Braaksma, Peter Chen, Luke Klassen, Horst Hartwich.

came back again the following summer. He's been with us ever since. He's an expert at learning things and an excellent designer. You have to put him at the top.

Repair Philosophy

Jim McLaren looks at the big picture when approaching Allied's repair work: any specific job needs to be considered in terms of the impact it will have on the entire vessel. According to Jim, "I've found that the majority of our customers are coming to us to identify the most cost-effective way to do their work. It's a total job. To do repairs or a refit cost-effectively, we need to find out how durable the work has to be, how long the boat's going to last, how the customer will be able to use this work in the future. In other words, we have to rationalize the installation or work to produce what the customer wants. I think that's what has enabled us to be successful in repair/refit. Sure, we don't get all of the jobs, but most of the time our repair crews are working to capacity."

The same is true for new vessel construction. "You have to have the customer explain his requirements and then interpret them in drawings and modify them until they're right. Then you pick the right components, the right suppliers and the right people to do the work, so that when the boat goes out for its trial, everything's successful. When a vessel leaves us and goes into service, we like to think that everything's been taken care of and that any potential problems were solved before construction even started."

As Malcolm McLaren points out, "We've kept the name Allied Shipbuilders, but that's not what we do now. For the last decade we've been ship repairers that also do shipbuilding. When we do get new build orders, we build even better vessels because of what we've learned doing repair. It's frustrating and expensive to work on equipment you can't take apart or service easily. We try to build the best vessel we can by incorporating those repair lessons into our new construction."

CHAPTER 9

Tugs and Barges:
Workhorses of the Coast

"If someone were writing a history of what we've done on the west coast, you'd have to put these self-loading, self-dumping log barges at the top of the list."

—*Arthur McLaren*

Tugs

British Columbia's economy has long been linked to the fortunes of the forest industry. From the earliest days of commercial logging, trees were felled into the many coastal inlets, rafted into flat booms and towed to the sawmills. To tow these booms, a distinctive type

The Kingcome Navigation tug *Ivanhoe*, built in 1907. The vessel, one of the longest-running tugs on the coast, was later converted to a yacht but still operating in the late 1990s.

of tug developed. It was of wooden construction, generally 60 to 80 feet long and fitted with a single coal-fired Scotch boiler and a steam engine of 150–350 ihp. The first of these tugs dates back to the 1870s. During the period 1900–1910, scores of utility steam tugs were launched.

At that time timber was plentiful and of sufficient size to make wood keels of 100 feet and planking 30 to 40 feet long. Engines and boilers were built in the UK or locally. In both cases, they were built by Scots. These tugs were workhorses, but as slow, steady plodders they were appropriate to the task—log booms would break up if towed at a speed of more than 2 knots or in rough water. Most of the south coast of mainland BC is very sheltered, but in the event of inclement weather, tug and tow sought refuge and were often tied up for days. Before the advent of the radio-telephone, owners had scant knowledge as to the location of their vessels.

There was plenty of towing work during World War II, but wartime government policy froze the towing rates and almost no tugs were built. Most of the aging fleet dated from the 1920s.

The wooden tug *Protective II*, an M.R. Cliff Towing vessel, aground on the BC coast, c. 1932. Murray Cliff's company was once one of BC's largest towboat operations. Before the advent of radar and other navigation devices, the ship repair business sometimes survived on the misery of others.

Changes in Towing

After the war the nature of towing began to change. Timber rights and the ownership of hundreds of small coastal sawmills became concentrated in the hands of fewer and larger corporations, and increasingly efficient machines meant more logs were harvested. The end result was a greater volume of logs had to be towed from more distant locations. In response, towboat companies devised new equipment and techniques for transporting logs. At the same time, as the demand for pulp product rose dramatically in proportion to sawn wood, numerous new chip barges were built for transporting wood chips.

The primary towing market on the BC coast has always been tied to forest products such as logs and wood chips. But other markets requiring tug and barge fleets emerged. Logging and processing

forest products required fuel, machinery and explosives, much of which was barged to logging and mill sites. Barges also delivered materials such as gravel and cement powder, as well as hauling finished products. Oil fuels, chemicals and hazardous materials not permitted on passenger ferries had to be towed to coastal communities. More recently, new industries such as fish farming have opened up further towing opportunities. Over the years, BC tug and barge operators have met the challenges of these various markets with all manner of innovations.

Changes in Tugs

The towboats working BC's rivers and coastal waters evolved continually from the slow, steady steam tugs of the early 1900s. These wooden vessels were re-powered with big, slow-speed diesels and required seven-man crews. Wooden US and Canadian war surplus tugs that became available after World War II helped update and re-equip the BC towing fleet. Since then, the trend in building coastal towboats has moved toward smaller boats with significantly more powerful engines, all operated by smaller crews. The late 1940s and '50s saw numerous upgrades and conversions on these vessels as owners became eager to increase the pulling power of their fleets.

John Manly was already building small steel tugs in BC when Arthur McLaren opened up his own yard in 1948. Allied's first hull, completed in 1949, was the relatively large 55-foot *Bering Straits*. Subsequent Allied tugs were mostly in the 20- to 35-foot range. It wasn't until the late 1950s and early '60s that such steel-hulled tugs became common in BC waters.

The development of smaller, lighter high-speed diesel engines meant that towing companies could pack considerably more power into a small tug. Arthur called this the "tin can phase," when a towboat was basically a noisy steel hull with a high-powered engine. Over the years, the capabilities of these new steel boats improved considerably. Living and safety conditions improved as well, with the addition of new equipment such as electronic navigation aids, sophisticated communications systems, improved propulsion devices, towline safety-release mechanisms, and anti-vibration materials to quiet engines.

The new breed of towboat was built by a number of yards in BC, including John Manly, Benson Brothers, Mercer's, BC Marine, Van Ship, Vito, Bel-Aire and Allied. Towing companies upgraded their fleets with new, higher-powered boats and specialized barges. Many owners took full advantage of the federal shipbuilding subsidy, introduced in 1961, for tugs exceeding 50 gross tons. Old wooden tugs were replaced with new steel ones at a rapid rate and steel tugboat construction entered its heyday—most of today's towboat fleet was built during the1960s and 1970s. Through the 1970s, equipment and construction costs escalated but new construction continued, with vessels being ordered for increasingly specialized work.

Government regulations played a significant role in the way the modern west coast tugboat fleet developed during this period. In the late 1960s, after several tugboat tragedies, federal safety regulations for new tug construction were enacted. These stipulated noise limits, minimum cabin size, use of approved exterior doors and hatches, and required that all crew be berthed above waterline. Other regulations were based on archaic requirements, among them "nominal horsepower," which was calculated according to the swept area of the main engine's pistons. The use of nominal horsepower was equitable at one time, with old slow-speed engines. But with the advent of the modern high-speed diesel, much more power was produced for an equivalent swept volume, the calculation being:

Nominal Horsepower (NHP) = $\dfrac{D^2 \times N}{60}$

where D = cylinder diameter in inches
     N = number of cylinders

Regulations also specified that the number of crew be determined in part by the overall size (gross tonnage) of a vessel. The larger a tug, the larger the crew required.

Therefore, a towboat owner in a competitive situation had only one economical choice when buying a new vessel: to order a relatively small tug with loud, high-speed diesel engines, run by a smaller crew. Government regulations effectively penalized him for building a large, spacious vessel with long-lasting medium-speed diesel engines.

In the 1980s and '90s, the pace of larger tug construction slowed dramatically, reflecting the "maturity" of the coastal forest industry. The timber harvest had levelled off and there were enough good vessels to meet the towing demand. It could be said that BC shipbuilders were victims of their own success and had worked themselves out of a job. Still, shipyards continued to take orders for smaller, high-powered tugs. Low operating cost became a priority: tugs built through the 1990s were mostly under 15 gross tons, with high power and low crew requirements.

Allied's Hard-Working Vessels

Island Comet (Hull #27)

The 40-foot *Island Comet* was the second largest tug Allied built in the company's early years. Island Tug & Barge wanted the single-screw tug for harbour work in Victoria. It was powered by two used 6-71 engines, supplied by the owner. "Those kinds of engines were regularly pulled out

The completed structure of the *Island Comet*. The vessel owner outfitted the tug in Victoria.

of World War II landing craft and other vessels," Arthur explained. "There were scads of them all over the country."

Kitmano (Hulls #38, #112, #119)

Allied built three *Kitmano* tugs. The original 42-foot tug (Hull #38) was built in 1955 for Bill Cogswell of Northern Salvage & Towing. In 1960 the second (Hull #112) was built to replace the original one. This new 50 x 14-foot tug wasn't satisfactory because the hull was not large enough to provide adequate buoyancy to support the weight of the machinery chosen, a large cast-iron medium-speed Alpha diesel. Underway the tug tried to behave more like a submarine. So Allied built a larger hull, Hull #119; at 51 x 19 feet it was 5 feet wider and 2 feet deeper. The machinery, deckhouse and all the equipment were transferred to this new hull and, in Arthur's words, "It worked just fine."

Hull #112 was then fitted with a lightweight GM diesel, which proved successful, and was sold to Harry Hansen.

Black Fir (Hull #107), G.M. Venture (#109)

Arthur McLaren designed the *Black Fir*, a 50-foot tug built for Doug Rust and Doug Fielding of Texada Towing Company. The tug was used for towing logs on the coast. The power was a B&W Alpha, built in Denmark. The 40-foot *G.M. Venture* was

Bill Cogswell with the final version of the *Kitmano* (Hull #119).

Above and at top: Installing the big B&W Alpha engine, 350 hp at 375 rpm, in the 51-foot Texada Towing Company tug *Black Fir* (Hull #107).

Arthur McLaren and Doug Rust (right), a principal of Texada Towing.

built for Frank Hole to one of Bill Brown's first designs. It was delivered to G.M. Flyer Towing Ltd. Both tugs were built in 1959.

Neva Straits (Hull #124)

This tug, designed by Robert "Bob" Allan, was equipped with a Dutch-built diesel engine and a controllable-pitch prop. At the time there was a man in Vancouver named Leo Vanderveen who supplied equipment from Holland. As Arthur McLaren remembered it:

He did a very good job selling even though he didn't have the foggiest notion of anything to do with engineering. One day Leo phoned to say he had a Dutch director in town and wondered if they could come by to look at the Neva Straits *under construction. I agreed and took them on a tour. We looked over the hull then went up top to*

Launch of the 93-foot, 900-hp tug Neva Straits.

TELEPHONE:
MU 5-0121

PURCHASE ORDER

THIS PURCHASE ORDER NO.

31838

MUST APPEAR ON ALL BILLS
OF LADING, INVOICES, DE-
LIVERY SLIPS & CONTAINERS

STRAITS TOWING LIMITED

2215 COMMISSIONER STREET,
VANCOUVER 6, B.C.
CANADA

Page 1 of 2

TO

Allied Builders Limited,
145 West First Avenue,
Vancouver 10, B.C.

SHIP TO

SHIP VIA	ORDER DATE 11/24/61	REG. VESSEL NEW TUG	JOB NO.	
QUANTITY	DESCRIPTION	PRICE	DELIVERY	CODE

CODE 1/17/05

This Purchase Order No.31838 shall constitute a firm
contract with Allied Builders Ltd.,to build and outfit
a 93 foot Single Screw Steel Tug as per plans and specifications prepared by Mr. Robert F. Allan, as submitted
to yourselves for tender. All conditions and guarantees
outlined in these specifications are to be considered as
binding in this contract.

The Tug is to be built under the Federal Government ship
building assistance program and, subject to Government
approval, the breakdown of responsibility for payment
will be as follows :-

Total cost as per your tender   189,360.00
Less Government Subsidy - 40%   75,744.00 $ 113,616.00
Balance due Allied Builders Ltd,
   payable by Straits Towing Ltd.

Hold-back to be paid on satisfactory
performance of tug, three (3) months
after launching date   - 10% $ 11,361.60
                                                       102,254.40
No interest to be charged on Hold-back.

Schedule of payments to be advanced by
   Straits Towing Limited :-
   Start of project   ...   15%   17,042.40
   90% Completion of tug   25%   28,404.00
   Launching 25%   28,404.00
   Delivery   ......   25%   28,404.00 $ 102,254.40

The following conditions are to be considered as binding
on both parties on acceptance of this Contract :-

(1)   Provincial Social Service Tax of 5% to be an extra.

(2)   Allied Builders Limited agree to make delivery of
      the completed Tug five (5) months from the date of
      this contract or April 24th 1962. Completion date
      to be -

OVER ..

1 RENDER INVOICES IN DUPLICATE.
2 PACKING SLIP MUST ACCOMPANY
   ALL MATERIAL.
3 THIS PURCHASE ORDER IS NOT VALID
   UNLESS SIGNED BY THE PURCHASING
   AGENT OR AUTHORIZED REPRESENTATIVE.

STRAITS TOWING LIMITED

STRAITS TOWING LIMITED

John Orr

PURCHASING AGENT

See Reverse For Terms and Conditions

In the early 1960s, the construction contract for a tug fit on one page. As Arthur McLaren said, "Business was straightforward and paperwork was kept to a minimum. Instead of sending the same piece of paper around seven times with no one producing anything, all that effort was put into production."

The tug *Neva Straits* under construction. Commercial Illustrators photo

September 29, 1961

93'-0" STEEL TUG FOR STRAITS TOWING
LIST OF TENDERS RECEIVED

Allied Builders Ltd.	$188,860
Mercer (Star)	202,000
Manly	206,000
Victoria Machinery Co. Ltd.	214,000
Yarrows Ltd.	243,000

(Above) Bid results for the tug *Neva Straits*, one of the first vessels Allied constructed under the federal subsidy program.

look down into the machinery access hole that was still open.

Leo peered in and said, "You have the engine there?"

"Yes," I said.

"And the propeller at the other end?"

"Yes," I said again.

"Well, what goes in between?" he asked.

"The flywheel normally goes there," I explained with some amazement.

"When does that go in?" he wanted to know.

I guess I decided to have a little fun, because I told him, "Oh, we aren't going to bother putting that in." And then I blathered on about the engine having four cylinders that would all run without the necessity of a flywheel.

About an hour later I got a call from Jack Scagel asking if I had really told Leo that the tug wouldn't need a flywheel. I told him that Leo had asked a stupid question so I'd given him an equally stupid answer. I didn't think he'd taken it all that seriously, but evidently Leo had wired Holland to see if it was really true that this engine didn't need a flywheel. Well, everybody straightened him out in short order about that.

The launch of the 1,800-hp berthing tug *Charles H. Cates VIII*.

The Cates Ship-Berthing Tugs
Hulls #225, #230, #237, #248, #253

Of the five ship-berthing tugs Allied has delivered to C.H. Cates & Sons, the first two were 1,800-hp

A Cates "1800" escorting a freighter in the Port of Vancouver.

Laying down the aft main deck plate on the construction jig for the *Charles H. Cates II*, a Z-peller tug. The modern shipbuilding method is to start assembly by laying the deck, not the keel. The vessel is constructed upside down.

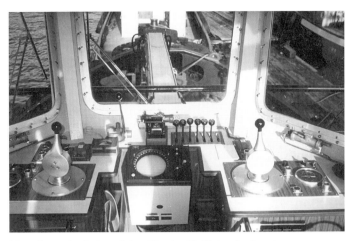

View from the helm of the *Charles H. Cates II*, showing radar (at centre), propulsion control joy sticks (at left and right), and winch and crane controls (the six levers centre forward).

Erecting the transverse frame and girders on the deck panel.

The *Charles H. Cates II* demonstrating amazing manoeuvrability at sea trials—rotating 360 degrees on the spot, 1983. Murray McLennan photo

The aft hull section is joined to the forward hull on the launchways.

The *Charles H. Cates II* at work. An articulated crane is used to lift the towline up to the ship. Murray McLennan photo

60-foot twin-screw tugs: the *Charles H. Cates VI* (Hull #225), built in 1979, and the *Charles Cates VIII* (#230), built in 1980. Robert "Rob" Allan designed these tugs; their shallow drafts and wide hulls allowed them to move sideways without rolling over and capsizing. Their sloped superstructures were set well back so they could get in close under the hulls of the ships being berthed.

The breakthrough came with the 72-foot *Charles H. Cates II* (Hull #237). It was the first Z-peller berthing tug of its type in BC and, at 2,400 bhp, a powerful tug for its size when built in 1982. Designed by Rob Allan, this berthing tug was enormously successful and has been imitated around the world since its launch. Naval architects in other countries had certainly designed modern ship-berthing tugs, but Allan's design was a true innovation in terms of its small size and high power. Two decades later, tugboat fleets in the USA and elsewhere were being renewed with vessels featuring 360-degree steerable drives.

Allied also built the smaller 1,300-bhp Z-peller *Cates X* (Hull #248) in 1987. Cates' management thought the services of this vessel, a smaller version of the 2,400-hp tugs, could be sold at a lower rate than those of the larger tugs and perhaps fill a niche. But pilots on deep-sea ships had become accustomed to the more powerful 2,400-hp Cates tugs. The *Cates X* cost the ship owner almost as much as those earlier ship-berthing tugs that featured twice the power. The construction price on the *Cates X* didn't come down in proportion to the amount of power, as it was as complex as its more powerful cousins.

Barges

The post-war period in BC was characterized by the expansion of industry and transportation of raw goods. One of the fastest growing sectors was the pulp and paper industry, generating a dramatic increase in the demand for pulp feedstock and the means to take it to the mills. By this time logs were being debarked prior to cutting and this bark, known as "hog fuel," was barged to mills for fuel.

Sawmill waste, being free of bark, was diced into wood chips—a valuable new commodity that was barged directly to paper mills. Hundreds of specialized chip barges were produced, most of them built by only a few shipyards. The typical customer was an independent owner who built a barge as an investment, then leased it out, applied accelerated depreciation and wrote off the cost in a few years. The chip barge played an essential role in the pulp and paper industry, particularly for sawmills with little or no storage capacity for chips or hog fuel. Barges were spotted at the loading wharf and filled with sawmill waste as it was produced. The chip barge is a standardized piece of equipment that doesn't require a long construction time. Basically it is a simple steel pontoon with a timber deck box about 12 feet high. The size varies depending on the owner's work. A company moving chips from the Fraser River up to Elk Falls, for example, would want a fairly big barge to make the trip pay off. Other companies needed smaller barges that would fit into specific berths for loading. In the 1960s barge sizes were standardized to 150 x 44 feet. At Yarrows Ltd., where most of the early chip barges were built, the "standard" barge size was set by the dimensions of the shipyard's covered building berth, which had been used during the war for building frigates.

Over time the original wood construction gave way to steel. The wooden deck boxes, which were too easily smashed, were replaced by wood boxes

The chip barge *Island Tug 61* being pulled by the *Island Comet*, also built by Allied.

reinforced with steel posts, and then by fairly robust steel boxes with steel posts. The chip barges being used in BC waters today are 200 x 50 feet in size, with a capacity of some 2,000 tons.

The reliance on tug and barge operations is a unique feature of the Northwest Coast marine scene. After World War II, tug and barge fleets replaced self-propelled cargo coasters as local workhorses, serving industrialized cities, small coastal communities and remote logging operations. At the start of the new millennium, hundreds of chip, gravel, oil and chemical barges continue operations in BC waters.

Allied's Barges

Rather than trying to break into high-volume production of standardized barges, Allied Shipbuilders went after the more complex specialty ones. These ranged from chemical barges to gravel barges with loading conveyors built into the structure. Arthur explained: "In the mid-'60s we saw a lot of future in building big barges that could carry a decent amount of cargo. Shipping 100 tons at one time wasn't particularly economical, but if you built barges that could carry 4,000 tons, they would certainly be a better idea."

Arrow Park (Hull #16), Deer Park (#17)
In 1952 Allied constructed the 99-foot barge *Arrow Park*. Arthur recalled:

The Arrow Park *was built for Ben Bowman and Grant McKenzie for service on the Arrow Lakes. They started a business there digging zinc ore out of the tailings from lead mines north of Revelstoke and then transporting the ore down the lakes to Trail. To do that, they got hold of two trucks and a series of dump bodies which they could load and then put on the barge and take off as necessary. They had a rig that lifted the body up, then the truck pulled away and the body was dropped down. They needed a barge to carry these loaded dump bodies down the rivers, and a tug to push it. Originally they used a boat called the* Minto *that the CPR had laid up in 1952. We built Hull #17,*

the 40-foot steel tug Deer Park *that pushed the* Arrow Park.

Later Allied worked on the *Arrow Park* a second time, changing it to self-propelled by installing two 265-hp engines. Eventually the *Arrow Park* was renamed the *Lardeau* and ran on the Arrow Lakes as a ferry.

Pitt Polder No. 1 (Hull #51)
After the war, Pitt Polder Ltd. opened up quite a bit of property in the Pitt River area. Much of it was marshy estuary at the time. The company used the vessel to reclaim low-lying land from the sea as it had done in Holland. *Pitt Polder No. 1* was based on drawings the owner supplied of a similar dredge used in Holland. Machinery for the dredge was brought over from Holland.

V.P.D. Derrick #2 (Hull #132)
When Hull #132 was built for Vancouver Pile Driving, it was based on the relatively new idea of a barge using a mobile crane instead of a purpose-built stationary crane. It was hoped that a mobile crane would be one way of cutting costs, and a 110-foot barge certainly qualified for the shipbuilding subsidy.

V.P.D. Derrick No. 2 at work, dredging in North Vancouver, 1962. The Second Narrows bridge and two freighters are in background. Commercial Illustrators photo

St. John Carrier (Hull #178)

Allied built this newsprint barge in 1971 for MacMillan Bloedel Ltd., and Yarrows built its sister ship. In terms of gross tonnage, the two barges were the largest vessels constructed in BC until the two Spirit Class ferries were built in the 1990s. The *St. John Carrier* took newsprint from MB's paper mill at St. John, New Brunswick, to US ports along the Atlantic seaboard. In Arthur's words:

Construction went well, and MacMillan Bloedel had agreed to use one of their tugs to tow the barge around to the east coast. But when it came time to paint, we ran into trouble with Mother Nature. We had to deliver the vessel by December, but that year it rained every day except one between the end of September and the end of December! We tried heating torches to try to dry the surfaces, but mostly we were just wasting our time.

One day a friend came into the yard and I was telling him our tale of woe. He asked how we were going to deliver it and I said via the Panama Canal. "In that case," he said, "you'll be going by Los Angeles, and I have a friend down there." He gave me the guy's card and told me to call him and explain my problem. I did, and the fellow in L.A. said he could paint it for us! So we loaded all the paint onto the barge when construction was complete and sent it down to L.A. The guy painted it within two weeks and we met our delivery date. That was one of the lucky things that happened.

Rail-Trailer Transport

Yorke No. 21 (Hull #126)

Allied built a number of vessels for F.M. Yorke, a company that concentrated on rail barge traffic. Their barges ranged in capacity from the 273-foot 18-rail car vessel *Yorke No. 21*, to small 4-car scows typically used by Fraser River mills that did not have direct rail access. These smaller barges would usually just tie up at the mill until all the rail cars were loaded and then get towed to F.M. Yorke's wharf near the foot of Campbell Avenue in Vancouver, where they would be switched to the Great Northern Railway tracks.

Greg Yorke (Hull #142)

The 1960s saw the construction of two rail-trailer ferries by Allied. Best described as self-propelled barges, these ferries had railway tracks welded to the deck, with asphalt laid flush with the top of the rails. This permitted the transport of either rail cars or transport trailers.

The *St. John Carrier* (Hull #178) on the ways. In terms of size, at 10,683 gross tons, this was one of the largest vessels ever built in BC.

The 325-foot rail car ferry *Greg Yorke*, outbound at the First Narrows, 1963. The vessel was later renamed the *Seaspan Greg*. Commercial Illustrators photo

The *Greg Yorke* was a 325 x 60-foot self-propelled rail barge. Yorke built it to transport rail cars loaded with pulp or paper on a daily service between Vancouver and the pulp mill at Powell River. Designed by Robert "Bob" Allan, it was the first self-propelled rail car vessel in the province. Arthur McLaren remembered that it worked very well.

The only trouble I had was with the owner. At the time F.M. Yorke was long gone and the company was run by Lorne Yorke. Now, Lorne was an awfully nice guy but he had some silly idea that the only one entitled to make a profit out of the thing was F.M. Yorke. Lorne was very active in the vessel's construction. He wanted to select the colour of the linings inside the deckhouse and came along one day with a sample of some arborite. I said, "What's that you've got?"

He said, "It's arborite."

"I can see that. What are you going to do with it?"

He replied, "It's not what I'm going to do with it, it's what you're going to do with it."

"What am I going to do with it?"

He told me I was to buy it and install it inside the cabins. It was a horrible pink colour with gold stars. "You don't really want that, do you?" I asked.

"Sure!" he said. "It's distinctive." Well, it was distinctive, all right.

By the time we got the accommodation linings half built, Lorne had a change of mind. "I don't think I'm going to like that arborite with the gold stars," he said.

"Why are you telling me now?"

"Because I want you to change it for something else."

I told him, "To hell we're going to change it. We bought all they had!"

"Well, send it back, then."

"Nobody wants it back," I told him. "They had to make a special order to get it in here for you." So we ended up using that awful stuff for years as the backing for more civilized colours of arborite.

We had the same kind of circus when it came to deciding which kind of engine he'd put in the Greg Yorke. We'd quoted a price for the self-propelled barge without the engine, listing separate prices for a Caterpillar, a GM and so on. Finally Lorne announced he'd settled on the Dutch engine. I told him that was fine and said the total price would be $110,000. He countered with $95,000. I explained that that was the price for the German engine. He said, "Arthur, you can take it from me, the Werkspoor will cost $95,000."

When I next saw the supplier, Leo Vanderveen, I congratulated him on getting the order for the engine but I asked him how come he had quoted me a price of $110,000 and then given it to Lorne for $95,000. He said, "Don't you know anything about a Dutch auction, McLaren?" He explained how you keep bidding the price down. "You start off with the highest price and the various contenders keep lowering their price until it gets to the point where nobody will take any more off. The guy who has the lowest price settles." So I learned something there.

Haida Transporter (Hull #162)

Allied built this rail car ferry in 1968 for Kingcome Navigation, the coastal marine division of the forestry giant MacMillan Bloedel. Designed by Jackson, Talbot, Walkingshaw &

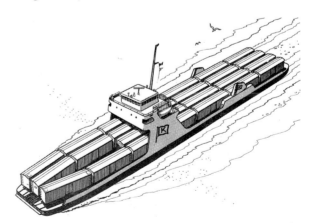

Cover of the invitation to the launch of the *Haida Transporter*. The artist's drawing shows the barge with a full load of twenty-six rail cars.

Arthur McLaren said, "Launching a ship is the most stressful operation in shipbuilding. It's a lot like parachute jumping—you have to get it right the first time. But it isn't until you're totally responsible for a launching that you get the full emotional experience of the event. As the launch hour approaches, you're filled with dread. You go over everything in your mind a dozen times, worrying about what you didn't allow for that can possibly go wrong. Will the ship start when the triggers are released? Will the ship continue to slide? Will the bow poppet carry the extra weight imposed when the stern rises and transfers weight onto the forward ways? Finally the waiting is over, the axemen chop the ropes and you watch as the ship accelerates down the ways and finally becomes fully waterborne. In about one and a half minutes, the whole burden of the launch is lifted from your shoulders and you have accomplished what few men are privileged to do. You've moved a 1,500-ton mass some 300 feet—and done so safely."

Arthur McLaren and launching foreman Ralph Burry, shaking hands after the launch of the *Haida Transporter*.

Associates Ltd., it was built to haul rail cars of newsprint from the MB paper mills at Harmac and Powell River to Vancouver. By the year 2000 it had been in continuous use for over thirty years.

Log Barges

The sheltered coastal waters of BC are well suited to the practice of moving logs in flat booms. But flat booms break up in the slightest seaway, so they can't be used to bring logs from the Queen Charlotte Islands or the exposed west coast of Vancouver Island.

Early on, enterprising towboat operators tried to deal with the hazards of open water by bundle-booming logs into Davis rafts or by loading them into hulks. However, building a Davis raft—a cigar-shaped bundle of hundreds of interlaced logs—was labour-intensive, and breaking one up at the completion of the voyage was extremely dangerous. The other alternative was to load logs into a hulk, usually an old sailing ship hull with its masts and decks removed. But their carrying capacity was limited, since they were entirely open to the weather and thus required good freeboard.

The late 1950s saw the introduction of the side-tipping log barge. Arthur recalled that the very first of these were used along the Columbia River, but they were not big barges. Floyd Kurtz, a superintendent for MacMillan Bloedel, saw them in operation and felt they could be useful in BC. Kurtz worked with Bob Allan to develop the design for a large side-tipping log barge. The first working version was the *Powell No. 1*, built by Burrard Dry Dock in 1957. From the start the 300-foot vessel was a success.

The concept behind the side-tipping log barge is relatively simple. Arthur explained:

Logs are loaded transversely onto the barge deck, restrained only by heavy log stops at the forward and aft ends. The barge has a flooding tank built into one side of the vessel. To unload the barge, the sea valves are opened and the tipping tank floods, causing the barge to list until there is sufficient transverse declivity to "launch" the logs. The flooding tank has a bottom at a somewhat higher level than the light draft of the barge. Once free of log cargo, the barge assumes a lighter draft and the ballast water in the tipping tank drains out. At this point the flooding valve is closed and the barge is ready for reloading and repeating the cycle. Later on, these barges were also equipped with one or two cranes, so they became self-loading as well as self-dumping.

Launching of the rail car barge *Haida Transporter*, April 27, 1968.

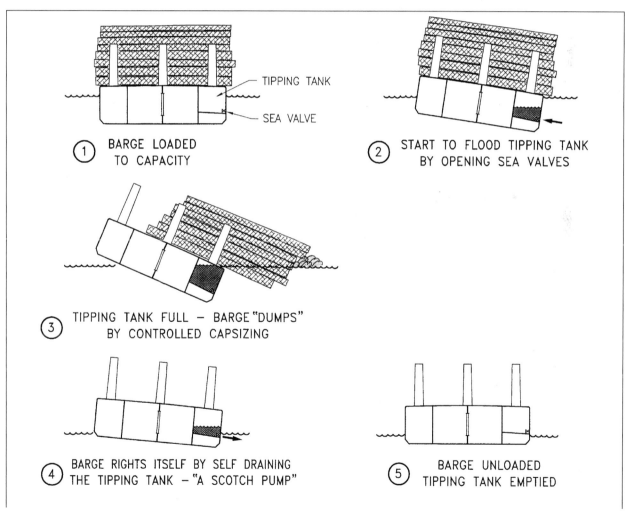

1. BARGE LOADED TO CAPACITY

   TIPPING TANK

   SEA VALVE

2. START TO FLOOD TIPPING TANK BY OPENING SEA VALVES

3. TIPPING TANK FULL — BARGE "DUMPS" BY CONTROLLED CAPSIZING

4. BARGE RIGHTS ITSELF BY SELF DRAINING THE TIPPING TANK — "A SCOTCH PUMP"

5. BARGE UNLOADED TIPPING TANK EMPTIED

Diagram of side-tipping log barge. Arthur McLaren referred to the self-draining of the "tipping tank" as a "Scotch pump." He often said the two most basic tenets of mechanical engineering are 1) water flows downhill and 2) you can't push on a rope.

The 220-foot self-dumping log barge *Island Pine* under construction, 1959. Commercial Illustrators photo

Island Pine (Hull #104)

Arthur McLaren designed the *Island Pine* (Hull #104) for Island Tug & Barge. Built in 1959, the 220-foot steel log barge was Allied's biggest barge to that time. "In those days," Arthur said, "private companies often didn't tender their jobs. The company would announce their intentions and ask for proposals. The customer would think over the proposal and then say, 'Yes, we'll go ahead with it' or 'No, we won't'."

The barge was built to bring logs in from the west coast of Vancouver Island. The company wanted a small self-dumping barge to service the many "gyppo" camps that produced smaller quantities of logs. The *Island Pine* was still haul-

ing logs in the late 1990s, being well suited to the smaller cutblocks typical of logging in this period.

Rayonier No. 1 (Hull #120), *Rayonier No. 2* (#121)

In 1961 Arthur designed two side-dumping log barges for Rayonier Ltd. With dimensions of 312 x 61 x 17 feet, these were by far the largest vessels Allied had constructed at the False Creek yard since the war. Each had a deadweight capacity of 7,000 tons and a lightship weight of some 1,125 tons.

The price for each was $425,000. As Arthur remembered it:

We gave them a price for each barge, but they hummed and hawed on the thing. We couldn't get a yes or no out of them, and time was going by. Foolishly we placed an order for the steel without having a firm order for the vessels. Each barge had 1,200 tons of steel in it, so that meant we had 2,400 tons of steel coming without an order. I think at the time steel only cost about 6 cents a pound, but it added up. For two or three weeks, we were on tenter hooks.

Anyway, we had no problem building these two barges. For a long time they were the biggest vessels we'd ever built. I made the down payment for the Coal Harbour Shipyard with the proceeds from that project.

Launching the *Rayoniers*

Building the two Rayonier log barges presented no major hurdles. "But," Arthur commented, "the launch was another story." Allied launched them on the 18-inch-wide ways that West Coast Ship-builders had put down during 1941 for the 10,000-tonners.

The pressure on the ways was calculated to be 1.5 tons per square foot, a figure similar to that used on the standard cargo ships. Unfortunately, we overlooked two serious points:

The launching of the log barge *Rayonier No. 1*. The bow poppet caught fire during the launch. Commercial Illustrators photo

a) Due to the fullness of the stern, at an early point of travel down the ways the buoyant stern would rise and put a concentrated weight of some 475 tons on the forward poppet.
b) Our shipwright foreman had put very short lengths of ways at the bow poppet so that when the stern lifted the pressure on the ways was in the order of 12 tons per square foot—far too high.

The owners invited some fifty guests from the forestry industry to the launching ceremony for the first barge. It was scheduled for 3:30 on a Saturday afternoon. As guests arrived, we took out the final bilge blocks, which were helping to restrain the vessel. Once the sponsor named the vessel and broke the bottle, we knocked out the trigger shores. Rayonier No. 1 started down the ways, but not with the acceleration we expected. In fact, the barge entered the water at a rather slow speed. The stern lifted, smoke rose from the ways under the bow poppet and the vessel came to a stop on the ways.

I quickly told my wife, "You look after the guests. I'm going to look after the ship."

We discovered that when the barge stalled, the forward sliding ways were intact. However, the aft ways had dislodged as the barge's stern lifted. The only solution was to add water ballast in the stern and tow the vessel backward off the ways at the next high tide. We got two of the largest local tugs onto lines and started pulling the barge. Slowly, slowly we got stern motion on Rayonier No. 1 and finally the barge was afloat, clear of the ways.

On the following Monday I had several phone calls from launch guests asking if we got the hull afloat. I told them, "Yes, about ten o'clock Saturday night." I also apologized for abandoning them at the ceremonies, but they assured me that my wife was an excellent hostess and everybody had a good time. I told the callers that attending a launch where everything went smoothly was commonplace, but to be at a launch where the vessel halted on the ways, well, that was a unique occasion!

When it was time to launch the sister ship, *Rayonier No. 2*, Arthur and his crew made sure that the mistakes of the first launching would not be repeated.

In fact, we were determined that there would be no mistakes at all. Now we knew we needed to ensure that the stern would not rise until the vessel had passed farther down the ways. To get the necessary stern trim, we ballasted the aft peak 80 percent full of water. This would reduce the loading of the bow poppet at this critical time. To that end, we used 24-foot ways under the bow poppets, so that the calculated loading on the ways at the point of stern raising was on the order of 5 tons per square foot, hopefully low enough so that the ship would keep sliding down the ways.

We launched again on a Saturday, but this time with no ceremony and no guests. The triggers were released and the hull accelerated down the ways like a racehorse freed at the starting gate. Once Rayonier No. 2 became waterborne, it continued across False Creek, where it eventually collided with and broke off a piling dolphin used for mooring log booms. It was a beautiful launching! The ship was in the water and we had proven that we were professionals at our job. As for the dolphin, so what.

Well, mid-morning on the following Monday I got a call from a gentleman who advised me he was manager of the Bay Lumber Company across the creek from the shipyard. He noted that we had launched a barge on Saturday which had wiped out his dolphin. I admitted to being responsible, but said that to my knowledge that piling had stood for twenty years so I should only have to pay for its depreciated value. My friendly neighbour had different news and views, stating that the piling structure was only two months old. And if I had any doubts, I should call Dave Milavsky at Greenlees Pile Driving. Well, I know Milavsky, so I phoned him and asked.

Dave told me, "The guy's right, Arthur. We drove that pile cluster six weeks ago and it consisted of creosoted logs. That will cost you twice as much."

Sometimes you cannot win.

The *Rayonier No. 1* dumps its logs. When he was maintenance systems manager at Rivtow, Marc McAllister made a study of log barge dumps and discovered that the *Rivtow Hercules* moves 350 feet sideways in seven seconds when dumping, an indication of the impressive forces at work.

SHIPS OF STEEL

The 363-foot 10,000 dwt capacity self-loading log barge *Crown Zellerbach No.1* (later renamed *Seaspan Harvester*) dumping.

Self-Unloading Carriers

Great West #2 (Hull #143), Great West #3 (#144)

Prior to the 1960s, self-dumping barges were loaded with land-based equipment or with a floating crane. Later, barges were constructed and equipped with their own cranes. In 1964 Allied built *Great West #2* and *Great West #3* for Great West Towing & Salvage. These 262-foot self-unloading log carriers were designed by Robert Allan Ltd. Each was equipped with a single crane, and the log dumping procedure was radio controlled.

Self-Propelled, Self-Loading, Side-Dumping Log Barges

The final chapter in the development of specialized log barges came in the late 1970s, when the

first self-propelled, self-loading, side-dumping log barge was designed by Gerry Talbot. The advantage of a self-propelled vessel was that it could maintain a better sea speed than the towed barge, particularly in heavier weather, and thus was capable of quicker turnaround time. The Burrard-Yarrows group built two of these unique ships—the *Haida Monarch* and the *Haida Brave*—for Kingcome Navigation, a subsidiary of MacMillan Bloedel. The *Haida Monarch*, capable of carrying 15,000 tons of logs at a speed of 12 knots, was built at a cost of $8,200,000. The second vessel was ordered in August 1977 at a cost of $14,000,000 with delivery in the fall of 1979. Well over two decades later, both are still in operation on the BC coast.

CHAPTER 10

The Business of Fish and Fishing Vessels

"In the early 1970s it made sense to build a bigger and better boat with all the modern technology and comforts."

—*John Lenic*

From earliest times of human habitation on the Northwest Coast, fishing has been a vital activity. Beginning in the 1870s, entrepreneurs recognized the commercial value of the fishery resource. At the same time, improved technology for preserving salmon was leading to the establishment of salmon canneries up and down the coast. From 1900 to 1910, some eighty fish-packing plants were in operation. These early companies owned hundreds of open wooden boats 18 to 30 feet in length, each outfitted with oars and a lug sail. A fisherman was allotted a boat and gillnet, and fished for the cannery on a share basis. The open boats were towed from the cannery out to the fishing grounds by a small tug or launch and were towed back at the end of the opening.

By the first decade of the 1900s, the gasoline engine had been introduced and many fishermen owned their own "gas boats." There was a great demand for gasoline engines, and two Vancouver shops—Easthope and Vivian—built simple one- and two-cylinder models of 5 to 10 hp output. These engines were manufactured and sold until the early 1950s.

The 1920s were good economic times in BC and the 50- to 60-foot seine boat, which had been introduced just prior to World War I, was becoming very popular for fishing pilchards, salmon and herring. During the 1930s and 1940s, little new construction in the towing and fishing industries took place. So when wooden war surplus, diesel-powered vessels were put up for disposal by the Canadian and US governments, there was a rush to buy and convert them for fish packers, as they were not suitable for the particular functions of fishing boats.

The 1950s saw the introduction of small welded steel craft, first for use in the forest industry, later

Per Englund's trawler *Sunnfjord* bucking. The wooden vessel was built at Matsumoto Shipyards in 1957. Carl Stace-Smith photo

In heavy weather, a wave breaks over the bulwarks of the trawler *Freeport*. Carl Stace-Smith photo

in the fishing industry. By the end of the decade, steel had replaced wood for construction of larger fishing vessels. However, it wasn't until the mid-1970s that building fishing boats was a steady business for many BC coastal yards. Strong earnings from the emerging herring roe fishery led to steel seiners being produced in the mid-1970s to replace the old wooden fleet.

Aluminum construction of fish boats and work boats also commenced during this period, first with Matsumoto Shipyards, followed by Shore Boatbuilders and later other small yards. Like Sam Matsumoto, Al Renke of Shore Boats kept to simple, effective designs and produced fishing vessels at a rate of up to seven a year. Malcolm McLaren notes that the success of yards such as Matsumoto and Shore stems from the fact that they were headed up by people who were superb tradesmen as well as good businessmen.

Matsumoto, Pioneer in Building Aluminum Boats

Sam Matsumoto led the way in building aluminum fish boats in BC. Prior to World War II he worked with his family building wooden boats in Prince Rupert, but in wartime, when residents of Japanese descent were removed from the coast, he ended up in Nelson, still building wooden fishing boats. In 1946 Arthur McLaren was also in Nelson, finishing up the Kootenay Lake ferry *Anscomb*. Across the lake he spotted what looked like the stern of a Columbia River fishing boat sticking out of a boat-building shed. When he got the chance, he went over to investigate. "A little Japanese fellow asked if he could help me. I introduced myself and asked him if he was the one building fishing boats here? And are there fish in the lake?"

Sammy Matsumoto told Arthur that he was the builder and that the lake had fish, but he explained these boats were destined for BC Packers in Vancouver. He said that the deal worked out very well for CPR, who charged $700 to ship a boat to Vancouver. Very little was left over to pay for construction of the boat, complete with engines and all the other gear. "That was my introduction to Sammy Matsumoto," Arthur said later.

He told me his family had come from Prince Rupert, and he was one of the people kicked off the coast when the war broke out. Sammy's family moved "behind the mountains," as they say, and he ended up on Kootenay Lake building wooden fishing boats.

After the war Sammy got re-established on the coast and set up building wooden boats on the Dollarton Highway in North Van. In the early 1960s he got in with an aluminum company and signed an arrangement to build gillnet boats for the Alaskan fishery. He got an order for fifty-two boats and set up quite a production line. He did them all in one season!

Sam Matsumoto, owner of Matsumoto Shipyards, designers and builders.

Arthur again stopped by and reintroduced himself. He noticed that the people working at the Dollarton yard were wooden shipwrights by trade. But that was no problem because Sam Matsumoto had discovered that making an aluminum boat wasn't a lot different than doing a wooden boat. You could even cut the aluminum on a band saw, just like plywood.

> *I never really talked to Sammy about the difficulties of getting aluminum boats accepted over wooden ones. Initially they might have been more expensive. But over the years, as wages went up and the cost of wood went up, an aluminum boat became relatively cheaper. First, there were a lot less hours expended in building an aluminum boat over a wooden one. Second, they seemed to stand up well, and nobody had any great complaints about them. Sammy did very well with those boats.*

Al Renke, Shore Boatbuilders

Al Renke recalled that the first ten aluminum fish boats for Alaska were built by Marco Shipyards of Seattle; then Sam Matsumoto went in and later Shore Boats got involved. "At the time Sam got that big contract to produce gillnetters for Alaska, we were building small 38- to 40-footers for individual fishermen. The Alaskan fishery called for a lot of boats, so we ended up building over a hundred 32- and 33-foot salmon gillnetters for Bristol Bay service."

Al explained that at the time Bristol Bay fishermen would tie up directly to the packing plant dock and, one at a time, unload their fish. This procedure was not only slow, but it required boats to wait out the big tidal fluctuations—all of which took a significant chunk out of a 72-hour opening. Harold Deubenspeck, an Alaskan packing plant owner, set up a fish transfer barge equipped with four hydraulic cranes and built-in scales, so boats could unload regardless of the tide. He also followed up on Al Renke's suggestion of fitting a net into each fish hold before placing fish in the hold, so the fish could be lifted easily by hydraulic crane. Fishermen using the new system could offload in a fraction of the time and head right back to the grounds. It didn't take long for skeptics' opinions about the "tin cans," as aluminum boats were called, to change. Furthermore, the owners of twelve of the twenty boats delivered that first year were able to pay off their boats by the end of the first fishing season.

Canadian yards like Matsumoto and Shore Boats could sell gillnetters to the US because they were all under the Jones Act commercial limit of 5 gross tons measurement. But occasionally there was trouble. Al related the story of the time he'd taken twenty 32-foot boats up to Bristol Bay for delivery.

> *One Fisheries officer measured them, including the 4-inch length of the bow roller in his calculations, and announced in an official tone that he couldn't license them because they were 32 feet 4 inches long. Harold Deubenspeck looked at a nearby concrete breakwater and said, "Al, I guess we will just have to run them all into that wall—then they'll be 32 feet." Finally, after a long silence, the officer said, "No, don't do that," and he issued the licences. It all depended on who was doing the measuring—on one occasion, I had to bring the whole load of twenty gillnetters back down to Seattle for modifications.*

Canadian builders lost their Bristol Bay gillnetter

A typical aluminum seiner built by Shore Boatbuilders.

markets when fishermen increased the beam on their boats and exceeded the 5-ton limit.

In the 1970s, fibreglass hulls for fishing vessels also became popular, and some wooden boatbuilders changed over to either fibreglass or aluminum construction. Their facilities, tools and skills readily adapted to specializing in building fishing vessels under 40 feet in length. Small yards such as Raider Aluminum Ltd., Frostad Boat Works and Hi-Line Aluminum Welding began cranking out aluminum boats as fast as they could. These were followed later on by a mix of small ferries, crew boats and a few yachts. Aluminum yards on Vancouver Island started up a little later and are still producing a variety of smaller aluminum boats today.

BC developed a thriving aluminum building industry, Al notes, with people coming from all over the world to see how it was done.

In the 1970s, Alcan used to bring delegations from Australia to tour our shop. Back then there was some small aluminum boat construction happening in Australia. But Alcan had built a rolling mill there and was starting to produce marine alloy plates, so they were looking to develop a market. We had seiners under construction on both sides of the shop and those guys would just look at them in amazement. The Australians had no idea boats that big could be built out of aluminum. When the Australian government began to support aluminum development in earnest, all of a sudden their industry took off and they passed us by.

The construction costs of smaller aluminum vessels are competitive with those of their steel counterparts. For larger vessels, the arguments for using aluminum over steel are weight and maintenance. Bringing a vessel's weight down means you can drive it faster with less power. So even though aluminum costs more than steel, building out of aluminum may be worth the difference since aluminum weighs only a third of the weight of a similar steel vessel, and a boat made of marine-grade aluminum does not require any painting.

Today there are a number of companies building aluminum boats in BC. But as Arthur McLaren explained, Sammy Matsumoto was the first, and he did it in a big way.

Boom Time Construction

The pace of fish boat construction accelerated between 1972 and 1980. Fish prices took off and money became abundant—it was the perfect time to build a new boat. This boom also affected many of the medium-sized steel yards such as Manly, Allied and Bel-Aire. During this period of prosperity, many backyard builders produced one or two seiners.

Prior to this construction boom in fishing boats, many of the larger fishing vessels on the coast were in need of major repair, if not replacement. The naval architect firm of Cleaver & Walkingshaw produced innovative designs suitable for a long-awaited upgrading of the seine fishing fleet, drawing vessels that were attractive, practical to build and functional. When the Department of Fisheries and Oceans started restricting vessels to the net tonnage of the previous fishing licence and later overall length, the result was some creative vessel design that would minimize net tonnage and meet length requirements. It was this need to comply with bureaucratic requirements that ushered in the era of short, stubby boats. Unfortunately not all of these unique design solutions were favourable to a vessel's appearance or sea-keeping ability.

From Fishermen to Businessmen

In the 1996 issue of *The Vessel Owner*, John Lenic, president of the Fishing Vessel Owners Association, wrote a summary of changes in the fishing industry. He named three specific events in 1972 that altered the nature of BC's commercial salmon fishery and consequently the shipbuilding industry:

The modern seine fleet is the product of a number of changes that started in 1969 with the Davis Plan. All of a sudden we had a tangible and transferable privilege, which really wasn't worth all that much until the changes of 1972. Three things happened that year. The herring roe fishery began, the 200-mile limit was created and the Japanese discovered BC as a source of fish products. The booming Japanese economy and the shifting westward of the Japanese "high seas fleet," because of the 200-mile limit, created a demand for sockeye far more lucrative than the historical canned market. This resulted in another change. Fishermen began to earn more than just a living. Before this, the attraction of fishing was the lifestyle. When you bought a boat, you were only buying what you hoped was a well-paying job. Suddenly, we were making enough money to call ourselves businessmen.

Hey, if we had tax problems we could use business write-offs. It made sense to build a bigger and better boat with all of the modern technology and comforts. In 1973, central heat on a seiner was a big deal as were wheelhouse windows and doors that didn't leak when you started to buck. As the seventies rolled along the salmon runs began to increase. Now we had better catches together with higher prices for salmon and roe herring—prices that were going through the roof! More boats were built, more licences were made productive and our incomes were still on the upward curve. Some scored big on herring—others lucked out on sockeye. This was great—more tax problems!

A successful fishing season depends on two factors—getting fish and getting a good price for those fish. For example, during 1963, fishermen were paid 16 cents a pound for pink salmon. When corrected for inflation, 16 cents/lb. is the current equivalent of $1.60/lb. By 1980, pinks were garnering 45 cents/lb., with fishermen paid an additional 15 cents/lb. for packing! Those flush times were only a distant memory by 1999, with fishermen being paid as little as 19 cents/lb. for good quality pinks. These low fish prices, along with limited catch, brought drastic changes to the commercial salmon fishing industry of BC.

Just as fish boat construction expands when times, prices and catch are good, the opposite is also true. During the 1990s, low fish prices and limited catch affected the entire marine industry. To survive in these difficult times, provincial shipyards had to switch their focus from new builds to refit and repair work. The harsh reality for all domestic BC shipyards is that there are fewer and fewer commercial fish boats of any vintage working coastal waters.

Allied's Steel Fishing Vessels

Foursome 1 (Hull #198)

Allied built this 200-ton herring barge for John Haugan & Associates of Prince Rupert. The *Foursome 1* was a repeat of three hulls Allied had built for the Prince Rupert Fisherman's Co-op in 1956 and 1957. The original herring barges were designed for packing herring destined for reduction, a relatively low use-value process whereby herring was caught, then transferred to shore and ground up for fish meal. Beginning in the 1970s, the herring roe fishery started up in BC because Japanese buyers considered processed roe a delicacy and were willing to pay a lot of money for it.

Star Pacific (Hull #199), Island Rogue (#200)

Arthur described these two 55-foot steel drum seiners as "in-breakers" for a number of fishing vessels that Allied built during the fishing boom of the mid-1970s. The *Star Pacific* was built for Risto Kaltio; the *Island Rogue* was for Chris Peterson of Sointula and Ewan Macmillan. Ewan was the principal of the Cassiar Packing Company. Both seiners were in the classic style of wooden fishing vessels of the 1950s and '60s, with relatively low freeboard and a small house, in contrast to the new designs with semi-raised or raised fo'c'sles. Part of the reason for higher fish prices

The *PRFC II* (Hull #55), November 1956, one of three herring packing barges built for the Prince Rupert Fisherman's Co-op.

in the 1970s was an improvement in the quality of the delivered fish. The seine fleet adopted the use of the "champagne" system, consisting of large "wet holds" chilled with ice. When the salmon were placed in the hold, compressed air was bubbled from the bottom of the tank in order to circulate the ice water, cooling the fish quickly to minimize spoilage.

At the time, Arthur modified the compound curves on the bow of the *Star Pacific*, changing the shape to a more easily built conical development. "We also changed the look of the house, but somehow then it resembled a tugboat. So we left the superstructure of the second vessel looking more like Allan's original design. In fact, young Rob Allan came in and we had a frank discussion about changing their designs."

Both fishing vessels went on to have quite successful careers. The *Island Rogue* was owned by Chris Peterson until the 1990s. Arthur remembered: "Shortly after delivery the *Island Rogue* was travelling in coastal waters quite near the shore

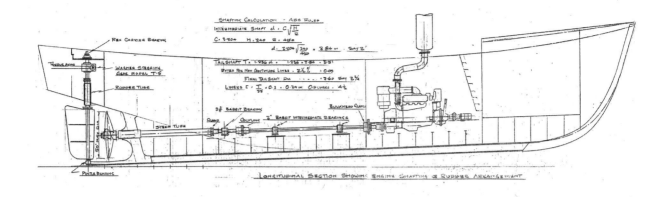

Arthur McLaren's construction drawing of the *Star Pacific* (Hull #199), a 55-foot steel drum seiner, showing engine, shafting and rudder arrangement.

and hit a rock. The impact put a big dent in one side of the hull and bent the beaver tail (net guard below the propeller). The boat was brought back to Vancouver and docked at Burrard Shipyard in Coal Harbour for repairs. It was then that young Chris Peterson, a great big fellow of Finnish descent, said to his partner and joint owner of the *Island Rogue*, 'Oh look, Ewan, your half of the boat has a dent in it!'"

Dual Venture (Hull #203), C. Venture No. 1 (#204)

These 76-foot drum seiners were built to Cleaver & Walkingshaw designs, Hull #203 for Nick Brajich and Hull #204 for Mario Carr, both independents who fished for the Cassiar Packing Company. The first launch was memorable, as Arthur recalled.

The C. Venture No. 1 *was all but empty, but we were eager to have the vessel in service soon after it was launched. So we filled the hydraulic oil tanks and some other tanks on the downward side of the launchways. Also, this design had a raised fo'c'sle on a 20-foot beam. Cleaver & Walkingshaw had done something similar on other vessels but these two were perhaps a little higher, and in true Allied tradition, everything was heavier or more robust on our vessel, which also contributed to top weight. Then we'd done some other things like move the batteries, which weighed close to half a ton, up to the fo'c'sle deck level.*

The launch was on a chilly February morning,

so the vessel's progress down the ways was slow, due to the cold launch grease and partly because we still had the ways set to the lower declivity we used to launch very large ships. When we let go, rather than gaining sufficient velocity to carry the boat into the water at the end, the vessel basically fell off the end of the side launchways. Upon launch, the C. Venture No. 1 *laid over until most people claimed they could see the keel. They also claimed that Arthur McLaren bit the end off his cigar!*

Slowly, slowly the boat righted, but it didn't become fully upright because of the unbalanced weights. Arthur said later:

The problem at the launching was aggravated because West Coast seiners are basically big breadboxes that have to be loaded to keep the full

The launching of the *C. Venture No. 1*, a 76-foot drum seiner. It was not a flawless launch.

stern in the water. When they are light (empty), they trim by the bow. When they do that, the shape of the waterplane is more like a wedge than a rectangle. One aspect of stability relates to the area of the waterplane, and the problem was that a wedge does not have near the waterplane of a rectangle. So when we launched the sister ship the next day, we filled the back ballast tanks so that when the boat passed the end of the ways, the boat was at a level trim instead of down by the head. We also had the transverse weights positioned so the vessel would come upright. I think everyone felt better after that launch. I certainly did!

With a launching such as the first one, both owners had misgivings. So after a brief fishing career both vessels were taken to Burrard Shipyard, where foreman Barry Piggot cut the sides off the seiners, pulled them out to a 24-foot beam and put in a new chine plate. As the 1990s ended, the

The C. *Venture No. 1* and *Dual Venture* running together after being widened.

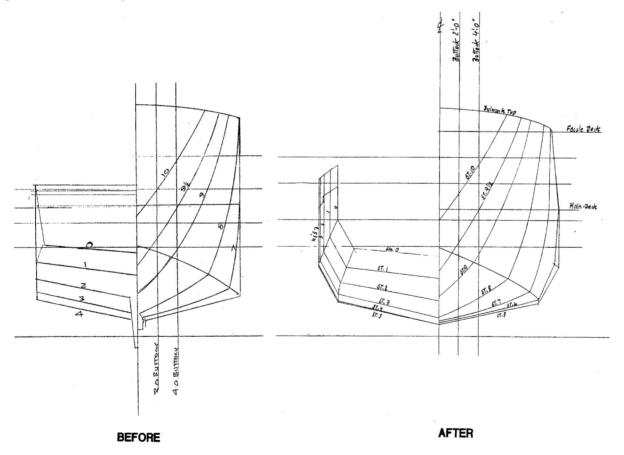

BEFORE

AFTER

The body plan of the C. *Venture No. 1* and the *Dual Venture*, before and after widening.

Dual *Venture* was operating in New Brunswick and *C. Venture No. 1* was active in BC waters.

Katrena Leslie (Hull #214), *Snow Drift* (#215), *Angela Lynn* (#216), *Bold Performance* (#218) *and Karenora* (#219), *Western Investor* (#223), *Ocean Invader* (#229)

The *Katrena Leslie* was the first in a series of seven attractive drum seiners that Allied built to a Cleaver & Walkingshaw design. These fishing boats were all made with a semi-raised fo'c'sle, which made for a racier looking vessel. They also had a clipper bow that had quite a bit of shape in it. Arthur regularly referred to this series of good-looking vessels as "the pretty ones." "They may not have packed as much," he said, "but they had nice bows, beautiful lines and a good turn of speed."

The *Katrena Leslie* was memorable for another reason. It was built for Mr. Alfred "Hutch" Hunt, who filled the boat with herring the first time he took it out fishing. At that time, the value of the fish he caught on that first trip was equivalent to the construction price of the seiner.

Arthur described the large master suite that took up half the main deck: "At first I thought that the owner was making himself very comfortable, but that wasn't really the case. Alfred is a Native fisherman from Fort Rupert who regularly brought his whole family along fishing. So the big master suite was actually a rumpus room to keep the kids out of the way while the crew were working. It made a great deal of sense."

Ocean Pearl (Hull #220)

At 110 feet, Allied's Hull #220 is one of the largest fishing vessels built in BC. The *Ocean Pearl* was built for blackcod fishermen Blair Pearl and Chris Hummel of the Gibsons area.

The 79-foot drum seiner *Katrena Leslie* (Hull #214), underway in fog in English Bay. It was built for Alfred "Hutch" Hunt in 1979.

The fishing vessel *Ocean Pearl* on sea trials.

The *Ocean Pearl* at sea, off Tasu, Moresby Island. The longline pot hauler hangs over the side.

Bruce Lenaker and other crew members clean their catch of blackcod before freezing it on board.

Blackcod had been fished for a long time on the BC coast, but previously the catch was just iced and brought to shore, often in less than pristine condition. Blair Pearl was one of the first to put high-quality freezing equipment on board a fishing vessel.

Catching the fish and fast-freezing them at sea after removing the head and entrails, meant that crews could wait until they had large quantities before coming back to port. Once ashore, this higher-quality frozen fish was packed into refrigerator containers and shipped direct to Tokyo. The two owners were able to catch enough fish and process them to a high standard to make a very good go of it.

Chris Hummel fell off a net loft ladder and died not many years after the *Ocean Pearl* was built. Blair Pearl worked his big boat until the mid-1990s, when it was sold to fish tuna in the Pacific Ocean, utilizing its 10,000-mile range.

It is interesting to note that most of the fishing vessels built in the boom of the 1970s were for salmon and herring, when prices were high. Ironically, some twenty years later these fisheries were in decline. But the lesser known fisheries like blackcod, halibut, trawl fish, prawns, shrimp, crab, geoduck and shellfish were doing all right.

Resolution II (Hull #221)

This hull, the only fishing vessel Allied built to a Cove-Dixon design, stood out as an example of Arthur's inventiveness. There was such a high demand for orders and such limited launchway space that this fishing boat was actually built inside the new drydock Allied had under construction, just so the company could take the order. After the drydock was launched, it was submerged and the *Resolution II* was launched. It was one of many fishing vessels with critical delivery dates: John LaPointe required his for the start of the herring season.

Tenacious (Hull #222)

This 70-foot seiner-dragger was built for Don Murray and Vigo Mark, both well-known BC fishermen. Some consider Vigo the granddaddy

of trawl fishing on this coast because many of the current generation of trawler fishermen who are not Europeans or east coast Canadians were in-breakers on one of Vigo's boats.

The *Tenacious* had a big B&W Alpha diesel engine and a controllable-pitch propeller. It also had large auxiliary engines for on-board refrigeration equipment. This seiner-dragger was similar to the semi-raised fo'c'sle vessels Allied had built earlier, but was much bigger, with a 24-foot beam and 13-foot depth. Malcolm McLaren dubbed it a big box. "Earlier vessels were built for speed but sometimes they had problems with not always having a high freeboard when fully loaded. Even when full of fish, this one had 2 feet of freeboard." *Tenacious* was lucky to make 9 knots, Malcolm added, but it was rumoured to be one of the best sea boats on the coast. Its big boxy shape was not at all like a classic hull design, but in heavy winds this fishing vessel would just ride up and down, hardly rolling at all. Those on board called it a very comfortable vessel.

Malcolm noted that Vigo Mark was one of those exceptionally hardworking fishermen who never let up. The *Tenacious* would regularly head out to its fishing grounds at Christmas time so the boat could deliver at the start of the new year, thereby getting a higher price for their catch because almost no one else was fishing. Once when Vigo was leaving Allied's yard on Christmas Eve to go fishing, someone asked him if he was going to miss Christmas. He told them, "No, we're taking a turkey with us."

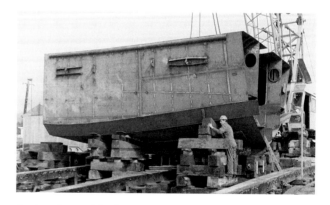

Setting the mid-body hull section of the fishing vessel *Tenacious* on the launchways.

The seiner–dragger *Tenacious* under construction. The aft hull unit is being lifted off the jig. Superintendent Barry Smith is in foreground.

The *Tenacious*, ready for launching.

Turning the aft hull unit.

Welding the overhead butt.

Vigo Mark, Don Murray and friends watching Sherril Murray break the bottle.

Queens Reach (Hull #224)

Queens Reach was launched in 1980 for its owner, John Legate. The vessel was built to take over a licence from the *Early Field*, an old-style wooden seiner. Previously, vessels taking over a Fisheries licence only had to match the original vessel's net tonnage, but by the time *Queens Reach* was built, the new fishing boat had to match both the tonnage and length of the original vessel. So *Queens Reach* was shorter than the other Allied vessels, with a 62-foot waterline rather than a 70-foot one.

This fishing vessel was different in another way. Most vessels were getting more and more sophisticated, with electric diesel generators that always had to be running and sophisticated electrical circuits. *Queens Reach* was a bit of a throwback in that it was strictly a DC vessel without 110 AC power, and it had an oil stove. Malcolm noted, "Many years later some of our customers told us it was perhaps one of the better vessels built during the period due to its simple machinery. Going back to basics minimized both construction and maintenance costs."

Ocean Achiever (Hull #246), E.J. Safarik (#247), Ocean Rebel (#252)

During the short boom of 1987–88, a number of trawlers and seiners were built. Shore Boats was quite busy, as was West Coast Manly and a number of other small coastal yards. Allied got an order for two vessels from Ocean Fisheries. The *Ocean Achiever* was a 65-foot combination seiner-dragger while the *E.J. Safarik*, named for the senior Mr. Safarik, founder of Ocean Fisheries, was a 70-foot dragger. A third sister ship, *Ocean Rebel*, was built in 1989.

The only problem, according to Arthur, was that they sold for far too little money. Both were designed in house by Chuck Ko and had fully raised fo'c'sles. They floated at the exact draft predicted and proved to be very good vessels. Both of these pocket draggers were considered to be relatively small at the time, but in hindsight it is clear they were just the right size boat. Once the trawl fishery went on quota, there was no great benefit to very large vessels with their higher operating costs. Smaller vessels can catch their share of a quota at a much lower cost.

Lifting the forward half of the *Queens Reach* (Hull #224) into position on the launchways. Note the main engine is already installed.

The *Queens Reach* seine fishing in Johnstone Strait, September 1993.

Launch of the pocket trawler *E.J. Safarik*, 1988.

CHAPTER 11

Ships for Offshore Oil and the Arctic

"I guess that sooner or later every shipyard chases a contract too hard, takes a gamble and has a catastrophe. Then you have to work even harder and try everything you can think of."

—*Arthur McLaren*

In the mid-1960s, British Columbia shipbuilders entered into the offshore oil exploration industry with the construction of the semi-submersible drilling platform *Sedco 135 F* at Victoria Machinery Depot and the building of two supply vessels by Allied Shipbuilders Ltd. At first they were employed in drilling off the west coast of Vancouver Island; later they were stationed in other parts of the world.

Offshore resource exploration requires massive purpose-built equipment. Early on, yards such as Allied, Bel-Aire and Mercer's built smaller supply ships. Then the sudden escalation of world crude oil prices in 1973 spurred the pursuit of offshore oil exploration. As drilling operations moved to the less hospitable waters of the North Sea and Arctic Ocean, the ships grew in size, power, sturdiness and complexity. Many were constructed in British Columbia for eastern Canadian owners. The 1970s were a buoyant decade for BC yards.

Offshore Vessels

Canadian Tide (Hull #157), Min Tide (#158)

Offshore oil supply vessels were originally developed to aid drilling operations and transport supplies to drill rigs in the Gulf of Mexico. These ships, affectionately known as "mud boats," were smaller and suited for work in calmer waters. The first offshore supply boats constructed in Canada were the *Canadian Tide* and *Min Tide*, both 165-foot supply vessels delivered in 1967 for Tidewater Marine Pacific Ltd., a Canadian subsidiary of a New Orleans company. Arthur recalled:

We built those two vessels at the same time that Victoria Machinery Depot was building a big drilling rig called the Sedco F. *It was a huge thing. I have an idea that by the time VMD finished it, they had a lot less money than what they started off with.*

Within a few weeks of finishing up the supply boats, I was asked to go over to Port Alberni, where they had towed this great big drilling rig. I had to straighten up a couple of things on one of our vessels. I got there by car and as I looked across the inlet, there was this huge rig sitting in the water alongside of our wee little supply boat. I remember thinking that we'd gotten $935,000 for building each supply boat and VMD didn't get much more than $10,000,000 for building this great big rig. Then I knew there was something *wrong. It was a case of we bid the right price and they didn't. It happens. After that launch VMD started building another vessel for Yorke, but about three-quarters into the rail car ferry* Doris Yorke *they gave up.*

Arthur and others from Allied attended a commissioning party hosted by Tidewater Marine Pacific at the Bayshore Inn, Coal Harbour, to celebrate taking over the vessels. George LaPorte, the boss at Tidewater, made a point of mentioning the fact that these were the most expensive vessels his company had ever had built. "I replied they were probably the best ones

they ever had, too!" Arthur commented some thirty years later. "And I think I was right—these ships were still running when their contemporaries weren't."

Sedco 135 F was enormous, as shown in this artist's drawing of the Sedco relative to the Empress Hotel in Victoria's inner harbour.

The Min Tide under construction, July 1966. The photo shows bottom plating and bulkheads.

IOS Supply Ships

Lady Joyce (Hull #180), Lady Lisbeth (#181), Lady Vivien (#182), Lady Jean (#183), Lady Alexandra (#184)

From 1971 to 1974, Allied worked on a series of five ships that could be classed as the first North Sea type vessels built in Vancouver. Hulls #180–184 were ordered by International Offshore Services (IOS) of Britain. Unfortunately, Allied's previous supply ship experience was with the lighter "mud boat" style ship, not the heavier, more complex supply ships required for drilling in the North Sea.

Arthur described the start of his yard's association with IOS:

The Canadian Tide on sea trials, March 17, 1967. This was the first offshore supply vessel built in Canada.

We saw a press article that said International Offshore Services was looking for a builder, so we answered the inquiry. We'd never dealt with people outside of North America. We submitted our proposal and the owner hummed and hawed and finally said they'd go with us. But they were

The oil drilling rig *Sedco 135 F* undergoing anchor trials off Victoria, attended by the *Min Tide* and *Gulf Joan*. At the time of building (the vessel was delivered May 1967), the *Sedco 135 F* was the largest semi-submersible oil drilling vessel in the world.

in a hurry so the contract stated we had to complete the ships within a two-year time allotment. These supply ships had to carry fuel oil, water, deck cargo and dry bulk cement powder out to the drill rigs; we'd had some cement experience building the cement barge Tsimshian Warrior *(Hull #174), but nothing as complex as these five vessels. We bid each one the same price, somewhere in the order of $1.5 million per ship—the biggest contract we'd ever had.*

Our offer was based on the owner's description, a brief outline arrangement of the ships, and an idea of what machinery they wanted to put in it. Unfortunately we did not have detailed specifications. The result was that we got into quite a bit of financial trouble on this job.

One problem was inflation: when Allied submitted its bid, wages were about $5 an hour, and by the time the work was done they had risen to $7.00—a 40 percent increase in just two years.

Also, I wouldn't say the project was at all well described. We'd based our bid on the successful Tidewater supply ships, but the IOS vessels were larger and far more complex. They had heavier scantlings, as well as incorporating multi-engine drives, controllable-pitch propellers and steering nozzles; there were numerous fuel tanks with lots of valves, for example, and a lot of auxiliary equipment we normally wouldn't put into a vessel. They were highly complex ships used to transport dry cement to the drilling rigs for drilling

Typical Canadian Westcoast Shipbuilding Wages
1949 - 1999

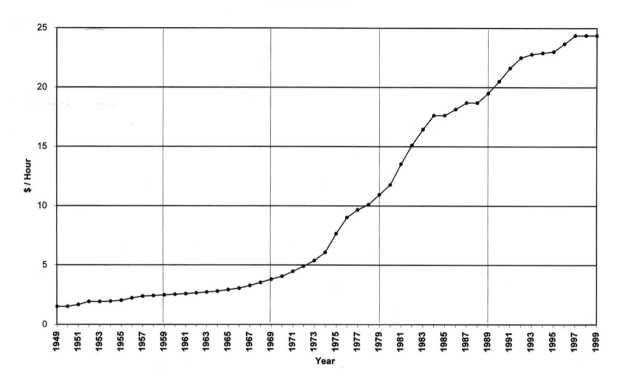

purposes, so they all had cement tanks built into the hull. The cement powder was in hoppers, with air blown in to make it flow down to conveyor belts and then to the unloading system. None of us appreciated the complexity of the cement system and we never did get proper pricing on it until the ships were finished.

Construction on the first vessel started in the summer of 1972, but we still hadn't delivered the Lady Joyce by the next summer. One problem was that we were still designing the first ship and settling details as we went along. There was a bigger problem—lack of money. Payment to the shipyard was made based on milestones such as launching, installation of engines, launching, completion, etc. We had to reach a major milestone in order to get a payment. Labour costs and inflation were eating away at any margins. Also purchases were costing more than anticipated.

By May of 1973 Allied simply could not pay what it owed to employees and suppliers. The company reported to IOS that it had run out of money. The owners met with Allied in Vancouver

and Allied's bank became involved.

The bank told us to finish the ship. They would meet the payroll, but they would not pay suppliers. Fortunately most suppliers kept on delivering but we were four to five months late in making their payments.

Despite the financial pressure of the IOS ships, Arthur managed to keep his wry sense of humour:

We had a memorable event with the first ship on sea trials. We had laid out a schedule of tests, but when we completed them the owner's representative wanted to do some other trials. These included running the vessel up to full speed in a maximum power condition and then putting the helm hard over. The result was that the propeller on one side got overloaded, stalling that engine, and the propeller on the other side was unloaded, ran far too fast and tripped out on overspeed. That manoeuvre left the Lady Joyce sitting dead in the middle of English Bay. Nothing running. Well, we didn't do that test on any future IOS ships.

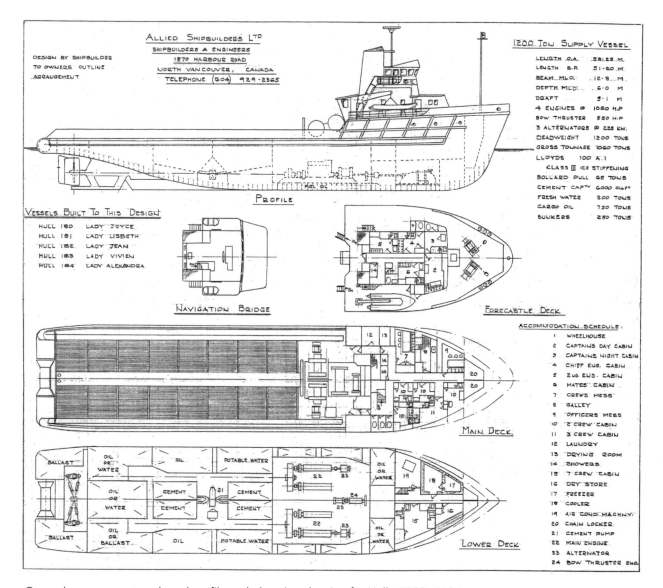

ALLIED SHIPBUILDERS LTD
SHIPBUILDERS & ENGINEERS
1870 HARBOUR ROAD
NORTH VANCOUVER, CANADA
TELEPHONE (604) 929-2365

DESIGN BY SHIPBUILDER
TO OWNERS OUTLINE
ARRANGEMENT

PROFILE

1200 TON SUPPLY VESSEL

LENGTH O.A.	58.28 M
LENGTH B.P.	51.20 M
BEAM MLD.	12.8 M
DEPTH MLD.	6.0 M
DRAFT	5.1 M
4 ENGINES @	1080 H.P
BOW THRUSTER	550 H.P
3 ALTERNATORS @	225 KW.
DEADWEIGHT	1200 TONS
GROSS TONNAGE	1060 TONS
LLOYDS	100 A.1
CLASS III ICE STIFFENING	
BOLLARD PULL	65 TONS
CEMENT CAP'TY	6000 CU.FT
FRESH WATER	200 TONS
CARGO OIL	750 TONS
BUNKERS	250 TONS

VESSELS BUILT TO THIS DESIGN

HULL 180	LADY JOYCE
HULL 181	LADY LISBETH
HULL 182	LADY JEAN
HULL 183	LADY VIVIEN
HULL 184	LADY ALEXANDRA

NAVIGATION BRIDGE

FORECASTLE DECK

MAIN DECK

LOWER DECK

ACCOMMODATION SCHEDULE:

1	WHEELHOUSE
2	CAPTAINS DAY CABIN
3	CAPTAINS NIGHT CABIN
4	CHIEF ENG. CABIN
5	2ND ENG. CABIN
6	MATES CABIN
7	CREWS MESS
8	GALLEY
9	OFFICERS MESS
10	2 CREW CABIN
11	3 CREW CABIN
12	LAUNDRY
13	DRYING ROOM
14	SHOWERS
15	7 CREW CABIN
16	DRY STORE
17	FREEZER
18	COOLER
19	AIR COND. MACHNY.
20	CHAIN LOCKER
21	CEMENT PUMP
22	MAIN ENGINE
23	ALTERNATOR
24	BOW THRUSTER ENG.

General arrangement, outboard profile and plan view drawing for Hulls #180–#184.

Aerial view of Allied's North Vancouver yard, showing the first two IOS ships on the ways. Hull sections for ships 3 and 4 are ready for erecting on the launchways.

Side launch of the *Lady Joyce*.

These ships were also equipped with bow thrusters, and the owner's rep wanted us to run a measured mile using only the bow thruster. So we did. I forget how many minutes it took, but it wasn't fast at a speed of 2 knots. Once completed, everybody said, "Well, don't bother doing it backwards."

Construction work on the second ship, the *Lady Lisbeth*, went faster, but by the summer of 1973 Arthur knew the company would have to try to renegotiate the contract.

We had two vessels launched but not entirely finished. Two more were on the ways and the last was in pieces throughout the yard. So several of us flew to Britain—our lawyer Ted Horsey, our accountant Peter Speer, Les Coward and myself. We met with Paul Negra, the managing director of IOS. Basically, International Offshore Services was a subsidiary of the Peninsular and Oriental Steam Navigation Company and didn't have much capital itself. The bank held possession, so the task was to try to renegotiate a contract to complete the vessels. A lot of money had already been paid out and IOS had a big investment in the ships— too much investment to walk away from. So we were all in a bad way.

If IOS stopped payments and work was cancelled, Allied would go into receivership. The bank was the only secured creditor, so "the ships would sit there." The owners would be entitled to come in and finish them, but at this point the ships were so far along that IOS had little choice but to salvage the job by paying more money.

Ted Horsey and Peter Speer were very professional and commanded the respect of the IOS people. They did a good job of pointing out where everybody stood and explaining the benefits of having Allied complete the contract. It would cost IOS more money to finish the ships themselves than to pay Allied additional money to have us do the work. Fortunately we all hung in there and five excellent supply ships were completed.

These vessels were built under the subsidy program, which was at 17 percent by then. At first the federal government was very shy about coming up with their share of the increase—the price per ship went from about $1.5 million to $2.1 million. However, Mr. Graham Lockheed and the people at the Department of Industry were reasonable to deal with, and eventually they agreed to increase the subsidy in accordance with the increase of the contract price.

We were able to complete the third, fourth and fifth vessels in record time. So we got the whole thing cleaned up in a space of less than twenty-four months, which is pretty good for building five such complex vessels. Fortunately we had Bill Arthur return to Allied from our repair yard on Georgia Street. He was legendary in his ability to push jobs through to completion. He did that by example— he set incredibly high standards of work and inspired people to work hard by going at it so hard himself.

At the time the five IOS vessels were built, they were among the most sophisticated supply ships in the world.

One technical problem I particularly remember was the trouble we had controlling the main

Within two hours after the launch of the *Lady Joyce*, the bow was fitted to the sister ship, *Lady Lisbeth*.

engines. There were four engines coupled up to two propeller shafts, with an electrical generator connected to the front of each inboard main engine. The engines were supposed to share the load equally between them, but it was difficult to share the load with one taking the propeller and generator and the other only the propeller. We got in touch with the company who supplied the system, and they sent their people out from Colorado, but they couldn't make it work either and finally gave up in disgust.

Finally we got ahold of John Bjorknis of Prime Mover Controls in Vancouver. He knew about sophisticated power controls and straightened the whole thing up for us so that it worked beautifully. It was the common case where the local fellow knew a lot more than the experts from far away. In the course of doing all these things, we did let the first two ships sail away from Vancouver with load control problems, so we had to go down to the Panama Canal to put things right. That cost money and took time, too.

Allied got into financial difficulties on the IOS job because of inflation. We also underbid because we did not properly consider and obtain pricing for all of the equipment that had to be purchased. As well it seemed that every day the owners came up with new ideas of how they wanted the ship built, even though we said that wasn't what the contract allowed for. I guess that's a common problem in shipbuilding. Many people think the naval architect's nice picture is the final design, and the shipyard only has to go ahead and build it. But it's far more complicated than that—the shipbuilder has to figure out the details of the construction. It doesn't go well if the owner is continually bringing up new ideas or changing the plans.

There was a sentimental side to the IOS saga, as Arthur described:

When I saw they were naming all their vessels Lady this and Lady that and Lady the next thing, I told the company rep that I'd like to have a chance to name one of the boats. The fellow told me it was usually the owner's privilege to name the vessel. "Oh, I quite appreciate that, but in this particular case I would like to name one of the vessels Lady Alexandra." He wanted to know why. I explained that my father's company, Coaster Construction of Montrose, Scotland, had built the original Lady Alexandra for Union Steamships out of Vancouver. I had seen it launched when I was just four years old and I thought it would be very nice to do the reverse–build a Lady Alexandra in Vancouver that was going to Dundee, which isn't far away from Montrose. The company rep told me that sounded reasonable and he'd think about it.

That was the last I heard. So by the time we got down to the final vessel, I thought he'd forgotten about it. But one day he came up to me and said, "By the way, this is the one you named. Lady Alexandra, you wanted to call it?" I confirmed the name and that was that. The rule I made was in order to be on the platform at the 1974 launch for this new vessel, you had to have attended the launching of the first Lady Alexandra in 1924. So there was myself, my brother and sister, who were in a pram the first time around, Howard Leeming's wife Jean, who went to school with me in Montrose and whose father came to Vancouver on the Lady Cynthia, and my mother, who broke a bottle and named the vessel. She certainly remembered the launch of the original Lady Alexandra in Montrose and thought this was just great.

The launch of the Lady Alexandra.

There was other work available at this time, which wouldn't have gotten us into the financial trouble that we had with the IOS vessels. But I guess that sooner or later every shipyard chases a contract too hard, takes a gamble and has a catastrophe. Then you have to work even harder and try everything you can think of.

Fortunately, soon after we secured an order to build a couple of thruster barges for Northern Construction and that gave the yard just enough money to start life over again. The IOS job almost took us under. We had a very tight time after that.

In shipbuilding there are two critical issues. The first is the challenge of building safe, efficient ships that can do their jobs. The second is that vessels have to be bid and built at a price that enables the yard to pay its employees and suppliers. A good job makes a profit that can be reinvested in equipment and facilities or cover other jobs that are not so profitable.

Staying financially solvent while building ships requires carefully thought-out bids and a fair degree of constancy in wages, supply costs, taxes, legislation and company operations. All seven of Allied's early supply vessels were well-built ships, but the financial impact of the two profitable

The launch party for Allied Shipbuilders' *Lady Alexandra*.

Tidewater ships was extremely different from that of the subsequent five IOS vessels, which almost bankrupted the company.

Ice Class Vessels

In the mid-1970s, the first tugs and supply vessels were produced for offshore oil drilling operations in the western Arctic Ocean. The Arctic Pollution Prevention Regulations introduced by the Canadian government specified hull construction standards to meet Arctic requirements and defined vessels as Class I, Class II, Class III, etc., based on the vessel's ability to steam continuously through 1 foot, 2 feet, 3 feet, etc. of ice.

Dome Petroleum ordered the first Ice Class supply vessels in 1974—one each from four BC shipyards. The first ship was delivered in 1975 and the other three in 1976. Oil company icebreakers were a fraction of the price of government icebreakers of similar capability. The "no frills" private sector vessels were built to get the job done, as compared to the government vessels, dubbed "floating hotels." The vessels working in Arctic waters were more powerful than any previous supply ships built in the province, many of them utilizing new, effective ways of breaking ice.

Canmar Supplier (Hull #192)

If the five IOS supply ships caused a bleak period for Allied, the mood improved with the yard's first

Arthur McLaren's mother, Eliza Louisa, at the launch of the second *Lady Alexandra*.

The *Canmar Supplier* under construction.

Pipefitting crew for *Canmar Supplier* on the foredeck.

View of the engine room in the *Canmar Supplier*.

Ice Class supply ship. The *Canmar Supplier* was a shipbuilder's dream—one of those extremely successful projects finished within budget and on time. It gave Allied Shipbuilders a high level of prestige, and positioned the yard for more Arctic work.

All the construction experience the yard had gained with the five IOS vessels proved to be invaluable when the yard began work on this complex icebreaker. That was a good thing, because the Arctic ships all had crucial delivery dates: vessels had to be ready to go to work as soon as the ice cleared off Point Barrow. Jim McLaren commented that the challenge and thrill of building the ship was in meeting the deadline. Once Allied's ships were launched and trialled, they all went to work and didn't come back for changes or bugs to work out. "You never heard from the icebreakers again," Jim said. "They just went to work immediately and that was it."

The 210-foot *Canmar Supplier* was one of four identical supply vessels that were built concurrently in Vancouver to a Robert Allan design. Dome ordered one ship from each of four yards—Allied,

Vito, Burrard Dry Dock and Yarrows. Like Allied, Bel-Aire and Mercer's had already built some supply vessels, but at this time Vito, Burrard and Yarrows had little experience with such ships. The Allied and Vito ships were built with Polar-Nohab engines and nozzles. The other two had EMD engines and no propeller nozzles. There were many other supply vessels in the world, but these were pretty much the first of the Ice Class supply ships.

Canmar (Canadian Marine Drilling), a subsidiary of Dome Petroleum, initially operated one drilling ship in the Canadian Arctic Ocean. The four supply vessels were used to set the anchors for the drilling rig and to carry consumables such as drill pipe, fresh water, diesel fuel and cement

Icebreaker *Canmar Supplier* at work in the Beaufort Sea.

powder to the ship from Tuktoyaktuk. Where the IOS vessels had carried cement powder in large hull tanks, the *Canmar Supplier* used a simpler system: cylindrical tanks were mounted vertically and the cement powder was blown out with pressurized air.

Jim noted:

Ours was the only ship of the four that was delivered on time and able to round Point Barrow in 1975. The other three were delivered later and couldn't get into the Arctic until the following summer. We had gained a lot of experience building the sophisticated IOS supply ships so we identified and solved construction problems on the Canmar ship. These techniques were then applied to the three sister ships. As a result, when we tendered projects we were known as people who could do the work and get it out on time.

All of that helped to put Allied Shipbuilders back on a sound financial footing.

The Arctic Tugs

Arctic Taglu (Hull #194), *Arctic Hooper* (#195)

Allied got the contracts for building the *Arctic Taglu* and the *Arctic Hooper* on December 31, 1975, after scrambling to get the subsidy application submitted by the end of the year. It was a clear case of catching the shipbuilding subsidy before it dropped another percent on January 1. Delivery was scheduled for July 1976.

These 110-foot tugs were designed by Dick Walkingshaw and Bill Cleaver with high wheelhouses so that crewmen could see over the top of an icebreaking pusher barge out in front. It was the first time Allied had built vessels designed by the new firm of Cleaver & Walkingshaw. "They were reasonable people to work with," Arthur said. "All you had to do was suggest how you wanted to do something and they accommodated.

The water route from southwestern BC to the rivers of Canada's northwest is many times longer than the land route.

They also got drawings out in a hurry, even if it meant working all weekend. Our relationship with C & W was different than with other naval architects in that they handled the general arrangement and structure of a vessel, and more importantly they created the right ship concept to do the job." Allied followed up with the mechanical, electrical and piping details, including layout and installation of machinery, shafting, stern tubes, electrical wiring and piping systems.

According to Jim McLaren, credit for the success of these Arctic jobs belongs to Arthur. "He was the driving force behind it all. Years later Chuck Ko was working with Arthur and they were a formidable team. They produced more drawings than an office of naval architects. It was just awesome! Everything fit and worked. In between pencil strokes, Arthur would be giving instructions to Guenter Christophersen and doing the review of the construction assembly."

Both of these Arctic tugs were designed to do all kinds of work, including hauling big, specially built barges for building up islands for oil drill rigs. Each barge hauled approximately 2,000 tons of sand and it split in the middle in order to drop its load down exactly where it was needed.

Turning the bow unit of the *Arctic Taglu*.

Shipbuilding contracts often provided for "milestone payments" when certain targets were met, such as launching, delivery and installation of the main engines. Arthur McLaren would build the hull section designed to support the engines first, then set the engines in place; at this point the project would qualify for a significant payment.

Hooking up the lift slings on the bow unit of the *Arctic Taglu*. Left to right: George MacPherson, Ray Aikia, shipyard superintendent Barry G. Smith.

The *Arctic Taglu* and the *Arctic Hooper* on sea trials. Commercial Illustrators photo.

Tug and barge stopped in ice.

The *Arctic Taglu*, in ice with the ice-breaking barge *Arctic Tarsuit*.

SHIPS OF STEEL

Canmar Tugger (Hull #231), Canmar Widgeon (#232), Canmar Teal (#233)

By the early 1980s, offshore oil exploration activity in the western Canadian Arctic was on the rise. Eleven tugs and supply vessels built to Arctic Class II or IV standards and ranging in size from 800 to 4,200 gross tons were delivered by BC yards. In addition to the Arctic Ice Class vessels, two Husky Oil supply vessels were constructed in Vancouver area yards for service on the east coast of Canada.

The order for the *Canmar Tugger* came in December 1980, just as the fishing vessel boom ended. This 116-foot Ice Class tug was basically a sister ship to the *Arctic Taglu* and *Arctic Hooper* that Allied had built four years earlier, although this vessel was ordered with a double bottom. "We enjoyed all our jobs for Canmar," Malcolm McLaren said later, although there was some dispute with Captain Jan Hurt over the price for the double bottom. When Captain Hurt completed overseeing the work at Allied, he stood by the

The *Canmar Tugger*'s steel deckhouse, with windows, ladders and other outfit all complete, is lifted into position in one piece.

The *Canmar Tugger* at rest in ice.

Left to right: *Canmar Teal, Canmar Widgeon* and *Canmar Tugger* on Allied's side launchways.

construction of the *Robert Lemeur* at Burrard Dry Dock. During that time, when Captain Hurt, Jim, Malcolm and their wives met for dinner, Malcolm recalled, "Captain Hurt admitted that although he might have complained about Allied's pricing, he later realized he had been with the sheep and now he was with the wolves!"

After the tug was underway, Canmar ordered two 130-foot standby vessels, the *Canmar Widgeon* and the *Canmar Teal*. Arthur remembered them as simple, inexpensive work boats, each having a clear aft deck. They were intended to stand by the oil drilling rig, as required by regulations. In case of an emergency on the rig, they could remove crew. Thus, these small boats would free up the larger, expensive icebreakers to transport supplies. That spring all three vessels were in a row on the launchways.

The Spoon-Shaped Bow

Between 1976 and 1984, Canadian icebreakers built for the private sector led the world in innovative ship design. Ben Johansson, director of Canmar's Arctic Technology Department, detailed those developments in a paper delivered at the 1994 SNAME Icetech Conference. He noted that the story actually goes back to the turn of the last century, when ice-breaking bow forms had split into two distinctly different types. The dominant shape was the wedge-shaped bow and sharp stem of sea-going icebreakers. Blunt bows were relegated to ships breaking level ice in sheltered areas.

This distinction was so pervasive that every sea-going icebreaker built between 1901 and 1979

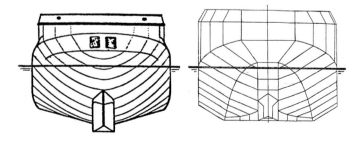

Left: Body plan showing the unconventional spoon bow of the *Canmar Kigoriak*, right; the similar but hard-chined spoon bow of icebreakers built for Arctic Transportation Ltd.

(those intended to operate in ridges and rubble as well as in level ice) had a distinct wedge-shaped bow and a sharp stem. The large size, power and exotic polar work environment of these sea-going icebreakers meant they easily dominated the news as well as technical conferences—so much so that their bow form became known as a "conventional" or "classic" ice-breaking bow. In contrast, by the early 1970s, blunt (spoon) bows were well established, but only for ships working in first-year ice in sheltered areas such as rivers. It wasn't until 1979 that a spoon bow was finally introduced on sea-going icebreakers.

In 1977 Canmar applied for a patent adapting the spoon-shaped bow for use on a large, single-screw sea-going icebreaker. Their plan was to combine the spoon-shaped bow that Weedermann had first patented in 1892 with an abrupt narrowing of the aft section of the ship. Because the maximum beam occurred in the forward third of the ship, a wide channel was created that reduced friction along the ship's sides and facilitated manoeuvring in solid ice with the box-shaped midbody.

The *Canmar Kigoriak* was delivered in 1979, the first twentieth-century sea-going icebreaker to be equipped with a spoon-shaped bow. The vessel's successful operation in ice ridges and rubble was copied on many other Canadian Beaufort Sea icebreakers built in the early 1980s. Certainly a ship equipped with a wedge-shaped bow could break ice, but a spoon-shaped bow allowed a ship to go right up onto the ice, breaking the ice with its weight. To prevent the ship from coming out of the water entirely, a large stop or ice knife was fitted low on the centreline in the forward quarter of the vessel.

Beginning in 1982, Allied built four ice-breaking ships for Arctic Transportation Ltd. The *Arctic Nanook*, *Arctic Nutsukpok*, *Arctic Nanabush* and *Arctic Ivik* were all equipped with the "new" blunt spoon bows, but these were constructed out of flat plates in order to reduce costs. The flat planes presented no problem: these ships functionally broke ice just like a curved spoon-shaped bow.

Dome Petroleum's ship *Canmar Kigoriak*, a Class 4 icebreaker, was the first icebreaker to operate year-round in the North American Arctic.

Arctic Nutsukpok (Hull #235), *Arctic Nanook* (#236)

In 1981 the price of oil was still high and there was concern that the world's oil supply would run out. Imperial Oil had a steel caisson built in Japan for use in oil drilling in the Arctic Ocean. Basically it was a giant donut made out of steel that was to be landed on a big dredged berm. Its steel sides would deflect and break ice that drifted onto it. After the caisson was in place, the centre was filled with sand to make a structure that ice could not push away.

Arctic Transportation Ltd. had three ships built to support this drilling island. Two were 154-foot Class II ice-breaking anchor handling tugs, Allied's hulls #235 and #236. Vancouver Shipyards built the third vessel, the *Arctic Ubleri-ak*, which was a lesser Ice Class. The *Nanook* and *Nutsukpok* were started in November 1981 and delivered in July 1982—on time and on budget. Propulsion power was 6,200 hp each. Arthur

The spoon bow of Allied's Hull #235, *Arctic Nutsukpok*.

Arctic Nanook under construction, winter 1982.

The *Arctic Nutsukpok* in light ice.

Arctic Nutsukpok in the Arctic Ocean, August 1982.

The *Arctic Nanook* and *Arctic Nutsukpok* pulling a floating steel caisson. To be used as a drilling island, the steel caisson was sunk upon an underwater dredged berm and the centre was backfilled with dredged material. The steel sides of the caisson were designed to resist the pressure of the Arctic ice.

explained, "This bow was simpler to build and shaped so that it was a more effective ice-breaking bow. It was designed so the ship could climb way up on the ice and use the weight of the ship to break the ice underneath."

Malcolm McLaren described an incident the following year, when the *Arctic Ubleriak* got a little too close to the caisson and hit a sharp edge, which punctured the hull through to the engine room. "This ship didn't have the double bottom subdivision of our Class II icebreakers, and before the crew realized what was going on, the engine room filled with water. The ship filled, foundered

and sank. There were memorable pictures taken of the crew stepping off the *Arctic Ubleriak* with their suitcases and getting onto one of our icebreakers, which was standing by." The ship was later recovered, although only a few components were usable.

A windy summer day in the Beaufort Sea.

Lowering the starboard main engine into the *Arctic Nanabush*.

Marine engineer Gary Shook tending to a main engine in the *Arctic Nanook*.

Arctic Nanabush (Hull #242)

After the *Arctic Ubleriak* sank, the underwriters in the London market paid out the insurance money quickly, enough so that in 1983 Arctic Transportation ordered the *Arctic Nanabush*. It was basically the same design as Hulls #235 and #236, which had been successful, but it had a much larger superstructure to house additional crew for surveying work. The *Nanabush* was also more powerful than the earlier vessels, having B&W Alpha main engines of 2 x 3,600 hp. This 154-foot anchor handling/survey vessel was delivered in July 1984.

Arctic Ivik (Hull #243)

In December 1984 Arctic Transportation put a new 1,500-dwt ice-breaking supply ship out for tender. Allied went after the job, bidding not only against local yards but against Japanese companies

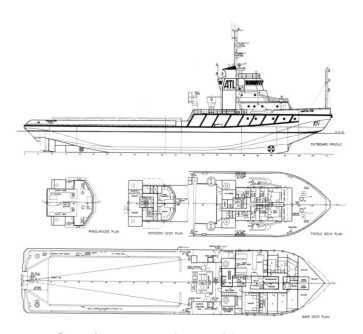

General arrangement drawing of the *Arctic Ivik*.

The *Arctic Ivik* just before delivery, with the outfitting crew who completed the ship.

as well. Malcolm explained, "At that period the federal shipbuilding subsidy was down to 9 percent and was slated to be removed entirely midway through 1985. It was clear that if we couldn't get the subsidy for this ship, we might lose the order to Japan."

Arthur and Jim McLaren and John O'Connell went to Ottawa, where their MP Chuck Cook helped steer the discussion through the minister of industry. The federal government told them that they could never get a vessel that big built in time for July and that the subsidy would be removed on June 30, so there was no use talking. "It took some negotiation," Malcolm said, "but eventually the federal government was convinced that it was indeed possible to build ships in this country in six months, provided that the federal government shipbuilding departments weren't involved."

Allied wanted an agreement that if they didn't get it done by June 30, they would get the subsidy on all the work done up until that date. But in order to qualify, the ship had to be registered. And in order to have it registered, it had to be afloat and complete.

Allied won the bid, and the *Arctic Ivik* was designed in-house. Arthur, who was very active in 1985, tutored Chuck Ko with this work. Dick Walkingshaw provided instruction on the hull form. The proposed Cleaver & Walkingshaw design had the engines midships and bulk tanks forward and aft. Allied built a ship very similar to the earlier ATL icebreakers but with all the tanks aft of the engine room. Although there was some disagreement about the layout, Allied went ahead with their own idea.

The first steel was cut on January 2, 1985, and the ship was launched by the end of June. Malcolm said later:

We went on sea trials, then came back and took the main reduction gears apart and changed the ratio—a big job in itself. Then we returned to sea trials and showed that the ship made an 80-ton bollard pull, as per the contract requirement. In the third week of July the ship sailed to the Arctic,

The *Arctic Ivik*, running in new ice. Ranson Photographers Ltd.

The End of the Arctic Boom

Innovative thinking resulted in BC shipyards producing the world's largest fleet of private sector icebreakers between 1976 and 1985. Alas, the offshore oil exploration boom, which began with the escalation of oil prices in 1973, did not last. When oil prices plummeted in the mid-1980s, the domestic market for specialized icebreakers evaporated, along with the hopes and fortunes of many BC shipyards. Within ten years these Arctic vessels had all been removed from western Arctic waters. With the exception of the *Terry Fox*, which works in eastern Canada for the Coast Guard, and its sister ship *Kalvik*, which was bought by Fednav of Montreal, all were sold for service elsewhere around the world.

where it worked continuously for some five years.

Building a ship that big in six months is an accomplishment anywhere. The difference between a Canadian yard and a Japanese yard is a Japanese yard probably would have taken three to four months to design the ship and then built it in three months. We started building immediately. In fact, the forward accommodation and the engine room were under construction before the final lines were established for the stern. We knew quite specifically the size of the propellers and we knew within 5 to 10 feet of length how to make the ship balance. If there had been a problem we would just have lengthened it a bit, but it worked out very well. It handled the full deadweight specified at the design draft.

After coming out of the Arctic, the *Ivik* was chartered by the Canadian Coast Guard for west coast and Arctic work. It then went to the North Sea. Later it was bought and converted in England to a seismic survey vessel by fully enclosing the aft deck in steel.

The *Kalvik*, built by Yarrows, Victoria. This Ice Class IV icebreaker was the sister ship to the *Terry Fox*, built at the Burrard Dry Dock site in North Vancouver.

CHAPTER 12

Slow Times

"If building ships has become simpler, I think that the business of building ships has become far more complex."
—*Arthur McLaren*

Shipyard workers know firsthand the boom-or-bust cycle that characterizes their industry. However, a decade and a half after the dramatic decline in new construction that began in the mid-1980s, there has been no substantial reversal. During those years the jubilation that accompanied the launch of a new ship was tempered by the sobering knowledge that there was nothing on the order books to take its place.

By the close of the 1990s, demand for new private sector ships was low all across Canada. The once-mighty fishing and logging industries of the west coast were cutting back. Furthermore, commercial vessels that once had an anticipated lifespan of twenty years were going strong at forty years of age, whether they were ferries, tugs, log barges or fishing vessels.

The situation in this country has been likened to that of sailors on a sinking ship with too few life rafts to save everybody. Eastern and western yards squabble over the few federal contracts like hungry dogs snapping over a single bone. And all of the big naval contracts of the 1980s and '90s went to the eastern yards, reflecting the focus of political power in Canada. As Arthur McLaren noted,

"Now every little job that comes along, we cut each other's throats for it. And it's not how much money you can make, it's how little you can lose."

Those few new build contracts that did materialize were often lured away from Canadian shipyards by foreign countries with considerably lower wages and other costs. Many maritime countries in similar situations consider shipbuilding an integral part of their national economic program and have come up with various strategies to combat cut-rate competition. For example, the European Community actively subsidizes its industry, and the USA restricts commercial shipping to US-built vessels.

Without supportive federal policy, Canadian shipyards simply cannot compete against predatory practices of other countries. As a result, at the start of the new millennium BC's remaining commercial shipyards face a challenge as great as any the industry has ever contemplated. In 1980 Canada had sixty-nine shipyards capable of new construction. By 1986 the number of big yards had fallen to twenty. Hand in hand with yard closures is the loss of an experienced workforce. If the specialized skills and expertise of the industry's aging workforce are not replaced, Canada will surely lose its capacity to build commercial ships—a strange predicament for a maritime nation.

The Price of Politics

It used to be that a shipyard that built good ships could be assured that more contracts would follow. But in the late 1990s, success in the shipbuilding industry was no longer that simple. Succeeding—or even just staying afloat—was based on factors far outside any one yard's control.

For example, the adoption of the Canada–US Free Trade Agreement delivered a powerful blow to Canadian shipbuilders. The FTA eliminated duties on US-built vessels entering Canada, but the reverse is not true: US shipbuilders have the Jones Act, which takes precedence over the FTA and thereby protects American maritime commerce. Passed in 1920, the law says that any vessel trading between US ports must be built in an American shipyard, registered in the US and crewed by Americans. Larger Canadian-built commercial vessels, new or used, may not be imported to work in US waters. The Jones Act, coupled with the Free Trade Agreement, have set up a one-way street that benefits US shipbuilders and sucks the economic life out of Canadian ones.

If cross-border politics clobbered the large commercial shipyards in Canada, such was not the case for companies willing to specialize in the booming luxury yacht market. Beginning in the early 1990s, the repeal of the US "luxury tax" led to a boom in Canadian luxury boat building for the US market. This change was a significant incentive for these specialized Canadian yards, where the sales ticket on a large fibreglass yacht starts at a million dollars.

Other Roadblocks to Recovery

Needing to build a new ship is one thing; financing it is quite another issue. Several years ago Lucille Johnstone, an executive from the tug and barge business, questioned how any towing companies could afford to renew their barge fleets. She noted that the existing barges were built for relatively low cost, when Canadian shipbuilding wages were still $5 an hour. Since then wages have risen significantly, but the earning power of barges has not kept pace. The good news is that the demand for coastal towing and freight is growing, and recent studies suggest that moving freight by water is not only economical, it alleviates traffic congestion on roads as well. Nonetheless, Lucille wonders how the towing industry can afford to justify the capital costs to renew their fleets.

These arguments are nothing new. A presentation to the federal government by the Canadian Shipbuilding and Ship Repairing Association in August 1944 included the following catechism:

> *Canada has a long and glorious record in the history of shipbuilding, ship-owning and seafaring. It can build ships and breed sailors. It is a nation of extensive sea-washed coasts on both oceans; it borders the greatest inland seas in the world; its domain boasts of over three hundred ports; its coastal and overseas trade is enormous and its diplomatic and commercial ties are extending throughout the globe. When the war ends, will Canada's navy dwindle to the status of a coast guard service; will its merchant marine be reduced and retire from ocean trading to purely domestic freighting, most of it in summer months; will the tens of thousands of young Canadians now at sea in Navy and Merchant Marine return after the war to the farm, office, factory, machine shop, because there are no ships in which they might continue their careers; will the grass grow once more in Canadian shipyards and the men who drove rivets, welded plates, shaped frames, turned and fitted, caulked and rigged, and exhibited their many skills in the fabrication of the most intricate task in the world—the building of a modern steel ship—be allowed to drift back to wherever they can find a job?*

Today, much that we do or consume still depends on the "old" production-based economy. British

Columbians travel on ferries. They live in homes built of materials often delivered by water. Dinner may be seafood, caught with the aid of fishing boats that are built and/or repaired at provincial yards. In their offices and schools they work with computers and fax machines and cellular phones, most of which have been imported on ships. Their reports, contracts, books, newspapers and other communications are printed on paper, manufactured with the aid of fleets of tugs and barges. They drive cars, some of which are imported by ship. For those who live on a coastal island community, even fuel is brought to them by tug and barge. The new high-tech world has not changed these daily facts of life for British Columbians.

Canada is still a maritime nation, dependent on marine businesses and vessels to move goods within our borders and beyond. Furthermore, Canadians have a growing reliance on the development of offshore energy projects, all of which require marine equipment, vessel technology and services. Certainly it makes sense to invest in that growth, before the facilities and expertise have disappeared.

Today Allied and the few remaining commercial yards in BC are basically ship repairers who occasionally build vessels. Some hope that this downturn is like that of the 1930s, when there was a long spell of no new contracts but eventually business picked up and the shipbuilding industry sprang back. "Of course we all hope that will happen," Malcolm McLaren said in late 1999. "But the other possibility is that the loss of skills and infrastructure will be so complete that the ability of Canadian yards to build new ships will be lost permanently."

Allied Vessels During the Slow Times

Floating Drydock (Hull #244)

From the mid-1980s to the present day, provincial yards have seen very little new commercial construction. Arthur McLaren characterized it as "an ongoing period of repairs with limited new

When shipbuilding began to give way to repair work as Allied's major source of business in the mid-1980s, Allied decided to build a new and larger floating drydock. It went into service in May 1986.

buildings." To him the message was clear—the BC shipbuilding industry was in a state of decline. In response, he decided to invest in a new and larger floating drydock.

Construction on Hull #244 started after the *Arctic Ivik* was built. The new drydock was 160 feet long with a 1,800-long-ton lift capacity. It went into service on May 2, 1986. Allied's investment in this facility and the resulting ship repair work is the reason the yard has remained in business despite the absence of new build orders.

Kla-Wichen (Hull #245)

Allied began construction of its first all-aluminum hull at the same time crews were building the yard's 160-foot floating drydock. This small harbour patrol boat was a Robert Allan design. "We bid on it against a number of the small yards," Malcolm McLaren recalled. "Al Renke, who owned and ran Shore Boatbuilders, was rather disappointed to see us turning our attention to the small aluminum vessel market. I thought that was odd because he certainly had the aluminum market locked up, but we did manage to get that one away from him. We also managed to build it for about what we thought it would cost. It's been a very good boat and is still in daily service."

Aft view of the *Kla-Wichen*. Murray McLennan photo

R.B. Young (Hull #250)

This 90-foot coastal survey vessel came near the end of the federal government's program of building ships for federal service. In the fall of 1989, while the *R.B. Young* was under construction, Arthur McLaren suffered a minor stroke. He went to a cardiac surgeon, who asked how many cigars he smoked in a day. Arthur replied "Ten," to which the surgeon said, "Oh, my God!" Before agreeing to schedule any bypass surgery, she laid down the law. "You can smoke cigars or you can have the bypass, but you are not going to do both." Arthur gave up cigars.

Ironically, it had been Hubert Wallace's advice

Airie Braaksma installing the starboard CPP tailshaft on the *R.B. Young*.

Launching the *R.B. Young*. The crew receive the launch command, "stand by your axes." The horn blows, the ropes are cut, then the ship slides down the ways.

The oceanographic survey vessel *R.B. Young* at sea. Murray McLennan photo.

years earlier—that all government contractors had to smoke cigars—that had gotten Arthur started. Now, the *R.B. Young* was one of the last government ship contracts—a fitting time to quit stogies. Arthur missed the launch of the *R.B. Young*: he was recovering from bypass surgery.

Spirit of British Columbia (Hull #254), Spirit of Vancouver Island (#255)

The Spirit Class ferries were the biggest self-propelled ships ever built in British Columbia. They were unique in another way: a consortium of three yards—Yarrows, Vito and Allied—built them. At the end of the project, two of those yards closed their doors.

Allied built the forward hull sections for each of the superferries. They were 200 feet long, 88 feet wide and 26 feet deep, complete with two 1,000-hp bow thrusters. These sections were outfitted with all the bilge and fire systems, stainless steel fresh water tanks, and were painted inside—all in all, quite a large piece of work.

Work on these ferries came during a very slow period for new construction. "We started the first one in the summer of 1991 and the work carried into 1993," Malcolm explained. "In years past we would have knocked these jobs off in half the time, but we stretched the job out somewhat to provide continuous employment to a small group of tradesmen—the other portion of the ship was not ready, so there was no point in manning excessively."

Inkster (Hull #256)

Allied's next contract didn't come until 1995, reflecting the industry-wide slowdown in new build orders. The $1.5-million *Inkster* was an aluminum catamaran for the Royal Canadian Mounted Police. Shore Boatbuilders had already built a series of three aluminum-hulled catamarans for the Mounties, but Al Renke, the owner, was thoroughly convinced that the boat would perform better if it were longer. So the *Inkster* was built to the 65-foot waterline he advocated and it worked out extremely well.

Allied delivered the *Inkster* in February 1996

The *Inkster* on sea trials, with the trials crew on deck. Murray McLennan photo

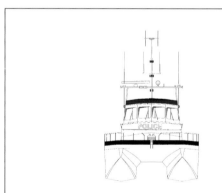

PATROL VESSEL "INKSTER" IS A HIGH SPEED ALUMINUM CATAMARAN BUILT BY ALLIED SHIPBUILDERS FOR OPERATION ON THE COASTAL WATERS OF BRITISH COLUMBIA.

PRINCIPAL PARTICULARS:

OWNER	ROYAL CANADIAN MOUNTED POLICE	
LENGTH OVERALL	19.75m	64' - 9"
LENGTH ON WATERLINE	17.75m	58' - 3"
BREADTH, MOULDED	6.7m	22' - 0"
DRAFT	0.67m	2' - 2"
CREW	3	
ENDURANCE	20 HRS @ 25 knots	
MAXIMUM SPEED	IN EXCESS OF 30 knots	

and it immediately went to work from its base in Prince Rupert. The longer aluminum catamaran gets better fuel economy than its shorter cousins and is more sea kindly. With a cruising speed of 25 knots and a range of 500 miles, the patrol vessel has had virtually no down time due to machinery problems since it has been in operation.

Skeena Queen (Hull #257)

McLaren & Sons, the design division of Allied Shipbuilders, won the bid to design a new "no-frills" commuter ferry in April 1995. The specs called for a 100-car, 600-passenger ferry able to manoeuvre in tricky tide and high-congestion areas while still delivering a fast turnaround time and efficient operation. Once the design was model tested and completed, the proposed ferry went to tender. Allied Shipbuilders won that bid as well, and the first steel for the *Skeena Queen* was cut in October 1995.

Reflections on a Lifetime of Shipbuilding

In 1998, Arthur McLaren noted that there wasn't much left of an industry that once employed more than 20,000 people in this province alone.

The industry is staying alive by attrition. Years ago everybody was getting a job as soon as they finished one. Now we are down to two yards of a size that can build these large vessels.

For much of the history of shipbuilding, the changes in the industry have not been earth-shattering. People are using different tools and methods, all directed at making the construction of steel ships more economical and certainly more productive. That's the main thing we've tried to do in fifty years.

Many people attribute the main changes in ship design to the use of the computer. I don't fall into that camp. I found out that people with computers could do wonderful things. But I didn't have a computer and I could design vessels just as effectively without one. The problems you have to solve are still basic problems. Two times two is four. You don't need to make it five and a half.

You often hear that the work has become more specialized, but in my point of view, it has become less specialized. In earlier times, a lot of people were employed in building ships and the work involved a great number of different trades and skills. In the past fifty years we have simplified the procedure so that today people do a broader spectrum of work. That's where advances in equipment and technology have helped. Also, the type of work has changed. For example, there is less emphasis on steelwork and more on other trades such as electronics.

If building ships has become simpler, I think that the business of building ships has become far more complex. In the early days, jobs were often done on the strength of a handshake or a phone call. We just went ahead and built the ship.

The 100-car, 600-passenger, no-frills ferry *Skeena Queen*.

Epilogue

"My paternal grandmother was adamant that my father and his two brothers get an education and make something of themselves. I, too, was very anxious that my own sons do the best they could. As for the fact that James, Douglas and Malcolm all ended up in the shipyard, well, it's exactly what I wanted! Of course, I never told them that."

—*Arthur McLaren*

Arthur McLaren died on February 19, 1999. From early childhood he had dreamed of building ships, and he did exactly that for nearly sixty years. As he later remarked, "I don't regret a day of it. In fact, it's been fun."

Some 560 family, friends, fellow shipbuilders, tradesmen, maritime business people and professional colleagues attended Arthur's funeral. The phrase "end of an era" echoed again and again, long after the bagpipes had stopped playing. Many people have their own stories to tell about this sometimes crusty, sometimes humorous, always determined shipbuilder. His funeral service featured anecdotes from six such people: Arthur's sister Ada, naval architect Peter Hatfield, Allied technical manager Chuck Ko and Arthur's three sons. Excerpts from their comments follow:

James McLaren

Life and work with my father has been an immense experience. He was a brilliant and prolific naval architect, marine engineer and shipbuilder.

May 22, 1991, was a very important date for Arthur. It was the anniversary of his 50th year of shipbuilding. Arthur's employees presented him with a builder's nameplate to recognize the length and quality of his career and the special achievement of having built a successful shipyard.

There have been many shipyards in BC that did good work, but most are no longer active. Arthur designed and built ships that are strong and will last. He also was able to build a very good shipyard and kept it operating successfully in British Columbia for over fifty years. The man who did that was a very special man. He was my father.

Peter Hatfield

My first knowledge of Arthur occurred when I was in high school in Penticton. Allied had built a small dredge for the Department of Public Works and Arthur hired a truck, equipment and some assistance from my dad to get the dredge up and running. When he learned that Arthur was a naval architect, my dad told Arthur that his son wanted to be a naval architect and asked what advice he could offer. Arthur's reply was typically short and to the point—drown him!

Arthur was a man of strong opinions, strongly

held and readily shared—and those opinions were nearly always on the mark. He was also generous of his time and support of the shipbuilding industry and engineering profession.

Some of my best memories are of times spent in Arthur's upstairs office at Allied. Firstly, you armed yourself with a cup of coffee (greatly improved from the awful stuff at the False Creek yard), headed up the stairs past the gallery of project photographs, then along the corridor down which Arthur's gaze continually swept as he kept an eye on goings-on, and finally into his room. There was always a cheerful welcome, an invitation to take a seat and, regardless of the occasion, a discussion.

On one sombre occasion, Arthur, Doug and Malcolm were on one side of the table. Along the other side was the might of Esso Resources Canada Ltd., supported by their awesome documentation including a small section with our tug design. In the middle of this seriousness, Jim poked his head in the door and asked, "Who's winning—the lions or the Christians?"

I trust Jim, Doug and Malcolm will continue to run Allied Shipbuilders with the same philosophy as Arthur, who summed up the yard's mission statement in the simple phrase, "Remember, the man wants his boat."

Chuck Ko

Arthur inspired great loyalty in everybody who knew him. My nineteen years of service drafting and designing ships is short compared to the many employees who have thirty or forty years of service at Allied. Many weekends and nights were spent toiling over an estimate or trying to get a job out. Without question, many of us would be working with Arthur to see that everything got finished. Somebody once summed up how we all felt about Arthur—"You'd go through a brick wall for the old man!"

As an employer, Arthur was very respectful of the talents and ingenuity of the people he trusted to build his ships. He fully appreciated the value of a good tradesman. He spoke proudly of his own apprenticeship as a boilermaker. He would chastise me if I made the tradesmen's job unnecessarily difficult.

He was a practical, common sense man, who abhorred unnecessary complexity. Many times he changed his own work to simplify the task and insisted others follow suit. I was one of many who benefitted from his wealth of knowledge and experience. I was also one of the many who benefitted from his good graces. He gave many of us opportunities so we could develop to our full potential.

Arthur led by his example of hard work, common sense and integrity. He was an inspiration to us all.

Douglas McLaren

My dad had a favourite spot in the corner of our living room in West Vancouver where he could look out of the big windows, through the trees and over the water to Point Grey. No boat, barge or ship could slip into or out of the harbour without his scrutiny.

Around his chair there would always be a big stack of newspapers, magazines and library books. My father did not like wasting time in traffic jams, so he would use that as an excuse to stay at work until rush hour traffic was over. Then he would go home to his favourite chair and pick up something to read and start absorbing all sorts of facts and knowledge that he somehow managed to retain better than most of us.

On the technical side, my father was big on basic principles. He told me that everything big and complicated was just a lot of simple things stuck together. If you were going to make or use something, you'd better be able to understand everything about it and know for yourself that it would be right before you start. Practising his philosophy led me to cut out a quote and stick it over my desk. It says, "The only problem with doing things right the first time is that no one appreciates how difficult it was."

Ada Berry

In our family there were three siblings—Arthur, me and my twin brother Jim. I am the one left to tell you about Arthur's earlier years.

Arthur had a capacity for storing facts. At age five he knew the names and distinguishing features of all the British steam trains. When the family immigrated to Canada in 1928, Arthur was put in a grade with children at least two years older than himself. So, making up for the size difference, he had to perform well in studies.

He was not athletic, so had other interests like building forts for refuge against the "gang" down the street. He also belonged to the Sea Scouts, and for a short time he became domesticated enough to iron the "7 seas" creases on those bell-bottom trousers. The family thought it a miracle when he became an "honour boy" at Chalmers Church Camp.

Yes, Arthur did have that Lloyd's registry book under his bed. Mother found something else, too—an empty sardine tin that had been there so long that the fork left in it was permanently tarnished.

Arthur's philosophy on life was "Keep working and producing until the end." Well done, Arthur!

Malcolm McLaren

My father inspired me to acquire his fondness of ships. As a child, he didn't take me camping or swimming or any such activities. But on Saturday mornings I often accompanied him to his shipyard in False Creek. On the way we would drive by the docks in Vancouver Harbour and look at the deep sea ships. At a glance, my father could identify the nationality of the different freighters.

"There's a German ship," he would say.

"How can you tell?" I would ask.

"Oh, just look at the shape of the funnel."

At the next dock, he would say, "There's a British ship."

"How can you tell?"

"By the shape of the bow."

I was so impressed that my father knew such things. It wasn't until years later that I figured out he was also looking at the ship's flag!

The last vessel designed and built at Allied during my father's life was the large steel ferry *Skeena Queen*. A documentary video was made of that ferry's construction. My mother has told me that my father watched that video over and over, his face beaming with delight. He was so pleased that the people at his shipyard were carrying on the tradition of using their best efforts to create something to be proud of.

Arthur McLaren relaxing on a cruise ship. Dorothy McLaren has always known that her husband loved building ships, but Arthur's pride in five decades of doing so was especially apparent on the eve of their second cruise. She recalled: "Our ship sailed about six o'clock at night and before we'd gotten to the First Narrows, we'd passed about seven or eight ships in the harbour, all of which Arthur had built or had something to do with. He was almost in tears. Underneath Arthur was a real softie and his pride in that accomplishment was very, very strong."

Appendices

Terms used in appendices:

Official No. is the unique vessel number issued by the government of Canada, as recorded in the Ships Registry.

Builder name is the name of the individual or the official registered or trade name of the company responsible for the construction. Please note that a shipyard at a certain location may have undergone several changes in ownership and name.

Location of each shipyard is British Columbia.

Ships (as opposed to boats) are defined here, as in the British tradition, as "sea-going vessels," regardless of size. Many shipyards have built both ships and boats, and we have included as many of these yards as possible.

Dates are generally the years during which the shipyard built metal vessels, from the date the first vessel was built to the date of the most recently built vessel, or the date the shipyard closed operations. Some companies operated before the period specified, as builders in wood, or after the period specified as ship repairers.

Number of ships built is as accurate as possible, based on information that could be confirmed (complete and accurate records from every shipyard for every year are not always available).

Tonnage: Gross tonnage (**GT**) refers to the volume of the ship's enclosed spaces and is not a measure of weight. Traditionally, a gross ton is equivalent to 100 cubic feet. Net tonnage (**NT**) is the gross tonnage less the volume of the ship devoted to stores, machinery, crew's quarters and other necessities. Deadweight tonnage (**Dwt**) refers to the number of long tons (2,240 lbs) of cargo a ship can carry before it reaches the maximum draft load line. **Lightship** is the weight (in long tons) of the complete ship, ready for sea but with no cargo, fuel or water on board.

Gross tonnage range is the range of vessels built, from smallest to largest.

Length range is the range of overall length (**OA**) or in some cases registered length (**Reg**) of vessels built, from shortest to longest.

The information presented in Appendix 2 is the most accurate and up-to-date that could be found and confirmed. Because of the number of firms that have come and gone over the years, it would be impossible to obtain figures that are completely free of minor errors and omissions. Nonetheless, these statistics give an accurate picture of general numbers, trends, and production of individual firms and the steel shipbuilding industry overall.

Appendix 1
Vessels built by Allied Shipbuilders Ltd.

For an overview of terms used in appendices, see page 218.

Hull No: 001   **Original name:** *Bering Straits*
Renamed: *Emerald Straits*   **Official No:** 190804

Type: Tug   **Designer:** McLaren & Sons   **Delivered:**
1949, Vancouver BC   **Built for:** Straits Towing Ltd.,
Vancouver BC   **Owner's representative:** Fred Mickey

Length: **OA** 55′   **Reg** 51.4′   **Beam mld:** 16.2′
Depth: 9′   **Design draft:** 7.75′   **Tonnage:**   **GT** 46
NT 6   **Material:** Steel hull and superstructure

Main engine: Cooper-Bessemer, 8 cylinder 8″x11″—1 @
600 hp @ 950 rpm   **Reduction ratio:** 1.94 : 1
Propeller: 1 - 76″ dia.

The Bering Straits.

At the time of build, the *Bering Straits* was one of the
larger locally built steel tugs in BC. The vessel, which was
renamed the *Emerald Straits* soon after commissioning,
sank in the waters of Howe Sound on the stormy night of
Friday, April 18, 1969. The *Emerald Straits* left Woodfibre
at 10:30 p.m., heading for Vancouver, with the scow *Straits
No. 153* (790 GT) in tow. Winds in the sound were gusting
to 35-40 mph. A commission of inquiry found the most
probable cause of the sinking was that the *Emerald Straits*
failed to maintain headway. As a result she fell to starboard,
was girded (pulled sideways by her own towline) and held
over for long enough to allow a flood of water to enter the
hull, causing her to go down almost immediately.

The mate, Barry Gordon, age 29, was swept overboard
while working the towing winch prior to the capsizing. He
swam to shore and was found on the Pacific Great Eastern
railway track by a track patrolman. The rest of the crew,
skipper Billie Rapitla, 32, engineer Joseph Kachkowski, 43,
and deckhand John Cords, 24, perished.

Shortly afterwards, due to a number of steel tug sinkings,
the Department of Transport introduced new safety
regulations, including certified closures and towline abort
systems, which have proven effective in reducing the
number of tragedies such as the sinking of the *Emerald
Straits.*

Hull No: 002   **Original name:** *Wee MacAdam*
Official No: 192905

Type: Tug, Boom Boat   **Designer:** McLaren & Sons
Delivered: 1950, Vancouver BC   **Built for:** Dumaresq
Bros. Ltd., Squamish BC

Length: **OA** 20′   **Reg** 18.1′   **Beam mld:** 8′
Depth: 4′   **Tonnage:**   **GT** 3.27   **NT** 2   **Material:**
Steel hull and superstructure

Main engine: 1 @ 100 hp   **Sister ships:** 003; 004

Hulls No. 2, 3 and 4 were simple 20-foot-long boom
boats built on speculation, during quiet times. At the time,
1950-51, Allied Builders and John Manly were the primary
builders of small steel tugs of this type.

Each of these boats cost about $3,500 to build and sold for
between $3,600 and $3,800, not including the engine. At that
price Allied was able to sell them fairly easily. Construction of
the first two was funded using income from building Hull
No. 1.

The vessels were powered by whatever the engine
supplier would provide in order to sell the boats on spec.
Chrysler Crown and Gray Marine engines were often used,
but one Packard gasoline engine was fitted.

Hull No: 003   **Original name:** *Wee MacAlpine*
Official No: 193798

Type: Tug, Boom Boat   **Designer:** McLaren & Sons
Delivered: 1950, Vancouver BC   **Built for:** Lions Gate
Lumber Co. Ltd., North Vancouver BC   **Owner's
representative:** J. Earl Wilcox

Length: **OA** 20′   **Reg** 18′   **Beam mld:** 8′   **Depth:** 4′
Tonnage: **GT** 3.21   **NT** 2.18   **Material:** Steel hull
and superstructure

Main engine: Packard—1 @ 100 hp   **Sister ships:** 002;
004; 009

Hull No: 004   **Original name:** *Wee MacAllister*
Official No: 193799

Type: Tug, Boom Boat   **Designer:** McLaren & Sons
Delivered: 1950, Vancouver BC   **Built for:** Cowdell
Towing Ltd., Squamish BC   **Owner's representative:**
Harry Head

Length: **OA** 20′   **Reg** 18.2′   **Beam mld:** 8′
Depth: 4′   **Tonnage:**   **GT** 3   **NT** 2   **Material:**
Steel hull and superstructure

Main engine: 1, gas-powered   **Sister ships:** 002; 003; 009

Hull No: 005   **Original name:** *Spica's Spanker*
Renamed: *I'm Alone III*   **Official No:** 193783

Type: Fishing, Longliner   **Designer:** McLaren & Sons

Delivered: 1950, Vancouver BC　　**Built for:** David M. McCormic, Vancouver BC

Length:　OA 50′　**Reg** 46.2′　**Beam mld:** 14′
Depth: 8′　**Material:** Steel

Main engine: Gardner diesel—1 @ 65 hp　**Reduction gear:** Snow-Nabstedt　**Propeller:** 1 @ 44″ dia. x 39″ pitch, 3-blade

Spica's Spanker was an all-steel fish boat with a single painted unlined fish hold. Allied had wanted to build a steel fish boat and talked the original owner into building the vessel. It was operated successfully for a while and was subsequently sold to Norman Ryall. The vessel then fished for crab off the west coast of Vancouver Island and albacore tuna off the coast of California. This vessel was one of the first locally built "modern" fishing boats. According to Arthur McLaren, "David Scott, who worked on Twigg (Mitchell) Island, built the first steel fishing boats in BC, nearly single-handed. He rivetted them together with the assistance of a youngster who came in and held the head of the rivet."

Hull No: 006　　**Original name:** *Dunvegan*

Type: Tug　**Designer:** Robert Allan
Delivered: 1950, Peace River, Dunvegan, Alberta
Built for: Department of Highways, Alberta

Length:　OA 48′　**Reg** 38′

Main engine: Gardner, 5L3—1 @ 95 hp @900 rpm

The *Dunvegan*.

The *Dunvegan* was a simple 38-foot tug that moved a catamaran-type barge ferry across the Peace River at Dunvegan, Alberta. This tug-barge ferry ran for many years until it was eventually replaced by a bridge.

Hull No: 007　　**Original name:** *Radium Franklin*
Official No: 194887

Type: Tug, Shallow Draft　　**Designer:** Milne, Gilmore & German　　**Delivered:** 1951, Fort McMurray, Alberta
Built for: Northern Transportation Co. Ltd., Edmonton, Alberta

Length:　OA 69′　**Beam mld:** 24.4′　　**Depth:** 4.6′
Tonnage:　GT 119　**NT** 81　　**Material:** Steel hull with aluminum superstructure　　**Speed:** 12 knots (max)

Main engines: General Motors—2 @ 250 hp

The *Radium Franklin* was a shallow-draft, twin-screw tug with an aluminum superstructure. It was the first vessel built by Allied that had aluminum construction in it. The aluminum was rivetted because welding techniques and equipment were not yet well developed.

Northern Transportation Co. Ltd. originally ordered this tug from Frank Ross of Western Bridge, but Western Bridge, represented by Syd Hogg, did not wish to do the job and passed it on to Allied.

The vessel was built to assist in uranium exploration and moved barges on the Bear River between Great Bear Lake and the Mackenzie River. It took barges with supplies in and brought uranium out.

Hull No: 008　　**Original name:** *Wee MacDonald*
Official No: 194939

Type: Tug, Boom Boat　　**Designer:** McLaren & Sons
Delivered: 1952, Vancouver BC　　**Built for:** Falt Bros. Agencies Ltd., Cowichan Bay BC

Length:　OA 20′　**Reg** 18′　**Beam mld:** 8′
Tonnage:　GT 2　**NT** 2　　**Material:** Steel hull and superstructure

Main engine: Chrysler, gasoline—1 @ 100 hp
Reduction ratio: 3.00 : 1　　**Sister ships:** 002; 003; 004; 009

The *Wee MacDonald* was built to the account of the Falt Brothers and MacMillan Bloedel Ltd., Shawnigan Division. The full price of the vessel including the engine and machinery was $5,993.21.

Hull No: 009　　**Original name:** *Dala (Kildala)*
Official No: 194901

Type: Launch　　**Designer:** McLaren & Sons
Delivered: 1951, Vancouver BC　　**Built for:** Kenneth Illingworth, West Vancouver BC　　**Length:　OA** 20′
Beam mld: 8.2′　　**Tonnage:　GT** 3　**NT** 2
Material: Steel hull and superstructure

Main engine: Gray diesel—1 @ 155 hp
Sister ships: 002; 003; 004; 008

The *Kildala* was built for the Morrison-Knudsen Company and was used to assist in construction of the Aluminum Co. of Canada (Alcan) smelter at Kitimat BC.

Hull No: 010　　**Original name:** *Kemano*　　**Official No:** 194902

Type: Tug　　**Designer:** McLaren & Sons　　**Delivered:** 1951, Vancouver BC　　**Built for:** Morrison Knudsen Co.

Length:　OA 30′　**Reg** 28.3′　　**Tonnage:　GT** 7
Material: Steel

Main engine: General Motors diesel 6-71—1 @ 165 hp @ 1800 rpm

Typical of the 30-foot steel tugs that Allied and Manly were making at the same time, the *Kemano* was used to assist in construction of the Aluminum Co. of Canada (Alcan) smelter at Kitimat.

Hull No: 011　　**Original name:** *Stamish Chief*
Official No: 194913

Type: Tug, Boom Boat　　**Designer:** McLaren & Sons

Delivered: 1952, Vancouver BC   **Built for:** Cowdell Towing Ltd., Squamish BC   **Owner's representative:** Norman F. Cowdell

Length: OA 25′   **Reg** 22.8′   **Beam mld:** 8′
Depth: 4′   **Tonnage: GT** 3   **NT** 2   **Material:** Steel hull and superstructure

Main engine: Caterpillar—1 @ 80 hp

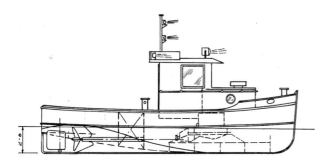

The *Stamish Chief*.

The *Stamish Chief* was a 5-ft longer version of the standard Allied 20-ft steel tug.

Hull No: 012   **Original name:** *Stave Lake II*
Renamed: *Reliable II*   **Official No:** 194917

Type: Launch   **Designer:** McLaren & Sons
Delivered: 1952, Stave Lake   **Built for:** Booth Logging Co., Ruskin BC   **Owner's representative:** A.E. Kearsly

Length: OA 25′   **Reg** 23.3′   **Beam mld:** 8′
Depth: 4′   **Tonnage: GT** 4.36   **NT** 3.62
Material: Steel hull and superstructure

Main engine: Paragon—1 @ 110 hp   **Reduction ratio:** 2.00 : 1   **Propeller:** 1 - 22″ dia.

This launch was used on Stave Lake, near Mission BC, after the lake was created by a dam. The launch was used to assist in cutting and removing trees that were left standing underwater when the lake was flooded.

The *Stave Lake II* cost $2,208 to build, excluding the owner-supplied gasoline engine and shaft. The vessel sold for $2,970, providing a contribution of $762 which equalled about 3 months' rent for the shipyard at the time.

Hull No: 013   **Original name:** *Alco Lad*
Official No: 195421

Type: Tug   **Designer:** McLaren & Sons
Delivered: 1952   **Built for:** Allison Logging Co. Ltd., North Vancouver BC

Length: OA 28′   **Reg** 26′   **Beam mld:** 10.2′
Depth: 3.7′   **Tonnage: GT** 5.62   **NT** 3.82

Main engine: Buda diesel, 6-BDMR-230—1 @ 45 hp @ 2000 rpm

The 45-hp, 1,000-lb. Buda engine installed in the vessel was made in Chicago, IL, and was purchased from Simson-Maxwell Ltd. of 1931 West Georgia St., Vancouver BC.

Hull No: 014   **Original name:** *Canim Clipper*
Official No: 195858

Type: Tug, Boom Boat   **Designer:** McLaren & Sons
Delivered: 1952   **Built for:** Canim Lake Sawmills Ltd., Canim Lake BC   **Owner's representative:** The Jens Brothers

Length: OA 25′   **Reg** 22′   **Beam mld:** 9.9′
Depth: 3.75′   **Tonnage: GT** 4.86   **NT** 3.3
Material: Steel hull and superstructure

Main engine: General Motors diesel, 2 cylinder 71 series— 1 @ 55 hp @ 1850 rpm

The *Canim Clipper* was originally used for logging around Canim Lake, in the Cariboo region of central BC. This tug, like many of its type, was shipped by rail to or near its work location. The vessel's name was intended to be "Canim Lake Clipper," but the owners registered it as *Canim Clipper* after the Owner's painters inadvertently painted the shorter name on the tug. Allied typically built a standard 20- to 25-ft. tug, like the *Canim Clipper*, in a four-week period.

Hull No: 015   **Original name:** *Lady Pauline*
Official No: 195248

Type: Fishing, Gillnet   **Designer:** McLaren & Sons
Delivered: 1952   **Built for:** Steve Shtrodl, Steveston BC

Length: OA 35′   **Reg** 33.2′   **Beam mld:** 10′   **Depth:** 5′
Tonnage: GT 10   **NT** 9

Main engine: 1 @ 36 hp

The *Lady Pauline* was one of the first salmon gillnet fishing boats in BC made of steel.

Hull No: 016   **Original name:** *I.T.T. No. 1*
Renamed: *Arrow Park; Lardeau*   **Official No:** 195240

Type: Self-Propelled Barge   **Designer:** McLaren & Sons   **Delivered:** 1952   **Built for:** Interior Tug & Transport Co. Ltd., Revelstoke BC   **Owner's representatives:** Ben Bowman/Grant McKenzie

Length: OA 80′   **Beam mld:** 25.5′   **Depth:** 6′
Design draft: 3.75′   **Tonnage: GT** 95.38   **NT** 95.38
Dwt 133 L.tons

Main engines: 2 @ 265 hp

The *Arrow Park* was a barge originally built for Ben Bowman and Grant McKenzie for service on the Arrow Lakes. Ben and Grant had started a business where they wanted to dig ore out of the country north of Revelstoke and take it down the Arrow Lakes to Trail, BC. To do that they got hold of two trucks and a series of dump bodies that they put on and took off the trucks. They then loaded the dump bodies on the barge for the trip down the lake. This lasted for about three years and then the mine folded up. The *Arrow Park* was originally pushed by the Allied-built tug *Deer Park* (Allied Hull No. 17).

In 1954 Bowman and McKenzie had Allied lengthen the barge to 99 feet and convert it to self-propelled. Allied fitted two 265 hp engines c/w shafts, rudders and deckhouse, etc. This self-propelled barge then provided a service crossing the lake between Nakusp and Arrowhead, on the Arrow Lake, previously provided by the CPR vessel *Minto*, which had been laid up in 1952.

Hull No: 017   **Original name:** *Deer Park*
Official No: 195329

Type: Tug, Tunnel Stern   **Designer:** McLaren & Sons
Delivered: 1952, Arrow Lakes   **Built for:** Interior Tug & Transport Co. Ltd., Revelstoke BC   **Owner's representatives:** Ben Bowman/Grant McKenzie

Length: OA 40′   **Reg** 36.3′   **Beam mld:** 11.5′
Depth: 4.75′   **Design draft:** 3.5′   **Tonnage: GT** 12
NT 8

Main engine: Caterpillar, 338—1 @ 170 hp @ 1600 rpm
Reduction ratio: 2.00 : 1   **Propeller:** 1 - 36″ dia.

The *Deer Park*.

The *Deer Park* was originally built for the purpose of moving the barge *Arrow Park* (Allied Hull No. 16). The dimensions of this tug permitted the complete vessel to be shipped by rail from Vancouver to the Arrow Lakes.

The matter of payment for work done often arises between the shipbuilder and ship owner. On October 6, 1952, Grant McKenzie, a principal of Interior Tug & Transport Co. Ltd., sent Arthur a letter, which started: "Dear Arthur, Received a letter from Miss Andrews re money (which we don't have) however we do have high hopes. . ."

Hull No: 018   **Original name:** *Andy's Bay No. 4*
Renamed: *Myrmac II*   **Official No:** 195470

Type: Tug, Captain   **Designer:** McLaren & Sons
Delivered: 1953, Vancouver BC   **Built for:** Coastal Towing Co. Ltd., Vancouver BC
Owner's representative: Oswald "Sparky" New

Length: OA 32.5′   **Beam mld:** 10′   **Depth:** 6′
Design draft: 5′   **Tonnage: GT** 9.8   **NT** 6.7
Material: Steel hull and superstructure

Main engine: General Motors, 6-71—1 @ 165 hp @ 1800 rpm   **Reduction ratio:** 3.00 : 1

Sparky New had this tug built for use at a logging camp-sorting ground on Howe Sound. Approximately 20,000 pounds of steel were used in the construction and tradesmen were paid $1.95 per hour.

Hull No: 019   **Original name:** *Yorke No. 9*
Renamed: *Marine Erector; Seaspan 911; Allied Barge*
Official No: 192903

Type: Rail Car Barge   **Designer:** McLaren & Sons
Delivered: 1953   **Built for:** F. M. Yorke & Son Ltd., Vancouver BC   **Owner's representative:** Lorne Yorke

Length: OA 270′   **Beam mld:** 10.5′   **Depth:** 43′

The original service of this vessel was moving rail cars carrying forest products. Allied's hull number was for a 90-ft-long section of hull used to lengthen an existing barge built by Yarrows in 1950. The barge is presently owned by Allied, in use as a large work float.

Hull No: 020   **Original name:** *Booth No. 2*
Official No: 195853

Type: Launch   **Designer:** McLaren & Sons
Delivered: 1953, Vancouver BC   **Built for:** Booth Logging Company Ltd., Vancouver BC

Length: OA 25′   **Reg** 22.7′   **Beam mld:** 8′
Depth: 4′   **Design draft:** 3′   **Tonnage: GT** 4.9
NT 3.9   **Material:** Steel hull and superstructure

Main engine: Chrysler Crown, gasoline—1 @ 100 hp @ 3200 rpm   **Propeller:** 1 - 24″ dia.

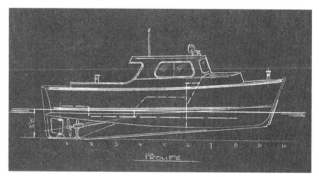

The *Booth No. 2*.

This 25-foot steel utility boat was designed primarily as a logging camp tender, capable of yarding logs or carrying passengers and freight.

Hull No: 021   **Original name:** *Sea Beaver No. 2*
Official No: 195865

Type: River Launch   **Designer:** McLaren & Sons
Delivered: 1953   **Built for:** Squamish Towing & Contracting Co. Ltd., Squamish BC

Length: OA 24′   **Reg** 22.8′   **Beam mld:** 7.7′
Depth: 2.2′   **Tonnage: GT** 3   **NT** 2
Material: Steel hull and superstructure

Main engine: Simplex gasoline—1 @ 205 hp @ 4200 rpm

Allied built the steel-hulled *Sea Beaver No. 2* to similar

lines as the Owner's previous wooden *Sea Beaver*. The vessel was used for handling logs in the Squamish River, including the very fast water in the upper part of the river.

Hull No: 022   **Original name:** *Rosalie*

Type: Tug, Boom Boat   **Designer:** McLaren & Sons
Delivered: 1953, Vancouver BC   **Built for:** Dumaresq Brothers Ltd.   **Owner's representative:** Mr. Dumaresq

Length: OA 22.5′   **Beam mld:** 8′   **Depth:** 3.38′
Tonnage: GT 3   **NT** 2   **Material:** Steel hull and superstructure

Main engine: General Motors, 4-55—1 @ 100 hp
Reduction ratio: 3.17 : 1   **Propeller:** 1 - 27″ dia.

This 22′-6″ tunnel stern shallow-draft steel work boat was designed primarily for boom work in such places as tidal flats, rivers, etc.

Hull No: 023   **Original name:** *Wee MacKay*
Official No: 198077

Type: Tug, Workboat/Tender   **Designer:** McLaren & Sons   **Delivered:** 1953   **Built for:** Interior Tug & Transport Co. Ltd.   **Owner's representatives:** Ben Bowman/Grant McKenzie

Length: OA 25′   **Reg** 23.7′   **Beam mld:** 8.2′
Depth: 4′   **Tonnage: GT** 4.7   **NT** 4.2
Material: Steel hull and superstructure

Main engine: Buda, gasoline - 1 @ 76 hp

Hull No: 024   **Original name:** *Mallard*
Renamed: *Sea Chase*   **Official No:** 320946

Type: Launch, Search & Rescue   **Designer:** U.S. Navy
Delivered: 1954, Vancouver BC   **Built for:** Department of National Defence, Ottawa, Ontario
Owner's representative: Royal Canadian Air Force

Length: OA 40′   **Reg** 38.4′   **Beam mld:** 11.5′
Tonnage: GT 13   **Material:** Steel hull with aluminum superstructure   **Speed:** 20 knots (max), 18 knots (service)

Main engines: Detroit diesel, 6-71—2 @ 225 hp

The Mallard.

The *Mallard* was a type of planing crash boat similar to numerous ones that had been built in the United States. Vessels of this type were of lightweight steel construction, except for a small pilothouse made of aluminum and rivetted

to the hull structure. The *Mallard* was stationed at the Kitsilano Coast Guard base from 1954 until the 1980s, after which it was replaced by the *Osprey*, an aluminum search and rescue vessel built by Matsumoto Shipyard in North Vancouver.

Hull No: 025   **Original name:** *Y.S.F. 217*

Type: Cargo, Ammunition   **Designer:** Department of National Defence   **Delivered:** 1954   **Built for:** Department of National Defence, Royal Canadian Navy

Length: OA 104′   **Beam mld:** 18′   **Tonnage:**
GT 116   **Material:** Steel hull and superstructure
Speed: 8.5 knots (service)

Main engines: Caterpillar diesel—2 @ 120 hp
Sister ship: 026

The *Y.S.F. 217.*

A total of three self-propelled ammunition lighters were built on the west coast to service warships at the Esquimalt Naval Base: two by Allied and one by Yarrows. Although Allied tendered the lower price, the Department of National Defence arranged for Yarrows to engineer and build the first vessel and for Allied to build the remaining two ships.

Victoria Machinery Depot (VMD) built a similar vessel, which, instead of being an ammunition lighter, was called a water lighter (*Y.S.W. 220*) since there were big water tanks in it.

Hull No: 026   **Original name:** *Y.S.F. 218*

Type: Cargo, Ammunition   **Designer:** Department of National Defence   **Delivered:** 1954   **Built for:** Department of National Defence, Royal Canadian Navy

Length: OA 104′   **Beam mld:** 18′   **Tonnage:**
GT 116   **Material:** Steel hull and superstructure
Speed: 8.5 knots (service)

Main engines: Caterpillar diesel—2 @ 120 hp
Sister ship: 025

Hull No: 027   **Original name:** *Island Comet*
Renamed: *Delta Fox*   **Official No:** 197844

Type: Tug   **Designer:** McLaren & Sons   **Delivered:** 1954   **Built for:** Island Tug & Barge Ltd., Victoria BC
Owner's representative: Harold Elworthy

Length: OA 40′   **Reg** 38′   **Beam mld:** 12″
Depth: 7′   **Design draft:** 6′   **Tonnage: GT** 14.9

NT 8.9   **Material:** Steel   **Speed:** 10 knots
Main engines: Detroit diesel 6-71-Tandem—2 @ 165 hp
Propeller: 1 - 54″ dia.

The *Island Comet* was a simple harbour tug with fire-fighting capability. Its primary duty was to serve as a tug in Victoria harbour but in an emergency it could act as a fire boat, pumping 1,500 gallons of seawater a minute through monitors on the house top and the foredeck. This deck monitor enabled crews to shoot water under a blazing wood wharf. The tug was fitted with two diesel engines coupled to a single reduction gear. For fire-fighting the forward engine was de-clutched from the reduction gear and used to power the fire pump. The pump was a gift from Victoria Machinery Depot in recognition of work done by other Island Tug ships and crews while battling an earlier blaze at VMD's plant.

Hull No: 028   **Original name:** *P.W.D. No. 324*
Renamed: *D.P.W. No. 224*   **Official No:** 197443

Type: Barge, Suction Dredge   **Designer:** Public Works
Delivered: 1954, Fort McMurray, Alberta   **Built for:**
Department of Public Works, Ottawa, Ontario

Length: **OA** 70′ **Beam mld:** 27′   **Depth:** 5′
Tonnage: **GT** 155

Public Works Dredge 324 was a "portable" dredge hull. On delivery of the barge to Fort McMurray, Public Works put 12″ suction dredging machinery on it for dredging shallow spots in the Hay River.

Hull No: 029A   **Original name:** *Wee Bernie*
Official No: 197402

Type: Tug, Boom Boat   **Designer:** McLaren & Sons
Delivered: 1953, Vancouver BC   **Built for:** Falt Bros.
Agencies Ltd., Cowichan Bay BC   **Owner's**
representatives: George & Albin Falt

Length: **OA** 14′ **Reg** 12.8′ **Beam mld:** 7′
Depth: 3′ **Design draft:** 2.5′ **Tonnage:** **GT** 1.66
NT 1.13 **Lightship** 2
Main engine: Chrysler Crown, gasoline—1 @ 104 hp
Reduction ratio: 2.00 : 1

The *Wee Bernie*, one of two Allied Hull No. 29s, was the first very small (14-foot) steel log-handling tug built by Allied. Various builders made many vessels of this type for use on the BC coast. The term originally used to describe this vessel was "Steel Bulldozer Boat."

Hull No: 029B   **Original name:** *Pewit*   **Official No:**
197451

Type: Tug, Shallow Draft   **Designer:** McLaren & Sons
Delivered: 1954, Thompson River BC   **Built for:**
Minister of Public Works, Ottawa, Ontario

Length: **OA** 32.6′ **Reg** 30.3′ **Beam mld:** 12′
Depth: 4′ **Tonnage:** **GT** 10 **NT** 7
Main engine: 1 @ 105 hp   **Reduction ratio:** 1.00 : 1

The *Pewit* was a simple steel tug of fairly shallow draft. It was of a size that could be shipped on a railway car and was

used with a dredge that worked on the Thompson River in BC.

Hull No: 030   **Original name:** *Falbro*   **Official No:**
197704

Type: Tug   **Designer:** McLaren & Sons   **Delivered:**
1954   **Built for:** Falt Bros. Agencies Ltd., Cowichan Bay
BC   **Owner's representatives:** George & Albin Falt

Length: **OA** 32.9′ **Reg** 30.6′ **Beam mld:** 10′
Depth: 6′   **Tonnage:** **GT** 7.88 **NT** 5.36
Main engine: Gray Marine, diesel—1 @ 165 hp @ 1800
rpm   **Reduction ratio:** 3.00 : 1

This 30-foot standard tug c/w hydraulic towing winch, 32-volt electric system, cabin with oil stove, compass, port lights, etc. was built for Falt Bros., as was Hull No. 29A. It was used for log sorting and towing. The Falt brothers had settled themselves in Cowichan Bay and were handling logs that came from the interior of Vancouver Island. The shipyard charge-out rate for additional work during construction was $3.25 per hour. Diesel fuel at the time cost 4 cents per litre.

Hull No: 031   **Original name:** *James L.H.*
Official No: 198097

Type: Tug, Log Towing   **Designer:** McLaren & Sons
Delivered: 1954, Nelson BC   **Built for:** Kootenay
Forest Products Ltd., Nelson BC

Length: **OA** 35.75′ **Reg** 34′ **Beam mld:** 12′
Depth: 7′ **Design draft:** 6′ **Tonnage:** **GT** 15
NT 9.83 **Material:** Steel hull and superstructure
Main engine: Caterpillar diesel—1 @ 170 hp
Propeller: 1 - 54″ dia.

The *James L.H.*

The *James L.H.*, a larger version of the standard Allied tug, was built in Vancouver and shipped via rail to Nelson, where it was used for log towing on Kootenay Lake. The total selling price of this tug was $19,753 plus tax.

Hull No: 032   **Original name:** *Marila*   **Official No:** 198656

Type: Fisheries Patrol Boat   **Designer:** Milne, Gilmore & German   **Delivered:** 1955, Great Slave Lake NWT
Built for: Department of Fisheries & Oceans, Ottawa, Ontario   **Owner's representative:** Mr. deLancey
Length: OA 45′ **Reg** 42.5′ **Beam mld:** 12′
Depth: 4′   **Design draft:** 3.5′   **Tonnage:** GT 15
NT 10   **Material:** Steel hull   **Speed:** 11 knots
Main engine: Cummins, NHMS-600—1 @ 175 hp @ 1800 rpm

The *Marila*.

This steel-hulled vessel was used to patrol Great Slave Lake for the purpose of enforcing fishing regulations.

Hull No: 033   **Original name:** *McMurray*
Official No: 198918

Type: Tug, Shallow Draft   **Designer:** Department of Public Works, Ottawa, Ontario   **Delivered:** 1955, Fort McMurray   **Built for:** Department of Public Works, Ottawa, Ontario   **Owner's representative:** Superintendent Corby
Length: OA 60′ **Beam mld:** 18′   **Depth:** 5.4′
Tonnage: GT 49 **NT** 33

Main engines: Cummins diesel - 2 @ 188 hp

The *McMurray* was a little pusher tug with square ends. It sat behind a barge-type dredge and pushed it up and down the Athabasca River between McMurray and Fort Fitzgerald. The vessel was assembled on the Hudson's Bay Company ways near Fort McMurray.

Hull No: 034   **Original name:** *Radium Dew*   **Official No:** 198913

Type: Tug, Shallow Draft   **Designer:** Milne, Gilmore & German   **Delivered:** 1955, Fort Smith   **Built for:** Northern Transportation Co. Ltd., Edmonton, Alberta
Owner's representative: Frank Broderick

Length: OA 120′ **Reg** 120′ **Beam mld:** 30′
Depth: 8′   **Design draft:** 3.67′   **Tonnage:** GT 289
NT 144   **Material:** Steel hull and superstructure
Capacity: 15 (crew)   **Speed:** 11 knots
Main engines: Enterprise diesel, DMG8—2 @ 770 hp @ 600 rpm

The *Radium Dew* was built for service on the Mackenzie River system. It operated from the Mackenzie River delta west to Herschel Island and east to Baillie Island, pushing N.T.C.L. barges carrying supplies for DEW (Distant Early Warning) line stations. On review of the design, T. A. McLaren determined that the tug's centre of buoyancy was aft of midship and its centre of gravity was forward of midship, which would cause the tug to trim by the bow. The vessel was built to somewhat different lines, which corrected this problem.

Hull No: 035   **Original name:** *Debby*   **Renamed:** *Debbie*   **Official No:** 198931

Type: Tug, Boom Boat   **Designer:** McLaren & Sons
Delivered: 1955   **Built for:** Dumaresq Bros. Ltd., Squamish BC

Length: OA 20′ **Reg** 18.2′ **Beam mld:** 8′
Depth: 4.5′   **Tonnage:** GT 3.35 **NT** 2.28
Material: Steel hull and superstructure

Main engine: Paragon 4 cylinder—1 @ 50 hp
Reduction ratio: 3.00 : 1   **Propeller:** 1 - 28″ dia.

The *Debby*, built for use by the Dumaresq brothers at their mill in Squamish, was a well-bottom-type boom boat. Such designs are now called "pod boats."

Hull No: 036   **Original name:** *R.L. 25*   **Renamed:** *V.T.N. No. 66; Seaspan 326; BYC Barge*   **Official No:** 198954

Type: Chip Barge   **Designer:** McLaren & Sons
Delivered: August 26, 1955   **Built for:** Red Line Barge Ltd., Vancouver BC   **Owner's representative:** Frank Ross

Length: OA 150′ **Beam mld:** 44′   **Depth:** 11′
Tonnage: GT 639.66   **Material:** Steel with wood superstructure   **Sister ship:** 040

The barge *R.L. 25* was a plain scow with a wooden box on it for carrying chips. Frank Ross wanted to have a fleet of barges. He had owned a fleet of barges in Montreal before the war, and he thought this was "the best thing since they made sliced bread." The Red Line fleet of barges included *R.L. 10, 11, 12 & 14*. Eventually they were all sold to Vancouver Tug.

Hull No: 037   **Original name:** *Esquimalt II*
Official No: 188212

Type: Tug, Berthing   **Designer:** T. A. McLaren/ Original   **Delivered:** 1955, Vancouver BC   **Built for:** Department of Public Works, Ottawa, Ontario
Length: OA 38′ **Reg** 35.3′ **Beam mld:** 12.2′
Tonnage: GT 13   **Material:** Steel
Main engine: Vivian—1 @ 80 hp @ 600 rpm

Built for use at the government graving dock in Esquimalt, the *Esquimalt II* was ordered by the Department of Public Works to replace a wooden tug that had grown old and decrepit. The vessel was essentially a repeat of the original wooden tug, but was made of steel, as this is what the customer wanted. They were not interested in anything else. Certain parts of the old vessel were removed and put on the new one.

Hull No: 038   **Original name:** *Kitmano*   **Renamed:** *Gulf Prince*   **Official No:** 188309

Type: Tug   **Designer:** McLaren & Sons   **Delivered:** 1955, Vancouver BC   **Built for:** Northern Towing & Salvage Co. Ltd., Kitimat BC   **Owner's representative:** Bill Cogswell

Length: OA 42′   Reg 39.2′   **Beam mld:** 14′
Depth: 7′   **Design draft:** 5.75′   **Tonnage:** GT 21
Material: Steel hull and superstructure   **Speed:** 8 knots

Main engines: General Motors diesel, 6-71 LH&RH—2 @ 165 hp @ 1800 rpm   **Reduction ratio:** 3.00 : 1
Propellers: 2 - 50″ dia.

A little twin-screw semi-tunnel tug with a towing winch, the *Kitmano* towed barges between Kitimat and Kemano for the building of the Alcan aluminum smelter and powerhouse at Kemano, BC.

Hull No: 039   **Original name:** Not Built

Type: Tug, Coastal/Offshore   **Designer:** McLaren & Sons   **Owner's representative:** Harold Jones

Length: OA 117.5′   **Design draft:** 13.5′
Material: Steel hull and superstructure

Main engine: Fairbanks-Morse—1 @ 1200 hp

Hull No. 39 was to have been a 110-foot tug for the Vancouver Tug Boat Co. Allied designed the vessel and had prepared steel cutting templates when the project was cancelled.

According to Arthur McLaren: "Harold Jones owned Vancouver Tug Boat Co. and he loved to fart around with all kinds of things. And he got all excited about building a great big tug. He had us (Allied) doing a lot of preliminary work on it—then he upped and died which made things difficult because the people who ran his estate were not the slightest bit interested in a big tug."

Hull No: 040   **Original name:** *R.L. 26*   **Renamed:** *Seaspan 327*   **Official No:** 188322

Type: Chip Barge   **Designer:** McLaren & Sons
Delivered: January 31, 1956, False Creek, Vancouver BC
Built for: Red Line Barge Ltd., Vancouver BC
Owner's representative: Frank Ross

Length: OA 150′   **Beam mld:** 44′   **Depth:** 11′
Tonnage: GT 640   **Material:** Steel with wood superstructure   **Sister ship:** 036

R.L. 26 was a simple 150-foot steel barge with a wooden box for moving wood chips. Allied installed the hog fuel box in February 1956.

Hull No: 041   **Original name:** *Gulf of Georgia 202*
Renamed: *S.N. Dock 2*   **Official No:** 188596

Type: Barge, Chip Scow   **Designer:** McLaren & Sons
Delivered: 1956, Vancouver BC   **Built for:** Gulf of Georgia Towing Co., Vancouver BC

Length: OA 130′   **Beam mld:** 43′   **Depth:** 10.6′
Tonnage: GT 512.2   **Sister ships:** 042; 068; 070

The *Gulf of Georgia 202*, which sold for $59,000, was a steel barge with a wood box for carrying hog fuel. It was divided into 8 compartments by one longitudinal bulkhead on centre and three transverse bulkheads; side and bottom shell plating was 3/8″ thick and increased to 1/2″ at the forward rake. A total of 365,100 pounds of steel were used in the construction.

Hull No: 042   **Original name:** *Gulf of Georgia 203*
Renamed: *Meldella*   **Official No:** 188659

Type: Barge, Chip Scow   **Designer:** McLaren & Sons
Delivered: 1956, Vancouver BC   **Built for:** Gulf of Georgia Towing Co., Vancouver BC

Length: OA 130′   **Beam mld:** 43′   **Depth:** 10.6′
Tonnage: GT 512.2   **Material:** Steel with wood superstructure   **Sister ships:** 041; 068; 070

Hull No: 043   **Original name:** *Gravelle Ferry*

Type: Reaction Ferry   **Designer:** McLaren & Sons
Delivered: 1956, Gravelle BC   **Built for:** Department of Public Works (Highways), Victoria BC

Length: OA 44′   **Beam mld:** 10′   **Depth:** 3′
Sister ships: 044; 052; 053

This simple catamaran ferry went across the river propelled by the current, hence the term "reaction."

Hull No: 044   **Original name:** *High Bar Ferry*

Type: Reaction Ferry   **Designer:** McLaren & Sons
Delivered: 1956   **Built for:** Department of Public Works (Highways), Victoria BC

Length: OA 44′   **Beam mld:** 10′   **Depth:** 3′
Sister ships: 043; 052; 053

West Coast Shipbuilders started building these catamaran ferries in 1946. The original vessels had wooden pontoons, but at the government's request, a steel one was designed by Arthur McLaren, and they just kept duplicating it.

Hull No: 045   **Original name:** *Cee Vee*
Official No: 189247

Type: Fishing   **Designer:** A naval architect in Seattle
Delivered: 1956, Vancouver BC   **Built for:** Tommy Wright, Vancouver BC

Length: OA 49.9′   Reg 45.2′   **Beam mld:** 14.3′
Depth: 7.6′   **Tonnage:** GT 36   NT 24
Material: Steel with wood superstructure

Main engine: General Motors diesel—1 @ 147 hp

According to Arthur McLaren: "Tommy Wright caught

dogfish and everything under the sun. The only thing I remember about him is a very funny story. He wanted a fishing boat made of steel. He got a very attractive design from an American naval architect in Seattle. We contracted to build the hull. Tommy wanted to put on a wooden house so he got a guy to come in and build a wooden house. We put the boat in the water and finished it up. And then Tommy had a problem keeping his engine cooled, so he wanted to put in a big heat exchanger. That was fine and we did all that. The boat, by this time, was in the water and he wanted us to put a big sea valve on the thing. How much was this going to cost? We gave him the price to install a new bronze sea valve and he said to hell with it. So over the weekend he brought in a valve from Seattle and put it on the boat. To this day I don't know how he installed the sea valve with the boat afloat!"

Hull No: 046   **Original name:** *Frank William*
Renamed: *Glacier No.1*   **Official No:** 198665

Type: Tug   **Designer:** McLaren & Sons   **Delivered:** 1956, Quesnel BC   **Built for:** F.W. Graham, Quesnel BC

Length: OA 30.25′   **Reg** 28.3′   **Beam mld:** 10′
Depth: 6′   **Design draft:** 5′   **Tonnage: GT** 6.39 **NT** 4.35

Main engine: Gardner diesel 6LW—1 @ 114 hp @ 1200 rpm   **Reduction ratio:** 2.00 : 1   **Propeller:** 1 - 38″ dia.

"*Frank William* was a little tug that a guy up in Quesnel wanted," said Arthur McLaren. "All he wanted was the hull. Not the machinery or anything else, just the hull. He wanted it sent up there so he could finish it up himself."

Hull No: 047   **Original name:** Work Skiff

Type: Work Skiff   **Designer:** McLaren & Sons
Delivered: 1956   **Built for:** Department of Public Works, Ottawa, Ontario

Length: OA 16′   **Material:** Steel   **Sister ships:** 059; 060; 075; 082; 086; 093

"Public Works used these open steel-hulled skiffs for work with their dredges and things like that, so they could go out and work on them."

Hull No: 048   **Original name:** *Sam*   **Official No:** 189235

Type: Tug, Boom Boat   **Designer:** McLaren & Sons
Delivered: 1956, Vancouver BC   **Built for:** Walden Sawmills Ltd., Minstrel Island BC

Length: OA 20′   **Reg** 18.3′   **Beam mld:** 8′   **Depth:** 5′   **Tonnage: GT** 4 **NT** 2   **Material:** Steel

Main engine: Paragon diesel—1 @ 95 hp

Hull No: 049   **Original name:** *Emil A. No. 2*
Renamed: *Fish Culture No. 1*   **Official No:** 189218

Type: Self-Propelled Barge   **Designer:** T. A. McLaren
Delivered: 1956, Hope BC   **Built for:** Emil Anderson Construction Co. Ltd., Hope BC

Length: OA 48′   **Reg** 48′   **Beam mld:** 20′
Depth: 4′   **Tonnage: GT** 28.27   **Material:** Steel

Main engine: Chrysler Crown gasoline—1 @ 100 hp

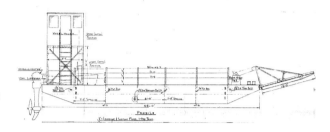

The *Emil A. No. 2.*

A single-screw self-propelled barge used for building of bridges and roads, this vessel divided along the centreline into two separate watertight hulls so that it could be dismantled and moved by truck. A 12-foot-long ramp was fitted at the bow. At the stern was a wheelhouse raised 8 feet above the deck. Propulsion was by a Harbour Master 360-degree steerable drive.

Hull No: 050   **Original name:** *Wyclees*   **Renamed:** *Timber Mac*   **Official No:** 189241

Type: Log Towing Tug   **Designer:** McLaren & Sons
Delivered: 1956, Vancouver BC   **Built for:** Vandale Logging Co. Ltd., Vancouver BC

Length: OA 30′   **Reg** 28.7′   **Beam mld:** 10′
Depth: 4.2′   **Tonnage: GT** 9 **NT** 6   **Material:** Steel hull and superstructure

Main engine: Cummins diesel—1 @ 165 hp @ 1800 rpm

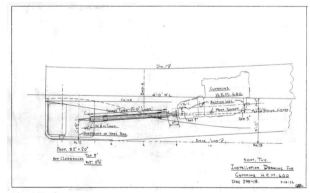

The *Wyclees.*

Hull No: 051   **Original name:** *Pitt Polder No. 1*
Renamed: *Sagra 2*   **Official No:** 189250

Type: Dredge   **Designer:** McLaren & Sons
Delivered: 1956, Pitt River BC

Length: Reg 71.7′   **Beam mld:** 17.3′
Tonnage: GT 39

The *Pitt Polder No. 1* was a barge fitted with Dutch-built

suction dredging equipment. It was made for a group of post-World War II Dutch immigrants to Canada who owned property on the Pitt River. This dredge was used to build polders—a Dutch term for a method of recovering land using dykes, channel dredging and draining. Prior to that time the Pitt River area was primarily marshland. Using land recovery practices similar to those they had employed in Holland, these people were able to recover a large amount of agricultural land, which is now known as the Pitt Polder Area.

Hull No: 052   **Original name:** *Blackpool Ferry*

Type: Reaction Ferry   **Designer:** McLaren & Sons
Delivered: 1956, Blackpool BC (by truck)
Built for: Department of Highways, Victoria BC

Length: OA 44′   **Beam mld:** 10′   **Depth:** 3′
Sister ships: 043; 044; 053

The *Blackpool Ferry* was a small vehicle ferry built to cross the North Thompson River.

Hull No: 053   **Original name:** *Little Fort Ferry*

Type: Reaction Ferry   **Designer:** McLaren & Sons
Delivered: 1956, Little Fort BC (by truck)
Built for: Department of Highways, Victoria BC

Length: OA 44′   **Beam mld:** 10′   **Depth:** 3′
Sister ships: 043; 044; 052

The *Little Fort Ferry* was a small vehicle ferry built to cross the North Thompson River at Little Fort, downriver from Clearwater, BC.

Hull No: 054   **Original name:** *P.R.F.C. No. I*
Official No: 198576

Type: Fish Packing Barge   **Designer:** McLaren & Sons
Delivered: 1956, Vancouver BC   **Built for:** Prince Rupert Fisherman's Co-operative

Length: OA 80′   **Beam mld:** 21.0′   **Depth:** 8.0′
Design draft: 6.5′   **Tonnage: GT** 104   **Dwt** 200 L. tons   **Sister ships:** 055; 057; 198

Three steel barges were built to transport herring to the processing plant. In this fishery, herring was ground into fish meal and oil rather then being processed for food use. In 1977 a fourth sister barge, *Foursome 1*, was built for service in the lucrative herring roe fishery. The barges had a spoon bow and were easily towed by a fishing vessel.

Hull No: 055   **Original name:** *P.R.F.C. No. II*
Official No: 198577

Type: Fish Packing Barge   **Designer:** McLaren & Sons
Delivered: 1956   **Built for:** Prince Rupert Fisherman's Co-operative

Length: OA 80′   **Beam mld:** 21.0′   **Depth:** 8.0′
Design draft: 6.5′   **Tonnage: GT** 104   **Dwt** 200 L. tons   **Material:** Steel   **Sister ships:** 054; 057; 198

Hull No: 056   **Original name:** *Island Tug 61*
Official No: 189157

Type: Barge, Chip Scow   **Designer:** McLaren & Sons

Delivered: 1957, Vancouver BC   **Built for:** Island Tug & Barge Ltd.

Length: OA 150′   **Beam mld:** 43.1′   **Depth:** 10.4′
Tonnage: GT 593.67   **Material:** Steel with wood superstructure

Hull No: 057   **Original name:** *P.R.F.C. No. III*
Official No: 198579

Type: Fish Packing Barge   **Designer:** McLaren & Sons
Delivered: 1956   **Built for:** Prince Rupert Fisherman's Co-operative

Length: OA 80′   **Reg** 80′   **Beam mld:** 21.0′   **Depth:** 8.0′   **Design draft:** 6.5′   **Tonnage: GT** 104
Dwt 200 L. tons   **Material:** Steel   **Sister ships:** 054; 055; 198

Hull No: 058   **Original name:** *Pacific Ocean*
Official No: 189993

Type: Fishing, Seiner   **Designer:** McLaren & Sons
Delivered: 1957, Vancouver BC   **Built for:** Kelly Fishing Company Ltd., Nanaimo BC   **Owner's representatives:** Robert and Nicholas Kelly

Length: OA 72′   **Reg** 67.2′   **Beam mld:** 21.1′
Depth: 10′   **Tonnage: GT** 105   **NT** 71.39   **Dwt** 120 L. tons   **Speed:** 10 knots

Main engines: General Motors 6-71 tandem—2 @ 145 hp @ 1800 rpm   **Reduction ratio:** 5.00 : 1

The *Pacific Ocean*.

The *Pacific Ocean* was the first relatively large fishing vessel built by Allied. It was lengthened 15 feet by Allied, in 1962.

Hull No: 059   **Original name:** Work Skiff

Type: Skiff   **Designer:** McLaren & Sons
Delivered: 1957   **Built for:** Department of Public Works, Ottawa, Ontario

Length: OA 16′   **Beam mld:** 6′   **Depth:** 2′
Material: Steel   **Sister ships:** 047; 060; 075; 082; 086; 093

These simple steel skiffs were made of 12-gauge plate.

Buoyancy chambers were fitted at the bow and stern. Each vessel weighed 1,335 lbs., took 64 hours to build and was sold for $239 plus taxes.

Hull No: 060   **Original name:** Work Skiff

Type: Skiff   **Designer:** McLaren & Sons
Delivered: 1957   **Built for:** Department of Public Works, Ottawa, Ontario

Length: OA 16'   **Material:** Steel   **Sister ships:**
047; 059; 075; 082; 086; 093

Hull No: 061   **Original name:** *Sagra*   **Official No:** 189979

Type: Tug, Dredge Tender   **Designer:** McLaren & Sons
Delivered: 1957   **Built for:** Pitt Polder Ltd.

Length: OA 30'   **Reg** 28.1'   **Beam mld:** 10'
Depth: 3.0'   **Tonnage: GT** 6   **NT** 4

Main engine: Lister diesel—1 @ 77 hp

Sagra was a 30-foot tug built to tend the dredge *Pitt Polder No. 1* (Hull No. 51). The design was a little different from a standard Allied steel tug, more or less to suit Dutch practice.

Hull No: 062   **Original name:** *Island Tanker No. 1*
Renamed: *Seaspan 810*   **Official No:** 310263

Type: Fuel Barge   **Designer:** McLaren & Sons (W. R. Brown)   **Delivered:** 1957   **Built for:** Island Tug & Barge Ltd., Victoria BC   **Owner's representative:** Norman Turner

Length: OA 165'   **Reg** 165'   **Beam mld:** 42.0'
Depth: 11.5'   **Design draft:** 10'   **Tonnage:**
GT 643.5   **NT** 645.4   **Dwt** 1320 L. tons

The *Island Tanker No. 1* was a 10,000-barrel capacity bulk carrier for transport of gasoline and diesel fuel. It was fitted with an engine and machinery dedicated to pumping out its cargo and had a ship-shape bow, double chines and a transom stern.

Hull No: 063   **Original name:** *Y.M.U. 118*

Type: Work Boat, Utility   **Designer:** Department of National Defence   **Delivered:** 1957, Vancouver BC
Built for: Department of National Defence, Ottawa, Ontario

Length: OA 48'   **Reg** 46'   **Beam mld:** 12.75'   **Depth:**
6'   **Design draft:** 3.75'   **Tonnage: GT** 13
Lightship 25 L. tons   **Material:** Steel   **Speed:** 9 knots
Main engine: Caterpillar—1 @ 120 hp @ 1000 rpm
Sister ship: 064

The *Y.M.U. 118* and *Y.M.U. 119* were utilitarian work boats built for the Canadian Navy. Crown Assets disposed of the *Y.M.U. 118* in September 1995 for approximately $23,000.

Hull No: 064   **Original name:** *Y.M.U. 119*

Type: Work Boat, Utility   **Designer:** Department of

National Defence   **Delivered:** 1957, Vancouver BC
Built for: Department of National Defence, Ottawa, Ontario

Length: OA 48'   **Beam mld:** 12.75'   **Depth:** 6'
Design draft: 3.75'   **Tonnage: GT** 13
Material: Steel   **Speed:** 9 knots

Main engine: Caterpillar—1 @ 120 hp @ 1000 rpm
Sister ship: 063

Hull No: 065   **Original name:** *Dumit*   **Renamed:**
Hay River No. 1   **Official No:** 188710

Type: Buoy Tender   **Designer:** Milne, Gilmore & German   **Delivered:** 1958, Waterways, Alberta
Built for: Minister of Transport, Ottawa, Ontario

Length: OA 67.5'   **Reg** 66.8'   **Beam mld:** 21.2'
Depth: 5.7'   **Design draft:** 2.5'   **Tonnage: GT** 98
NT 41.74   **Lightship** 57   **Dwt** 13 L. tons   **Material:**
Steel hull and superstructure   **Capacity:** 5 (crew)
Speed: 10 knots (max) 8.5 knots (service)

Main engines: Cummins HRMS 600—2 @ 225 hp
Reduction ratio: 3.38 : 1   **Sister ship:** 066

"What had happened up in the northern rivers," Arthur McLaren remembered, "was that at first they didn't have any means of putting channel marker buoys in the river at all. And then they contacted a fellow who lived at McMurray. He put in a boat to lift buoys in and out. The trouble was that the season was half over before he got the buoys in. So the federal government decided to build two buoy tenders for themselves. One to operate on the Athabasca River from McMurray down to Fort Fitzgerald and the other one to operate from Fort Fitzgerald down as well as on the Mackenzie River. When we finished the boats we took them for trials on the Clearwater River outside Waterways. The bloody boats wouldn't go straight at all. They'd go every which way except straight! It was because they were built like saucers! To fix it we took the two rudders and made them diverge toe out to put some drag at the aft end, like skegs on a barge."

Hull No: 066   **Original name:** *Miskanaw*
Official No: 310126

Type: Buoy   **Designer:** Milne, Gilmore & German
Delivered: 1958, Waterways, Alberta   **Built for:**
Minister of Transport, Ottawa, Ontario

Length: OA 67.5'   **Reg** 66.8'   **Beam mld:** 21.2'
Depth: 5.7'   **Design draft:** 2.5'   **Tonnage: GT** 98
NT 41.67   **Lightship** 57 L. tons   **Dwt** 13 L. tons
Material: Steel hull and superstructure   **Capacity:** 5
(crew)   **Speed:** 10 knots (max) 8.5 knots (service)

Main engines: Cummins HRMS 600—2 @ 225 hp
Reduction ratio: 3.38 : 1   **Sister ship:** 065

Hull No: 067   **Original name:** Pontoon

Type: Float   **Designer:** McLaren & Sons
Delivered: 1957   **Built for:** LaFarge Cement Ltd.

Length: OA 24′ **Beam mld:** 11′ **Depth:** 4′
Material: Steel

This small barge was built to support a conveyor boom.

Hull No: 068 **Original name:** *Gulf of Georgia No. 204*
Renamed: *Crown Forest No. 11; Sunshine Transporter II*
Official No: 310355

Type: Barge, Scow **Designer:** McLaren & Sons
Delivered: 1957 **Built for:** Gulf of Georgia Towing
Co., Vancouver BC

Length: OA 150′ **Reg** 150′ **Beam mld:** 43.0′
Depth: 10′ **Design draft:** 9′ **Tonnage:**
GT 589.51 **Dwt** 1322 **Sister ships:** 041; 042; 070

Hull No: 069 **Original name:** Pontoon

Type: Barge, Clay slurry **Designer:** McLaren & Sons
Delivered: 1957 **Built for:** Lafarge Cement Ltd.

Length: OA 24′ **Beam mld:** 18′ **Depth:** 4′

A small barge built to support a clay slurry pump.

Hull No: 070 **Original name:** *Gulf of Georgia No. 205*
Renamed: *MBM 17* **Official No:** 189265

Type: Barge, Clay slurry **Designer:** McLaren & Sons
Delivered: Vancouver BC

Length: OA 130′ **Reg** 130′ **Beam mld:** 43.0′
Depth: 10.5′ **Tonnage: GT** 651.02 **NT** 651.0
Dwt 1138 L. tons

Gulf of Georgia Towing Company had this barge built
for the carriage of liquid clay slurry for Lafarge Cement
Ltd. The slurry tank was arranged with a bottom that sloped
to a trough at the low point at centre, lengthwise.

Hull No: 071 **Original name:** *P.W.D. No. 253*
Renamed: *D253* **Official No:** 311167

Type: Suction Dredge **Delivered:** 1957, Waterways,
Alberta **Built for:** Department of Public Works

Length: OA 80′ **Beam mld:** 30′ **Depth:** 5′
Tonnage: GT 131

The *P.W.D. No. 253.*

This steel barge was fitted with a 64′x24′x8′ steel house
to enclose the machinery that powered the 10″ suction
dredge. It was used to dredge northern rivers for navigation.

Hull No: 072 **Original name:** *Island Princess*
Renamed: *North Island Princess* **Official No:** 310431

Type: Vehicle Ferry **Designer:** Robert Allan
Delivered: 1958, Vancouver BC **Built for:** Gulf Islands
Navigation Ltd.
Owner's representative: Captain Oswald "Sparky" New

Length: OA 131.3′ **Reg** 120′ **Beam mld:** 34.0′
Depth: 10.75′ **Design draft:** 7′ **Tonnage:**
GT 502 **Material:** Steel **Capacity:** 300
(passengers); 20 (vehicles) **Speed:** 11 knots
Main engines: Rolls Royce diesel—2 @ 256 hp @ 1800 rpm

Hull No: 073 **Original name:** *Clowhom*
Official No: 310391

Type: Passenger Launch **Designer:** McLaren & Sons
Delivered: 1958 **Built for:** BC Electric (later BC Power
Corp), Vancouver BC **Owner's representative:**
P.E. MacBride

Length: OA 25′ **Reg** 23.2′ **Beam mld:** 8′
Depth: 3′ **Tonnage: GT** 4.87 **NT** 3.31
Material: Steel hull and superstructure **Capacity:** 1
(crew); 10 (passengers) **Speed:** 16 knots (max) 14 knots
(service)
Main engine: Chrysler Imperial gasoline—1 @ 225 hp

This steel personnel launch was built for use by the BC
Electric Company to access the Clowhom Falls power plant
on Salmon Inlet off Sechelt Inlet. The *Clowhom* was
launched at 11:45 a.m. on March 4, 1958. The sale price was
$9,950 excluding taxes.

Hull No: 074 **Original name:** *Green Lake*
Official No: 310423

Type: Tug, Boom Boat **Designer:** McLaren & Sons
Delivered: 1958, Vancouver BC **Built for:** L&K
Lumber Co., Vancouver BC **Owner's representative:**
G.M. Lyttle

Length: OA 15′ **Reg** 14′ **Beam mld:** 7.5′
Depth: 3.2′ **Design draft:** 3′ **Tonnage: GT** 1.77
NT 1.2 **Material:** Steel
Main engine: Chrysler Crown gasoline—1 @ 110 hp
Reduction ratio: 2.95 : 1 **Propeller:** 1 - 28″ dia.

The *Green Lake* was one of Allied's standard boom boats
used to service a wood mill. The complete boat was built
and trialled in a 5-week period and sold for $4,725. The
Chrysler gasoline engine c/w reverse gear and 12-volt
system cost $1,807 and was sold by Dave Simpson of White
Marine Engines. Simpson sold hundreds of Chrysler engines
for use in forestry and fishing vessels.

Hull No: 075 **Original name:** Work Skiff

Type: Work Boat **Designer:** McLaren & Sons
Built for: Department of Public Works, Ottawa, Ontario
Length: OA 16′ **Beam mld:** 6′ **Depth:** 3′
Material: Steel **Sister ships:** 047; 059; 060; 082; 086; 093

Hull No: 076　　**Original name:** *Paddy D*
Official No: 320060

Type: Tug, Boom Boat　　**Designer:** McLaren & Sons
Delivered: 1958　　**Built for:** Victoria Plywood Ltd.,
Victoria BC

Length:　**OA** 15′　**Reg** 14′　**Beam mld:** 7.6′
Depth: 3.5′　　**Tonnage:**　**GT** 1　**NT** 1　　**Material:**
Steel

Main engine: Chrysler gasoline—1 @ 115 hp

Hull No: 077　　**Original name:** *Yorke No. 12*
Renamed: *DHT B No.1; Aquamex*

Type: Rail Car Barge　　**Designer:** McLaren & Sons
Delivered: 1958, Vancouver BC　　**Built for:** F. M. Yorke
& Son Ltd., Vancouver BC　　**Owner's representative:**
Lorne Yorke

Length:　**OA** 90′　**Beam mld:** 34′　　**Depth:** 10.5′
Tonnage:　**GT** 264　　**Capacity:** 4 (rail cars)　　**Sister
ships:** 078; 079; 080; 085

The *Yorke No. 12* and its sister ships were built to move
the rail cars used at many of the lumber mills on the BC
south coast. In 1958 Allied was commissioned to build five
rail car barges for F. M. Yorke & Son. Four were 4-railcar
barges and one was a 6-railcar barge.

Hull No: 078　　**Original name:** *Yorke No. 14*
Official No: 311188

Type: Rail Car Barge　　**Designer:** McLaren & Sons
Delivered: 1958, Vancouver BC　　**Built for:** F. M. Yorke
& Son Ltd., Vancouver BC　　**Owner's representative:**
Lorne Yorke

Length:　**OA** 90′　**Beam mld:** 34′　　**Depth:** 10.5′
Tonnage:　**GT** 264　　**Capacity:** 4 (rail cars)
Sister ships: 077; 079; 080; 085

Hull No: 079　　**Original name:** *Yorke No. 15*
Renamed: *Arcnav No. 101*　　**Official No:** 311196

Type: Rail Car Barge　　**Designer:** McLaren & Sons
Delivered: 1958, Vancouver BC　　**Built for:** F. M. Yorke
& Son Ltd., Vancouver BC　　**Owner's representative:**
Lorne Yorke

Length:　**OA** 90′　**Beam mld:** 34′　　**Depth:** 10.5′
Tonnage:　**GT** 264　　**Capacity:** 4 (rail cars)　　**Sister
ships:** 077; 078; 080; 085

Hull No: 080　　**Original name:** *Yorke No. 16*
Renamed: *Seaspan 905; Delcat 203*　　**Official No:** 311204

Type: Rail Car Barge　　**Designer:** McLaren & Sons
Delivered: 1958, Vancouver BC　　**Built for:** F. M. Yorke
& Son Ltd., Vancouver BC　　**Owner's representative:**
Lorne Yorke

Length:　**OA** 100′　**Beam mld:** 42′　　**Depth:** 9.5′
Tonnage:　**GT** 351　　**Material:** Steel　　**Capacity:** 6
(rail cars)

Hull No: 081　　**Original name:** *Snauq*　　**Renamed:**
Red Baron No. 1　　**Official No:** 311199

Type: Work Boat, Harbour Patrol　　**Designer:** John
Brandlmayer　　**Delivered:** 1958, Vancouver BC
Built for: National Harbours Board, Ottawa, Ontario
Owner's representative: Capt. D. B. L. Johnson

Length:　**OA** 22.3′　**Reg** 21.4′　**Beam mld:** 9′
Depth: 2.8′　　**Tonnage:**　**GT** 4.18　**NT** 2.84
Material: Steel hull and superstructure

Main engine: Nordberg Norseman 6 cylinder gasoline—1
@ 155 hp　　**Reduction ratio:** 2.50 : 1　　**Propeller:** 1 -
20″ dia.

The *Snauq*.

The *Snauq* was built to patrol the waters of False Creek
and remove debris that could block the channel. It replaced
the 35-foot wood tug *Burnaby*, which was built in 1925.
Captain Charlie Cates, an expert on local Indian lore,
suggested the unusual name "Snauq," which is the Native
name for the entrance to False Creek.

Hull No: 082　　**Original name:** Work Skiff

Type: Work Skiff　　**Designer:** McLaren & Sons
Length:　**OA** 16′　**Beam mld:** 6′　　**Depth:** 3′
Material: Steel　　**Sister ships:** 047; 059; 060; 075; 086;
093

Hull No: 083　　**Original name:** *Halcyon Bay*
Renamed: *Beaver Delta II*　　**Official No:** 311266

Type: Tug, Dredge Tender　　**Designer:** McLaren & Sons
Delivered: 1958　　**Built for:** Department of Public
Works, Ottawa, Ontario

Length:　**OA** 37.5′　**Beam mld:** 12′　　**Depth:** 5.75′
Material: Steel hull and superstructure

Main engines: Cummins—2 @ 160 hp　　**Reduction
ratio:** 2.00 : 1　　**Propellers:** 2 - 29″ dia.

This twin-screw shallow-draft tender was built to assist a
Federal Public Works dredge on the Arrow Lakes. It was
designed to be transportable in one piece, by rail. Up until
the early 1970s there was not enough clearance on the
highways to permit sizable sections to move by road.

Hull No: 084　　**Original name:** *V.P.D. No. 4*
Renamed: *Dillingham No. 50; Delcat No. 50*
Official No: 311209

Type: Barge, Pile Driving Scow **Designer:** McLaren & Sons (D. G. Cowie) **Delivered:** 1958 **Built for:** Vancouver Pile Driving & Contracting Co., North Vancouver BC

Length: **OA** 65' **Reg** 65' **Beam mld:** 24' **Depth:** 4.5' **Material:** Steel

This barge was used as a pile-driving scow. Allied built the basic barge only; the equipment was installed by the owner.

Hull No: 085 **Original name:** *Yorke No. 17*
Renamed: *Arcnav No. 102* **Official No:** 311218

Type: Rail Car Barge **Designer:** McLaren & Sons **Delivered:** 1958, Vancouver BC **Built for:** F. M. Yorke & Son Ltd., Vancouver BC **Owner's representative:** Lorne Yorke

Length: **OA** 90' **Beam mld:** 34' **Depth:** 10.5' **Tonnage:** **GT** 264 **Material:** Steel **Capacity:** 4 (rail cars) **Sister ships:** 077; 078; 079; 080

Hull No: 086 **Original name:** Work Skiff

Type: Work Skiff **Designer:** McLaren & Sons **Delivered:** 1958, Monte Creek BC **Built for:** Department of Public Works, Ottawa, Ontario

Length: **OA** 18' **Beam mld:** 8' **Depth:** 3' **Material:** Steel **Sister ships:** 047; 059; 060; 075; 082; 093

Hull No: 087 **Original name:** Launch

Type: Passenger Launch **Designer:** McLaren & Sons **Delivered:** 1958, Hudson's Hope BC **Built for:** Department of Highways, Victoria BC

Length: **OA** 26.25' **Beam mld:** 8' **Depth:** 3' **Material:** Steel

Hull 87 was a little steel open launch with a canopy over it. It was used for ferrying people on the Peace River at Hudson's Hope.

Hull No: 088 **Original name:** *B.A. Logger*
Renamed: *Pacific Barge 99; Seaspan 802; J.S.M. Transporter*

Type: Fuel Barge **Designer:** McLaren & Sons **Delivered:** 1958 **Built for:** British American Oil Co.

Length: **OA** 100' **Beam mld:** 35' **Depth:** 9.5' **Tonnage:** **GT** 300

The *B.A. Logger* was a 3,000-barrel capacity barge built for the British American Oil Co. It was used for transporting oil products to marine service stations located on the coast of BC. The vessel caught fire soon after delivery and was sold by the insurance company to the Pacific Tanker Company, which contracted Allied to rebuild it under the name *Pacific Barge 99*. Later, British American Oil had Allied build a second *B.A. Logger* (*B.A. Logger (II)*—Hull 116) to replace the damaged barge.

Hull No: 089 **Original name:** *Colleen L*
Renamed: *Canyon Clipper* **Official No:** 311249

Type: Harbour Tug **Designer:** McLaren & Sons **Delivered:** April, 1959 **Built for:** Lyttle Bros. Ltd., Vancouver BC **Owner's representative:** Doug Dixon

Length: **OA** 30' **Reg** 29' **Beam mld:** 11' **Depth:** 5.5' **Design draft:** 4' **Tonnage:** **GT** 8.49 **NT** 5.77 **Material:** Steel

Main engine: General Motors 671—1 @ 165 hp **Propeller:** 1 - 42" dia.

This harbour tug was used at L&K Lumber's mill at the foot of Pemberton Avenue in North Vancouver.

Hull No: 090 **Original name:** *T.B.D. No. 1*
Renamed: *Dillingham No. 251* **Official No:** 311225

Type: Barge **Designer:** McLaren & Sons **Delivered:** 1959 **Built for:** Tide Bay Dredging Co. Ltd. **Owner's representative:** P.T. Cote

Length: **OA** 60' **Beam mld:** 20' **Depth:** 5' **Tonnage:** **GT** 45.95 **NT** 45.95

T.B.D. No. 1 was a bare barge on which the owners fitted dredging equipment to suit their needs. The damage caused by the Fraser Valley flood of 1948 was so great that lots of small government-tendered dredging jobs were available. Following the flood a dredging program was established; it ran for at least fifteen years, during which numerous people with small dredges built most of the sloughs and dikes that exist in the Fraser Valley today.

Hull No: 091 **Original name:** *Scacon* **Official No:** 312080

Type: Tug **Delivered:** 1959 **Built for:** Jack Scagel, Vancouver BC **Owner's representatives:** Jack Scagel & Hughie Connacher

Length: **OA** 31' **Reg** 29' **Beam mld:** 11' **Depth:** 5.5' **Tonnage:** **GT** 8 **NT** 6 **Material:** Steel

Main engine: 1 @ 225 hp

Jack Scagel had Allied build the hull of this tug and the owners outfitted it themselves.

Hull No: 092 **Original name:** *Daleo* **Official No:** 312068

Type: Fishing Packer **Designer:** McLaren & Sons **Delivered:** 1959, Vancouver BC **Built for:** Donald C. Cameron, Madeira Park BC **Owner's representative:** Donald Cameron

Length: **OA** 47' **Reg** 42.7' **Beam mld:** 14.3' **Depth:** 6.58' **Tonnage:** **GT** 33.22 **NT** 22.59 **Lightship** 23 L. tons **Material:** Steel hull and superstructure **Speed:** 8.5 knots (max)

Main engine: General Motors 6-71—1 @ 147 hp @ 1800 rpm **Reduction ratio:** 3.00 : 1

The *Daleo* was used by Mr. Cameron to service fish buying stations in the vicinity of Pender Harbour, and to bring the fresh fish into Steveston and Vancouver. She was named after the Owner's daughter Dale. The vessel sank in shallow waters on August 12, 1997. The crew of 5 reached shore by the time search and rescue craft arrived.

Hull No: 093   **Original name:** Work Skiff

Type: Work Skiff   **Designer:** McLaren & Sons
Delivered: Nakusp, BC   **Built for:** Department of Public Works, Ottawa, Ontario
Length: **OA** 16′   **Beam mld:** 6′   **Depth:** 3′
Material: Steel   **Sister ships:** 047; 059; 060; 075; 082; 086

Hull No: 094   **Original name:** *Cook Bay*
Official No: 312046

Type: Tug, Boom Boat   **Designer:** McLaren & Sons
Delivered: 1959   **Built for:** Forbes Bay Logging Co. Ltd., Vancouver BC   **Owner's representative:** Mr. McDonagh
Length: **OA** 15′   **Reg** 14′   **Beam mld:** 7.5′
Depth: 3.5′   **Tonnage:**   **GT** 1.8   **NT** 1.23
Material: Steel

Main engine: Chrysler Crown gasoline—1 @ 110 hp

This standard Allied boom boat took 559 hours to build and was sold for $4,750 plus tax.

Hull No: 095   **Original name:** *P.W.D. No. 328*
Renamed: *D.P.W. No. 328*   **Official No:** 311263

Type: Barge   **Designer:** McLaren & Sons
Delivered: 1959   **Built for:** Department of Public Works, Ottawa
Length: **OA** 35′   **Reg** 35′   **Beam mld:** 15′
Depth: 2.8′   **Tonnage:**   **GT** 12

This steel scow was used on the Fraser River in aid of government dredging operations. When dredging the river they placed the soil up on the river bank. This barge was used to support the pipeline going ashore.

Hull No: 096   **Original name:** *Gulf Scamp*
Official No: 311270

Type: Tug   **Designer:** McLaren & Sons   **Delivered:** 1959   **Built for:** River Towing Co. Ltd., Vancouver BC
Owner's representative: L. M. MacDonald
Length: **OA** 32′   **Reg** 29.8′   **Beam mld:** 11.2′
Depth: 4.5′   **Tonnage:**   **GT** 10   **NT** 7
Material: Steel hull and superstructure

Main engine: General Motors—1 @ 147 hp

Hull No: 097   **Original name:** *Sandy L II*
Renamed: *Candy L II; Barbie L II*   **Official No:** 312071

Type: Tug, Boom Boat   **Designer:** McLaren & Sons
Delivered: 1959   **Built for:** L&K Lumber Ltd., North Vancouver BC   **Owner's representative:** Doug Dixon
Length: **OA** 15′   **Reg** 14′   **Beam mld:** 7.5′
Depth: 3.5′   **Tonnage:**   **GT** 1.88   **NT** 1.28
Material: Steel

Main engine: Chrysler Crown gasoline—1 @ 125 hp
Reduction ratio: 4.00 : 1   **Propeller:** 1 - 28″ dia. x 22″ pitch

This typical Allied 15-foot steel bulldozer boom boat was built for use at the North Vancouver mill.

Hull No: 098   **Original name:** *Bull Block*
Official No: 312084

Type: Tug Camp Tender   **Designer:** McLaren & Sons
Delivered: 1959, Vancouver BC   **Built for:** Albert J. Stroud, Bella Coola BC
Length: **OA** 31′   **Reg** 29′   **Beam mld:** 11′
Depth: 5.5′   **Tonnage:**   **GT** 9   **NT** 6   **Material:** Steel hull and superstructure

Main engine: General Motors 6-71—1 @ 147 hp @ 1800 rpm

The *Bull Block*.

Albert Stroud sent Arthur a letter in 1960 describing the challenge of operating a small business: "Dear Sir: Enclosed is my cheque for the amount owing you. I am very sorry I was so long in paying my debt. I did not make you wait till last to be paid and I had several debts who waited to. I have found that the work for my boat is easy to come by but another thing to get paid."

Hull No: 099   **Original name:** *P. No. 1*   **Official No:** 312093

Type: Tug   **Designer:** McLaren & Sons   **Delivered:** 1959, Vancouver BC (on truck)   **Built for:** Percy Logging Co. Ltd., Vancouver BC
Owner's representative: G.E. Percy
Length: **OA** 15′   **Reg** 14′   **Beam mld:** 7.5′
Depth: 3.5′   **Tonnage:**   **GT** 1.85   **NT** 1.26
Material: Steel

Main engine: Chrysler Crown gasoline—1 @ 125 hp

This standard boom boat was sold complete for $4,839 plus taxes. Full payment was delayed due to the effects of a major forest industry strike in the summer of 1959.

Hull No: 100   **Original name:** *Yorke No. 18*
Renamed: *Seaspan 906; Evco 100*

Type: Rail Car Barge   **Designer:** McLaren & Sons

Delivered: 1959, Vancouver BC   **Built for:** F. M. Yorke & Son Ltd., Vancouver BC   **Owner's representative:** Lorne Yorke

Length: OA 100'   **Beam mld:** 43'   **Depth:** 10'
Tonnage: GT 351   **Capacity:** 6 (rail cars)   **Sister ships:** 080; 101; 106

Hull No: 101   **Original name:** *Yorke No. 19*
Official No: 312786

Type: Barge, Rail Car   **Designer:** McLaren & Sons
Delivered: 1959   **Built for:** F.M. Yorke & Son Ltd., Vancouver BC   **Owner's representative:** Lorne Yorke

Length: Reg 100'   **Beam mld:** 42'   **Depth:** 10'
Tonnage: GT 350

Arthur McLaren remembered: "Allied built a number of simple barges for F.M. Yorke & Son. When Yorke went out of business, the barges all passed over to Vancouver Tug, who kept what they wanted and sold the ones that they weren't attracted to. Harold Jones was the principal of Vancouver Tug until he died. Then his sidekick Jim Stewart took over. The other one in there was Arthur Lindsey. He was the businessman of the group. He watched the dollars. In the end there was Vancouver Tug and there was Island Tug & Barge, two similar companies, and in the middle 1960s they combined forces to form a joint operation, which eventually became Seaspan."

Hull No: 102A   **Original name:** *Triad II*
Official No: 312082

Type: Ferry, Reaction   **Designer:** McLaren & Sons
Delivered: 1959   **Built for:** Triad Oil Co. Ltd., Calgary, Alberta   **Owner's representative:** Dr. T. C. Richards

Length: OA 44'   **Reg** 43.8'   **Beam mld:** 10'
Depth: 2.7'   **Tonnage: GT** 8   **Sister ships:** 043; 053; 044; 052

This catamaran "reaction" ferry was built to transport oil exploration equipment across Pine River in northern Alberta.

Hull No: 102B   **Original name:** *Triad III*
Official No: 312083

Type: Ferry, reaction   **Designer:** McLaren & Sons
Delivered: 1959   **Built for:** Triad Oil Co. Ltd., Calgary, Alberta

Length: OA 44'   **Reg** 43.8'   **Beam mld:** 10'
Depth: 2.7'   **Tonnage: GT** 8

Hull No: 103   **Original name:** *Attu*
Official No: 312815

Type: Fishing, Seiner/Longliner   **Designer:** Robert Allan   **Delivered:** 1959, Vancouver BC   **Built for:** Arnet Boat Co. Ltd., West Vancouver BC   **Owner's representative:** Edgar Arnet

Length: OA 76'   **Reg** 69.5'   **Beam mld:** 21'
Depth: 11.25'   **Tonnage: GT** 115   **NT** 78

Material: Steel with aluminum superstructure   **Speed:** 10.5 knots (max) 10.2 knots (service)

Main engine: Stork AR216—1 @ 282 hp @ 650 rpm
Reduction ratio: 2.00 : 1   **Propeller:** 1 - controllable pitch

Built for halibut fishing in the Bering Sea, *Attu* was one of the first BC fishing vessels to be fitted with an aluminum deckhouse (alloy 57S or 65S—salt water resistant) and bilge keel rolling chocks. This vessel was a replacement for the *Kodiak*, which was lost in a storm.

Hull No: 104   **Original name:** *Island Pine*
Renamed: *Seaspan 701; Island Pine*   **Official No:** 312266

Type: Barge, Self-Dumping Log   **Designer:** McLaren & Sons   **Delivered:** 1959, Vancouver BC   **Built for:** Island Tug & Barge Ltd., Victoria BC   **Owner's representative:** Harold Elworthy

Length: OA 220'   **Reg** 220'   **Beam mld:** 54'
Depth: 14.5'   **Design draft:** 12'   **Tonnage: GT** 1509   **Dwt** 3125 L. tons

The *Island Pine*.

The vessel's first operational trip in November 1959 was to Nootka Sound on the west coast of Vancouver Island, where she loaded a log cargo at Mooyah Bay for delivery to Howe Sound. In 1999, the Island Pine was still in active service as a self-dumping log barge.

Hull No: 105   **Original name:** *T.B.D. No. 2*
Renamed: *Dillingham No. 250; Delcat 250*   **Official No:** 311279

Type: Barge   **Designer:** McLaren & Sons
Delivered: 1959   **Built for:** Tide Bay Dredging Co. Ltd., New Westminster BC

Length: OA 75'   **Beam mld:** 30'   **Depth:** 6'
Tonnage: GT 111

This barge was originally used for bunkering dredges being used to build the BC Ferry terminal at Tsawwassen beach.

Hull No: 106   **Original name:** *Yorke No. 20*
Renamed: *Seaspan 905; Valley No. 2*   **Official No:**
312814

Type: Barge, Rail Car   **Designer:** McLaren & Sons
Delivered: 1959, Vancouver BC   **Built for:** F.M. Yorke
& Son Ltd., Vancouver BC

Length: **OA** 100′   **Beam mld:** 42′   **Depth:** 7.5′
Tonnage: **GT** 274   **Material:** Steel

Hull No: 107   **Original name:** *Black Fir*
Official No: 312116

Type: Tug, Log Towing   **Designer:** McLaren & Sons
Delivered: 1960, Vancouver BC   **Built for:** Texada
Towing Co. Ltd., Vancouver BC   **Owner's**
representatives: Doug Rust and Doug Fielding

Length: **OA** 51′   **Reg** 45.7′   **Beam mld:** 17.3′
Depth: 11′   **Design draft:** 10′   **Tonnage:**   **GT** 41
NT 28   **Lightship** 58   **Dwt** 21 L. tons   **Material:**
Steel hull and superstructure

Main engine: B & W Alpha 405V0 2-cycle—1 @ 350 hp @
375 rpm

Launched on Saturday morning, January 30, 1960, the
vessel was christened by April Cochran, daughter of D.W.
Cochran, one of 3 partners. The other partners were Capt.
Doug Rust of Vancouver and Capt. H. D. Fielding of
Pender Harbour. The *Black Fir* sank, by down-flooding, in
1962.

Hull No: 108   **Original name:** *Quadra Queen*
Renamed: *Cortes Queen; Nicola*   **Official No:** 312279

Type: Ferry, Vehicle   **Designer:** McLaren & Sons
Delivered: 1960   **Built for:** Department of Highways,
Victoria BC   **Owner's representative:** Ken Gann

Length: **OA** 110′   **Reg** 101.7′   **Beam mld:** 38′
Depth: 10.5′   **Tonnage:**   **GT** 255   **NT** 174
Material: Steel hull and superstructure   **Capacity:** 4
(crew); 99 (passengers); 15 (vehicles)   **Speed:** 12 knots
(max) 9.8 knots (service)

Main engines: Cummins HRMS—2 @ 240 hp @ 1800 rpm
Sister ship: 117

The *Quadra Queen* was the first public vehicle ferry to
operate between Campbell River and Quathiaski Cove,
Quadra Island. A total of 4 ferries were built to this basic
design, 2 by Allied (*Quadra Queen* and *Garibaldi*), 1 by BC
Marine (*Nimpkish*) and 1 by McKenzie Barge (*Garibaldi II*).

Hull No: 109   **Original name:** *G.M. Venture*
Official No: 312848

Type: Tug, Log Towing   **Designer:** W. R. Brown
Delivered: 1960, Vancouver BC   **Built for:** G.M. Flyer
Towing Ltd., Campbell River BC   **Owner's**
representative: Frank L. Hole

Length: **OA** 40′   **Reg** 37.4′   **Beam mld:** 15.6′
Depth: 9.5′   **Tonnage:**   **GT** 15   **NT** 10   **Material:**
Steel hull and superstructure   **Speed:** 10.6 knots (max)

Main engines: Detroit diesel Tandem Twin 6-110—2 @
220 hp @ 1800 rpm   **Reduction ratio:** 4.50 : 1
Propeller: 1 - 65″ dia.

This tug had a deep draft for its length. "The midship
section looked like a top," said Arthur McLaren. "It was a V,
a straight V. Sadly, the man who inspired her design did not
live to see her in service. Alva 'Curley' Snider died just a
week before the launch."

Hull No: 110   **Original name:** *Schwatka*
Official No: 312895

Type: Passenger   **Designer:** McLaren & Sons
Delivered: 1960, Whitehorse, Yukon   **Built for:** Yukon
River Industries Ltd., Whitehorse YT
Owner's representative: John Scott

Length: **OA** 48.9′   **Reg** 46.5′   **Beam mld:** 12′
Depth: 4′   **Tonnage:**   **GT** 28   **NT** 23   **Material:**
Steel hull and superstructure   **Capacity:** 2 (crew); 38
(passengers)   **Speed:** 11 knots

Main engines: BMC—2 @ 90 hp   **Propellers:** 2

Arthur McLaren remembered: "A fellow walked in the
yard and started talking. The result was a little boat,
Schwatka. It was sent north on the coastal container ship
Frank Brown. At Skagway it was put on a rail car for the trip
to Whitehorse. The boat has since been in use every
summer for tourist excursion trips from Whitehorse, Yukon,
to Miles Canyon."

Hull No: 111   **Original name:** *No. 111*

Type: Work boat   **Designer:** McLaren & Sons
Delivered: 1960   **Built for:** Monarch Marine Products
Owner's representative: M. Judd

Length: **OA** 20′   **Reg** 19′   **Beam mld:** 7.5′
Depth: 3.5′   **Tonnage:**   **GT** 2.92   **NT** 1.99
Material: Steel hull and superstructure   **Speed:** 7 knots

Main engine: Chrysler gasoline—1 @ 125 hp

According to Arthur McLaren, "Judd was a great big guy.
At the time, there was a bounty on killing sea lions. He
wanted a boat so he could go up and down the coast and
shoot sea lions, drag them in and recover what you get out
of the carcasses. That's what he went after. He did that, but
only for two years. Then the government withdrew the
bounty on shooting the animals. There wasn't any incentive
to do that any more."

Hull No: 112   **Original name:** *Kitmano*   **Renamed:**
*Hull 112; Nanoose Bay; La Banque; Seaspan Rover; Mountain
Rover*   **Official No:** 312117

Type: Tug   **Designer:** McLaren & Sons   **Delivered:**
1960   **Built for:** Western Tug & Barge Ltd., Nanaimo
BC   **Owner's representative:** Harry Hansen

Length: **OA** 51′   **Reg** 47.2′   **Beam mld:** 15.9′
Depth: 8.5′   **Tonnage:**   **GT** 39   **Material:** Steel
hull and superstructure

Main engine: General Motors 16V-71—1 @ 457 hp @ 1800
rpm

Hull 112 was originally built for Bill Cogswell of Kitimat. The tug was fitted with a large, heavy medium-speed diesel engine. Unfortunately there was more engine than boat. A new hull was built for Bill and Hull 112 was fitted with a light GM diesel and sold. It worked well with the lighter machinery.

Hull No: 113   **Original name:** *Radium 701*   **Other name:** *Radium 256*   **Official No:** 175558

Type: Barge, Shallow Draft   **Delivered:** 1960   **Built for:** Northern Transportation Co. Ltd., Edmonton, Alberta

Length: OA 155′   **Beam mld:** 45′   **Depth:** 7′
Tonnage: GT 449   **Sister ship:** 114

"Those are the two barges that the Hudson's Bay Company had up in the northern rivers and they sold the barges to Northern Transportation," Arthur McLaren remembered. "Northern Transportation said these barges are oddballs and they don't fit into our plans at all and we would like bigger barges. So we cut the barges up and built them up in size. The original small hulls were built in Trenton, Ontario, in 1946. These were the only 700 series barges NTCL had. There were numerous 600 series barges (i.e. 600-ton capacity). The next size built was the 1000 series."

Hull No: 114   **Original name:** *Radium 702*
Other name: *Radium 257*   **Official No:** 175559

Type: Barge, Shallow Draft   **Delivered:** 1960   **Built for:** Northern Transportation Co. Ltd., Edmonton, Alberta

Length: OA 155′   **Beam mld:** 45′   **Depth:** 7.1′
Tonnage: GT 449   **Sister ship:** 113

Hull No: 115   **Original name:** *Eckaloo*   **Renamed:** *Hay River II; Arctic Duchess*   **Official No:** 313125

Type: Buoy, Shallow Draft   **Designer:** Gilmore, German & Milne   **Delivered:** 1961, Bell Rock, Alberta **Built for:** Ministry of Transport, Ottawa, Ontario
Owner's representative: J. R. Goodwin, Marine Agent

Length: OA 84′   **Reg** 79.6′   **Beam mld:** 22′
Depth: 7′   **Design draft:** 4′   **Tonnage:** GT 133 **NT** 45   **Lightship** 100 L. tons   **Speed:** 10.5 knots
Main engines: Rolls Royce C8TLFM—2 @ 255 hp @ 1600 rpm   **Reduction ratio:** 3.07 : 1   **Propellers:** 2 - 42″ dia.

The *Eckaloo* was built to tend buoys and do related work on the Mackenzie River system, down which almost all supplies for the western Arctic are moved each summer by barge. The name *Eckaloo* is from a Slave Indian word meaning "track" or "trail."

Hull No: 116   **Original name:** *B.A. Logger (II)*
Renamed: *Gulf Logger; Petro-Canada Logger*
Official No: 313708

Type: Barge, Oil   **Designer:** McLaren & Sons
Delivered: 1961, Vancouver BC   **Built for:** British American Oil Co.

Length: OA 100′   **Beam mld:** 35′   **Depth:** 9.5′
Tonnage: GT 312   **Sister ship:** 088

Hull No: 117   **Original name:** *Garibaldi*
Renamed: *Westwood; Albert J. Savoie*   **Official No:** 314008

Type: Ferry, Vehicle   **Designer:** McLaren & Sons
Delivered: 1961, Vancouver BC   **Built for:** Department of Highways, Victoria BC

Length: OA 110′   **Reg** 101.7′   **Beam mld:** 41′
Depth: 10.5′   **Tonnage:** GT 256   **NT** 174
Material: Steel hull and superstructure   **Capacity:** 4 (crew); 150 (passengers); 15 (vehicles)   **Speed:** 10.5 knots

Main engines: Allis Chalmers—2 @ 200 hp
Sister ship: 108

The *Garibaldi*.

Garibaldi was built to link the reopened sulphite pulp and paper mill of Rayonier Canada Ltd. at Woodfibre with Darrell Bay, across Howe Sound.

Hull No: 118   **Original name:** Pontoon

Type: Barge, Drilling Platform   **Designer:** McLaren & Sons   **Delivered:** 1961   **Built for:** Department of Highways, Victoria BC

Length: OA 32′   **Beam mld:** 15′   **Depth:** 3.5′

This steel pontoon was used as a drilling platform.

Hull No: 119   **Original name:** *Kitmano*
Official No: 313732

Type: Tug, Berthing & Coastal   **Designer:** McLaren & Sons   **Delivered:** 1961   **Built for:** Northern Salvage & Towing Ltd., Kitimat BC   **Owner's representative:** Bill Cogswell

Length: OA 51′   **Reg** 47.9′   **Beam mld:** 18′
Depth: 10′   **Design draft:** 8.5′   **Tonnage:** GT 48 **NT** 32   **Lightship** 61 L.tons   **Dwt** 22 L. tons
Material: Steel hull and superstructure   **Capacity:** 4 (crew); 12 (passengers)

Main engine: B & W Alpha 404-VO 4 cylinder—1 @ 280 hp @ 375 rpm   **Propeller:** 1 controllable pitch

The *Kitmano*.

The primary duty of the *Kitmano* was to assist in the berthing of deep-sea vessels at the Port of Kitimat. The tug was also licensed to carry twelve passengers and cargo on Home Trade III voyages between Kitimat and Kemano, BC.

Hull No: 120   **Original name:** *Rayonier No. 1*
Renamed: *McAllister 130; Sea Barge III*   **Official No:** 314792

Type: Barge, Self-Dumping Log   **Designer:** McLaren & Sons   **Delivered:** 1961   **Built for:** Rayonier Canada (BC) Ltd., Vancouver BC   **Owner's representative:** H.R. Homewood

Length: **OA** 315′   **Beam mld:** 62′   **Depth:** 17′
Design draft: 13′   **Tonnage:**   **GT** 2970   **Dwt** 5700 L. tons   **Sister ship:** 121

The two *Rayonier* barges initially operated between the Queen Charlotte Islands and the company's booming grounds in Howe Sound. The loaded towing speed was 8 knots. Capacity was 1,400,000 fbm of logs.

Hull No: 121   **Original name:** *Rayonier No. 2*
Renamed: *Straits Traveller*   **Official No:** 314818

Type: Barge, Self-Dumping Log   **Designer:** McLaren & Sons   **Delivered:** 1961   **Built for:** Rayonier Canada (BC) Ltd., Vancouver BC

Length: **OA** 315′   **Beam mld:** 62′   **Depth:** 17′
Tonnage: **GT** 2970   **Dwt** 5700 L. tons   **Sister ship:** 120

Hull No: 122   **Original name:** *Hugh A. Young*
Official No: 193256

Type: Research Survey   **Designer:** Robert Allan
Delivered: 1962, Hay River NWT   **Built for:** Department of Public Works, Ottawa, Ontario

Length: **OA** 87′   **Beam mld:** 22′   **Depth:** 6.6′
Design draft: 3.68′   **Tonnage:**   **GT** 150   **NT** 45
Material: Steel hull and superstructure   **Capacity:** 4 (crew); 4 (passengers)   **Speed:** 11 knots
Main engines: Dorman—2 @ 296 hp   **Reduction ratio:** 4.00 : 1   **Propellers:** 2 - 45″ dia. x 42″ pitch

Hull 122 was a shallow-draft twin-screw survey vessel built to conduct survey work on the Mackenzie River system, in order to improve navigation. Major General H. A. Young was a former commissioner of the Northwest Territories. In his youth, General Young was instrumental in establishing radio stations in the North, including Aklavik, Berens River, Pelican Narrows, Isle a la Crosse and Larder Lake.

Hull No: 123   **Original name:** *Harrop Ferry*

Type: Ferry, Cable   **Delivered:** 1961, Kootenay Lake BC   **Built for:** Department of Highways, Victoria BC
Owner's representative: P. T. Brown, Chief Engineer

Length: **OA** 90′   **Beam mld:** 38′   **Depth:** 4.5′
Tonnage: **GT** 120   **Material:** Steel

This simple barge is fitted with a winch that pulls on a steel cable lying across the bottom of the lake, which moves the barge back and forth across the west arm of Kootenay Lake, near Nelson.

Hull No: 124   **Original name:** *Neva Straits*
Official No: 319346

Type: Tug, Coastal   **Designer:** Robert Allan
Delivered: 1962, Vancouver BC   **Built for:** Straits Towing Ltd., Vancouver BC   **Owner's representative:** G. B. McKeen

Length: **OA** 92.5′   **Reg** 86.6′   **Beam mld:** 23.33′
Depth: 12.83′   **Design draft:** 12.5′   **Tonnage:** **GT** 150   **NT** 24   **Material:** Steel with aluminum superstructure   **Capacity:** 6 (crew)

Main engine: Stork-Werkspoor 4 cylinder (290x400)—1 @ 800 hp @ 450 rpm   **Propellers:** Controllable pitch

Built for coastal towing from Portland, Oregon, to Alaska, this tug was the first vessel Allied Shipbuilders built with the aid of government subsidy. Canadian-built equipment for the *Neva Straits* included steering gear by Wagner Engineering, towing winch by Burrard Iron Works, fibreglass lifeboat by Davidson Manufacturing, pumps by Pumps & Power and radios by Spilsbury & Tindall.

Hull No: 125   **Original name:** *Rayonier No. 3*
Renamed: *Forest Camp No. 1*   **Official No:** 319344

Type: Barge, Wood Pulp   **Delivered:** 1962
Built for: Rayonier Canada Ltd., Vancouver BC

Length: **OA** 150′   **Beam mld:** 42′   **Depth:** 12.5′
Tonnage: **GT** 651   **Dwt** 1200 L. tons   **Material:** Steel

This barge was built to transport pulp from Port Alice and Woodfibre to ports on the Lower Mainland. *Rayonier No. 3* had a large steel house on deck for the 1,200-ton pulp cargo and was equipped with three sets of doors.

Hull No: 126   **Original name:** *Yorke No. 21*
Renamed: *Seaspan 913*   **Official No:** 319419

Type: Barge, Rail Car/Fuel   **Designer:** Robert Allan
Delivered: 1963, Vancouver BC   **Built for:** F. M. Yorke

& Son Ltd., Vancouver BC   **Owner's representative:** Lorne Yorke

Length: OA 273' **Beam mld:** 43' **Depth:** 12'
Tonnage: GT 1277   **Material:** Steel

Yorke No. 21 was built to transport rail cars from the Great Northern Railway wharf in Vancouver to industries on the southern BC coast without railway service such as oil refineries, pulp and paper plants and lumber and shingle mills. The vessel had a capacity of 18 rail cars on deck and an internal capacity of 160,000 gallons of fuel oil. Dual pumps could discharge the oil cargo at the rate of 1,000 gallons per minute. The commissioning of *Yorke No. 21* on January 24, 1963, was a novel affair. Three posh lounge rail cars, one each—Canadian Pacific's "Canadian," Canadian National's "Super Continental" and Great Northern's "Seattle-Portland Service"—were set on board for the guests, as the barge was towed around the Port of Vancouver.

Hull No: 127   **Original name:** *Gulf Diane*
Renamed: *Gulf Dianne*   **Official No:** 319436

Type: Tug, Coastal Towing   **Designer:** Robert Allan
Delivered: 1963, Vancouver BC   **Built for:** Gulf of Georgia Towing Co. Ltd., Vancouver BC

Length: OA 64' **Reg** 59.8' **Beam mld:** 19' **Depth:** 10.6' **Tonnage: GT** 67 **NT** 11   **Material:** Steel hull and superstructure   **Capacity:** 5 (crew) **Speed:** 10.5 knots

Main engine: Caterpillar D398—1 @ 760 hp
Propeller: 1 - 76" dia.

The *Gulf Diane.*

The *Gulf Diane* was one of two identical tugs built for Gulf of Georgia Towing Co. Ltd. A simultaneous launch occurred in January 1963, the *Gulf Diane* launched by Allied in False Creek and her sister ship, *Gulf Muriel*, at Star Shipyards (Mercer's) Ltd. on Annacis Island, New Westminster. The *Gulf Dianne* was sighted in June 1999 in the Canso Strait, Nova Scotia, with a gravel barge in tow.

Hull No: 128   **Original name:** *YBZ 61*

Type: Barge, Tank Cleaning   **Designer:** Naval Headquarters   **Delivered:** 1963, Esquimalt BC   **Built for:** Royal Canadian Navy, Ottawa, Ontario

Length: OA 120' **Beam mld:** 36' **Depth:** 8.5'
Design draft: 6'   **Tonnage: GT** 450 **Dwt** 320 L. tons   **Material:** Steel hull and superstructure

The tank cleaning barge *YBZ 61* was built to ventilate, clean and gas-free ship's fuel tanks and bilges during refit and repair work at the Esquimalt navy base. Equipment on the barge for tank cleaning consisted of boilers generating steam, which was used to steam the tank surfaces. Next, the tanks were washed down with a mixture of 175 degrees Fahrenheit hot sea water, mixed with detergent. The tanks were emptied to the barge by use of a vacuum on board the barge. The tank slops were transferred to settling tanks where the water component was dischargd overboard via an oily water separator. The oil remaining was used as fuel for the boilers which provide the steam necessary for the continuous operation of the craft. A sister ship, *YBZ 60* (built by the Davie Yard in Quebec) is based at the naval dockyard in Halifax.

Hull No: 129   **Original name:** *N.S.T. No. 1*   **Official No:** 319349

Type: Barge, Deck Cargo Barge   **Designer:** McLaren & Sons   **Delivered:** 1962   **Built for:** Northern Salvage & Towing Co. Ltd., Kitimat BC

Length: OA 84' **Beam mld:** 32' **Depth:** 9'
Design draft: 7'   **Tonnage: GT** 206 **Dwt** 350 L. tons   **Material:** Steel

---

Hull No: 130   **Original name:** *Evco No. 1*
Official No: 319164

Type: Barge, Self Unloading   **Designer:** Robert Allan
Delivered: 1963   **Built for:** Evans, Coleman & Evans Ltd., Vancouver BC

Length: OA 190' **Beam mld:** 46' **Depth:** 13.1'
Design draft: 10'   **Tonnage: GT** 1087 **Dwt** 2000 L. tons   **Material:** Steel hull and superstructure

The *Evco No. 1* was built to carry aggregate from the company's Mary Hill quarry, down the Fraser River to their concrete manufacturing plant at Marpole. This $250,000 steel hopper barge featured an automated 900-ton-per-hour mechanical unloading system. Aggregate was carried in 8 hoppers discharging through hydraulically operated doors onto a longitudinal conveyor belt, which in turn fed onto a transverse belt unloading over the side at the bow. The system was electrically powered from shore. A total of 3 sister barges were built, the first by Allied and the other two by Yarrows, Victoria and Bel-Aire Shipyard, North Vancouver.

Hull No: 131   **Original name:** *Crown Zellerbach Log Sorter No. 1*   **Renamed:** *Downie No. 1*   **Official No:** 320214

Type: Barge, Log Sorter   **Designer:** Mc&Mc Manufacturing Co./Allied   **Delivered:** 1963
Built for: Crown Zellerbach Canada Ltd.
Owner's representative: Ernie Pederson

Length: OA 138'   **Beam mld:** 32'   **Depth:** 6'
Tonnage: GT 206   **Material:** Steel

This novel piece of floating machinery was used to sort logs by size, species and quality, into selected areas of the booming ground. In effect, the barge was a dry-land log sorter, adapted to marine use at the Ocean Falls Pulp & Paper Mill.

Hull No: 132   **Original name:** *V.P.D. Derrick No. 2*
Renamed: *Dillingham No. 2; Delcat No. 2*   **Official No:** 319505

Type: Barge, Crane   **Designer:** McLaren & Sons
Delivered: 1963   **Built for:** Vancouver Pile Driving & Contracting Co., North Vancouver BC

Length: OA 110'   **Beam mld:** 44'   **Depth:** 8'
Tonnage: GT 356

At the time of building, *V.P.D. Derrick No. 2* was the largest crane barge in BC. A 50-ton mobile crane was fitted on one end. A steel house at the other end enclosed the 2 - 100 kw generators and the 5-drum winch which raised and lowered the spuds and worked the anchor lines.

Hull No: 133   **Original name:** *K.F.P. No. 1*
Official No: 319450

Type: Barge, Icebreaking, Deck Cargo   **Designer:** McLaren & Sons   **Delivered:** 1963, Nelson BC
Built for: Kootenay Forest Products, Nelson BC
Owner's representative: G. Barnes

Length: OA 70'   **Beam mld:** 27'   **Depth:** 5'
Design draft: 3'   **Tonnage:**   GT 82   **Dwt** 100 L. tons

This small barge was built in Vancouver and delivered to Nelson for $23,000, six weeks after order. The barge was designed and reinforced so that it could be pushed through winter ice by a tug at the stern. To ease turning when in the ice, the bow was wider (30') than the stern (27').

Hull No: 134   **Original name:** *Skidegate*   **Renamed:** *Casaco; Marine Voyager*   **Official No:** 320939

Type: Buoy, Coastal   **Designer:** Campbell, Montreal
Delivered: 1964   **Built for:** Department of Transport, Ottawa, Ontario   **Owner's representative:** Capt. E. O. Ormsby

Length: OA 87.3'   **Reg** 79.6'   **Beam mld:** 21.5'
Depth: 10.5'   **Tonnage:**   GT 136   **NT** 35
Material: Steel hull, aluminum superstructure
Capacity: 9 (crew)   **Speed:** 10.5 knots
Main engines: Cummins 525, V12—2 @ 340 hp @ 1600 rpm   **Reduction ratio:** 2.20 : 1

The *Skidegate*, named after an inlet in the Queen Charlotte Islands, went into service for the federal Department of Transport's Prince Rupert agency on April 1, 1964, replacing the *Katerine B*. After about five years, the

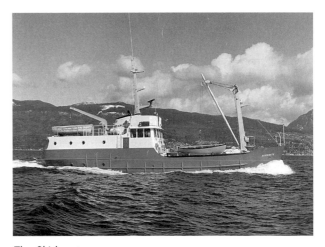

The *Skidegate*.

Skidegate was transferred to the Arctic, where she worked out of Tuktoyaktuk for a decade. Transferred yet again to Newfoundland, the *Skidegate* traversed the Northwest Passage. After being lengthened, the ship ended its government service in Newfoundland waters. Subsequent private sector owners included the Canadian Saltfish Corporation and Puddister Trading Co. Ltd.

Hull No: 135   **Original name:** *Tembah*   **Official No:** 320934

Type: Buoy, Shallow Draft   **Designer:** Gilmore, German & Milne   **Delivered:** 1963, Fort Smith NWT
Built for: Department of Transport, Ottawa, Ontario

Length: OA 123.8'   **Beam mld:** 26'   **Depth:** 5'
Design draft: 3.13'   **Tonnage:**   GT 178   **NT** 53
Lightship 124 L. tons   **Dwt** 30 L. tons   **Material:** Steel hull, aluminum superstructure   **Capacity:** 8 (crew)
Speed: 12.8 knots (max) 10.5 knots (service)
Main engines: Cummins 525M V12—2 @ 340 hp @ 1600 rpm   **Reduction ratio:** 3.00 : 1   **Propellers:** 2 - 42" dia.

The name *Tembah* is a Slave Indian word meaning "rapids." Designed for very shallow draft operations, especially to work up to the edges of the river, the $677,000 *Tembah* covered the 563 miles from the start of the Mackenzie on the west end of the Great Slave Lake to Norman Wells, NWT. At the time of launching, one of the old-time river boat skippers "hoped she will be able to float on a heavy dew."

Hull No: 136   **Original name:** *G. of G. 237*
Renamed: *Seaspan 131*   **Official No:** 320216

Type: Barge, Deck Cargo   **Designer:** Robert Allan
Delivered: 1963, Vancouver BC   **Built for:** Gulf of Georgia Towing Co. Ltd., Vancouver BC

Length: OA 120'   **Beam mld:** 44'   **Depth:** 12.5'
Design draft: 10.83'   **Tonnage:**   GT 563   **Lightship** 205 L. tons   **Dwt** 1295 L.tons   **Sister ship:** 137

This simple steel scow, typical of the era, was constructed of 5/16" plate on deck, sides and bottom. The deck was sheathed with 2x6″ fir, on edge. The box wall was made of steel pillars clad with 4x12″ fir. The hull was subdivided by 3 transverse watertight bulkheads.

Hull No: 137   **Original name:** *G. of G. 238*
Renamed: *MBM 15; Arrow Marine #2; Walco*
Official No: 320231

Type: Barge, Deck   **Designer:** Robert Allan
Delivered: 1963, Vancouver BC   **Built for:** Gulf of Georgia Towing Co. Ltd., Vancouver BC

Length: OA 120′   **Beam mld:** 44′   **Depth:** 12.5′
Design draft: 10.83′   **Tonnage: GT** 563
Lightship 205 L. tons   **Dwt** 1295 L. tons
Material: Steel hull and superstructure   **Sister ship:** 136

Hull No: 138   **Original name:** *Kemat*   **Official No:** 320171

Type: Tug, Boom Boat   **Designer:** McLaren & Sons
Delivered: 1963, Vancouver BC   **Built for:** Kitimat Tug & Barge Co. Ltd.   **Owner's representative:** Bill Cogswell

Length: OA 26′   **Reg** 24′   **Beam mld:** 10′
Depth: 4.13′   **Design draft:** 3.5′   **Tonnage: GT** 6 **NT** 4

Main engine: General Motors 6-71—1 @ 165 hp @ 1800 rpm   **Reduction ratio:** 2.00 : 1   **Propeller:** 1 - 32″ dia.

Hull No: 139   **Original name:** *Barnston Island No. 1*
Renamed: *Shelter Bay; Keefe*   **Official No:** 320049

Type: Tug   **Designer:** McLaren & Sons   **Delivered:** 1963, Vancouver BC   **Built for:** Minister of Highways, Victoria BC   **Owner's representative:** Ken Gann, Superintendent of Ferries

Length: OA 37.6′   **Reg** 34.7′   **Beam mld:** 12′
Depth: 6.75′   **Design draft:** 6′   **Tonnage: GT** 11 **NT** 7   **Lightship** 20 L. tons

Main engine: General Motors 6-71—1 @ 134 hp @ 1600 rpm   **Propeller:** 1 - 42″ dia.

The *Barnston Island No. 1.*

This vessel was originally built to move a barge-type vehicle ferry across the Fraser River to Barnston Island. The tug has performed service in a variety of locations in the interior of BC.

Hull No: 140   **Original name:** *Big Beaver II*
Official No: 320242

Type: Tug, Boom Boat   **Designer:** McLaren & Sons
Delivered: 1963, Vancouver BC   **Built for:** Saskatchewan Power Corp., Regina, Saskatchewan

Length: OA 26′   **Reg** 23.8′   **Beam mld:** 10.1′
Depth: 3.1′   **Tonnage: GT** 5 **NT** 3

Main engine: Allis-Chalmers 11000—1 @ 210 hp @ 1800 rpm   **Reduction ratio:** 2.00 : 1   **Propeller:** 1 - 30″ dia.

"The owners wanted a tug that they could put a bow blade on," Arthur McLaren remembered, "a special blade in front of it. When they went on to some lakes in northern Saskatchewan which had logs floating on them, you could go and push them like a bulldozer." The tug was shipped to Regina via rail car.

Hull No: 141   **Original name:** *B.P. 451*
Official No: 320056

Type: Tug, Assist   **Designer:** McLaren & Sons
Delivered: 1963   **Built for:** Department of Highways, Victoria BC

Length: OA 26′   **Reg** 23.8′   **Beam mld:** 10′
Depth: 5′   **Design draft:** 3.75′   **Tonnage: GT** 5 **NT** 3   **Material:** Steel hull, aluminum superstructure
Main engine: Cummins JN-6-M—1 @ 100 hp
Propeller: 1 - 32″ dia.

Hull 141 was a standard 26-foot tug that was used to push a ferry barge on the Trans-Canada Highway, just west of Revelstoke, where there is a chain of three lakes. The Rogers Pass Highway wasn't finished, so they used this vessel during highway construction and then it was moved on. The tug was built using much of the machinery from the decommissioned tug *Barnston Island*, including the main engine, propeller and steering quadrant. The aluminum wheelhouse was attached with bolts so it could be removed when transporting the tug.

Hull No: 142   **Original name:** *Greg Yorke*
Renamed: *Seaspan Greg*   **Official No:** 323224

Type: Ferry, Rail Car   **Designer:** Robert Allan
Delivered: 1964, Vancouver BC   **Built for:** F. M. Yorke & Sons Ltd., Vancouver BC
Owner's representative: Lorne Yorke

Length: OA 325′   **Reg** 304.2′   **Beam mld:** 55.5′
Depth: 18.75′   **Design draft:** 11.2′   **Tonnage: GT** 2443 **NT** 1229   **Lightship** 1348 L. tons   **Dwt** 2161 L. tons   **Capacity:** 9 (crew)   **Speed:** 11 knots
Main engines: Stork-Werkspoor RUB 1616 16 cylinder—2 @ 976 hp @ 1400 rpm   **Reduction ratio:** 6.00 : 1

The *Greg Yorke* was the first self-propelled rail car ferry built in BC. The idea came from the San Francisco area, where there was a big barge with engines in it and house spanning over the top for moving rail cars across San Francisco Bay. The vessel has four tracks on deck and can carry twenty-five 80-ton rail cars, or trailer trucks.

Hull No: 143　　**Original name:** *Great West No. 2*
Official No: 323246

Type: Barge, Self-Dumping Log　　**Designer:** Derek S. Cove　　**Delivered:** 1964　　**Built for:** Great West Towing & Salvage Ltd., Vancouver BC

Length:　OA 262.5′　**Beam mld:** 62′　　**Depth:** 17′
Design draft: 13′　　**Tonnage:　GT** 2443　**NT** 2437
Sister ship: 144

With a carrying capacity of 1,000,000 board feet of logs, this vessel was smaller than contemporary log barges, some of which had a capacity of more than 2,000,000 board feet. *Great West No. 2* was a fully self-contained log-loading unit complete with a single pintle-type Washington Iron Works crane and its own small boom boat, *Little West No. 2*.

Hull No: 144　　**Original name:** *Great West No. 3*
Renamed: *Panaclete*　　**Official No:** 323299

Type: Barge, Self-Dumping Log　　**Designer:** Derek S. Cove　　**Delivered:** 1964　　**Built for:** Great West Towing & Salvage Ltd., Vancouver BC

Length:　OA 262.5′　**Reg** 262.5′　**Beam mld:** 62′
Depth: 17′　　**Design draft:** 13′　　**Tonnage:　GT** 2444
NT 2438　　**Sister ship:** 143

Hull No: 145　　**Original name:** *Rockgas Propane No. 1*
Renamed: *Nootka Barge*　　**Official No:** 322483

Type: Barge, Propane Gas　　**Designer:** McLaren & Sons
Delivered: 1964, Vancouver BC　　**Built for:** Rockgas Propane Ltd., Vancouver BC　　**Owner's representative:** Pat Martin

Length:　OA 100′　**Beam mld:** 40′　　**Depth:** 7.5′
Tonnage:　GT 254

Built to ship liquid petroleum gas to customers along the south coast of BC, *Rockgas Propane No. 1* was the first liquid petroleum gas carrier in Canada. Previously, propane had been transported to users by means of tank trucks and railway tank cars, but restrictions on carrying inflammable substances made distribution difficult. Use of a tank barge made it possible to supply propane gas more frequently and with a wider distribution. *Rockgas Propane No. 1* was in service for some thirty years. The completion of the natural gas pipeline to Vancouver Island in the mid-1990s rendered the barge obsolete. Fabrication of the three 30,000-US-gallon tanks was one of the last jobs done by the once prolific False Creek shop of Vancouver Iron Works.

Hull No: 146　　**Original name:** *Rayonier No. 4*
Official No: 325652

Type: Barge, Self-Dumping Log　　**Designer:** Derek S. Cove　　**Delivered:** 1965, Vancouver BC
Built for: Rayonier Canada (BC) Ltd., Vancouver BC

Length:　OA 340′　**Reg** 340′　**Beam mld:** 64′
Depth: 19′　　**Tonnage:　GT** 3745

The *Rayonier No. 4* was built to transport logs between Rayonier's Queen Charlotte Islands camps to their Howe Sound booming grounds. Launched on September 22, 1965, the barge was delivered on September 26. The vessel, perhaps the last self-dumping log barge built in BC that was not fitted with a log-loading crane, had a capacity of 1,800,000 board feet.

Hull No: 147　　**Original name:** *D.O.T. 147*
Official No: 320960

Type: Barge, Dumb　　**Delivered:** 1964, NWT
Built for: Department of Transport, Ottawa, Ontario

Length:　OA 80′　**Beam mld:** 24′　　**Depth:** 3′
Design draft: 1.75′　　**Tonnage:　GT** 61　**Lightship** 53
L. tons　Dwt 23 L. tons　　**Sister ship:** 148

Two 80-foot "dumb barges" (a term coined from British practice) were built to be pushed by the relatively short buoy vessels *Dumit* and *Miskanaw*. The barges were of very shallow draft and each was fitted with a diesel generator and a 5-ton folding hydraulic crane. Use of the barge greatly improved the capability of the buoy vessels.

Hull No: 148　　**Original name:** *D.O.T. 148*
Official No: 320961

Type: Barge, Dumb　　**Designer:** German & Milne
Delivered: 1964　　**Built for:** Department of Transport, Ottawa, Ontario

Length:　OA 80′　**Beam mld:** 24′　　**Depth:** 3′
Design draft: 1.75′　　**Tonnage:　GT** 61
Sister ship: 147

Hull No: 149　　**Original name:** *Malibu Princess*
Official No: 326618

Type: Ferry, Passenger　　**Designer:** Phil Spaulding
Delivered: 1966, Vancouver BC　　**Built for:** Young Life of Canada, Vancouver BC

Length:　OA 126′　**Reg** 119.5′　**Beam mld:** 32.5′
Depth: 10.5′　　**Design draft:** 7.5′　　**Tonnage:**
GT 505　**NT** 319　　**Material:** Steel hull and superstructure　　**Capacity:** 250 (passengers)
Speed: 12 knots (service)

Main engines: Caterpillar D-343—2 @ 325 hp @ 1800 rpm
Reduction ratio: 3.00 : 1　　**Propellers:** 2- 46″ dia.

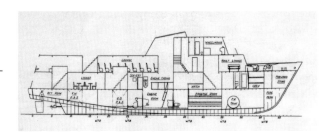

The *Malibu Princess*.

The *Malibu Princess* was built for Young Life Inc. to transport teenage passengers between Vancouver and Young Life's Malibu Camp, situated near the head of Jervis Inlet, some 78 nautical miles northwest of Vancouver. The site of the Malibu Camp was developed shortly after World War II as a luxury resort, but failed to attract the anticipated clientele. The Young Life organization, whose aim is to develop the moral character of teenagers, operates youth camps in other parts of Canada and the United States.

Hull No: 150　　**Original name:** *Moyie*　　**Official No:** 325590

Type: Passenger, Excursion　　**Designer:** Phil Spaulding
Delivered: 1965, Calgary, Alberta　　**Built for:** Heritage Park Society, Calgary, Alberta

Length: OA 89′　**Reg** 75′　**Beam mld:** 23′
Depth: 6.9′　**Design draft:** 4′　**Tonnage:** GT 122
NT 82　　**Material:** Steel hull, wood superstructure
Capacity: 4 (crew); 182 (passengers)

Built to resemble Kootenay Lake's sternwheeler of earlier days and to keep alive memories of the once popular vessels, *Moyie* was built to carry passengers on short cruises on Glenmore Reservoir, near Calgary, in connection with the "Living Museum" created at Heritage Park. The paddlewheel was turned not by steam, but by a hydraulic motor driven by a diesel engine. "It got broken up into sections and taken up to Calgary by train," Arthur McLaren said, "and arrangements were made with a fellow who had a machine shop there called Barber Engineering Company. Inside his shop we reassembled the boat. Then we took it through the streets of Calgary and launched it into the reservoir." The original *Moyie* was built in 1898 for $41,285 and served travellers on Kootenay Lake for fifty-nine years. The name "Moyie" comes from a BC mining community on the Crowsnest Pass railway line.

Hull No: 151　　**Original name:** *North Arm Explorer*
Official No: 323306

Type: Barge, Fuel and Deck　　**Designer:** Derek S. Cove
Delivered: 1965, Vancouver BC　　**Built for:** North Arm Transportation Ltd., Vancouver BC
Owner's representative: Stradiotti Brothers

Length:　OA 105′　**Beam mld:** 28.5′　　**Depth:** 7.75′
Tonnage:　GT 201.3

Built between Februry and April 1965, the *North Arm Explorer* was originally slated to sail on the relatively shallow Stikine River to transport fuel oil in six hull tanks and mining equipment on deck for the operation of Kennco (Stikine) Mining Ltd. in Northern BC. A pusher-type tug, also designed by Derek Cove, was built by John Manly Ltd. This was the first pusher-type tug barge combination in BC. An extra during the construction involved 340 lbs of steel charged at 10.5 cents/lb, and labour charged at $5.50/hour.

Hull No: 152　　**Original name:** *Tutsie No. 1*
Official No: 325542

Type: Barge, Oil　　**Designer:** McLaren & Sons
Delivered: 1965, Hay River NWT　　**Built for:** Imperial Oil Ltd., Toronto, Ontario　　**Owner's representative:** Capt. S. S. Martin

Length:　OA 95′　**Beam mld:** 26′　　**Depth:** 5′
Tonnage:　GT 99.3

This oil transport barge was designed for use in the Norman Wells oil fields, located on the Mackenzie River. Arthur McLaren remembered: "It was made in halves and shipped up by truck to McMurray. Not by train. By that time, we had lost all interest in trains. It was much cheaper to go by truck. Trucks gave you the opportunity to take the parts for building the barge right down to site where you wanted it. If you went by rail, you still had to move them down somehow." Allied bid $47,850. The only other bid was from McKay Cormak for $60,987. Estimated steel weight was 59 S. tons. Design capacity was 1,325 barrels of 41 A.P.I. crude oil.

Hull No: 153　　**Original name:** *Gulf Mary*
Renamed: *Squamish Rambler*　　**Official No:** 325616

Type: Tug, Harbour　　**Designer:** McLaren & Sons
Delivered: 1965, Vancouver BC　　**Built for:** Gulf of Georgia Towing Co., Vancouver BC

Length:　OA 37.5′　**Beam mld:** 12′　　**Depth:** 6.5′

The *Gulf Mary*.

Design draft: 6.3′ **Tonnage:** **GT** 9.8 **NT** 7
Material: Steel hull, aluminum superstructure
Capacity: 2 (crew)
Main engine: General Motors 12V-71—1 @ 335 hp @ 1800 rpm **Reduction ratio:** 3.00 : 1 **Propeller:** 1 - 48″ dia.

Work on this tug commenced early in June 1965 and the vessel was launched into False Creek on August 3, 1965. A small tug, with an unmanned engine room, *Gulf Mary* was part of a modernization and reconstruction program of the Gulf of Georgia Towing Company. The tug was named by Miss May Cooper, who held the record for longest employment with the Gulf of Georgia organization.

Hull No: 154 **Original name:** *V.P.D. No. 25*
Renamed: *Dillingham 100; Delcat 100* **Official No:** 325663

Type: Barge Self Dumping **Designer:** McLaren & Sons
Delivered: 1965 **Built for:** Vancouver Pile Driving Ltd., North Vancouver

Length: **OA** 128′ **Beam mld:** 30′ **Depth:** 11′
Tonnage: **GT** 381 **NT** 381

This barge, designed and built to the owner's requirement, was used for the deep-sea dumping of materials dredged from Vancouver and other harbours. It was made, remembered Arthur McLaren, "so that the vessel was hinged in halves. It opened up to dump. Whereas in the ordinary dump barge you build a false bottom that drops out and lets everything dump, this one the whole boat opens in half like a clamshell. There were people down in the States, Milwaukee or somewhere like that, that had built barges of this type and I saw a magazine article about them. The guy at Vancouver Pile Driving saw the same article and came over and asked if we could build one like it." Allied designed and built the first one. Then McKenzie Barge took over and built some for their own use. At the time of build, it was common practice to dispose of unwanted material by deep-sea dumping, which was done with bulldozers on flat scows—an operation that took several hours. The new hydraulically controlled dump scows were able to dump their load in minutes.

Hull No: 155 **Original name:** *V.T. No. 70*
Renamed: *Seaspan 640* **Official No:** 326602

Type: Barge, Covered/Pulp **Designer:** Robert Allan
Delivered: 1966, Vancouver BC **Built for:** Vancouver Tugboat Co. Ltd., North Vancouver BC

Length: **OA** 242′ **Beam mld:** 54′ **Depth:** 15′
Tonnage: **GT** 3757.4 **Dwt** 2500 L. tons

The *V.T. No. 70* was built to transport pulp, in pallet form, from BC to San Francisco (or between Vancouver and Port Alice). "That was a big barge," Arthur McLaren remembered. "It was a paper barge and it had a deckhouse on it. It had a great big warehouse or hold that had two cargo decks. Later on, pulp barges that were much bigger and more sophisticated were built."

Hull No: 156 **Original name:** *K.N. No. 29*
Renamed: *FMC 100; Chief* **Official No:** 326512

Type: Barge, Rail Car **Designer:** Derek S. Cove
Delivered: 1966, Vancouver BC **Built for:** Kingcome Navigation Company Ltd., Vancouver BC **Owner's representatives:** Bill Dolmage and R. D. Henderson
Length: **OA** 120′ **Beam mld:** 45′ **Depth:** 10.1′
Tonnage: **GT** 460

This simple steel barge was built to move chemicals to Powell River on railway cars. The deck had three railway tracks and wood sheathing.

Hull No: 157 **Original name:** *Canadian Tide*
Official No: 327856

Type: Offshore Supply **Designer:** Tidewater
Delivered: 1967 **Built for:** Pacific Tidewater Marine Ltd., Vancouver BC

Length: **OA** 168′ **Reg** 159′ **Beam mld:** 38′
Depth: 13.5′ **Design draft:** 11.3′ **Tonnage:**
GT 635 **NT** 335 **Lightship** 492 L. tons **Dwt** 833 L. tons **Material:** Steel hull and superstructure
Capacity: 9 (crew) **Speed:** 13 knots (max) 12.5 knots (service)

Main engines: General Motors 12-645-E—2 @ 1300 hp @ 800 rpm **Reduction ratio:** 3.00 : 1 **Propellers:** 2 - 96″ dia. **Sister ship:** 158

The *Canadian Tide* and the *Min Tide* were the first offshore drilling rig supply vessels to be built in Canada. These twin-screw vessels operated under contract to Shell Canada Ltd. for the purpose of supplying the semi-submersible oil-drilling platform *Sedco 135 F*. The *Canadian Tide* and *Min Tide* were in service on the west coast of Canada for about four years. Then they moved the whole drilling rig, supply vessels, etc. to New Zealand; then they moved them to Malaysia. At that time there was a war going on and the *Min Tide* got a couple of shells through its funnel.

Hull No: 158 **Original name:** *Min Tide* **Renamed:** *Atlas; Swift; Nettie; Mahal* **Official No:** 327883

Type: Offshore Supply **Designer:** Tidewater
Delivered: 1967 **Built for:** Pacific Tidewater Marine Ltd., Vancouver BC **Owner's representative:** John La Borde

Length: **OA** 168′ **Reg** 159′ **Beam mld:** 38′
Depth: 13.5′ **Design draft:** 11.3′ **Tonnage:**
GT 635 **NT** 335 **Lightship** 492 L. tons **Dwt** 833 L. tons **Sister ship:** 157

Hull No: 159 **Original name:** *George Black*
Official No: 328870

Type: Ferry, Vehicle **Designer:** Robert Allan
Delivered: 1967, Dawson City, Yukon **Built for:** Minister of Indian Affairs, Ottawa, Ontario

Length: **OA** 83′ **Beam mld:** 30′ **Depth:** 6′
Design draft: 3.5′ **Tonnage:** **GT** 106 **NT** 72

Dwt 64 L. tons   **Material:** Steel hull and superstructure
Capacity: 40 (passengers); 15 (vehicles)

Main engines: Caterpillar D333—2 @ 200 hp

The *George Black* was built to handle the growing number of tourists visiting the scenes of the Klondike gold rush. First assembled in Vancouver, the ferry was transported in sections north to Whitehorse, where she was re-erected on the banks of the Yukon. The vessel was named *George Black* in memory of the former speaker of the House of Commons. His wife Martha was then elected as Member of Parliament and a Coast Guard icebreaker was later named *Martha Black* in her honour.

Hull No: 160   **Original name:** *Metlakatla*
Official No: 328913

Type: Barge   **Designer:** Robert Allan Ltd.
Delivered: 1967   **Built for:** Hooker Chemicals Ltd., North Vancouver BC

Length: OA 272.5' **Beam mld:** 64'   **Depth:** 22'
Design draft: 15'   **Tonnage: GT** 3261 **Dwt** 4800 L. tons

The *Metlakatla*.

In 1967 Allied built this chemical barge for Hooker Chemical Co. Ltd. It carried chemicals from a chemical plant in North Vancouver to the pulp mill in Prince Rupert. Chlorine was transported in large tanks on deck. Big tanks inside the hull carried sodium chlorate and sodium chloride. Allied got the contract while the yard was still located in False Creek. Crews built the panels for the barge there, then transferred them by scow to the yard's new Seymour Creek location, so the barge was erected in North Vancouver and was the first vessel launched there.

Hull No: 161   **Original name:** *Scimitar*   **Official No:** 328945

Type: Tug, Coastal   **Designer:** Stan Nicholson
Delivered: 1967, North Vancouver BC   **Built for:** Blue Star Towing Co.   **Owner's representative:** Fred Delgarno

Length: OA 40'   **Tonnage: GT** 25.5 **NT** 17
Material: Steel hull and superstructure   **Capacity:** 5 (crew)

Main engines: Detroit diesel—2

The original owner, Fred Delgarno, was the shore superintendent for Northland Navigation. Blue Star Towing was a company Fred had for operating the tug. He had secured an order from the B.A. Oil Company to move their oil delivery barge up and down the coast. It had quite a tall deckhouse on it—two decks high. Since the boat was only 40 feet long, it was a huge-looking superstructure. On January 31, 1994, while transiting Draney Narrows, the *Scimitar* heeled to starboard, took on water and sank about 5 minutes later. The crew of five abandoned the sinking tug into an inflatable life raft and were all rescued.

Hull No: 162   **Original name:** *Haida Transporter*
Official No: 329516

Type: Ferry, Rail Car   **Designer:** Jackson, Talbot, Walkingshaw & Associates Ltd.   **Delivered:** 1968, North Vancouver BC   **Built for:** Kingcome Navigation Co. Ltd., Vancouver BC

Length: OA 326.5' **Reg** 306' **Beam mld:** 55.5'
Depth: 19'   **Design draft:** 11.25'   **Tonnage: GT** 2553 **NT** 1624 **Dwt** 2700 L. tons   **Material:** Steel hull and superstructure   **Speed:** 15 knots (max) 14 knots (service)

Main engines: Werkspoor TM 6 cylinder—2 @ 1550 hp
Propellers: 2 - 86.5" dia. controllable pitch

With a capacity for twenty-six 40-foot railway cars, the

The *Haida Transporter*.

Haida Transporter was built to transport chemicals from Vancouver to MacMillan Bloedel's pulp mills at Harmac and Powell River, returning with rail cars of pulp, newsprint and lumber. This self-propelled vessel reduced by half the time needed to transport rail cars by the tug and barge method. Kingcome Navigation, originally a division of MacMillan Bloedel Ltd., had been engaged in towing operations on the BC coast since 1910. In 1968 Kingcome Navigation handled a larger volume of logs than any other towing company in the world. In 1997 Kingcome was sold to the Washington Marine Group. In 1999 the BC Forestry icon MacMillan Bloedel was sold to the American forestry giant Weyerhaueser.

Hull No: 163   **Original name:** *Galena*   **Official No:** 329232

Type: Ferry, Vehicle   **Designer:** Case Existological Laboratories   **Delivered:** 1968   **Built for:** Minister of Highways, Victoria BC

Length: OA 165′   **Beam mld:** 61′   **Depth:** 9′
Design draft: 5′   **Tonnage:** GT 571   NT 388
Dwt 86 L. tons   **Material:** Steel hull and superstructure
Capacity: 200 (passengers); 35 (vehicles)   **Speed:** 10 knots

Main engines: Caterpillar D343—4 @ 250 hp

The *Galena* makes a 6-mile crossing from Shelter Bay to Galena Bay at the northern end of Upper Arrow Lake, created by the High Arrow Dam, which was built in the late 1960s. Prefabricated in Allied's North Vancouver shipyard, some thirty-five pieces were shipped by CPR rail car to the assembly point, north of Castlegar. *Galena* is propelled by two 350-hp Voith Schneider cycloidal propellers, which are electric motor-driven via four 250-kw diesel electric generators. The *Galena* was similar to but larger than the ferry *Needles*, built by John Manly Ltd.

Hull No: 164   **Original name:** *Texada Queen*
Renamed: *Tachek*   **Official No:** 330601

Type: Ferry, Vehicle   **Designer:** Greenwood & McHaffie   **Delivered:** 1969   **Built for:** Department of Highways, Victoria BC

Length: OA 162.5′   **Beam mld:** 48′   **Depth:** 14.5′
Design draft: 7.75′   **Tonnage:** GT 751   NT 501
Lightship 555 L. tons   **Dwt** 150 L. tons   **Material:** Steel hull and superstructure   **Capacity:** 200 (passengers), 30 (vehicles)   **Speed:** 12 knots

Main engines: Ruston-Hornsby 6 cylinder—2 @ 600 hp
Reduction ratio: 2.00 : 1   **Sister ship:** 165

The *Texada Queen* originally ran between Powell River and Blubber Bay on Texada Island. The vessel was launched at 7:22 on May 17, 1969. The sponsor was Hon. Isobel Dawson, MLA for Powell River, who had presided at the keel laying in October, making the first weld. She broke a bottle of champagne to mark the launch.

Hull No: 165   **Original name:** *Quadra Queen II*
Official No: 330610

Type: Ferry   **Designer:** Greenwood & McHaffie
Delivered: 1969   **Built for:** Department of Highways, Victoria BC

Length: OA 162.5′   **Beam mld:** 48′   **Depth:** 14.5′
Design draft: 7.75′   **Tonnage:** GT 752   NT 502
Lightship 555 L. tons   **Dwt** 150 L. tons   **Material:** Steel hull and superstructure   **Capacity:** 250 (passengers), 30 (vehicles)   **Speed:** 12 knots

Main engines: Ruston-Hornsby 6 cylinder—2 @ 600 hp
Sister ship: 164

The 30-car capacity *Quadra Queen II* replaced the 16-car ferry *Quadra Queen* on the short route between Campbell River on Vancouver Island and Quathiaski Cove on Quadra Island.

Hull No: 166   **Original name:** *Mule-1*

Type: Work Boat, Beaching   **Designer:** McLaren & Sons   **Delivered:** 1969   **Built for:** Northern Transportation Co. Ltd., Edmonton, Alberta

Length: OA 28′   **Beam mld:** 9′   **Depth:** 3.5′

Main engine: Detroit diesel 3-71—1 @ 85 hp @ 1800 rpm
Propellers: 1 - 18″ dia.   **Sister ship:** 167

Two "Mules" were built for Northern Transportation Co. Ltd., for use in general duties and to access the beach. Of all-steel construction, with ³/₁₆″ plate bottom and sides and ¹/₈″ deck, they were robust vessels. A draft of 1 foot, made possible by the tunnel stern, permitted shallow-draft operation. The rudder was transom-mounted per usual northern river practice.

Hull No: 167   **Original name:** *Mule-2*

Type: Work Boat, Beaching   **Designer:** McLaren & Sons   **Delivered:** 1969   **Built for:** Northern Transportation Co. Ltd., Edmonton, Alberta

Length: OA 28′   **Beam mld:** 9′   **Depth:** 3.16′
Sister ship: 166

Hull No: 168   **Original name:** *Angus Sherwood*
Renamed: *Kitikmeot*   **Official No:** 330881

Type: Tug, Shallow Draft   **Designer:** McLaren & Sons   **Delivered:** 1969, NWT   **Built for:** Northern Transportation Co. Ltd., Edmonton, Alberta
Owner's representative: Henry Christopherson

Length: OA 160′   **Beam mld:** 40′   **Depth:** 10.5′
Design draft: 6.5′   **Tonnage:** GT 669   NT 442
Material: Steel hull and superstructure   **Capacity:** 17 (crew)

Main engines: EMD 645—2 @ 2000 hp   **Reduction ratio:** 1.50 : 1   **Sister ships:** 169; 170

This vessel was designed and built for service on the Mackenzie River and western Arctic Ocean from Point Barrow to Spencer Bay.

Hull No: 169   **Original name:** *Kelly Hall*
Renamed: *Pisurayak Kootook*   **Official No:** 330880

Type: Tug, Shallow Draft   **Designer:** McLaren & Sons   **Delivered:** 1969, NWT   **Built for:** Northern Transportation Co. Ltd., Edmonton, Alberta

Length: OA 160′   **Beam mld:** 40′   **Depth:** 10.5′
Design draft: 6.5′   **Tonnage:** GT 668   NT 442

Main engines: EMD 645—2 @ 2000 hp   **Reduction ratio:** 1.50 : 1   **Sister ships:** 168; 170

Hull No: 170   **Original name:** *Knut Lang*
Renamed: *Nunakput*   **Official No:** 331298

Type: Tug, Shallow Draft   **Designer:** McLaren & Sons   **Delivered:** 1969, NWT   **Built for:** Northern

Transportation Co. Ltd., Edmonton, Alberta

Length: **OA** 172′ **Beam mld:** 47.9′ **Depth:** 10.5′
Tonnage: **GT** 789 **NT** 524 **Material:** Steel hull and superstructure

Main engines: EMD 645—2 @ 2000 hp **Reduction ratio:** 1.50 : 1 **Sister ships:** 168; 169

The *Knut Lang.*

Originally constructed to be an identical sister ship to Hulls 168 and 169, Hull 170 was increased in size during construction in an effort to make it float at a lighter draft.

Hull No: 171 **Original name:** *Crown Zellerbach No. 1*
Renamed: *Crown Forest No. 1; Seaspan Harvester*
Official No: 344635

Type: Barge, Self-Dumping Log **Designer:** Robert Allan Ltd. **Delivered:** 1970, Vancouver BC **Built for:** Crown Zellerbach Canada Ltd., Vancouver BC

Length: **OA** 363′ **Beam mld:** 80′ **Depth:** 24′
Design draft: 18.5′ **Tonnage:** **GT** 5881 **Dwt** 10160 L. tons **Material:** Steel

Delivered July 18, 1970, *Crown Zellerbach No. 1* had a capacity of 2.2 million board feet of wood and was intended for transport of logs in BC coastal service. The two Washington Iron Works loading cranes, model 121-RM-95, were each capable of lifting up to 40 tons. Carried on board were two 16-foot Manly boom boats. *Crown Zellerbach No. 1* was the seventh log barge built by Allied. Arthur McLaren noted that this was a large barge and not many BC shipyards had the facilities to build it. Allied won the contract, bidding against Burrard Dry Dock and Yarrows.

Hull No: 172 **Original name:** *Mitco No. 2*
Official No: 331271

Type: Barge, Ramp **Designer:** McLaren & Sons
Delivered: 1969 **Built for:** Misty Island Transportation Co. Ltd., Skidegate BC

Length: **OA** 48′ **Beam mld:** 24′ **Depth:** 5.25′
Design draft: 2.5′ **Tonnage:** **GT** 44 **NT** 44

Mitco No. 2 was a barge fitted with a steel ramp, used in

transporting logging and construction equipment around the Queen Charlotte Islands. The hull was subdivided about centre to provide 4 oil tanks. The bow structure was constructed to enable beaching.

Hull No: 173 **Original name:** *Vic Ingraham*
Official No: 344735

Type: Tug, Shallow Draft **Designer:** Robert Allan Ltd.
Delivered: 1970 **Built for:** Northern Transportation Co. Ltd., Edmonton, Alberta

Length: **OA** 154.6′ **Beam mld:** 50′ **Depth:** 9.5′
Tonnage: **GT** 711 **NT** 484 **Material:** Steel hull and superstructure

Main engines: Caterpillar—4

The *Vic Ingraham.*

Hull No: 174 **Original name:** *Tsimshian Warrior*
Official No: 345180

Type: Barge, Bulk Cement **Designer:** Robert Allan Ltd. **Delivered:** 1971 **Built for:** LaFarge Concrete Ltd., Vancouver BC

Length: **OA** 166.5′ **Beam mld:** 48′ **Depth:** 15′
Design draft: 11′ **Tonnage:** **GT** 2301 **Dwt** 1518 L. tons

This barge incorporated stowage for 1,000 tons of bulk cement within six compartments in the hull and stowage of up to 1,500 tons of palletized cargo such as bagged cement or concrete blocks within a deckhouse on the main deck. The bulk cement was unloaded via airslides at the bottom of the tanks, which led to forward and aft cement pumps. The pumps were powered via a shore powerline. In 1980 the *Tsimshian Warrior* was being towed north to Alaska with a load of cement and may have gone over a reef. The crew of the tug later reported they felt a jerk on the towline. The barge was observed to be sinking and was beached against a dropoff, but the barge then sank in about 600 feet of water, some 60 miles north of Campbell River. It was not recovered.

Hull No: 175 **Original name:** *Mitco No. 3*
Official No: 345236

Type: Barge, Ramp **Designer:** McLaren & Sons

Delivered: 1971 **Built for:** Misty Islands Transportation Co. Ltd., Skidegate BC **Owner's representative:** Dalby Thomas Kendall
Length: OA 59.5′ **Beam mld:** 30′ **Depth:** 6′
Design draft: 3.25′ **Tonnage: GT** 78.03 **Dwt** 100 L. tons

Launched on April 27, 1971, *Mitco No. 3* was used to move logging and construction equipment around the Queen Charlotte Islands. She was larger than her predecessor, *Mitco No. 2*. Separate houseworks forward contained a waiting room/washroom on the port side and a machinery space starboard.

Hull No: 176 **Original name:** *Mary Lu Spencer*
Renamed: *Miller Mission* **Official No:** 345584

Type: Tug, Shallow Draft **Designer:** Robert Allan Ltd.
Delivered: 1971 **Built for:** North Western Dredging Co. Ltd., Vancouver BC

Length: Reg 57′ **Tonnage: GT** 69 **NT** 47

Hull No: 177 **Original name:** *Captain G.O. Sutherland*
Official No: 345653

Type: Tug, Log Towing Tug **Designer:** Cove, Hatfield & Co. Ltd. **Delivered:** 1971, Robson, Arrow Lakes BC
Built for: Columbia Cellulose (Celtran Equipment Ltd.), Vancouver BC

Length: OA 52′ **Beam mld:** 20′ **Depth:** 10′
Design draft: 8.5′ **Tonnage: GT** 71 **NT** 48
Material: Steel hull and superstructure **Capacity:** 4 (crew)

Main engines: Caterpillar D343TA—2 @ 365 hp @ 1800 rpm
Reduction ratio: 5.17 : 1 **Propellers:** 2 - 60″ dia.

The *Captain G.O. Sutherland.*

Captain G.O. Sutherland was built to haul log tows of up to 9,600 units down the Arrow Lakes from Arrowhead to the Keenleyside Dam, where they were sorted and delivered to the Columbia Cellulose sawmill and pulp mill at

Castlegar. The tug was pre-built in Vancouver. The hull was then split lengthwise into two pieces for transport to the Interior. The tug was named after Capt. Gordon Sutherland, who came to the Arrow Lakes in 1918 from his home in Pictou County, Nova Scotia. He commanded the lake tug *Elco II* for the Waldie Lumber Co. for many years.

Hull No: 178 **Original name:** *Saint John Carrier*
Renamed: *Irving Carrier; Nitinat Carrier; Kent Carrier*
Official No: 345408

Type: Barge, Newsprint **Designer:** Robert Allan Ltd.
Delivered: 1971 **Built for:** Kingcome Navigation Co. Ltd., Vancouver BC

Length: OA 363′ **Beam mld:** 82′ **Depth:** 22.25′
Design draft: 16′ **Tonnage: GT** 10687 **NT** 8643
Dwt 7250 L. tons **Material:** Steel

The *St. John Carrier* was built to transport rolls of newsprint from Saint John, New Brunswick, to US east coast ports. Loading and unloading was done by forklift-type vehicles via four access doors in the side of the enclosed deckhouse. A sister barge was built by Yarrows in Victoria. These two barges were enormous, being of a larger gross tonnage than any other vessels built in BC until 1993, when a consortium of builders constructed the *Spirit of British Columbia* and *Spirit of Vancouver Island* for BC Ferries.

Hull No: 179 **Original name:** *N.W.D. 204*
Renamed: *Miller 101* **Official No:** 345246

Type: Barge, Anchor Handling **Designer:** McLaren & Sons **Delivered:** 1971, Hay River NWT **Built for:** Northern Construction Co. Ltd., Vancouver BC

Length: OA 40′ **Beam mld:** 20′ **Depth:** 4′
Tonnage: GT 21

Hull No: 180 **Original name:** *Lady Joyce*
Renamed: *Joyce Tide; HMCS Moresby (MSA 112)*

Type: Offshore Supply **Designer:** IOS/McLaren & Sons **Delivered:** 1973, Vancouver BC **Built for:** International Offshore Services (Liberia) Ltd., London
Owner's representative: Gustaaf Oudijk

Length: OA 191.1′ **Beam mld:** 41.9′ **Depth:** 19.67′
Design draft: 16.77′ **Tonnage: GT** 1067 **NT** 307
Lightship 1182 L. tons **Dwt** 1180 L. tons **Material:** Steel hull and superstructure **Capacity:** 22 (crew)
Speed: 14 knots
Main engines: Nohab SF16RS-F—4 @ 1050 hp @ 750 rpm
Propellers: 2 - 120″ dia. **Sister ships:** 181; 182; 183; 184

Simultaneous with the building of the five IOS vessels at Allied, two other 185′ offshore vessels were under construction at Bel-Aire Shipyard, North Vancouver, to the order of Zapata Canada Ltd., and three supply vessels were under construction at Star Shipyards (Mercer's) Ltd. in New Westminster. Hulls 180 and 182, *Lady Joyce* and *Lady Jean*, were purchased from Tidewater by the Canadian Department of National Defence in 1989. Renamed *Moresby* and *Anticosti*, the vessels underwent conversion to minesweepers for training Canada's Naval Reserve in mine warfare countermeasures. After a decade of naval service, *Moresby (MSA 112)* was paid off at Canadian Forces Base, Pacific, Esquimalt, BC on March 10, 2000, and put up for sale.

Hull No: 181   **Original name:** *Lady Lisbeth*

Type: Offshore Supply   **Designer:** IOS/McLaren & Sons   **Delivered:** 1973, Vancouver BC   **Built for:** International Offshore Services (Liberia) Ltd., London

Length: OA 191.1′   **Beam mld:** 41.9′   **Depth:** 19.67′   **Design draft:** 16.77′   **Tonnage: GT** 1067   **NT** 307   **Lightship** 1182 L. tons   **Dwt** 1180 L. tons

Main engines: Nohab—4 @ 1050 hp @ 750 rpm
Sister ships: 180; 182; 183; 184

The *Lady Lisbeth* sailed for Europe on Thursday, June 28, 1973, taking in tow the barge *Charlotte Vessels*, a 250x75′ barge equipped for laying electric power cables.

Hull No: 182   **Original name:** *Lady Jean*
Renamed: *Jean Tide*; HMCS *Anticosti*

Type: Offshore Supply   **Designer:** IOS/McLaren & Sons   **Delivered:** 1973   **Built for:** International Offshore Services (Liberia) Ltd., London

Length: OA 191.1′   **Beam mld:** 41.9′   **Depth:** 19.67′   **Design draft:** 16.77′   **Tonnage: GT** 1067   **NT** 307   **Lightship** 1182 L. tons   **Dwt** 1180 L. tons

Main engines: Nohab SF16RS-F—4 @ 1050 hp @ 750 rpm
Sister ships: 180; 181; 183; 184

On Tuesday, September 25, 1973, three new offshore supply vessels sailed out of Vancouver Harbour. The *Lady Jean* was in transit to the United Kingdom. The *Hudson Service* and *Baffin Service*, built by Bel-Aire Shipyards for Zapata Canada Ltd., were on their way to eastern Canada. The two 185-foot ice-strengthened vessels were designed by W. R. (Bill) Brown.

Hull No: 183   **Original name:** *Lady Vivien*
Renamed: *Vivien Tide*; *Auriga Tide*; *Putford Achilles*

Type: Offshore Supply   **Designer:** IOS/McLaren & Sons   **Delivered:** 1973, Vancouver BC   **Built for:** International Offshore Services (Liberia) Ltd., London

Length: OA 191.1′   **Beam mld:** 41.9′   **Depth:** 19.67′   **Design draft:** 16.77′   **Tonnage: GT** 1067   **NT** 307   **Lightship** 1182 L. tons   **Dwt** 1180 L. tons

Main engines: Nohab S16RS-F—4 @ 1050 hp @ 750 rpm
Sister ships: 180; 181; 182; 184

Lady Vivien was launched in August 1973, sea-trialled in November and sailed for Dundee, Scotland, in early December.

Hull No: 184   **Original name:** *Lady Alexandra*
Renamed: *Alexandra Tide*

Type: Offshore Supply   **Designer:** IOS/McLaren & Sons   **Delivered:** 1974, Vancouver BC   **Built for:**
International Offshore Services (Liberia) Ltd., London

Length: OA 191.1′   **Reg.'   Beam mld:** 41.9′   **Depth:** 19.67′   **Design draft:** 16.77′   **Tonnage: GT** 1067   **NT** 307   **Lightship** 1182 L. tons   **Dwt** 1180 L. tons

Main engines: Nohab SF16RS-F—4 @ 1050 hp @ 750 rpm
Sister ships: 180; 181; 182; 183

The *Lady Alexandra* was launched Saturday, November 10, 1973. On the launching platform were five people who had attended the launching of the first *Lady Alexandra* at Montrose, Scotland, in 1923.

Hull No: 185   **Original name:** *P.L. Transporter*
Official No: 346315

Type: Barge, Transport   **Designer:** Cove, Hatfield & Co.   **Delivered:** 1972, Powell Lake BC   **Built for:** Percy Logging Co. Ltd., Vancouver BC
Owner's representative: Mr. Percy

Length: OA 80′   **Beam mld:** 30′   **Depth:** 6′   **Tonnage: GT** 121   **Dwt** 170 L. tons

This barge was built for use as a general purpose equipment carrier and for delivery of fuel oil in service on Powell Lake, BC. Internal tanks carried 9,000 imperial gallons of diesel fuel and 6,750 imperial gallons of gasoline.

Hull No: 186   **Original name:** *Nahidik*
Official No: 347496

Type: Buoy Tender, Shallow Draft   **Designer:** McLaren & Sons   **Delivered:** 1974, Vancouver BC
Built for: Ministry of Transport, Ottawa, Ontario

Length: OA 175′   **Beam mld:** 50′   **Depth:** 10.5′   **Design draft:** 6′   **Tonnage: GT** 856   **NT** 392   **Lightship** 551 L. tons   **Dwt** 400 L. tons   **Material:** Steel hull, aluminum superstructure   **Speed:** 14.5 knots (max)

Main engines: GM-EMD 12-645-E5—2 @ 2100 hp
Propellers: 2 - 60″ dia.

In the native tongue, *Nahidik* means pathfinder or trail blazer. The *Nahidik* is a twin-screw, dual draft buoy/supply vessel, built for operation on both the Mackenzie River and in the Beaufort Sea (western Arctic Ocean). Duties to be performed were the maintenance of buoys and other aids to navigation, particularly in the Beaufort Sea, where a large amount of offshore oil exploration work was underway. Allied Shipbuilders Ltd. was awarded the contract, from the Department of Supply and Services, to build this ship in January 1974, and the vessel sailed around Point Barrow and into the Arctic Ocean in late August. The hull is of steel construction, subdivided with eight watertight bulkheads and reinforced forward for navigation in light ice conditions. The upper houses are of welded aluminium construction. A feature of the vessel is the tunnel stern, wherein the propellers are located in recesses or tunnels, allowing the diameter of the propellers to be greater than the light draft of the vessel. (This is common to all vessels operating in the Mackenzie River.)

Hull No: 187   **Original name:** *Thruster 3*
Official No: 347546

Type: Barge, Thruster   **Designer:** Robert Allan Ltd.
Delivered: 1973, Vancouver BC   **Built for:** Northern Transportation Co. Ltd., Edmonton, Alberta
Length: OA 105′   **Beam mld:** 35′   **Depth:** 7′
Tonnage: GT 214   NT 160   **Sister ship:** 188

Four *Thruster* barges were built, two by Allied and two by Yarrows in Victoria. These remote-controlled barges were placed at the head of a number of 1500 Series barges (250x56′) being pushed by large river tugs. The purpose of the thruster barges was to enhance manoeuvrability of the barge train. The two Allied barges were loaded on top of a new 1500 series barge for the sea voyage to the Canadian Arctic.

Hull No: 188   **Original name:** *Thruster 4*
Official No: 347547

Type: Barge   **Designer:** Robert Allan Ltd.
Delivered: 1973   **Built for:** Northern Transportation Co. Ltd., Edmonton, Alberta
Length: OA 105′   **Reg** 103′   **Beam mld:** 35′
Depth: 7′   **Tonnage:** GT 214   NT 160
Sister ship: 187

Hull No: 189   **Original name:** *Carlyn McMurren*
Renamed: *Miller Richmond*   **Official No:** 348856

Type: Tug, Shallow Draft   **Designer:** Robert Allan Ltd.
Delivered: 1974   **Built for:** Northern Construction Co.
Owner's representative: Douglas Coulter
Length: OA 70′   **Beam mld:** 25′   **Depth:** 9.25′
Design draft: 4.5′   **Tonnage:** GT 131   NT 49
Material: Steel hull, aluminum superstructure
Capacity: 5 (crew)
Main engines: Caterpillar D348—2 @ 725 hp @ 1800 rpm
Reduction ratio: 3.54 : 1   **Propellers:** 2 - 49″ dia.
Sister ships: 190; 191

The sister tugs, based at Tuktoyaktuk, pushed or pulled 2,000-yard self-dumping barges that were employed in the construction of artificial islands in the Beaufort Sea for Imperial Oil Ltd. The islands were used as stationary oil drilling platforms. A total of four tugs were built, three by Allied and one by Zenith Steel Fabricators Ltd. Five self-dumping barges were built by Burrard Dry Dock. The work season started about July 10 and ran for about ninety days. Northern Construction, a division of the US firm Morrison Knudsen Co., had done work in the Northwest Territories since 1946, including building about one-third of the DEW line, the defence early warning radar system.

Hull No: 190   **Original name:** *Dorothy Robinson*
Renamed: *Miller Surrey; Dorothy Robinson*   **Official No:** 348857

Type: Tug, Shallow Draft   **Designer:** Robert Allan Ltd.
Delivered: 1974   **Built for:** Northern Construction Co.

Length: OA 70′   **Reg** 65′   **Beam mld:** 25′
Depth: 9.25′   **Design draft:** 4.5′   **Tonnage:**
GT 131   NT 49   **Sister ships:** 189; 191

Hull No: 191   **Original name:** *Beverly Lambert*
Renamed: *Miller Delta*   **Official No:** 348855

Type: Tug, Shallow Draft   **Designer:** Robert Allan Ltd.
Delivered: 1974   **Built for:** Northern Construction Co.
Length: OA 70′   **Reg** 65′   **Beam mld:** 25′
Depth: 9.25′   **Design draft:** 4.5′   **Tonnage:**
GT 131   NT 49   **Sister ships:** 189; 190

Hull No: 192   **Original name:** *Canmar Supplier*
Renamed: *Supplier*   **Official No:** 370255

Type: Offshore Supply Vessel   **Designer:** Robert Allan Ltd.   **Delivered:** 1975, Vancouver BC   **Built for:** Dome Petroleum Ltd., Calgary, Alberta
Owner's representatives: Noel Broom; Capt. Colin Insh
Length: OA 210′   **Reg** 185′   **Beam mld:** 45′
Depth: 18.25′   **Design draft:** 14.25′   **Tonnage:**
GT 1188   NT 384   **Dwt** 1200 L. tons   **Material:** Steel hull and superstructure   **Capacity:** 14 (crew)
Speed: 15 knots (max) 13 knots (service)
Main engines: Nohab Polar F216V-D—2 @ 3510 hp

The *Canmar Supplier.*

The *Canmar Supplier* was the first of four similar ice-breaking supply vessels built in BC yards for Dome Petroleum. These ships, each with an excess of 7000 hp installed, were among the most powerful supply vessels being built and some of the first to be built for navigation in ice. The *Canmar Supplier* was intended for operation in the Beaufort Sea, i.e. the western Arctic Ocean, and serviced drilling ships that were operated in that area by Canadian Marine Drilling, a subsidiary of Dome Petroleum.

The vessel sailed from Vancouver, light boat, on September 1, 1975, directly for its base in Tuktoyaktuk, NWT. Of four sister ships built in Vancouver, she was the only one completed in time to enter the Arctic, ready for work the following spring.

Hull No: 193   **Original name:** *Omineca Princess*
Official No: 370059

Type: Ferry, Vehicle   **Designer:** Talbot, Jackson
Delivered: 1976, François Lake   **Built for:** Department of Highways, Victoria BC

Length: OA 192'   **Reg** 168'   **Beam mld:** 56'
Depth: 10'   **Design draft:** 6.5'   **Tonnage: GT** 765
NT 438   **Dwt** 406 L. tons   **Material:** Steel hull and superstructure   **Capacity:** 200 (passengers); 34 (vehicles)
Speed: 12 knots

Main engines: Caterpillar D-379—2 @ 565 hp @ 1225 rpm
Reduction ratio: 3.60 : 1

This vehicle ferry was built for service on François Lake in northern BC.

Hull No: 194   **Original name:** *Arctic Taglu*
Official No: 368381

Type: Tug, Anchor Handling   **Designer:** Cleaver & Walkingshaw   **Delivered:** 1976   **Built for:** Arctic Transportation Ltd., Calgary, Alberta
Owner's representative: John Mattson

Length: OA 110'   **Beam mld:** 34'   **Depth:** 16'
Design draft: 13.5'   **Tonnage: GT** 394   **NT** 44
Dwt 250 L. tons   **Material:** Steel hull and superstructure
Speed: 12 knots

Main engines: Caterpillar D399TA—2 @ 1125 hp @ 1225 rpm   **Reduction ratio:** 4.75 : 1   **Propellers:** 2 - 83" dia.   **Sister ship:** 195

The twin tugs *Arctic Taglu* and *Arctic Hooper* were built to assist in the construction of artificial islands for Imperial Oil. The islands were used as bases for oil drilling. At the time Arctic Transportation had joint owners: Seaspan International, Vancouver; Federal Commerce & Navigation, Montreal; and Crowley Maritime Corp., offshore division, Seattle Washington, USA.

Hull No: 195   **Original name:** *Arctic Hooper*
Official No: 368382

Type: Tug, Anchor Handling   **Designer:** Cleaver & Walkingshaw   **Delivered:** 1976   **Built for:** Arctic Transportation Ltd., Calgary, Alberta
Owner's representative: John Mattson

Length: OA 110'   **Beam mld:** 34'   **Depth:** 16'
Tonnage: GT 394   **Dwt** 250 L. tons   **Sister ship:** 194

Hull No: 196   **Original name:** *Storm Wave*
Official No: 383402

Type: Tug, Coastal   **Designer:** A. G. McIlwain Ltd.
Delivered: 1977, Vancouver BC   **Built for:** Egmont Towing & Sorting Ltd., Vancouver BC   **Owner's representative:** Gerry Rendall

Length: OA 63.75'   **Reg** 59'   **Beam mld:** 22.5'
Depth: 11.7'   **Tonnage: GT** 97.9   **NT** 2   **Lightship** 148 L. tons   **Dwt** 42 L. tons   **Material:** Steel hull, aluminum superstructure   **Capacity:** 4 (crew)
Speed: 10 knots (service)

Main engines: Caterpillar D346—2 @ 480 hp @ 1800 rpm
Reduction ratio: 5.17 : 1   **Propellers:** 2 - 61" dia.

The *Storm Wave*.

Allied built the hull and the aluminum wheelhouse, fitted the joiner work and installed the stern gear, but the rest of the vessel was finished by Summer Equipment crews. *Storm Wave* and the 72-foot *Bandera* (Hull #226) were built to a similar A. G. McIlwain design.

Hull No: 197   **Original name:** *C.F. Co. No. 66*
Renamed: *Western Transfer VI*   **Official No:** 371833

Type: Barge, Fish Unloading   **Delivered:** 1977
Built for: Canadian Fishing Co. Ltd. Vancouver BC

Length: OA 70'   **Beam mld:** 30'   **Depth:** 5'
Tonnage: GT 87   **Sister ships:** 205; 206

This was the first of three special barges built to facilitate gentle unloading of fish from catcher boats.

Hull No: 198   **Original name:** *Foursome No. 1*
Renamed: *Big Bay*   **Official No:** 371851

Type: Barge, Fish Packing   **Designer:** McLaren & Sons
Delivered: 1977   **Built for:** Foursome Fishing Co. Ltd., Prince Rupert BC   **Owner's representative:** John Haugan

Length: OA 87'   **Beam mld:** 21'   **Depth:** 8.25'
Design draft: 6.5'   **Tonnage: GT** 117   **Dwt** 200 L. tons   **Sister ships:** 054; 056; 057

Hull No: 199   **Original name:** *Star Pacific*
Official No: 372658

Type: Fishing, Seiner   **Designer:** Robert Allan Ltd.
Delivered: 1977, Vancouver BC   **Built for:** Mar-Pat Fishing Ltd.   **Owner's representative:** Risto Kaltio

Length: OA 54.75'   **Reg** 50'   **Beam mld:** 16.4'
Depth: 8.25'   **Tonnage: GT** 42.6   **NT** 13.62
Lightship 58 L. tons   **Dwt** 23 L. tons   **Material:** Steel hull, aluminum superstructure

Main engine: Detroit diesel 8V-71   **Sister ship:** 200

Hull No: 200   **Original name:** *Island Rogue*   **Official No:** 372701

Type: Fishing, Seiner   **Designer:** Robert Allan Ltd.
Delivered: 1977, Vancouver BC   **Built for:** Macmillan
Agencies Ltd., Vancouver BC   **Owner's representative:**
Chris Peterson, Ewen Macmillan

Length: OA 54.75′   **Reg** 50′   **Beam mld:** 16.4′
Depth: 8.25′   **Tonnage: GT** 43   **NT** 14   **Lightship**
58 L. tons   **Dwt** 23 L. tons   **Material:** Steel hull,
aluminum superstructure

Main engine: Detroit diesel 8V-71   **Sister ship:** 199

Hull No: 201   **Original name:** Work Boat

Type: Work Boat, Shallow Draft   **Designer:** McLaren
& Sons   **Delivered:** 1977   **Built for:** Dept. of Public
Works, Ottawa, Ontario   **Owner's representative:** Jack
Gilmore

Length: OA 17′   **Beam mld:** 7.6′   **Depth:** 4.75′
Design draft: 2.5′   **Tonnage: Lightship** 4 L. tons
Material: Steel

Main engine: Bedford 330 6 cylinder—1 @ 85 hp @ 2500
rpm   **Reduction ratio:** 3.00 : 1   **Propeller:** 1 - 29″
dia.

This small, robust single-screw workboat was carried on
board the *Essington II*, a 120-foot federal government vessel
with a crane mounted on the forward end, used to maintain
the many federal government wharves on the BC coast.
Bollard pull was 2,400 lbs.

Hull No: 202   **Original name:** *F.R.P.D. 20*
Official No: 348560

Type: Barge, Pile Driver   **Designer:** McLaren & Sons
Delivered: 1977 Vancouver BC   **Built for:** Fraser River
Pile Driving Co. Ltd., New Westminster BC

Length: OA 72′   **Beam mld:** 24.16′   **Depth:** 4′
Design draft: 1.75′   **Tonnage: GT** 57

Allied built this simple 72-foot spud barge for Fraser
River Pile Driving.

Hull No: 203   **Original name:** *Dual Venture*
Official No: 383455

Type: Fishing, Seiner   **Designer:** Cleaver &
Walkingshaw   **Delivered:** 1977, Vancouver BC
Built for: Our Own Investments Ltd., Vancouver BC
Owner's representative: Nick Brajich

Length: OA 76′   **Beam mld:** 20′   **Depth:** 11′
Tonnage: GT 129   **NT** 42   **Lightship** 131 L. tons
Dwt 135 L. tons   **Material:** Steel hull, aluminum
wheelhouse

Main engine: Caterpillar 3412—1 @ 520 hp @ 1800 rpm
Sister ship: 204

Hull 203 was one of the many new herring/salmon
seiners built during the bountiful west coast fishing boom of
the 1970s.

Hull No: 204   **Original name:** *C. Venture No. 1*
Official No: 383456

Type: Fishing, Seiner   **Designer:** Cleaver &
Walkingshaw   **Delivered:** 1977, Vancouver BC
Built for: Carr Fishing Co. Ltd., Burnaby BC
Owner's representative: Marijo Carr

Length: OA 76′   **Beam mld:** 20′   **Depth:** 11′
Tonnage: GT 119   **NT** 31   **Material:** Steel hull and
superstructure

Main engine: Caterpillar 3412—1 @ 520 hp @ 1800 rpm
Sister ship: 203

Hull No: 205   **Original name:** *C.F. Co. No. 67*
Renamed: *Western Transfer IV*   **Official No:** *383420*

Type: Barge, Fish Unloading   **Delivered:** 1977
Built for: Canadian Fishing Co. Ltd., Vancouver BC

Length: OA 70′   **Beam mld:** 30′   **Depth:** 5′
Tonnage: GT 86   **Sister ships:** 197; 206

Hulls 205 & 206, two 70-foot fish unloading scows, were
like the *C.F. Co. No. 66* (Hull #197) that Allied had built a
year earlier for Canadian Fishing Co. Ltd. Allied's steelwork
foreman Barry Piggot and George MacPherson, who later
became union president, worked on them together. "They
were very precise," Malcolm McLaren noted, "and they tell
me they quite enjoyed it because they were left alone to do
the work. Everything fitted perfectly—no muss, no fuss."

Hull No: 206   **Original name:** *C.F. Co. No. 68*
Renamed: *Western Transfer V*   **Official No:** 383421

Type: Barge, Fish Unloading   **Delivered:** 1977
Built for: Canadian Fishing Co. Ltd., Vancouver BC

Length: OA 70′   **Reg** 70′   **Beam mld:** 30′
Depth: 5′   **Tonnage: GT** 86   **Sister ships:** 197;
205

Hull No: 207   **Original name:** *T. L. Sharpe*
Official No: 384121

Type: Barge, Pile Driver   **Delivered:** 1978
Built for: Fraser River Pile Driving Co. Ltd., New
Westminster BC

Length: OA 105′   **Tonnage: GT** 356

The *T. L. Sharpe* was a 105-foot spud barge. This big
barge can handle a large crawler crane and is still in service.

Hull No: 208   **Original name:** *Allied 208*
Official No: 393380

Type: Floating Drydock   **Designer:** McLaren & Sons
Delivered: 1979   **Built for:** Allied Shipbuilders, North
Vancouver BC   **Owner's representative:** T. A. McLaren

Length: OA 119.5′   **Beam mld:** 62′   **Depth:** 29.6′
Design draft: 5′   **Tonnage: GT** 683   **NT** 506
Lightship 335 L. tons   **Dwt** 760 L. tons   **Material:** Steel

Arthur McLaren had intended to name this floating
drydock *Archimedes*, but the name was already taken.

Hull No: 209   **Original name:** *Ocean Cavalier*
Official No: 384020

Type: Fishing, Seiner **Designer:** Cleaver & Walkingshaw **Delivered:** 1978 **Built for:** Walter Carr, North Vancouver BC

Length: OA 86.4' **Beam mld:** 23' **Depth:** 12.33' **Tonnage: GT** 124 **NT** 39 **Lightship** 119 L. tons **Dwt** 130 L. tons **Material:** Steel hull, aluminum wheelhouse

Main engine: Caterpillar 3412—1 @ 520 hp @ 1800 rpm

Hull No: 210 **Original name:** *Viking Star*
Official No: 391345

Type: Fishing, Seiner/Longliner **Designer:** Cleaver & Walkingshaw **Delivered:** 1978 **Built for:** Westfjord Fishing Ltd., Prince Rupert BC
Owner's representative: Egil Elvan

Length: OA 88.9' **Beam mld:** 23' **Depth:** 12' **Tonnage: GT** 138.15 **NT** 57 **Lightship** 145 L. tons **Dwt** 176 L. tons **Material:** Steel

Main engine: Caterpillar 3412—1 @ 520 hp @ 1800 rpm
Propeller: 1 - 68" dia.

Allied built the 81-foot offshore longliner *Viking Star* for Egil Elvan of Prince Rupert. Longlining enables fishermen to specifically target the type of fish they want to catch. This particular vessel boasted a Mustad Autoline system, one of the first installed on the BC coast. Malcolm McLaren explained that the Norwegian system was different than the traditional way of hand-baiting longline hooks. Instead, this one automatically baited hooks. When the fish were hauled on board, the hooks and line returned to storage racks. Although they never gained much popularity in BC, a few of these automatic systems are still at work on the coast.

Hull No: 211 **Original name:** *Naden Drydock Gate*

Type: Caisson Gate **Designer:** Department of National Defence **Delivered:** 1978, Naden Drydock, Esquimalt BC **Built for:** Department of National Defence, Ottawa, Ontario **Owner's representative:** Tom Kirsop; Vic Booth

Length: OA 12' **Beam mld:** 71' **Depth:** 34.46' **Design draft:** 33.1' (max) **Tonnage: GT** 290 **Lightship** 401 L. tons **Dwt** 381 L. tons **Material:** Steel

Hull 211 was a replacement caisson-type gate, specifically designed for use to seal the Naden graving dock at the Esquimalt naval base. The gate was equipped with electric-driven pumps to pump out the water ballast used to "sink" the gate in position at the opening of the graving dock. Permanent ballast was of concrete made with Magnetite iron ore, rather than the usual rock aggregate.

Hull No: 212 **Original name:** *Imperial Nootka*
Official No: 391372

Type: Oil Transporter, Harbour Supply **Designer:** Cove, Dixon & Co. Ltd. **Delivered:** 1978, Vancouver BC **Built for:** Imperial Oil Ltd., Toronto, Ontario

Length: OA 82' **Beam mld:** 26.24' **Depth:** 7.22' **Tonnage: GT** 126 **NT** 122 **Material:** Steel hull and superstructure

Main engine: Caterpillar 3408 T/A—1 @ 365 hp @ 1800 rpm

The *Imperial Nootka*.

This self-propelled lube oil carrier was built to provide various grades of crankcase and lubricating oils, as well as diesel fuel, to visiting deep-sea ships in the Port of Vancouver. The main propulsion unit is a "Murray & Tregurtha" series 6 "Harbour Master" drive unit mounted on the aft deck of the vessel. The drive leg rotates 360 degrees.

Hull No: 213 **Original name:** *C.T. Titan*
Official No: 391718

Type: Tug **Designer:** Robert Allan Ltd. **Delivered:** 1979, Vancouver BC **Built for:** Chemainus Towing Co. Ltd., Chemainus BC **Owner's representatives:** Gary Urton; Graham Constable

Length: OA 53' **Reg** 50' **Beam mld:** 19' **Depth:** 9' **Design draft:** 8.5' **Tonnage: GT** 54 **NT** 30 **Lightship** 79 L. tons **Dwt** 24 L. tons **Material:** Steel hull, aluminum superstructure

Main engines: Cummins KTA-1150M—2 @ 470 hp @ 1800 rpm **Reduction ratio:** 5.17 : 1 **Propellers:** 2 - 58" dia.

The *C.T. Titan*.

Built for a combination of services—yarding, barge towing and ship assistance/berthing—this tug is operated by two people on 12-hour operations. It is still active towing log booms.

Hull No: 214   **Original name:** *Katrena Leslie*
Official No: 391846

Type: Fishing, Seiner   **Designer:** Cleaver & Walkingshaw   **Delivered:** 1978   **Built for:** Hunt Fishing Co. Ltd., Richmond BC
Owner's representative: Alfred (Hutch) Hunt

Length: OA 79.67′   **Beam mld:** 23′   **Depth:** 11′
Tonnage: GT 115   **NT** 35   **Lightship** 116 L. tons
Dwt 129 L. tons   **Material:** Steel hull, aluminum superstructure   **Capacity:** 6 (crew)   **Speed:** 10.5 knots (max) 10 knots (service)
Main engine: Caterpillar 3412—1 @ 520 hp @ 1800 rpm
Reduction ratio: 4.67 : 1   **Propeller:** 1 - 66″ dia.
Sister ships: 215; 216; 218; 219; 223

Hull No: 215   **Original name:** *Snow Drift*
Official No: 391861

Type: Fishing, Seiner   **Designer:** Cleaver & Walkingshaw   **Delivered:** 1978   **Built for:** Snow Drift Fishing Ltd., et al, Prince Rupert BC
Owner's representatives: Rodney Pierce, Aubrey Innes, Bill Seymour

Length: OA 79.67′   **Beam mld:** 23′   **Depth:** 11′
Tonnage: GT 115   **NT** 32   **Lightship** 116 L. tons
Dwt 129 L. tons   **Material:** Steel hull, aluminum superstructure
Main engine: Caterpillar 3412—1 @ 520 hp @ 1800 rpm
Reduction ratio: 4.67 : 1   **Propeller:** 1 - 66″ dia.
Sister ships: 214; 216; 218; 219; 223

The 1970s were boom times for salmon fishing on the BC coast. The combination of high rates of return of salmon coupled with high prices for the catch, led to a renewal of the existing fleet.

Hull No: 216   **Original name:** *Angela Lynn*
Official No: 391847

Type: Fishing, Seiner   **Designer:** Cleaver & Walkingshaw   **Delivered:** 1978   **Built for:** Snow Drift Fishing Ltd. & East West Fishing Co. Ltd., Prince Rupert BC   **Owner's representative:** Angus Tobin

Length: OA 79.67′   **Reg** 72′   **Beam mld:** 23′
Depth: 11′   **Tonnage: GT** 115   **NT** 49   **Lightship** 116 L. tons   **Dwt** 130 L. tons   **Material:** Steel hull, aluminum superstructure   **Sister ships:** 214; 215; 218; 219; 223

Hull No: 217   **Original name:** *Dumit*   **Official No:** 391902

Type: Buoy Tender, Shallow Draft   **Designer:** McLaren & Sons   **Delivered:** 1979   **Built for:** Ministry of

Transport, Ottawa, Ontario   **Owner's representative:** James Kirk, Victoria

Length: OA 160′   **Beam mld:** 40′   **Depth:** 8.5′
Design draft: 4′   **Tonnage: GT** 568.58   **NT** 176.1
Lightship 381 L. tons   **Dwt** 86 L. tons   **Material:** Steel hull, aluminum superstructure   **Capacity:** 10 (crew)
Speed: 13.58 knots (max) 12 knots (service)

Main engines: Caterpillar D399—2 @ 1125 hp

The *Dumit*.

Dumit was the sixth vessel Allied built for Canadian Coast Guard service on the northern river system. Launched on the night of Tuesday, July 10, 1979, the vessel was named by Pat Siddon, wife of Richmond Conservative MP Tom Siddon.

Hull No: 218   **Original name:** *Bold Performance*
Official No: 392246

Type: Fishing, Seiner   **Designer:** Cleaver & Walkingshaw   **Delivered:** 1979   **Built for:** Abbott Enterprises Ltd. et al, Vancouver BC   **Owner's representative:** Eric Abbott

Length: OA 79.67′   **Beam mld:** 23′   **Depth:** 11′
Tonnage: GT 115   **NT** 64   **Lightship** 116 L. tons
Dwt 129 L. tons
Main engine: Caterpillar 3412—1 @ 520 hp @ 1800 rpm
Sister ships: 214; 215; 216; 219; 223

Hull No: 219   **Original name:** *Karenora II*
Renamed: *Karenora*   **Official No:** 392757

Type: Fishing, Seiner   **Designer:** Cleaver & Walkingshaw   **Delivered:** 1979   **Built for:** Trinity Enterprises Ltd. et al, Nanaimo BC
Owner's representative: Don Smith

Length: OA 79.67′   **Beam mld:** 23′   **Depth:** 11′
Tonnage: GT 112   **NT** 32   **Lightship** 112 L. tons
Dwt 129 L. tons
Main engine: Caterpillar 3412—1 @ 520 hp @ 1800 rpm
Sister ships: 214; 215; 216; 218; 223

Hull No: 220   **Original name:** *Ocean Pearl*
Official No: 393497

Type: Fishing, Longliner   **Delivered:** 1979
Built for: R & B Fishing Co. Ltd. & Arran Sea Fishing Co. Ltd., Gibsons BC   **Owner's representatives:** Blair Pearl, Chris Hummel

Length: OA 116' **Beam mld:** 32' **Depth:** 15'
Design draft: 14.8' **Tonnage: GT** 374.9 **NT** 194.7
Lightship 274 L. tons **Dwt** 448 L. tons **Material:**
Steel hull and superstructure

Main engine: Caterpillar D398—1 @ 850 hp @ 1225 rpm
Propeller: 1 - 72" dia.

The *Ocean Pearl*.

This longliner was built to catch, and freeze at sea, blackcod (sablefish), a high-quality product for export to Japan. In recent years, the vessel has put its 10,000-mile cruising range to use in the longline tuna fishery of the mid-Pacific Ocean.

Hull No: 221 **Original name:** *Resolution II*
Official No: 393511

Type: Fishing, Seiner **Designer:** Cove, Dixon & Co.
Ltd. **Delivered:** 1979 **Built for:** Pisces Marine Ltd.,
North Vancouver BC **Owner's representative:** John La
Pointe

Length: OA 66.5' **Beam mld:** 22' **Depth:** 10.5'
Tonnage: GT 81 **NT** 24 **Material:** Steel hull,
aluminum wheelhouse **Capacity:** 6 (crew)
Speed: 10.5 knots

Main engine: Cummins KTA-1150-M—1 @ 470 hp @
1800 rpm **Reduction ratio:** 4.50 : 1 **Propeller:** 1 -
58" dia.

Hull No: 222 **Original name:** *Tenacious*
Official No: 392896

Type: Fishing, Trawler/Seiner **Designer:** Cleaver &
Walkingshaw **Delivered:** 1980 **Built for:** D. F.
Murray Consultants Ltd. & Mark Fishing, Prince Rupert
BC **Owner's representative:** Don Murray, Vigo Mark

Length: OA 86.7' **Beam mld:** 25' **Depth:** 13.5'
Tonnage: GT 149 **NT** 44 **Lightship** 184 L. tons
Dwt 134 L. tons **Material:** Steel hull, aluminum
superstructure **Speed:** 9.2 knots (max) 8.3 knots
(service)

Main engine: B & W Alpha 405—1 @ 765 hp
Propeller: 1 controllable pitch

Hull No: 223 **Original name:** *Western Investor*
Official No: 393512

Type: Fishing, Seiner **Delivered:** 1979
Built for: BC Packers Ltd., Richmond BC
Owner's representative: Aubrey Roberts

Length: OA 79.67' **Beam mld:** 23 **Depth:** 11'
Tonnage: GT 119.26 **NT** 46 **Lightship** 125 L. tons
Dwt 115 L. tons **Material:** Steel hull, aluminum
superstructure **Capacity:** 6 (crew) **Speed:** 11.1
knots (max)

Main engine: Caterpillar D-348—1 @ 700 hp @ 1800 rpm
Reduction ratio: 4.67 : 1 **Propeller:** 1 - 72" dia.
Sister ships: 214; 215; 216; 218; 219

This vessel was nearly identical to the other five vessels of the *Katrena Leslie* class. However, being first on the fishing grounds could often provide a competitive advantage. For increased speed, the *Western Investor* had about 35 percent more power than her sister ships; the increase in speed was 6 percent.

Hull No: 224 **Original name:** *Queens Reach*
Official No: 394194

Type: Fishing, Seiner **Designer:** Cleaver &
Walkingshaw **Delivered:** 1980 **Built for:** Legate
Enterprises Ltd., West Vancouver BC
Owner's representative: John Legate

Length: OA 76' **Beam mld:** 22' **Depth:** 10.5'
Tonnage: GT 93.63 **NT** 26.08 **Lightship** 100 L. tons
Dwt 107 L. tons **Material:** Steel hull, aluminum
superstructure **Capacity:** 6 (crew) **Speed:** 10.3
knots (max)

Main engine: Cummins KTA 1150-M—1 @ 470 hp @
1800 rpm **Reduction ratio:** 4.50 : 1 **Propeller:** 1 -
61" dia.

Queens Reach replaced the 62x14' 1926 wood seiner *Early Field*, which was suffering the effects of old age: rot, expensive repairs and a difficulty in competing against other newly built fishing machines.

Hull No: 225 **Original name:** *Charles H. Cates VI*
Official No: 395353

Type: Tug, Berthing **Designer:** Robert Allan Ltd.
Delivered: 1980 **Built for:** C. H. Cates & Sons Ltd.,
North Vancouver BC **Owner's representative:** Terry
Waghorn

Length: OA 60' **Beam mld:** 22' **Depth:** 9.4'
Design draft: 9' **Tonnage: GT** 69 **NT** 2.38

Main engines: Detroit diesel 16V-149—2 @ 900 hp @ 1800
rpm **Reduction ratio:** 5.17 : 1 **Propellers:** 2 - 66"
dia. **Sister ship:** 230

This tug was built for ship handling duties in the Port of Vancouver, BC. The tug is nearly identical to *C.H. Cates V* and *C.H. Cates VII*, previously built by Bel-Aire Shipyards.

Hull No: 226   **Original name:** *Bandera*
Official No: 394166

Type: Tug, Coastal   **Designer:** A. G. McIlwain Ltd.
Delivered: 1980   **Built for:** Broughton Towing Co. Ltd., Nanaimo BC   **Owner's representative:** Ridge Wilson

Length: OA 72′   **Beam mld:** 24′   **Depth:** 11.67′
Design draft: 12.5′   **Tonnage: GT** 144.21   **NT** 0.09
Lightship 162 L. tons   **Dwt** 76 L. tons   **Material:** Steel hull, aluminum wheelhouse   **Capacity:** 5 (crew)
Speed: 10.3 knots

Main engines: Detroit diesel 12V-149—2 @ 675 hp @ 1800 rpm   **Reduction ratio:** 6.18 : 1   **Propellers:** 2 - 72.9″ dia.

The *Bandera*.

Designed by A. G. MacIlwain, this vessel was originally going to be called *Vulcan*. Malcolm McLaren recalled that the nameplate was already welded on the hull when someone in the Wilson family decided that name wouldn't do. So steelworkers cut *Vulcan* off and the tug was renamed *Bandera* before being launched. The tug is now operated by Pacific Towing and is one of the many proven workhorses of this coast.

Hull No: 227   **Original name:** *Nor-Roi*   **Official No:** 393067

Type: Fishing, Seiner   **Designer:** Peter S. Hatfield Ltd.
Delivered: 1980   **Built for:** Les Pecheries Marc Ltee., Caraquet NB   **Owner's representative:** Don Dawson

Length: OA 78.08′   **Beam mld:** 24.33′   **Depth:** 11.5′
Design draft: 13′   **Tonnage: GT** 129   **NT** 37.17
Lightship 147 L. tons   **Dwt** 133 L. tons

Material: Steel hull, aluminum wheelhouse   **Speed:** 10.6 knots (max)

Main engine: Cummins VTA-1710-M—1 @ 545 hp @ 1800 rpm   **Reduction ratio:** 4.97 : 1
Propeller: 1 - 62″ dia.

The *Nor-Roi*.

Built for fishing herring on the east coast of Canada, this vessel had a refrigerated salt water system for cooling the catch of fish.

Hull No: 228   **Original name:** Nor-Roi (Skiff)

Type: Fishing, Power Skiff   **Designer:** Peter Hatfield Ltd.   **Delivered:** 1980   **Built for:** Les Pecheries Marc Ltee., Caraquet NB   **Owner's representative:** Don Dawson

Length: OA 22.4′   **Beam mld:** 11.1′   **Depth:** 5.2′
Material: Aluminum

Main engine: Cummins V-555-M—1 @ 185 hp @ 2800 rpm
Reduction ratio: 3.50 : 1   **Propeller:** 1 - 34″ dia.

This large aluminum power skiff was built to assist the seiner *Nor-Roi* in the east coast herring fishery. Total weight of the skiff was about 3.34 L. tons.

Hull No: 229   **Original name:** *Ocean Invader*
Official No: 395763

Type: Fishing   **Designer:** Cleaver & Walkingshaw
Delivered: 1980   **Built for:** Ocean Invader Fishing Ltd., Port Simpson BC   **Owner's representative:** Bill Johnson

Length: OA 76′   **Beam mld:** 23′   **Depth:** 11′
Design draft: 12′   **Tonnage: GT** 100   **NT** 34.58
Lightship 105 L. tons   **Dwt** 108 L. tons   **Material:** Steel hull, aluminum superstructure   **Speed:** 10 knots

Main engine: Caterpillar 3412—1 @ 520 hp @ 1800 rpm
Reduction ratio: 4.67 : 1   **Propeller:** 1 - 66″ dia.

Launched in 1980, this was one of the last of the fishing vessels that Allied constructed during the 1970s fishing boom. It was built for Bill Johnson, originally from Port Simpson. He liked the *Katrena Leslie* style of earlier vessels but he didn't have a fishing licence for a long boat. The solution was to take 7 feet out of the standard design. Unfortunately, as Arthur McLaren noted, losing that much flat deck and retaining the aft shear put in the *Western Investor* meant that the vessel looked somewhat like a banana. Since then, the vessel has been lengthened.

Hull No: 230   **Original name:** *Charles H. Cates VIII*
Official No: 395948

Type: Tug, Berthing   **Designer:** Robert Allan Ltd.
Delivered: 1980   **Built for:** C. H. Cates & Sons Ltd., North Vancouver BC   **Owner's representative:** Terry Waghorn

Length: OA 60′   **Beam mld:** 22′   **Depth:** 9.4′
Tonnage: GT 69   **NT** 2   **Speed:** 11.4 knots (max) 11 knots (service)
Main engines: Detroit diesel 16V-149—2 @ 900 hp @ 1800 rpm   **Reduction ratio:** 5.17 : 1
Propellers: 2 - 66″ dia.   **Sister ship:** 225

With delivery of *Cates VIII*, Cates Tugs now had four 1800-hp exceptionally manoeuvrable ship-berthing tugs. A bollard pull of 28 tons from a 60-foot, 2-person crew tug was a significant milestone in the ship-berthing business.

Hull No: 231   **Original name:** *Canmar Tugger*
Renamed: *Atlantic Oak*   **Official No:** 395515

Type: Tug, Anchor Handling   **Designer:** Cleaver & Walkingshaw   **Delivered:** 1981   **Built for:** Dome Petroleum Ltd., Calgary, Alberta
Owner's representative: Capt. Jan Hurt

Length: OA 116′   **Beam mld:** 34′   **Depth:** 16.66′
Design draft: 14′   **Tonnage: GT** 464   **NT** 132
Material: Steel hull and superstructure
Main engines: EMD 647-E7—2 @ 1525 hp @ 900 rpm
Reduction ratio: 3.50 : 1   **Propellers:** 2 - 96″ dia.

This vessel is a modified version of the *Arctic Taglu* and *Arctic Hooper*, built in 1976 for Arctic Transportation Ltd. The dome vessel had 50 percent more propulsion power, double bottoms in way of the forward fuel tanks and larger electrical generators. The construction contract was signed December 18, 1980. The keel was laid on February 17, it was launched June 3 and the vessel was delivered, after completing all trials, on July 8, 1981.

Hull No: 232   **Original name:** *Canmar Widgeon*
Renamed: *Toisa Widgeon*   **Official No:** 395516

Type: Offshore Supply, Standby   **Designer:** Cleaver & Walkingshaw   **Delivered:** 1981   **Built for:** Dome Petroleum Ltd., Marine, Calgary, Alberta
Owner's representative: Capt. Jan Hurt

Length: OA 131.25′   **Beam mld:** 29′   **Depth:** 13.6′
Design draft: 11′   **Tonnage: GT** 401.83   **NT** 124.8
Lightship 311 L. tons   **Dwt** 400 L. tons   **Material:**

Steel hull and superstructure   **Capacity:** 10 (crew)
Speed: 12.6 knots (max) 10 knots (service)
Main engines: Caterpillar D398—2 @ 850 hp @ 1225 rpm
Reduction ratio: 3.64 : 1   **Propeller:** 2 - 78″ dia.
Sister ship: 233

The *Canmar Widgeon*.

On December 30, 1980, Allied signed a contract with Dome Petroleum Ltd. of Calgary for two standby vessels. These were simple, inexpensive ships. It was intended that these vessels would fulfill the requirement to have at all times a "standby" vessel alongside the drilling rigs, thereby freeing up the larger, more capable Dome ice-breaking supply vessels for more rigorous work. The total construction time, for both vessels, was four months from laying of keels.

Hull No: 233   **Original name:** *Canmar Teal*
Renamed: *Toisa Teal*   **Official No:** 395517

Type: Offshore, Standby   **Designer:** Cleaver & Walkingshaw   **Delivered:** 1981   **Built for:** Dome Petroleum Ltd., Calgary, Alberta
Owner's representative: Capt. Jan Hurt

Length: OA 131.25′   **Beam mld:** 29′   **Depth:** 13.6′
Tonnage: GT 402   **NT** 124   **Dwt** 400 L. tons
Material: Steel hull and superstructure   **Capacity:** 10 (crew)   **Speed:** 11.6 knots (max) 10 knots (service)
Main engines: Caterpillar D398—2 @ 850 hp @ 1225 rpm
Reduction ratio: 3.64 : 1   **Propellers:** 2 - 78″ dia.
Sister ship: 232

This vessel was fitted with a large steel gantry over the main deck cargo area. It was intended that large balloons would be handled, via a tether, from this gantry. An ice-detecting radar scanner was to be carried by the balloon, thereby providing a method to monitor the movement of pack ice toward the nearby drilling ship.

Hull No: 234   **Original name:** *Britannia III*
Renamed: *Britannia*   **Official No:** 801531

Type: Ferry, Passenger   **Designer:** Robert Allan Ltd.
Delivered: 1981   **Built for:** Harbour Ferries Ltd.,

Vancouver BC	**Owner's representative:** Graham Clarke

**Length:	OA** 134.25′	**Beam mld:** 31.67′
Depth: 11.75′	**Design draft:** 7.5′	**Tonnage:**
GT 668	**NT** 460.0	**Lightship** 255 L. tons
Dwt 55 L. tons	**Material:** Steel	**Capacity:** 500
(passengers)	**Speed:** 12.8 knots (max)

Main engines: Caterpillar 3408 TA—2 @ 420 hp @ 1800 rpm	**Reduction ratio:** 4.50 : 1	**Propellers:** 2 - 56″ dia.

The *Britannia III*.

Britannia was originally intended to carry workers across Howe Sound from a landing at the old copper mining town of Britannia Beach to the otherwise inaccessible pulp mill at Woodfibre, in support of a major expansion. The ship later became a fixture in the tourist excursion business in Vancouver Harbour, working in conjunction with a popular boat/steam train trip between Vancouver and Squamish, BC.

Hull No: 235	**Original name:** *Arctic Nutsukpok*
Renamed: *Gal Beaufort Sea*	**Official No:** 801804

Type: Tug, Anchor Handling	**Designer:** Cleaver & Walkingshaw	**Delivered:** 1982	**Built for:** Arctic Transportation Ltd., Calgary, Alberta
Owner's representative: John Mattson, Hugh Hutton

**Length:	OA** 153′	**Beam mld:** 40′	**Depth:** 17.5′
Design draft: 14′	**Tonnage:	GT** 841.26	**NT** 254.9
Lightship 972 L. tons	**Dwt** 520 L. tons	**Material:**
Steel	**Speed:** 13.8 knots (max) 10 knots (service)

Main engines: Mak 8M-453—2 @ 3260 hp @ 600 rpm
Reduction ratio: 2.95 : 1	**Propellers:** 2 - 104″ dia.
Sister ships: 236; 242

This vessel was representative of the many innovative Canadian designed and built ice-breaking vessels which, by their capability, extended the season for firms building the drilling islands needed to exploit the vast oil and gas pools in the Beaufort Sea and the Mackenzie River delta. The name *Nutsukpok* means tugging heavily (or pull like hell).

Hull No: 236	**Original name:** *Arctic Nanook*
Renamed: *Gal Ross Sea*	**Official No:** 801805

Type: Tug, Anchor Handling	**Designer:** Cleaver & Walkingshaw	**Delivered:** 1982	**Built for:** Arctic Transportation Ltd., Calgary, Alberta
Owner's representatives: John Mattson, Hugh Hutton

**Length:	OA** 153′	**Beam mld:** 40′	**Depth:** 17.5′
Design draft: 14′	**Tonnage:	GT** 841.26	**NT** 254.9
Dwt 520 L. tons	**Speed:** 13.8 knots (max)

Main engines: Mak 453—2 @ 3260 hp @ 600 rpm
Reduction ratio: 2.95 : 1	**Propellers:** 2 - 104″ dia.
Sister ships: 235; 242

The word *Nanook* means polar bear.

Hull No: 237	**Original name:** *Charles H. Cates II*
Official No: 803541

Type: Tug, Ship Berthing	**Designer:** Robert Allan Ltd.
Delivered: 1983	**Built for:** C. H. Cates & Sons Ltd., North Vancouver BC	**Owner's representative:** Terry Waghorn, Hank Lum, Claire Johnston

**Length:	OA** 73.67′	**Beam mld:** 28′	**Depth:** 11.25′
Design draft: 12′	**Tonnage:	GT** 127	**NT** 83
Material: Steel hull, aluminum wheelhouse	**Capacity:** 2
(crew)	**Speed:** 11.7 knots (max)

Main engines: Detroit diesel 16V-149T—2 @ 1200 hp @ 1900 rpm	**Reduction ratio:** 3.05 : 1	**Propellers:** 2 - 76″ dia.	**Sister ship:** 253

This "revolutionary" tug design was one of the first ship-berthing tugs in North America having 360-degree steerable propulsion drives, providing exceptional manouevrability and thrust in all directions. This small tug achieved an ahead bollard pull of 38 tonnes. Speed ahead was 11.7 knots. Speed astern was 10.7 knots. The towing winch was located forward. A crane was fitted on the foredeck to lift the towline up to the ship being handled. The two right-angle drives were Niigata model ZP-2A.

Hull No: 238	**Original name:** *Constitution*
Official No: 803552

Type: Tourist Passenger Vessel	**Delivered:** 1983
Built for: Harbour Ferries, Vancouver BC

The *Constitution*.

Owner's representative: Graham Clarke

Length: OA 93.75′ **Beam mld:** 23.75′ **Depth:** 5.88′
Design draft: 4.25′ **Tonnage: GT** 187 **NT** 187
Lightship 113 L. tons **Dwt** 16 L. tons **Material:** Steel
hull and superstructure **Capacity:** 100 (passengers)

Main engine: Gardner 8-L3—1 @ 250 hp @ 1200 rpm
Paddlewheel: 1

Constitution was built for tourist excursions in Vancouver
Harbour. Incorporating the style and features of an
historical sternwheel vessel, she was propelled by a
paddlewheel, hydraulically driven from a diesel engine.

Hull No: 239 **Original name:** *Arctic Tender*
Official No: 802939

Type: Barge, Standoff **Designer:** Cleaver &
Walkingshaw **Delivered:** 1983 **Built for:** Arctic
Transportation Ltd., Calgary, Alberta
Owner's representative: John Mattson

Length: OA 50′ **Beam mld:** 7.88′ **Tonnage:
GT** 28 **Material:** Steel **Sister ship:** 240

Four small, irregular-shaped barges were moored against
the Imperial Oil steel drilling island in the Beaufort Sea.
These barges enabled service vessels to safely come
alongside the slope-sided caisson. Although designated Hulls
#239 and 240, there were four barges in total: two type A
and two type B barges (each hull number represented two
hulls). All were 50 feet long by 7 feet 10 1/2 inches wide.

Hull No: 240 **Original name:** *Arctic Tender II*
Official No: 802940

Type: Barge, Standoff **Designer:** Cleaver &
Walkingshaw **Delivered:** 1983 **Built for:** Arctic
Transportation Ltd., Calgary, Alberta

Length: OA 50′ **Beam mld:** 7.88′ **Tonnage:
GT** 28 **NT** 28 **Sister ship:** 239

Hull No: 241 **Original name:** *Tsekoa II*
Official No: 804446

Type: Workboat, Coastal **Designer:** Robert Allan Ltd.
Delivered: 1984 **Built for:** Public Works Canada
Owner's representative: Jack Gilmore, Hector Allan

Length: OA 87.58′ **Beam mld:** 23.75′

Depth: 10.67′ **Design draft:** 6.56′ **Tonnage:
GT** 160.75 **NT** 53.68 **Lightship** 137 L. tons **Dwt** 112
L. tons **Material:** Steel hull, aluminum superstructure
Capacity: 7 (crew) **Speed:** 12.2 knots (max) 11 knots
(service)

Main engines: Caterpillar 3408 TA—2 @ 335 hp @ 1800 rpm
Reduction ratio: 3.50 : 1 **Propellers:** 2 - 49″ dia.

The *Tsekoa II*.

The *Tsekoa II* was intended for operation as a workboat for
use in the maintenance and repair of public wharves and
similar structures controlled by Public Works Canada. The
area of operation encompassed all coastal waters of BC, from
sheltered waters to the exposed west coast of Vancouver
Island. The vessel functioned on a fourteen-day roundtrip
basis. The mix of cargo included 40-foot dock gangways, 8-
ton concrete anchors, chain, lumber, etc. A 10-short-ton
capacity knuckle boom crane was fitted on the aft deck.

Hull No: 242 **Original name:** *Arctic Nanabush*
Renamed: *Britoil 7* **Official No:** 804411

Type: Tug, Anchor Handling **Designer:** Cleaver &
Walkingshaw **Delivered:** 1984 **Built for:** Arctic
Transportation Ltd., Calgary, Alberta **Owner's
representatives:** John Mattson, Hugh Hutton

Length: OA 154.42′ **Beam mld:** 40′ **Depth:** 17.5′
Design draft: 14.83′ **Tonnage: GT** 879 **NT** 263
Dwt 520 L. tons **Speed:** 15.5 knots (max) 12.5 knots
(service)

Main engines: B & W Alpha 12V28/32VO—2 @ 3600 hp

@ 775 rpm   **Reduction ratio:** 3.36 : 1   **Propellers:** 2 - 118″ dia.   **Sister ships:** 235; 236

This vessel was ordered to replace the 1982-built, 139-foot tug *Arctic Ubleriak*, which sank in the Beaufort Sea in 1983, following a brush with a steel-encased drilling island. The *Nanabush* shares a hull design with the *Arctic Nutsukpok* and *Arctic Nanook*; however, the accommodation was enlarged to enable the vessel to carry additional crew when acting as a survey vessel.

Hull No: 243   **Original name:** *Arctic Ivik*
Renamed: *Geco Snapper*   **Official No:** 805517

Type: Offshore Supply, Icebreaker   **Designer:** Cleaver & Walkingshaw/McLaren & Sons   **Delivered:** 1985, Vancouver BC   **Built for:** Arctic Transportation Ltd., Calgary, Alberta   **Owner's representatives:** John Mattson, Hugh Hutton, Michael Bell

Length: **OA** 221′ **Beam mld:** 46′ **Depth:** 19′
Design draft: 16′ **Tonnage:** **GT** 1564.5 **NT** 793.2
Lightship 1650 L. tons **Dwt** 1500 L. tons
Capacity: 12 (crew)

Main engines: B & W Alpha 12V28/32—2 @ 3600 hp @ 775 rpm   **Reduction ratio:** 4.05 : 1   **Propellers:** 2 - 122″ dia.

The *Arctic Ivik*.

Intended for service in the Arctic and east coast of Canada, the *Arctic Ivik* is a Canadian Ice Class II vessel, being capable of continuous steaming in 2 feet of ice cover. The hull form, developed for ice-breaking capability, incorporates straight line framing with multi-chine knuckles, a form originated by Cleaver & Walkingshaw and proven to be most successful in negotiating ice. The hull framing is arranged so that there is a grid pattern of 8x24″ supporting the shell plating in way of ice pressure areas. The Lloyd's certified continuous bollard pull was 80.9 tonnes. The multi-purpose ship had a 7,060-cubic-feet bulk system for transport of drilling mud or cement, and was equipped for anchor handling or towing and fire fighting to FI-FI 1 standards. In 1997, at Tyne Tees Dockyard, UK, the *Arctic Ivik* was converted to the seismic survey vessel *Geco Snapper* for Norwegian owners.

Hull No: 244   **Original name:** *Allied 244*
Official No: 806685

Type: Drydock, Floating   **Designer:** McLaren & Sons
Delivered: 1985   **Built for:** Allied Shipbuilders Ltd., North Vancouver BC   **Owner's representative:** T.A. McLaren

Length: **OA** 159′ **Beam mld:** 83.33′ **Depth:** 7.92′
Tonnage: **GT** 1609 **NT** 1114 **Lightship** 777 L. tons
Dwt 1835 L. tons

This drydock was built to enhance Allied's ability to do ship repair work in the face of a declining market for new Canadian-built commercial vessels.

Hull No: 245   **Original name:** *Kla-Wichen*
Official No: 806746

Type: Harbour Patrol   **Designer:** Robert Allan Ltd.
Delivered: 1986   **Built for:** Vancouver Port Corp., Vancouver BC

Length: **OA** 45.25′ **Beam mld:** 14′ **Depth:** 6.67′
Design draft: 4′ **Tonnage:** **GT** 15 **NT** 10
Lightship 13 L. tons **Dwt** 2 L. tons **Material:** Aluminum **Speed:** 20 knots (max) 10 knots (service)

Main engines: Volvo Penta TAMD70E—2 @ 300 hp @ 2500 rpm   **Reduction ratio:** 1.98 : 1   **Propellers:** 2 - 26″ dia.

This vessel performs various patrol, inspection and yarding functions within the Port of Vancouver.

Hull No: 246   **Original name:** *Ocean Achiever*
Official No: 810482

Type: Fishing, Seiner/Trawler   **Designer:** McLaren & Sons (C. Ko)   **Delivered:** 1988   **Built for:** Ocean Fisheries Ltd., Vancouver BC   **Owner's representatives:** Peter Neuman, Ed Safarik

Length: **OA** 65′ **Beam mld:** 23′ **Depth:** 11.5′
Tonnage: **GT** 112 **NT** 31.73 **Lightship** 118 L. tons
Dwt 110 L. tons **Material:** Steel hull, aluminum wheelhouse **Speed:** 10.5 knots (max)

Main engine: Mitsubishi S6R—1 @ 590 hp @ 1600 rpm
Reduction ratio: 5.00 : 1 **Propeller:** 1 - 66″ dia.
Sister ships: 247; 252

The *Ocean Achiever*.

In 1987 and 1988, there was a brief fishing boat boom in BC. Shore Boatbuilders was quite busy; the BC Marine/West Coast Manly group had several orders, as did a number of other small coastal yards. Allied got an order for two seiner/draggers from Ocean Fisheries. The *Ocean Achiever* was a 65-foot combination seiner/dragger while the *E.J. Safarik* was a 70-foot dragger. This second vessel was named in honour of the senior Mr. Safarik, founder of Ocean Fisheries. A third sister ship, *Ocean Rebel* (Hull #252), was built in 1989.

Hull No: 247   **Original name:** *E.J. Safarik*
Official No: 810483

Type: Fishing, Stern Trawler   **Designer:** McLaren & Sons (C. Ko)   **Delivered:**   **Built for:** Ocean Fisheries Ltd., Vancouver BC   **Owner's representatives:** Ed Safarik; Ed Put

Length: OA 69.63′   **Beam mld:** 23.16′   **Depth:** 11.5′
Tonnage: GT 115   **NT** 33.7   **Lightship** 145 L. tons
Dwt 124 L. tons   **Material:** Steel hull, aluminum wheelhouse   **Speed:** 10.5 knots (max)

Main engine: Mitsubishi S6R—1 @ 590 hp @ 1600 rpm
Reduction ratio: 5.00 : 1   **Propeller:** 1 - 66″ dia.
Sister ships: 246; 252

A relatively small trawler when built in 1988, the *E.J. Safarik* turned out to be well sized for the "downsized" quota fishery of the late 1990s. The establishment of a strict quota for groundfish stocks, coupled with the security of a known volume of fish production, enabled smaller vessels with their smaller crew, fuel and maintenance costs, to outperform many of the larger vessels.

Hull No: 248   **Original name:** *Charles H. Cates X*
Official No: 811176

Type: Tug, Ship Berthing   **Designer:** Robert Allan Ltd.
Delivered: 1987   **Built for:** C.H. Cates & Sons Ltd., North Vancouver BC   **Owner's representatives:** Terry Waghorn, Claire Johnston

Length: OA 57.75′   **Beam mld:** 24.33′   **Depth:** 9.88′
Design draft: 10′   **Tonnage: GT** 76   **NT** 51
Material: Steel hull, aluminum wheelhouse   **Speed:** 11 knots (max)

Main engines: Caterpillar 3508 TA—2 @ 650 hp @ 1600 rpm
Reduction ratio: 4.23 : 1   **Propellers:** 2 - 55″ dia.

Hull No: 249   **Original name:** *Oil Spill Barge*

Type: Barge, Self-Propelled   **Designer:** B. McDonald & Assoc. Ltd.   **Delivered:** 1988, Vancouver BC
Built for: Canadian Coast Guard, Victoria BC
Owner's representatives: Colin Hendry, CCG; Dick Danyluk, DSS

Length: OA 31.5′   **Beam mld:** 10′   **Depth:** 3.25′
Design draft: 2′   **Tonnage: Lightship** 11.6 L. tons
Material: Steel

Main engine: Ford 2711E-4 cylinder   **Propeller:** 1 - 20″ dia.

This self-propelled landing barge was configured for use in oil recovery. A slicklicker was mounted at the front of the barge. Recovered oil was to be stored in oil drums on deck. Propulsion was via a 360-degree right angle drive.

Hull No: 250   **Original name:** *R.B. Young*
Official No: 811822

Type: Survey, Hydrographic & Oceanographic
Designer: Robert Allan Ltd.   **Delivered:** 1990, Vancouver BC   **Built for:** Department of Fisheries & Oceans   **Owner's representatives:** Ron Parkinson, Inam Majid

Length: OA 105.6′   **Beam mld:** 26.25′   **Depth:** 11.5′
Design draft: 7.5′   **Tonnage: GT** 304.96   **NT** 76.24
Lightship 226 L. tons   **Dwt** 172 L. tons   **Material:** Steel hull, aluminum superstructure   **Capacity:** 6 (crew); 5 (passengers)   **Speed:** 11.6 knots (max) 11 knots (service)

Main engines: Caterpillar 3406B—2 @ 322 hp @ 1800 rpm
Reduction ratio: 3.96 : 1   **Propellers:** 2 - 51.2″ dia.

Named by his wife in honour of one of the west coast's leading hydrographers, the late Robert B. Young, this vessel replaced the CSS *Richardson*. The *R.B. Young* was built to support scientific activities in the coastal waters of BC. In a hydrographic survey mode, the ship carried two launches under davits. In oceanographic mode, an aft A-frame articulated deck crane and deck-mounted survey winches were utilized. The flexible mounting of propulsion and generator engines made for a remarkably quiet vessel.

Hull No: 251   **Original name:** *A.M.E. Biname*
Official No: 810511

Type: Tug, Shallow Draft   **Designer:** Peter S. Hatfield Ltd.   **Delivered:** 1988, Norman Wells NWT
Built for: Esso Resources Canada Ltd., Calgary, Alberta
Owner's representative: Malcolm Comyn

Length: OA 42.9′   **Reg** 39.1′   **Beam mld:** 21′
Depth: 7′   **Design draft:** 3.5′   **Tonnage: GT** 59.03
NT 40.14   **Lightship** 53 L. tons   **Dwt** 7 L. tons
Material: Steel hull, aluminum superstructure

The *A.M.E. Biname*.

Main engines: Detroit diesel 8V-71—2 @ 239 hp @ 1800 rpm   **Reduction ratio:** 3.00 : 1
Propellers: 2 - 36″ dia.

Esso Resources Canada operates an oil field/oil refinery on the Mackenzie River in the Northwest Territories. Refined oil products are shipped south by pipeline. The shallow water of the Mackenzie River must be crossed to access the oil wells. Named after a well-known local priest, the *A.M.E. Biname*'s primary duty was pushing a ramp barge to provide transportation services between the mainland and the islands over the oil field.

Hull No: 252   **Original name:** *Ocean Rebel*
Official No: 812313

Type: Fishing, Seiner   **Designer:** McLaren & Sons (C. Ko)   **Delivered:** 1989, Vancouver BC
Built for: Ocean Fisheries Ltd., BC

Length: OA 65′   **Beam mld:** 23.16′   **Depth:** 11.5′
Tonnage: GT 123   **NT** 39.55   **Lightship** 113 L. tons
Dwt 126 L. tons   **Material:** Steel hull, aluminum wheelhouse

Main engine: Cummins KTA-19M—1 @ 500 hp @ 1800 rpm   **Reduction ratio:** 5.07 : 1   **Propeller:** 1 - 66″ dia.   **Sister ships:** 246; 247

The *Ocean Rebel* is nearly identical to Hull #246, *Ocean Achiever*.

Hull No: 253   **Original name:** *Charles H. Cates III*
Official No: 814182

Type: Tug, Ship Berthing   **Designer:** Robert Allan Ltd.
Delivered: 1993, Vancouver BC   **Built for:** C. H. Cates & Sons, North Vancouver BC   **Owner's representative:** Claire Johnston, Ken Yamashita

Length: OA 73.67′   **Beam mld:** 28′   **Depth:** 11.25′
Design draft: 12′   **Tonnage: GT** 80.99   **Lightship** 185 L. tons   **Dwt** 30 L. tons   **Material:** Steel hull, aluminum wheelhouse   **Speed:** 11.44 knots (max)

Main engines: Caterpillar 3512—2 @ 1175 hp @ 1600 rpm
Sister ship: 237

Hull #253 was the third of three 2400-hp sister ships built in Vancouver for C. H. Cates & Sons. The first of class *C.H. Cates II* was built by Allied in 1983. The 360-degree propulsion drives are Niigata Model ZP-2A. At maximum rpm the vessel makes 11.4 K ahead and 10.6 K astern. Bollard pull is 37 short tons ahead and 34 short tons astern. Perhaps unusual for a shipbuilding project, the vessel was delivered on time, for the exact amount of the contract price.

Hull No: 254   **Original name:** *Spirit of British Columbia*

Type: Ferry, Vehicle   **Designer:** Knud Hansen/Polar Design   **Delivered:** North Vancouver BC   **Built for:** BC Ferry Corp., Victoria BC   **Owner's representative:** Roland Webb, Lucille Johnston

Length: OA 194′   **Beam mld:** 88′   **Depth:** 26′
Tonnage: Lightship 820 L. tons   **Capacity:** 470

(vehicles—complete ship)   **Sister ship:** 255

This new building was the forward hull section of the first superferry built for the BC Ferry Corporation. The section contained about 800 tons of steel. The 550-foot "S" Class ferry was built by three yards: Allied Shipbuilders, Yarrows and Pacific Rim Shipbuilders (Vito Travesi and Dan Hengeveld).

Hull No: 255   **Original name:** *Spirit of Vancouver Island*

Type: Ferry, Vehicle   **Designer:** Knud Hansen/Polar Design   **Delivered:** North Vancouver, BC
Built for: BC Ferry Corp., Victoria BC   **Owner's representatives:** Roland Webb, Lucille Johnston

Length: OA 194′   **Beam mld:** 88′   **Depth:** 26′
Tonnage: Lightship 820 L. tons   **Sister ship:** 254

Hull #255 was the forward hull section of the second 470-car "S" Class ferry built for the Tsawwassen–Swartz Bay route (BC Ferry Corp. Route 1).

Hull No: 256   **Original name:** *Inkster*

Type: Catamaran Patrol Vessel   **Designer:** Brandylmayer Marine/Robert Allan Ltd.   **Delivered:** 1996, North Vancouver BC   **Built for:** Royal Canadian Mounted Police   **Owner's representatives:** Don Van Dusen, Sgt. Peter Attrell

Length: OA 70.8′   **Beam mld:** 22′   **Depth:** 6.5′
Design draft: 2.16′   **Tonnage: Lightship** 28 L. tons
Dwt 5 L. tons   **Material:** Aluminum   **Capacity:** 4 (crew)   **Speed:** 32 knots (max) 25 knots (service)

Main engines: M.A.N. D2840LE-401—2 @ 820 hp @ 2300 rpm   **Reduction ratio:** 2.00 : 1   **Propellers:** 2 - 34″ dia. surface piercing   **Original service:** Coastal patrol, northern BC

The Inkster.

Inkster is the fifth of a series of high-speed aluminum patrol vessels commissioned by the Royal Canadian Mounted Police. She is 7 feet longer than her four predecessors and the accommodation arrangement has been reconfigured. With an operating range of 500 miles at 25 knots, the *Inkster* operates as a mobile detachment with police constables on board, carrying out a variety of duties including investigations of criminal offences and local policing of coastal communities.

Hull No: 257   **Original name:** *Skeena Queen*
Official No: 819521

Type: Ferry, Vehicle (Century Class)   **Designer:** McLaren & Sons   **Delivered:** 1997, North Vancouver BC   **Built for:** BC Ferry Corp., Victoria BC
Owner's representatives: Frank Rhodes, Tom Ward, John Jones

Length: **OA** 360.8′   **Beam mld:** 77.1′   **Depth:** 17.2′
Design draft: 13.1′   **Tonnage:**   **GT** 2653   **NT** 795
Dwt 984 L. tons   **Material:** Steel   **Capacity:** 8 (crew); 594 (passengers); 100 (vehicles)   **Speed:** 17 knots (max) 14.5 knots (service)

Main engines: Mitsubishi S12R-MPTK—4 @ 1394 hp @ 1650 rpm   **Propellers:** 4 - 75″ dia. in nozzles

The *Skeena Queen*.

Conceived as a spartan, utilitarian vessel, the MV *Skeena Queen* is intended for use on a number of short-distance ferry routes serviced by the BC Ferry Corporation. These routes are 1 to 5 miles long and predominantly commuter-oriented with heavy early-morning and late-afternoon rush hour traffic patterns.

Appendix 2

BC Builders of Steel and Aluminum Commercial Vessels

For an overview of terms used in appendices, see page 218.

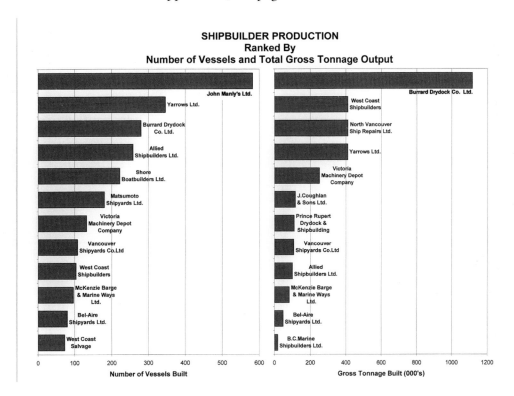

SHIPBUILDER PRODUCTION
Ranked By
Number of Vessels and Total Gross Tonnage Output

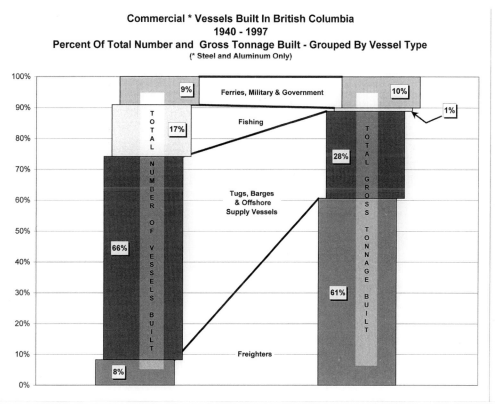

Commercial * Vessels Built In British Columbia
1940 - 1997
Percent Of Total Number and Gross Tonnage Built - Grouped By Vessel Type
(* Steel and Aluminum Only)

Commercial * Vessels Built In British Columbia
1940 - 1997
Number Of Vessels Built Ranked By Gross Tonnage Range
(* Steel and Aluminum Only)

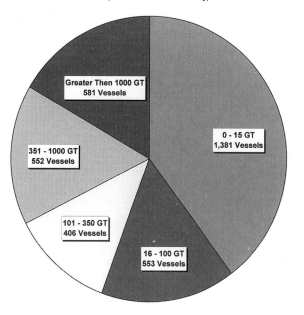

Greater Then 1000 GT
581 Vessels

351 - 1000 GT
552 Vessels

101 - 350 GT
406 Vessels

16 - 100 GT
553 Vessels

0 - 15 GT
1,381 Vessels

BC Built Metal Ships
Summary Statistics by Type of Vessel
1940–1997

Vessel Type	Total Gross Tonnage Built	Total Length Built (ft)	Total No. of Vessels Built
Barge	779,873	139,612	988
Ferry	165,628	18,873	143
Fishing Boat	34,191	26,867	581
Freighter	1,923,785	112,653	287
Government	66,718	8,199	95
Navy	85,743	13,824	77
Oil Explorer	55,646	6,550	39
Other	5,929	2,267	30
Tug	48,130	29,014	777
Work Boat	5,867	10,747	456
	3,171,510	368,606	3,473

Steel and Aluminum Vessels Only (excludes skiffs and yachts)

Commercial * Vessels Built In British Columbia
1940 - 1997
(* Steel and Aluminum Only)

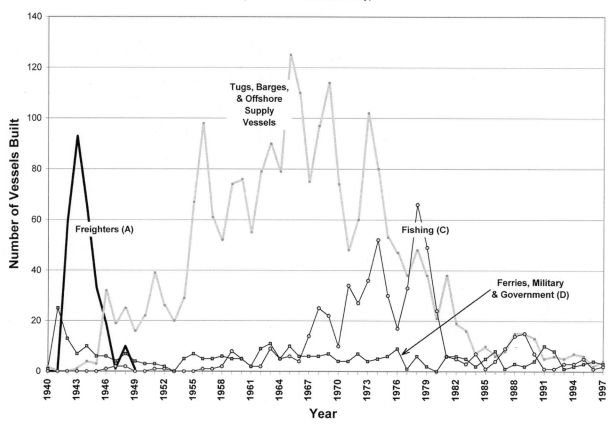

Builder	Dates	No. of Vessels Built	Total Gross Tonnage Built	Length Range (ft)	Gross Tonnage Range	Typical Vessel
A.A. Conner Ganges	1988	1	87	61	87	*Pacifica*
A.B.D. Aluminum Boats N. Vancouver	1992–	57	438	63–90	78–131	*Malaspina Express*

Owners Alan Dawson and Burton Drody established this company on the former site of Bel-Aire Shipyards, after many years working in the aluminum boatbuilding industry. Builders of luxury yachts, fishing vessels and other work boats, A.B.D. formed the joint venture A & F Aluminum Catamarans in 1996 and assembled the superstructure of the three high-speed catamaran ferries built for the BC Ferry Corporation.

Builder	Dates	No. of Vessels Built	Total Gross Tonnage Built	Length Range (ft)	Gross Tonnage Range	Typical Vessel
A.R. Sharcott Nanaimo	1971	1	8	30	8	*Lisa D*
A.V. Horth Victoria	1963	1	21	39	21	*Rana*
A.W. Casserly Vancouver	1947	1	11	29	11	*Southern Cross II*
ABC Boatcharters Ltd Vancouver	1997	1	350	127	350	*Queen of Diamonds*
Admiral Shipyards Ltd Port Hammond	1973	1	6	26	6	*River Imp*
Adrenalin Marine Ltd North Vancouver	1996–	2	22	45	11	*J/V Wind*

Peter Mitchell, principal of the company and a well-established participant in the BC aluminum boatbuilding industry, built a number of successful small high-performance vessels.

Builder	Dates	No. of Vessels Built	Total Gross Tonnage Built	Length Range (ft)	Gross Tonnage Range	Typical Vessel
Advance Marine Ltd New Westminster	1975	2	10	23	5	*Conuma Adriane*
Alberni Engineering & Shipyard Port Alberni	1964–	39	833	25–48	3–119	*Stormcrest*

Alberni was established in 1914, built steel vessels from 1964 to 1989, went out of business, then returned as a subsidiary of Nanaimo Shipyard. The company has specialized in tugs, side winders, fishing boats, skiffs, small barges and fast aluminum passenger boats, as well as participating in the high-speed catamaran building project of the BC Ferry Corporation.

Builder	Dates	No. of Vessels Built	Total Gross Tonnage Built	Length Range (ft)	Gross Tonnage Range	Typical Vessel
Alfab Marine Products Port Moody, loco, North Vancouver	1965–1978	9	53	26–31	5–9	*Columbus No. 1*
Allied Shipbuilders Ltd Vancouver, North Vancouver	1949–1999	257	89,217	13–360	1–10,687	*Radium Dew, Skeena Queen*

Originally named Allied Builders Ltd., this company was founded in Vancouver in 1948 by T.A. McLaren and moved to North Vancouver in 1967. To date Allied has built 257 commercial vessels.

Builder	Dates	No. of Vessels Built	Total Gross Tonnage Built	Length Range (ft)	Gross Tonnage Range	Typical Vessel
Alu-Craft Products Steveston, Surrey	1973–1988	10	134	18–53	4–74	*Native Joye*

Through the fishing boom of the 1970s, Alu-Craft built aluminum fishing boats—mostly seine skiffs and gillnetters but also larger ones such as the drum seiner *Native Joye*.

Builder	Dates	No. of Vessels Built	Total Gross Tonnage Built	Length Range (ft)	Gross Tonnage Range	Typical Vessel
Argo Marine Builders North Vancouver, Port Coquitlam	1975–1995	14	104	23–36	5–14	*Mercury XI*

Argo concentrated on building standard high-quality crew boats, water taxis and 20- to 30-foot fishing boats. Lorne Smith operated it for twenty years before closing in 1995 and embarking on a career in consulting on vessel construction.

Builder	Dates	No. of Vessels Built	Total Gross Tonnage Built	Length Range (ft)	Gross Tonnage Range	Typical Vessel
Argyle Machine Works Port Alberni	1963	1	52	48	52	*T.T.B. No 1*

Builder	Dates	No. of Vessels Built	Total Gross Tonnage Built	Length Range (ft)	Gross Tonnage Range	Typical Vessel
Armour Salvage (1949) Ltd Prince Rupert	1959	1	13	30	13	Naskeena No. 1
Armstrong & Morrison Vancouver	1898	1	10	40	10	Old Pioneer
Atom Welding Ltd Richmond	1971–1974	2	16	26	8	Go-Getter No. 1
Axton Industries Richmond	1977	1	30	51	30	Sea Love
BC Forest Products Youbou	1950	1	58	40	58	B.C.F.P. 617
BC Marine Railway Co Esquimalt	1907–1914	6	4,831	98–260	155–1,777	Princess Maquinna

Originally established as the Esquimalt Railway Company in 1893 by the Bullen family and subsequently renamed the BC Marine Railway Company in 1898, this company was purchased in 1914 by Alfred Yarrow and became Yarrows Ltd.

Builder	Dates	No. of Vessels Built	Total Gross Tonnage Built	Length Range (ft)	Gross Tonnage Range	Typical Vessel
BC Marine Shipbuilders Ltd Vancouver	1963–1983	45	19,059	–	3–2,912	Canmar Supplier V

This company was originally associated with the BC Marine Railway Company of Esquimalt until the latter was sold; BC Marine Shipbuilders of Vancouver was then bought by the McKeene family of Straits Towing.

Builder	Dates	No. of Vessels Built	Total Gross Tonnage Built	Length Range (ft)	Gross Tonnage Range	Typical Vessel
BC Packers Ltd Richmond, Steveston	1978–1979	9	110	30–41	6–15	Calvert Isle
Baker Island Logging Burnaby	1966	1	8	–	8–8	Baker Island No. 1
Balmer Bros. Vancouver	1949	1	14	39	14	Remlab
Banks Marine Industries Ltd. Parksville	1979–1980	4	195	46–61	38–77	Lasqueti Steeler
Barry Brown Boats Ltd Langley	1994	1	10	49	10	Westminster Apache
Beaumont Timber Co Revelstoke	1975	1	91	67	91	Beaumont No. 1
Behan Marine Richmond	1987	1	317	128	317	Richmond Carrier
Bel-Aire Shipyards Ltd Regent; John P. Tully Vancouver, North Vancouver	1963–1985	80	47,794	129	6–2,769	Lawrence L; Seaspan

Incorporated in 1956 in Coal Harbour, Vancouver, Bel-Aire built their first steel vessel in 1963. Under the owner, George Fryatt, the yard became a significant builder of offshore supply vessels, Arctic oil exploration support craft, tugs, barges and fishing vessels. Bel-Aire closed in 1986 after delivery of the 226-foot Fisheries & Oceans Canada survey vessel John P. Tully.

Builder	Dates	No. of Vessels Built	Total Gross Tonnage Built	Length Range (ft)	Gross Tonnage Range	Typical Vessel
Bellavance Welding Salt Spring Island	1970s–					Island Minnow

Owner Gene Bellavance built a large number of small aluminum boats (power skiffs and dead skiffs) for use in the BC fishing industry.

Builder	Dates	No. of Vessels Built	Total Gross Tonnage Built	Length Range (ft)	Gross Tonnage Range	Typical Vessel
Benson Bros Shipbuilding Co Ltd Vancouver, New Westminster	1959–1981	43	4,578	16–73	3–421	Jose Navarez; Nemesis; Caledonian

Originally a builder of wooden boats, Benson's took up steel shipbuilding in 1959. First located in Coal Harbour, Vancouver, they moved to the former Star Shipyard site in New Westminster. Many of the company's high-quality steel and wood vessels remain in service along the BC coast.

Builder	Dates	No. of Vessels Built	Total Gross Tonnage Built	Length Range (ft)	Gross Tonnage Range	Typical Vessel
Benton Navigation Co Beaton	1945	1	42	50	42	Beaton No. 3
Bertram Engineering Works/CPR Nelson	1898	2	1,664	162	829–835	Minto; Moyie
Blue Water Systems Ltd Delta	1996	1	150	88	150	Pile Driving Barge
Blueline Boatbuilders Coquitlam	1972	1	15	36	15	Creole
British Pacific Engineering & Construction Barnett, Vancouver	1916–1917	11	3,905	150	355	"H" Class submarine

This company, which quietly assembled US-made components into 150-ft submarines for Russia, was set up during World War I. Due to the Russian Revolution, British Pacific's second order for submarines was never delivered to Russia, and the subs were completed in Puget Sound for the the US Navy.

Builder	Dates	No. of Vessels Built	Total Gross Tonnage Built	Length Range (ft)	Gross Tonnage Range	Typical Vessel
Burrard Dry Dock Co Ltd North Vancouver	1925–1973	56	93,071	54–425	44–8,100	Powell No. 1; Tsawwassen; Terry Fox

Burrard Drydock was the predominant shipbuilding company on the west coast of Canada. In the 1890s, Alfred Wallace founded a shipyard in Vancouver at the foot of Granville Street on the north shore of False Creek. The company moved to North Vancouver and the shipyard went under different ownership and the names of: Wallace Shipbuilding Co., Burrard Drydock Co. Ltd., Burrard-Yarrows Corporation and Versatile Pacific Shipyards Inc. For a variety of reasons, including a plunge in market demand, the shipyard closed in 1992.

Builder	Dates	No. of Vessels Built	Total Gross Tonnage Built	Length Range (ft)	Gross Tonnage Range	Typical Vessel
Burrard Shipyard & Marine Ways Vancouver	1964	1	10	30	10	Service XI

Located in Coal Harbour near Vancouver's Stanley Park, "Little Burrard" was established in 1924, primarily as a repair facility.

Builder	Dates	No. of Vessels Built	Total Gross Tonnage Built	Length Range (ft)	Gross Tonnage Range	Typical Vessel
C. Lang Steveston	1975	1	12	34	12	Whale Bird
C. Mayer Victoria, Sidney	1966–1968	3	70	–	10–31	Valiant Lady
C. & H. Steel Fabricators Victoria	1977	2	56	46	28	Ambitious
C.E. Sahl Coquitlam	1969	1	6	–	6	Gayle IV
Canada Marine Industries Ltd New Westminster	1980	1	62	47	62	Pacific Force
Canadian Development Co Ltd Lake Bennett	1898	2	441	64–115	21–420	Australian

This company built two sternwheelers for service on Lake Bennett during the Klondike gold rush.

Builder	Dates	No. of Vessels Built	Total Gross Tonnage Built	Length Range (ft)	Gross Tonnage Range	Typical Vessel
Canadian Vickers Ltd Nelson	1928–1929	3	1,590	92–233	164–745	Granthall

Two barges and a tug for CPR service were prefabricated in Montreal, and assembled in Nelson.

Builder	Dates	No. of Vessels Built	Total Gross Tonnage Built	Length Range (ft)	Gross Tonnage Range	Typical Vessel
Cassiar Packing Co Richmond	1965	1	14	28	14	*Cassiar Dredger*
Catamaran Ferries International Inc North Vancouver	1996–2000	3				*PacifiCat Discovery*
A subsidiary of the BC Ferry Corporation, CFI managed the construction of three 250-vehicle 122-m high-speed aluminum catamaran 250-vehicle ferries.						
Celtic Shipyards (1988) Ltd Vancouver	1991–1995	9	245	34–59	5–175	*Fireboat I*
Celtic was formed when the Musqueam First Nation took over the BC Forest Service yard near the mouth of the north arm of the Fraser River. Under the leadership of Al Dickey, the company built five high-speed aluminum fireboats to serve municipalities in Greater Vancouver.						
Center Shipyard Ltd Victoria	1974–1975	4	340	53–76	50–123	*Sun Maiden*
Colin R. Smith	1992	1	13	40	13	*Hayley Jay*
Columbia Shipyards North Vancouver, New Westminster	1955–1956	3	26	23–34	5–15	*Jean L*
Comox Logging Ltd Ladysmith	1952–1954	4	22	15–29	4–10	*Carol Lee II*
Cooper Barging Service Fort Nelson	1974	1	221	115	221	*C.T. 110*
Cowichan Professional Installations & Welding Duncan	1990	1	67	47	67	*Royal Fisher*
D. Baldwin Richmond	1968	1	7	–	7	*Lorac*
D.R. Dickerson Lantzville	1967	1	15	–	15	*Wanderlust*
D. Skidmore Richmond	1976	1	15	40	15	*Skidmore Brothers No. 1*
David Thom Scott New Westminster, Mitchell Island	1931–1949	8	234	31–55	10–57	*Treasure Island*
David Thom Scott was born in Aberdeen, Scotland, in 1877 and was a pioneer steel fish boat builder in BC. From 1931 to 1949, Scott built eight steel rivetted vessels, some of which are still in operation.						
David L. Cawley Nanaimo	1969	1	6	26	6	*Pacific Chaser*
Dean Wilson Barnston Island	1977	1	11	30	11	*Razor Point*
Denford Metals Victoria	1976	1	5	24	5	*Ripoff*
Derek Verhey Victoria	1971	1	31	50	31	*Pacific Hunter*
Derrick Machinery Ltd Fort Nelson	1965	1	52	65	52	*C.T. 105*
Dominion Bridge Co Ltd Esquimalt, Vancouver, Burnaby	1943–1973	26	15,981	60–250	35–1,252	*N.T. 1510*
Dominion built barges, many of which were shipped to northern Canada for use by Northern Transportation Company Ltd.						

Builder	Dates	No. of Vessels Built	Total Gross Tonnage Built	Length Range (ft)	Gross Tonnage Range	Typical Vessel
E. Van Wort Lake Bennett	1898	1	7	34	7	*Alert*
E. Greozmiel Richmond	1958	1	50	57	50	*Centennial II*
Edward Cooper Fort Nelson	1965	1	14	–	14	*Barbara J. II*
Edward Kurz Vancouver	1974	1	15	37	15	*London Tramp*
Elmer McEachern Langley	1967–1973	4	36	36	12	*All Seasons*
Fairfield Fabricators North Vancouver	1966	3	45	37	15	*North Arm Surveyor*
Fauchon Engineering Works Ltd Campbell River	1965–1981	4	238	20–121	6–208	*Iron Mac II*
Finlay Navigation Ltd Mackenzie	1995–	1	4,252	360	425–4,252	*Williston Transporter*

This company, owned by John Harding, built and operates a fleet of large self-propelled barges that transport logs and ore on Williston and Babine Lakes, including the 5,000 dwt, 360x100' *Williston Transporter*, one of the largest vessels built in BC during the 1990s.

Builder	Dates	No. of Vessels Built	Total Gross Tonnage Built	Length Range (ft)	Gross Tonnage Range	Typical Vessel
Fisherman's Boat Works Albion	1966	1	10	30	10	*Dorothy Helena*
Folkes Manufacturing Port Coquitlam	1974–1975	3	104	40–70	15–60	*Co-op Dispatcher*
Frank E. Hall Vancouver	1940	1	38	32	38	*Gold Digger No. 1*
Fraser Marine Shipyards Vancouver	1961	1	14	37	14	*Sea Crab*
Fraser Shipyard & Industrial Centre Ltd New Westminster	1990–	2	80	47–50	9–71	*Yucata*

Primarily a repair yard operating on the former site of Star Shipyard, Fraser built a small tug and a fish boat hull outfitted by the owner.

Builder	Dates	No. of Vessels Built	Total Gross Tonnage Built	Length Range (ft)	Gross Tonnage Range	Typical Vessel
Frostad Boat Works Delta	1973–1975	8	507	39–64	25–87	*Carmanah No. 1*

Kris Frostad is a prolific, hands-on builder of small vessels. He designs, lofts and personally oversees construction of his vessels made of wood, fibreglass, aluminum or steel.

Builder	Dates	No. of Vessels Built	Total Gross Tonnage Built	Length Range (ft)	Gross Tonnage Range	Typical Vessel
G.E. Parsons Prince Rupert	1960	1	4	22	4	*Bob D.*
G.W. Ledingham Vancouver	1968	1	24	28	24	*Ledingham II*
Galbraith & Salley Vancouver	1968	1	73	40	73	*Carrier No. 3*
George A. Foster Vancouver	1951	1	11	31	11	*Blue Steel*
Gilpin Construction Vancouver, Richmond	1955–1956	3	865	70–120	88–448	*G.C. 26*

Builder	Dates	No. of Vessels Built	Total Gross Tonnage Built	Length Range (ft)	Gross Tonnage Range	Typical Vessel
Golden Eagle Marine Port Moody	1980	1	21	39	21	*Kinbasket Queen*
Greenwich Shipyards Port Hammond	1979	2	54	48	27	*Senji*
Gulf of Georgia Towing Vancouver	1975	1	46	40	46	*Pacific Enterprise*
H. Longland Richmond	1969	1	9	45	9	*Shore Gleaner*
H.C. Rogers Vancouver	1962	1	12	34	12	*Betty L-II*
Halliday Marine Ltd Nanaimo	1968–1973	9	1,162	43–97	31–345	*Golden Fleece*

This company set up shop during the boom times, building barges and fish boats. When the new-build market went sour, Halliday closed.

Builder	Dates	No. of Vessels Built	Total Gross Tonnage Built	Length Range (ft)	Gross Tonnage Range	Typical Vessel
Hamilton Bridge (Western) Vancouver	1939–1944	5	389	48–122	26–238	*Pendozi*

Located in False Creek next to the site of West Coast Shipbuilders, Hamilton was primarily a bridge and structural steel fabricator and did the fabricating for West Coast during World War II. Hamilton became Western Bridge & Steel Fabricators, which later became Canron. Canron fabricated numerous barges and built the engine room double-bottom units for the BC Ferry Corporation's *Spirit of British Columbia*.

Builder	Dates	No. of Vessels Built	Total Gross Tonnage Built	Length Range (ft)	Gross Tonnage Range	Typical Vessel
Hampton Lumber Mills Boston Bar	1972	2	10	25	5	*Scuzzy Belle*
Harbour Marine Co Victoria	1920–1921	3	12,021	270–400	112–5,455	*Canadian Traveller*
Harris Built Products Lantzville	1966	1	10	32	10	*Recovery II*
Hausot Bros. Ltd Prince George	1973	1	138	100	138	*W.D. No. 1*
Hills Machine Shop Gibsons	1969	1	5	20	5	*Tactician No. 1*
Hodder Tug Boat Richmond	1992	1	9	42	9	*Jessie Hodder*
Howie's Marine Service Prince George	1970	1	4	33	4	*K.C. No. 1*
Hunt & Nielson Delta	1976	1	77	57	77	*Dia-O-Mia*
Hyak Marine Gibsons Landing	1981	1	106	70	106	*Tillyak*
Igis Boatbuilders Pitt Meadows	1975	1	72	58	72	*Westview*
Industrial Welding Prince Rupert	1959	1	11	28	11	*E. Marie*
Integrated Ferry Constructors Vancouver/Victoria	1991–1994	2	–	–	–	*Spirit of British Columbia*

IFC was established by the BC Ferry Corporation as a management company to oversee the construction of two Spirit Class ferries.

Builder	Dates	No. of Vessels Built	Total Gross Tonnage Built	Length Range (ft)	Gross Tonnage Range	Typical Vessel
International Shipbuilders Ltd North Vancouver	1964	3	75	34–48	12–50	*Gulf Margaret*
Irwin Manufacturing Ltd Port Hammond	1977–1978	7	171	31–48	9–27	*Terry Lou*
Island Sand Sales Richmond	1974	1	33	41	33	*Sandpiper VI*
J. Sawyer Burnaby	1967	1	49	–	49	*Sans Peur*
J. Coughlan & Sons Vancouver	1917–1921	21	117,940	400–412	5,391–5,757	*War Charger*

Coughlan's, established on the southwest shore of False Creek, was a bridge builder and structural steel company that went into shipbuilding in 1917. Coughlan built freighters, including one that was built in less than a month, setting a world record.

Builder	Dates	No. of Vessels Built	Total Gross Tonnage Built	Length Range (ft)	Gross Tonnage Range	Typical Vessel
J. Crawford & F. Perello Lake Cowichan	1977	1	9	36	9	*Mitco Surf*
J.D. Pieters Port Mellon	1955	1	64	66	64	*The Little Giant*
J.E. McEachern Surrey	1967	1	12	35	12	*Eoinmor*
J.F. Moore North Vancouver	1964	1	9	32	9	*Golden Hair*
J.H. Calvert Lake Bennett	1898	2	174	50	87	*F.H. Kilbourne*
Jall Marine Transport Vancouver	1959	1	10	32	10	*Point Grey Prince*
Jenkins Marine Ltd Victoria	1988–	1	95	66	95	*Marine Link II*
John A. King Victoria	1964	1	25	42	25	*Five Kings II*
John Manly's Ltd New Westminster, Vancouver	1945–1983	569	14,468	16–34	1–860	*Bering Sea; Jervis Crown*

John Manly began building small welded steel tugs, and after many years as an independent builder he sold his company to Rivtow Marine Ltd. in 1972. Rivtow relocated the company to the foot of Victoria Drive on the Fraser River, where they also relocated West Coast Salvage. By 1990 West Coast Manly Shipyard was the result of consolidating numerous shipyards, including John Manly, West Coast Salvage, BC Marine Shipbuilders and Point Grey Shipyard.

Builder	Dates	No. of Vessels Built	Total Gross Tonnage Built	Length Range (ft)	Gross Tonnage Range	Typical Vessel
Kallahan Marine Ventures Port Coquitlam	1977–1978	3	21	25–29	6–8	*Point Tyee*
Kamma & Blake Industries Ltd Port Alberni	1998	12	–	24	–	Army work boats
Keith Notte Sooke	1983	1	37	52	37	*Strider*
Kimoli Ventures New Westminster	1989	1	74	59	74	*Sunset Bay II*

Builder	Dates	No. of Vessels Built	Total Gross Tonnage Built	Length Range (ft)	Gross Tonnage Range	Typical Vessel
Kootenay Tug Boat Nelson, New Westminster	1976–1981	2	84	25–49	9–75	*Kootenay No. 1*
L. & P. James Deroche	1966–1969	3	67	38–61	12–41	*Riverwood II*
L.B. Krutop Port Coquitlam	1970	1	29	–	29	*Twila Dawn*
L.E. Hill Sidney	1974	1	51	56	51	*Westerly Wind*
Lasqueti Fishing Co Nanaimo, Lasqueti Island	1973–1989	6	274	42–61	28–86	*Lasqueti; Gambler*
Peter Forbes and Tom Millicheap together with their sons built a number of drum seiners for use by their fishing company.						
Leader Marine Ltd Vancouver	1973–1978	4	153	19–72	4–98	*Leader IV*
Lincoln Steel Products Richmond	1981	1	54	90	54	*Explorer*
Lobnitz/Morgan & Co/VDM Victoria, Vancouver	1911–1914	2	741	100	229–512	*PWD Rockbreaker No. 1*
These two 100-ft barges were prefabricated in Scotland and assembled in BC, for use in building the graving dock in Esquimalt.						
M. Schroeder Lasqueti Island	1957	1	7	24	7	*S.L.*
M. & R. Forrest & Halliday Marine Vancouver	1972	1	67	50	67	*Hustler II*
Mardon Fabricators Richmond	1969	3	30	32	10	*Croatian Star*
Marine Mining & Engineering Richmond	1968	1	27	40	27	*Golden Tide No. 1*
Marine Pipeline & Dredging New Westminster, Port Coquitlam, Richmond	1955–1962	7	306	23–84	6–116	*Marine Pipeliner #104*
Marlin Marine Industries Ltd New Westminster, Vancouver	1977–1979	12	533	32–78	10–103	*Elora James*
Marlin Marine built modern fishing vessels in steel and aluminum, to the designs of Cleaver & Walkingshaw and Peter Hatfield.						
Matsumoto Shipyards Ltd North Vancouver	1960–1988	180	2,758	12–82	1–182	*Evening Star; Pemex 652; Nechako*
Perhaps best known for its aluminum boats, the Matsumoto family built a lot of wooden vessels as well. The hulls number at least 455, many of which were exported to the USA or not registered.						
Mayer Steel Boat Ltd Sidney	1973–1981	22	728	33–60	9–53	*Twin J*
A builder of fishing boats in the 1970s, the company built a number of bare hulls, leaving them unfinished for others to complete.						
McDougall Jenkins Ltd North Vancouver	1911	1	163	80	163	*Point Ellice*

Builder	Dates	No. of Vessels Built	Total Gross Tonnage Built	Length Range (ft)	Gross Tonnage Range	Typical Vessel
McKay Cormack Ltd Victoria	1962–1970	15	5,654	–	5–1,686	Island West No. 1

This company goes back at least to the 1930s. It was called Armstrong Brothers and Falconer Industries before becoming McKay Cormack. The company built wooden vessels through the 1940s and 1950s, then in 1962 started building in steel, including large barges and self-righting life boats for the Coast Guard.

Builder	Dates	No. of Vessels Built	Total Gross Tonnage Built	Length Range (ft)	Gross Tonnage Range	Typical Vessel
McKenzie Barge & Marine Ways Ltd North Vancouver	1959–	97	84,077	120–256	9–4,863	Imperial Tofino; Empire 60

Formerly McKenzie Barge & Derrick Co Ltd., located next to BC Marine in Vancouver Harbour, this company built wooden barges before converting to steel construction in 1959.

Builder	Dates	No. of Vessels Built	Total Gross Tonnage Built	Length Range (ft)	Gross Tonnage Range	Typical Vessel
McTavish Welding Ltd Campbell River	1964–1982	2	24	25–35	5–19	Island Prowler
Metal Vessels Ltd New Westminster	1951–1952	4	44	36–39	9–15	Cellulose
Nahanni Manufacturing New Westminster, Surrey	1970–1976	6	587	48–80	30–358	Western Mist

This company, which started out as a truck-body builder, constructed fishing vessels, a ferry and a barge.

Builder	Dates	No. of Vessels Built	Total Gross Tonnage Built	Length Range (ft)	Gross Tonnage Range	Typical Vessel
Nanaimo Shipyard Ltd Nanaimo	1970–1993	3	107	67	14–93	

Established in the 1930s, Nanaimo has had a variety of owners. It was acquired in 1985 by Gerry van Wachem, whose family also operates Alberni Engineering & Shipyard. Nanaimo is primarily a repair yard.

Builder	Dates	No. of Vessels Built	Total Gross Tonnage Built	Length Range (ft)	Gross Tonnage Range	Typical Vessel
New Method Welders Vancouver	1952–1966	9	55	15–31	3–9	Naskeena III
Newnes Machine & Iron Works Salmon Arm	1960	1	10	33	10	Raven III
Nielson Machine Works Ltd Richmond	1969	2	6	14	3	Cree
Noble Towing Ltd North Vancouver	1964	1	8	29	8	Western Yarder
Nordel Custom Marine Delta	1993	1	40	15	40	Jet Set I
North Arm Transportation Vancouver	1966	1	32	29	32	S.O.B.C. No. 24
North Vancouver Ship Repairs Ltd North Vancouver	1941–1946	71	411,306	172–425	672–8,580	HMCS Chignecto; Fort Babine; Kitsilano Park

Located on the west side of Lonsdale Avenue and initially named Vancouver Drydock & Salvage, North Van Ship Repairs built minesweepers at the start of World War II, then fifty-four North Sands type 10,000-ton freighters. The company was renamed Pacific Drydock at the end of the war, then was bought out by Burrard Dry Dock in 1950, following which the yard was closed.

Builder	Dates	No. of Vessels Built	Total Gross Tonnage Built	Length Range (ft)	Gross Tonnage Range	Typical Vessel
Northern Welding Co Ltd Fort Nelson	1967–1970	4	378	90–91	40–115	C.T. No. 108
O.C. Ferguson Ltd Vancouver	1968–1987	8	443	23–73	5–130	Vampy II

"Fergy" Ferguson was a designer and builder of small fishing vessels, which he constructed at sites all over the Lower Mainland. Each vessel he built he eventually sold, then built a bigger one.

Builder	Dates	No. of Vessels Built	Total Gross Tonnage Built	Length Range (ft)	Gross Tonnage Range	Typical Vessel
Osborne Shipyards Ltd North Vancouver	1965	1	10	30	10	*Service XII*
Pacific Marine Construction Nanaimo	1966–1967	3	88	47	15–58	*L.O. Larsen*
Pacific Shipyard Ltd Vancouver	1994–1997	3	43	44–45	14–15	*Tiger Pride*
Pacific Western Shipbuilders Co North Vancouver	1988–1993	5	48	35–50	9–10	*Ocean Monarch*

This company was originally located on the former site of Bel-Aire Shipyard, where it built tugs to the design of W.R. Brown. In 1990 the company moved to the former site of Matsumoto and operated until 1994 under principals Art Noble and Kris Frostad.

Builder	Dates	No. of Vessels Built	Total Gross Tonnage Built	Length Range (ft)	Gross Tonnage Range	Typical Vessel
Pacific Whaling Co Victoria	1910	1	103	93	103	*W. Grant*
Pelletier Welding & Fabrication Port Alberni	1975	1	59	59	59	*Windward Star*
Point Ellice Shipyard Ltd Victoria	1969	1	14	–	14	*Peace Piper*
Point Grey Towing Co Ltd Vancouver	1958–1965	6	58	16–40	3–13	*Point Grey King*
Polson Iron Works Nakusp, New Westminster	1908–1911	2	2,238	108–201	538–1,700	*Bonnington*
Poplar Island Marine Services Ltd Richmond	1998	1	–	45	–	*R.N. Hodder*
Prince Rupert Drydock & Shipbuilding Prince Rupert	1921–1946	27	111,608	66–425	56–7,171	*Canadian Scottish; HMCS Clayoquot; Fort Rupert*

The Grand Trunk Pacific Railway built this shipyard, including a 15,000-ton floating drydock, just before World War I. Two cargo ships for the Canadian Government Merchant Marine were built in the early 1920s, and during the next two decades it was the largest steel shipyard in BC. Prince Rupert built Bangor minesweepers and North Sands type 10,000-ton cargo ships during World War II. At the end of the war the yard closed and the drydock was sold to Seattle Ship Repairers.

Builder	Dates	No. of Vessels Built	Total Gross Tonnage Built	Length Range (ft)	Gross Tonnage Range	Typical Vessel
Progressive Marine Ltd New Westminster	1984–1990	13	406	36–72	8–118	*Cadal*

Les Woodward operated this company on the former site of the Star Shipyard, building a number of 15-ton tugs.

Builder	Dates	No. of Vessels Built	Total Gross Tonnage Built	Length Range (ft)	Gross Tonnage Range	Typical Vessel
Q.M. Machine Works Prince George	1968	1	21	–	21	*Ruby No. III*
R. Erickson Quathiaski Cove	1966	1	9	31	9	*Teakerne Wind*
R.F. Mann Bowser	1978	1	78	60	78	*Osprey No. 1*
R.H. Helenius Richmond	1979	1	100	50	100	*Hel Barge No. 1*
R.L. Ratcliffe Victoria	1968	1	11	–	11	*Wee Toot*
R.O. Scott Vancouver	1964	1	15	37	15	*Ice Breaker*

Builder	Dates	No. of Vessels Built	Total Gross Tonnage Built	Length Range (ft)	Gross Tonnage Range	Typical Vessel
R.W. Grumbach Port Alberni	1959	1	110	82	110	*S.B.T.*
Raider Aluminum Ltd Delta	1973–1979	21	197	19–39	4–27	*Silver Poacher*

Raider was a builder of aluminum seine skiffs and fish boats during the boom of the 1970s.

Builder	Dates	No. of Vessels Built	Total Gross Tonnage Built	Length Range (ft)	Gross Tonnage Range	Typical Vessel
Ray Adams Machine Works New Westminster	1961	1	2	13	2	*Sorter VII*
Raymond Lowres Sooke	1971	2	37	46	12–25	*Dori Louise*
Reyse Marine Ltd Surrey	1996	1	21	45	21	*Orca Spirit*
Ribco Leasing Ltd Vancouver	1971	1	29	32	29	*Ribco No. 1*
River Towing Co Ltd Harrison Lake, Hope	1960–1963	8	60	25–30	5–9	*Red Fir*
Robert Scott Nanoose	1975–1978	2	51	43–50	15–36	*Lady Lian*
Rodewoldt & Pellott Penticton	1964	1	370	129	370	*Ookpik*
Rogers & Sinclair Port Coquitlam	1978–1979	4	42	28–37	4–14	*Gungho*
Rosedale Machine Shop Rosedale	1971	1	8	26	8	*Chilako VII*
Roy Pardiac	1997	1	15	36	15	*Simba II*
S. Toth Nanaimo	1978	1	15	36	15	*Pamy-Rose*
S.I.B. Towing Sechelt	1987	1	98	60	98	*Aqua Transporter*
S. Madill Ltd Nanaimo	1951–1970	67	544	21–64	5–65	*Eager Beaver No. 1*

Madill designed and produced a number of small tugs during the 1950s and 1960s as part of their wide range of logging equipment, such as mobile spars.

Builder	Dates	No. of Vessels Built	Total Gross Tonnage Built	Length Range (ft)	Gross Tonnage Range	Typical Vessel
Sceptre Dredging Ltd New Westminster	1966–1970	2	621	48–160	39–582	*Sceptre Squamish*
Scott Ross	1997	1	15	34	15	*A New Millennium*
Sea Lane Towing Co Vancouver	1960	1	10	32	10	*Sea Lane II*
Selkirk Machine Works Vancouver	1972	2	1,548	192	774	*N.W.D. 205*
Shore Boatbuilders Ltd Burnaby, Richmond	1968–1992	223	5,674	17–67	2–123	*Kwawkewith Producer;* *Cape Morien*

Al Renke and his partner McEachern started off as an aluminum fabricator, and in 1967 began building aluminum gillnetters. Eventually Renke became sole owner, producing a tremendous number of vessels in the 1970s and '80s. When he foresaw the downturn in the fishing industry he shut down the company and leased out the site.

Builder	Dates	No. of Vessels Built	Total Gross Tonnage Built	Length Range (ft)	Gross Tonnage Range	Typical Vessel
Shoreline Metalcraft Sidney	1975	1	19	40	19	*Leviathan*
Sidney Steel Sidney	1968–1973	5	184	46–56	27–49	*War Nipper*
Sikanni Oilfield Construction Fort Nelson	1973–1975	11	4,092	49–200	55–876	*S.B.M.T. 801*

In the 1970s, as the oil exploration business in the North expanded due to high oil prices, more equipment was built at nearby sites. This northern BC company built barges and one tug for the northern river systems.

Builder	Dates	No. of Vessels Built	Total Gross Tonnage Built	Length Range (ft)	Gross Tonnage Range	Typical Vessel
Somass Shipyard Alberni	1958	1	74	61	74	*Ethel Hunter*
Sooke Machine Shop Sooke	1975	2	76	40–55	15–61	*Rebel Isle*
South Side Repairs Delta	1969	1	13	36	13	*Early Bird II*
Spectrum Charter Vancouver	1994	1	344	87	344	*Princess Tianna*
Star Shipyards (Mercer's) Ltd New Westminster	1957–1971	48	6,904	17–162	4–518	*Royal City; Harold A. Jones;* *Mercer Straits*

Star Shipyards, owned by the Mercer brothers, built hundreds of wooden vessels starting before World War I. In 1957 the company began producing steel vessels, including government vessels and fishing boats. A man named Horton, a fabricator from Ontario, bought the business in 1971 but eventually went broke.

Builder	Dates	No. of Vessels Built	Total Gross Tonnage Built	Length Range (ft)	Gross Tonnage Range	Typical Vessel
Star Shipyards Ltd New Westminster	1971–1973	6	4,329	95–215	390–1,392	*Federal 7*
Sterling Shipyards Ltd Vancouver	1974	11	44	17	4	*Power Skiff #21*

A long-established repair shipyard located in Vancouver, Sterling built eleven aluminum power skiffs for the yard's owner, the Canadian Fishing Co.

Builder	Dates	No. of Vessels Built	Total Gross Tonnage Built	Length Range (ft)	Gross Tonnage Range	Typical Vessel
Stradiotti Bros. Ltd Vancouver	1951	1	15	36	15	*Strady VII*
Streeper Bros. Marine Transport Dawson Creek, Fort Nelson	1960–1973	9	779	40–126	14–234	*S.B.M.T. 101*

This northern BC transportation company built barges for their own use.

Builder	Dates	No. of Vessels Built	Total Gross Tonnage Built	Length Range (ft)	Gross Tonnage Range	Typical Vessel
Summer Equipment Vancouver	1979	1	5	24	5	*Workmate*
Sunset Coast Fabricators Parksville	1981–1982	4	87	27–45	10–52	*Westview Chinook*
Superior Welding Inc. Sechelt	1976–1977	2	24	32–40	10–14	*Gambier Scout*
Swiftsure Towing Co New Westminster	1958–1961	4	35	20–38	3–14	*Swiftsure VI*
Sylte Shipyard Ltd Maple Ridge	1989–	12	709	30–140	7–326	*Seaspan Scout;* *Viking Moon*

Sylte was one of the few successful shipyards to open in the late 1980s. Run by Erling Sylte, the yard has built a number of small tugs, fish boats and barges.

Builder	Dates	No. of Vessels Built	Total Gross Tonnage Built	Length Range (ft)	Gross Tonnage Range	Typical Vessel
T.D. Manufacturing Port Coquitlam	1979–1989	4	170	46–65	38–54	Lukwa
T.J. Scoretz North Vancouver	1961–1974	2	146	56–73	39–107	Mr. Wind
Tahsis Co Gold River	1957	1	14	39	14	Jenkins
Taku Welding Maple Bay	1979	1	11	32	11	Rudee
Tanaboat Enterprises Ltd Vancouver	1974–1976	3	34	26–32	8–13	Blue Ocean
The Welding Shop & Engineering Vancouver	1946	3	27	28–38	6–14	Wolco
Thompson Machine Works Ltd Parksville	1973–1978	13	727	25–96	9–219	Nimpkish Producer No. 1

From an inland shipyard located on the Island Highway, Thompson built fishing vessels and tugs. Its name was later changed to Banks Marine.

Builder	Dates	No. of Vessels Built	Total Gross Tonnage Built	Length Range (ft)	Gross Tonnage Range	Typical Vessel
Tom Harper Sidney	1971	1	28	47	28	Pacific Warrior
Trinity Marine Ltd North Vancouver	1976–1977	2	13	24–30	5–8	Sea Farmer
Tristar Marine Port Hammond	1977–1978	2	184	69–72	91–93	Viking Sunrise
Trites Marine Services Ltd Richmond	1990	1	14	36	14	Brockton
Union Steamship Co Vancouver	1891–1892	3	588	101–120	101–256	Capilano; Comox; Coquitlam
Union Steamships Ltd Vancouver	1955	3	42	20–40	4–19	U.S.L. No. 1
United Barge Builders Vancouver	1972–1973	4	3,744	65	111–1,211	G. of G. 490
United Engineering Co Ltd Victoria	1974	1	15	32	15	Sooke Prince
United Engineering Works Ltd Victoria	1967	1	9	32	9	Albern
Vagabond Marine Steveston	1975	1	7	25	7	McGinty McGee
Vancouver Island Log Salvage Ltd Esquimalt	1950	1	25	67	25	V.I. Logger No. 1
Vancouver Island Shipyard Nanaimo	1977–1978	2	290	75–96	82–208	H.P.D. No. 1
Vancouver Pile Driving North Vancouver	1965–1968	3	888	105	270–333	V.P.D. Derrick No.3

Builder	Dates	No. of Vessels Built	Total Gross Tonnage Built	Length Range (ft)	Gross Tonnage Range	Typical Vessel
Vancouver Shipyards Co Ltd North Vancouver	1968–	108	108,982	40–438	49–7,761	Seaspan Commodore; Queen of Alberni; Queen of Capilano

"Van Ship" started as a small shipyard in Coal Harbour that worked on wood vessels. Vancouver Tugboat Company then bought out the company, and principals Jim Stewart and Rod Lindsey created a modern shipyard on the North Shore in 1967, primarily to build Vancouver Tugboat's own barges. After several mergers and name changes, the company is now owned by the Washington Corporation of Montana, USA.

Builder	Dates	No. of Vessels Built	Total Gross Tonnage Built	Length Range (ft)	Gross Tonnage Range	Typical Vessel
Vancouver Steel Fabricators Ltd Vancouver	1953–1969	32	535	24–77	2–148	Point Grey Maid

This early builder of small steel tugs was also engaged in other fabricating, and gave up shipbuilding in the 1960s.

Builder	Dates	No. of Vessels Built	Total Gross Tonnage Built	Length Range (ft)	Gross Tonnage Range	Typical Vessel
Vancouver Structural Steel Vancouver	1949	2	14	21–30	4–10	H & R
Victoria Machinery Depot Co of Esquimalt; Sedco 135 F Victoria	1898–1968	132	250,293	16–425	6–8,676	HMCS Terra Nova; Queen

This company started out as Albion Iron Works, one of the earliest foundry and engine builders in BC. The shipyard was set up in about 1880 and by 1900 they had built a number of composite hulls with steel frames and wooden planks. The company built steamers for the Canadian government and a rail car barge for the CPR. During World War II the company built a new shipyard at Ogden Point, and it operated there until 1968 when the company was sold to Burrard Dry Dock.

Builder	Dates	No. of Vessels Built	Total Gross Tonnage Built	Length Range (ft)	Gross Tonnage Range	Typical Vessel
Village of Harrison Harrison	1965	1	36	45	36	Harrison Dredge
Vito Steel Boat & Barge Construction Delta	1964–1987	43	13,364	73–100	8–2,769	Comox Crown; Canmar Supplier 2; Samuel Risley

Vito Trevisi was a determined and innovative shipbuilder who did things the way he saw it.

Builder	Dates	No. of Vessels Built	Total Gross Tonnage Built	Length Range (ft)	Gross Tonnage Range	Typical Vessel
Voyageur Aluminum Products Ltd Port Coquitlam	1973–1975	6	50	23–35	2–12	Swift Invader
W. Smith East Sooke	1973	1	5	25	5	Steele Smith
W.H. Arnett Vancouver	1950	–	9	30	9	Sea Mule III
W. Sampson Nanaimo	1974	1	8	25	8	Misty Surge
Wellen Building Supplies Vancouver	1967	1	16	48	16	Triumph No. 1
West Bay Boatbuilders Delta	1973–1978	6	56	21–43	4–23	Celtic

West Bay Boatbuilders, builders and repairers of relatively small commercial vessels, evolved into the firm West Bay Sonship, an enormously successful manufacturer of large fibreglass yachts.

Builder	Dates	No. of Vessels Built	Total Gross Tonnage Built	Length Range (ft)	Gross Tonnage Range	Typical Vessel
West Coast Manly Shipyard Ltd Vancouver	1982–1991	44	6,177	13–75	2–2,243	Rivtow Capt. Bob; Leonard J. Cowley; Rivtow Cecil
West Coast Salvage Vancouver	1965–1981	73	710	19–47	3–73	Conuma Trojan

Builder	Dates	No. of Vessels Built	Total Gross Tonnage Built	Length Range (ft)	Gross Tonnage Range	Typical Vessel
West Coast Shipbuilders Vancouver	1942–1950	104	411,366	271–425	5–8,580	*Fort Chilcotin; Anscomb; Radium Gilbert*
Western Aluminum Craft Sidney	1988–1989	3	325	46–65	63–164	*Tantrum No. 1*
Western Bridge & Steel Fabricators Vancouver	1946–1956	66	14,498	44–150	54–654	*Radium 600*
Western Drill-Dredging & Mfg Coquitlam, Prince George	1966–1971	3	43	30–35	10–18	*W.P.D. III*
Western Drydock & CPR Nelson, Okanagan, Port Arthur	1913–1914	3	3,806	90–201	150–1,869	*Nasookin*
Prefabricated in Port Arthur, Ontario, three steam-driven vessels were built for CPR lake service.						
Western Shipbuilders Ltd Victoria	1978	2	104	49	52	*Pacific Lad No. 1*
Wilfab Construction North Vancouver	1975	1	70	54	70	*Pacific Crest*
Williston Lake Navigation Hudson's Hope	1971	1	45	–	45	*Williston III*
Yarrows Ltd Esquimalt	1917–1979	332	364,535	89–425	10–9,911	*HMCS Nootka; Haida Monarch; Queen of Cowichan*
Yule Marine Contractors Vancouver	1961	1	57	53	57	*Chris Kringle*
Zenith Steel Fabricators Ltd Richmond	1969–1974	15	1,870	51–150	9–415	*Betty Coulter*

Index

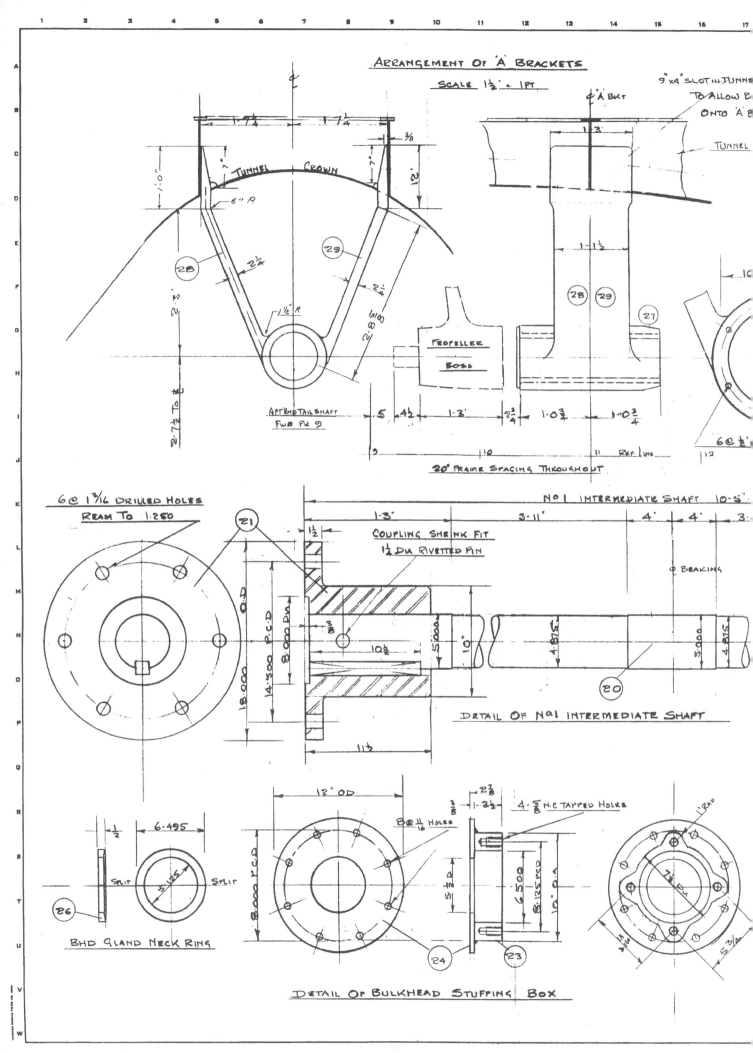